The Great Tradition in
English Literature
from
SHAKESPEARE
to
SHAW

Volume I
William Shakespeare to Jane Austen

ANNETTE T. RUBINSTEIN

(MR)

MODERN READER PAPERBACKS
NEW YORK AND LONDON

For
JEAN RUBINSTEIN
Mother, Teacher, Comrade

FOREWORD TO THE 1980 EDITION

It is with some trepidation that I return to a work completed over a quarter century before in order to write a note heralding a reprint edition. True, the subject matter was such that few new discoveries or developments could have been expected to upset former judgments, but what about the changes and developments in the author? Would I still agree with my former conclusions and approve my choice of the evidence selected to validate them? To a surprising degree, I have found that the answer was "yes."

Happily, a recent European university lecture tour supported this personal affirmative. English departments in Eastern Europe — Hungary, Czechoslovakia, the German Democratic Republic — are still regularly using the volume. A visit to Bonn found that in the Federal Republic the chapter on Dickens had just been assigned as background reading for an intensive *explication de texte* of *Oliver Twist*, and when my trip ended with a week in Cambridge I learned, amazingly, that an advanced tutorial on Milton was grateful for the unusual material from his relatively neglected prose, here correlated with his life and poetry.

My return to New York in January 1980 provided a climax. A letter awaited me from the head of the English Department of the Institute for Foreign Languages in Peking asking my help in "tracking down copies of the *Great Tradition*, the more the better, new or second-hand."

Since the book first appeared in the United States at the height —or depth—of the cold war, when any serious materialist interpretation of history was anathema and the separation between life and literature in academic circles was all but absolute, the four printings (two hardcover and two paperback) have found their readers largely outside university walls. This was not altogether regrettable since every teacher is glad to have students attracted by their interest in the subject rather than by their need for credits. Nevertheless, in today's freer atmosphere, with its general emphasis on an interdisciplinary approach, it is perhaps not unreasonable to hope that this new edition will find a place in college classrooms and libraries, at home as well as overseas.

Annette T. Rubinstein

New York, N.Y.
April, 1980

FOREWORD TO THE 1953 EDITION

The great tradition in English literature is the tradition of those great writers who could, as Shakespeare said, "sense the future in the instant." The future is always stirring beneath the heart of the present and it is therefore those who live closest to the heart of their own time who can most surely sense the pulse of the life-to-be.

The great tradition in English literature is the tradition of the great realists; that is to say, of the writers who know and are concerned with the vital current which moves steadily beneath the innumerable eddies and confusing crosscurrents of life's surface.

This feeling for the essential direction of history, this profound understanding of the significant events and potentialities of one's own age, has little relation to any skill at observing and reproducing its minutiae. Snobbish or sentimental writers like Pope, Thackeray and Trollope, angry and honest ones like Zola or Gissing or Morrison, can often create an impressive facsimile of the life led by the men and women whom they have had occasion to observe. But, as Bacon said in another context, "a crowd is not company; and faces are but a gallery of pictures; and talk but a tinkling cymbal, where there is no love." And it is in the love which makes them sensitively aware of their fellows' needs, in the respect they feel for man's potentialities, that the work of the great realists is rooted. It is this deep assurance of man's strength, this ardent concern for his rights, that has so often enabled them to "look into the seeds of time and say which grain will grow and which will not." It is this which paradoxically makes their work, written out of the most immediate care for contemporary events, most relevant to those of a far distant future.

This seemingly prophetic insight has taken many forms. One was the daring, closely reasoned scientific prevision of a Bacon or a Huxley. Another was the equally daring, less fully conscious, anticipation of a Blake or a Burns. At some periods we find that this central conviction of man's power to shape his own future expresses itself in the common religious mythology of his time, as with Bunyan. At other periods the writer is forced to create his own myths as Dickens does in his metaphorical use of an apparently factual plot. Often the great humanist was also a fiercely indignant revolutionary like Milton or Hazlitt or Shelley; less often he shared the brief serenity of an optimistic postrevolutionary age like Defoe or Fielding or Jane Austen. But always the great writers have, in one way or another, participated in the essential struggles of their own times. The old miners' song has it, "They say in Harlan County, there are no neutrals here," and that is also so in the great world of art.

True, it has long been a dogma in the academies that art and politics are two separate worlds; that the value of a work of art is unaffected by the artist's relation to the social movements of his own time, his concern with human needs, or his hopes of future progress. And in the last three quarters of a century the artist himself has too often concurred in this belief. But his acceptance of his separation from society, whether melancholy or defiant, was always only a special instance of that alienation of man from himself which has characterized the end of the great bourgeois epoch.

The representative art of the great epochs of human culture have always been political and partisan. Aristotle defined man as *the* political animal, and surely the most human of men—the great artist—are not the least political.

The following pages attempt a rapid survey of one of the greatest of such epochs—that of the expanding bourgeois world in its hopeful youth and its troubled but still rich maturity. The twenty-odd major figures here examined are all chosen from those acknowledged, by the most conservative academicians and critics, to be the greatest writers of their own times, and among the greatest of all time. Yet almost invariably scholarly discussions as well as popular biographies and anthologies minimize, distort, or altogether ignore the political concern and activity which lay at the root of the art they praise. And so, inevitably, they misunderstand and misrepresent vital elements in it, no matter how great their admiration.

A full consideration of the life and work of any of these major figures in the history of English literature soon shows us just how clear, conscious and complete the great writer's consistently progressive partisanship in the political and social conflicts of his own time has always been. But it is difficult for the nonacademic reader to find the time and factual material for such a consideration, and the nonpolitical literary student too often himself unquestioningly accepts the retired tradition of the academies.

This book grew out of one student's attempt first to learn in concrete detail, and then to teach in convincing summary, the part played by the great writers in man's continuing fight for freedom.

It begins with a brief synopsis of the social and political background for the great literature of Shakespeare and his contemporaries, and proceeds to a more detailed consideration of perhaps the two most important Elizabethans—Shakespeare himself and Bacon.

Each of the four succeeding sections similarly opens with a rapid sketch of its age, with emphasis upon those aspects of its history most directly related to the literary development of the period, and proceeds to a more specific consideration of its most representative figures.

There has been little attempt to impose any formal uniformity on the material presented. In some instances a rather full biographical account seemed desirable; in others more space has been devoted to a consideration of certain specific works. Nor is the length of any one chapter an indication of the relative importance of the writer to whom it is devoted. Here again the story to be told determined the manner of its telling. For example, the tragic fact that Keats died at twenty-six, after barely six writing years, made it possible to treat his life and work in less than half the space demanded by Hazlitt or Dickens or Shaw.

In many of the discussions my conclusions as to a writer's political and social attitude necessarily run counter to the conventional impression, so I have thought it best to use the impeccable evidence of direct quotation as far as possible. There are, therefore, substantial extracts from personal letters and diaries as well as from more deliberate literary works included in every chapter but the one on Shakespeare, and even in that there is an unusual amount of such quotation from more or less intimate contemporary sources. I believe that anyone judicially considering these great writers' own statements must conclude, whatever his own opinion may be, that they all felt "that those who are above the struggle are also beside the point."

Finally, although the book presents a continuous development, each of the five major sections of which it is composed can really be read as an independent unit. It may, in fact, be advisable for those readers not well acquainted with the earlier periods of English history and literature to begin with the discussion of the more familiar modern world in the third section, and then to turn back to the Elizabethan Age.

To those lovers of literature who already "think continually of those who are truly great," the book's approach may suggest a different interpretation of familiar beauty, and reveal another dimension in the well-known lives of many long beloved masters. To those men and women who are themselves deeply immersed in the political life of our stirring and difficult age it will, I think, introduce new allies and fresh sources of strength. That, at least, is the hope with which I here complete this long and rewarding labor of love.

ANNETTE T. RUBINSTEIN

New York, N. Y.
September, 1953

ACKNOWLEDGMENTS

For arrangements made with various authors and publishing houses whereby certain copyrighted material was permitted to be reprinted, and for the courtesy extended by them, the following acknowledgments are gratefully made:

D. Appleton & Co., *Bernard Shaw: Playboy and Prophet* by Archibald Henderson; Jonathan Cape, *The Aesthetic Adventure* by William Gaunt; Chanticleer Press, Inc., *John Milton* by Rex Warner; Chatto & Windus, Ltd., *Mliton* by E. M. Tillyard; The Citadel Press, *The Hidden Heritage* by John Howard Lawson; William Collins Sons & Co., Ltd., *The Life of William Cobbett* by G. D. H. and M. Cole; Columbia University Press, *John Bunyan, Mechanick Preacher* by W. Y. Tindall; Cresset Press, Ltd., *Jane Austen and Some Contemporaries* by Mona Wilson; Dodd, Mead & Co., *Charles Dickens* by G. K. Chesterton; Gerald Duckworth & Co., Ltd., *Huxley* by E. W. MacBride; Victor Gollancz, Ltd., *Bernard Shaw: Art and Socialism* by E. Strauss; Harcourt, Brace & Co., Inc., *The Poet in the Theatre* by Ronald Peacock, *The Common Reader* by Virginia Woolf; Harper & Brothers, *Color* by Countee Cullen, *The Poems of Emily Dickinson* by Emily Dickinson; Hodder & Stoughton, Ltd., *Men of Letters* by Dixon Scott; Horizon Press, *Modern Greek Poetry* by Rae Dalven; Hutchinson & Co., Ltd., *Introduction to the English Novel* by Arnold Kettle; International Publishers, *The Novel and the People* by Ralph Fox; The Kenyon Review, "Fiction and the 'Matrix of Analogy'" by Mark Schorer; Alfred A. Knopf, Inc., *Shelley* by Neuman Ivy White; John Lane, The Bodley Head, Ltd., *George Bernard Shaw* by G. K. Chesterton; Lawrence & Wishart, Ltd., *Charles Dickens—The Progress of a Radical* by T. A. Jackson, *A People's History of England* by A. L. Morton, *Crisis and Criticism* by Alick West, *A Good Man Fallen Among Fabians* by Alick West; The Macmillan Co., *Shakespeare and the Rival Tradition* by Alfred Harbage, *Collected Poems* by Thomas Hardy, *History of English Literature* by Legouis and Cazamian, *Science and the Modern World* by A. N. Whitehead; Macmillan & Co., Ltd., *Political Characters of Shakespeare* by John Palmer; McGraw-Hill Book Co., Inc., *Shakespeare Without Tears* by Margaret Webster; Methuen & Co., Ltd., *John Bunyan—Maker of Myths* by Jack Lindsay; New Statesman & Nation, "The Economic Deter-

minism of Jane Austen" by Leonard Woolf; The New Yorker,
"Charles Dickens" by Martha Keegan; Oxford University Press,
Shelley, Godwin and Their Circle by H. N. Brailsford, *The
Dickens World* by Humphrey House; Philosophical Library,
Charles Dickens by Jack Lindsay; Princeton University Press,
Prefaces to Shakespeare by H. Granville-Barker, *Jane Austen,
Irony As Defense and Discovery* by Marvin Mudrick, *The
Court Wits of the Restoration* by J. H. Wilson; G. P. Putnam's
Sons, *Ellen Terry and Bernard Shaw* by Ellen Terry; The
Quarterly Review, "Jane Austen" by Reginald Farrer; Rout-
ledge & Kegan Paul, Ltd., *Biography of Bacon* by Mary Sturt;
Henry Schuman, Inc., *Francis Bacon* by Benjamin Farrington;
Scrutiny (Magazine), "Regulated Hatred" by D. C. W. Hard-
ing; Secker & Warburg, *William Blake: A Man Without a
Mask* by J. Bronowski; Society of Authors (London), *William
Morris As I Knew Him* by Bernard Shaw, *The Works of Ber-
nard Shaw* by Bernard Shaw; George W. Stewart, Inc., *The
Great Tradition* by F. R. Leavis; University of California Press,
Swift and Defoe by John Frederick Ross; Viking Press, Inc.,
Collected Works by Dorothy Parker.

CONTENTS

THE GREAT TRADITION IN ENGLISH LITERATURE

VOLUME II

ROBERT BURNS TO BERNARD SHAW

includes the Index to both volumes

The Elizabethan Age and the
Bourgeois Revolution

THE ELIZABETHAN AGE

It is difficult for us today to imagine the reality and vigor of England's great Renaissance age, and of that early period of triumphant revolution which ushered in our modern world.

Sixteenth century England, and especially, its capital city London, were in the full enjoyment of a belated Renaissance, a humanist flowering of secular learning like that which had, a little earlier, reached Italy and France. But partly because of certain political events sketched below and the strong feeling of somewhat aggressive patriotism they engendered, partly because of the powerful current of the Reformation which had affected England almost as much as it did the Netherlands (and had inspired such martyred Protestant leaders as John Wyclif, William Tyndale, and Hugh Latimer) England wore its Renaissance with a difference. As the excellent French critic, Emile Legouis, says in his *History of English Literature*:

> While in France the Renaissance was eminently aristocratic, in England it was always regardful of the masses. It preserved and increased the vogue of the ballads. The theatre, the home of the most magnificent product of the period, was accessible to all men, appealed to the humble as well as to the great.

A striking example of this English integration of the new Renaissance emphasis on learning with the older popular cultural traditions is shown by the development of the medieval morality play in the early sixteenth century. (In France, on the contrary, this flourishing medieval folk art died out entirely during the Renaissance, and after 1548 popular performances of the other medieval religious plays, the mystery plays, were forbidden by law.)

One of the first of these new English morality plays was written by John Skelton in 1516. A famous humanist, noted as a Latinist and grammarian, and appointed tutor to the future Henry VIII, Skelton turned his back on the language of the court and university to write poetry in the still unrespected English vernacular. Thomas More's famous *Utopia*, for example, was written in Latin in 1516 and although widely known in his own time, was not translated into English until 1551. But Skelton said:

> Though my rime be ragged,
> Tatter'd and jagged,
> Rudely raine-beaten
> Rusty and moth-eaten;
> If ye take wel therewith,
> It hath in it some pith.

His morality play, *Magnificence*, does not represent the medieval struggle between heaven and hell for the soul of man. It represents a kingly Renaissance hero, Magnificence, who is almost ruined by following the advice of bad counselors but is saved by the help of such good, but equally worldly, ones as Hope, Circumspection and Perseverance.

An even more interesting secular adaptation of the old religious form, printed anonymously three years later, is called *The Four Elements*. It has as its devil, Ignorance, and as its hero, Humanity, son of the "Natura Naturata" who is saved by his guardian, Studious Desire.

In the late forties *The Play of Wyt and Science* was performed. In this a noble father, Reason, wishes to marry his daughter, Science, to the poor and low-born Human Wit, son of Nature. He answers arguments about the disparity of the match:

> Wherefore, syns they both be so meet matches
> To love each other, strawe for the patches
> Of worldly muckel syence [science] hath inowghe [enough]
> For them both to lyve.

In this play, too, one of the villains is Ignorance, born of Idleness.

About the same time another form of literature which deeply affected the developing Elizabethan drama began to appear.

In 1548 Edward Hall published his *Chronicles* which treated the history of the Civil Wars of Lancaster and York (the Wars of the Roses) and the reigns of Henry VII and VIII. Shakespeare's two great series of History Plays, which we will soon consider, drew much of their material from these very popular *Chronicles*. In 1561 another *Summarie of English Chronicles* was printed and ran into eleven editions in the following half century.

From 1578-1586 Raphael Holinshed's *Chronicles*, to which Shakespeare was also greatly indebted, appeared and were enthusiastically received by a public deeply interested in political affairs and avid for any lessons that might be learned from history.

The history which those who could not read were soon eagerly following on the bare Elizabethan stage was indeed a thrilling one.

The intoxication of freedom from feudal ties, and the excitement of the new horizons and possibilities which were opening up before the rising young bourgeoisie all over England, were already the very breath of the great Elizabethan Age when Elizabeth came to the throne in 1558.

Her grandfather, Henry VII, founder of the Tudor dynasty, had with his victory ended the hundred and fifty year fratricidal "Wars of the Roses" in which the feudal nobility had been largely destroyed. His need for support and his fear of any reviving rival power in the remnants of the old nobility made his Tudor monarchy from the beginning closely ally itself with the growing new power and wealth of the "middle class." His policies naturally fostered this growth and in many respects met the needs and paralleled the thinking of the most advanced sections of the bourgeoisie.

For example, the only way in which the notoriously thrifty Henry VII willingly spent royal funds was in bounties to encourage shipbuilding. And a century before Geoffrey Chaucer had already noted that, of all the pilgrims en route to Canterbury, only the prosperous "new man"—an active bourgeois merchant—was typically concerned about the neglect of England's sea power.

Henry's son, Henry VIII, had, in the course of England's opposition to Spain, then the center of European reaction, been led to defy the medieval power of the Catholic Church. With amazingly general support and virtually no internal opposition he had succeeded in asserting England's independence of that till then almost unchallenged supernational feudal authority.

By his confiscation and immediate piecemeal resale of the vast church estates, Henry VIII had enormously increased the power of the new monied men, now become landowners as well as merchants, had greatly stimulated trade, and had accelerated the formation of a new nobility whose origins were bourgeois and whose class interest promised loyalty to the throne, which then also meant to the principle of national unity.

At Henry VIII's death in 1547 commerce had grown so enormously that, according to some accounts, the population of London was quadrupled within one generation. The noble Council of Regency, appointed to rule in the name of his young son, did not have, among all its sixteen members, a single one whose title dated back even to the beginning of the century!

It is easy for us today to overlook the genuine advance involved in this substitution of a bourgeois for a feudal nobility.

But we must remember that when we speak of the Elizabethan Age as a revolutionary one we do not refer to a revolution of the miserably poor peasants or of the surprisingly large number of even more miserable "sturdy vagabonds"—the future mechanicks—forced off the land by early capitalist farming.

As Barrows Dunham's profound and witty *Giant in Chains* reminds us: "Feudalism fell . . . not by strength of the class which it directly exploited, but by strength of another class with which it merely interfered." This other class was, of course, the small but rapidly increasing bourgeoisie—some skilled craftsmen, some shipbuilders, some professionals, and above all the merchants.

And in many ways the demands made by this class were more progressive than its predominant composition would lead one to expect.

For, as the history of our own American Revolution and that of the French Revolution have amply illustrated, whenever any such middle class begins to struggle for its own emancipation and the freedom to develop itself, it must, at the beginning, state its case so as to seem to include universal emancipation and freedom of development. That it, as a class, invariably recoils in horror from this broad program as soon as the realization becomes a practical possibility, does not affect the statement's initial validity. And so, in the Elizabethan statement of the essential dignity of generic man, (a statement made in varying ways by Renaissance humanism everywhere at the beginning of the bourgeoisie's assumption of power), we find a universality from which three centuries of bourgeois power were to retreat, leaving its actual realization to a later more comprehensive revolution.

The reality of Tudor progress was emphasized when Edward

VI's death in childhood, and the accession of Elizabeth's older half-sister, the Catholic Mary, ushered in a bloody five years' attempt to reverse the movement of history.

The essential futility of this attempt is evident in the fact that there was never, during her entire reign, any concrete proposal to return even an acre of the confiscated land to the church! But a few of the most public spirited and courageous Protestant Church leaders, and over three hundred small farmers and artisans were burnt at the stake for refusing to disown their heresy. One of these, the brilliant Bishop Latimer, himself a small farmer's son, cried out as the fire was lit, to his colleague and companion in death:

> Play the man, Master Ridley; we shall this day by God's grace, light such a candle in England, as I trust shall never be put out.

The unpopularity of these persecutions was capped by Mary's marriage to the feared and hated king of Spain. Only the knowledge of her fatal illness prevented an uprising in 1558.

Elizabeth's accession was therefore welcomed with great relief and enthusiasm by almost all sections of the population. Even the large number of sincere Catholics were in general more afraid of Spanish domination and renewed civil war than they were of the results of a return to the very "Anglo-Catholic" Episcopalianism of Henry VIII. The event proved them correct. Elizabeth herself was, like her father and grandfather, untroubled with any particular religious convictions, and she was even more superbly gifted with the political sense that created the Tudor "absolutism by consent."

The church settlement she effected was planned to antagonize as few people as possible. The definitions of dogma were deliberately left vague, and the words of the Church services were carefully written so as to make several alternative interpretations equally plausible. A. L. Morton, in his *A People's History of England* summarizes her achievement:

> In the Elizabethan settlement Protestantism assumed the form most compatible with the monarchy and with the system of local government created by the Tudors. The parson in the villages became the close ally of the squire and almost as much a part of the State machine as the Justice of the Peace.

Elizabeth was thus in the happy position of a ruler attuned both temperamentally and intellectually to the tastes as well as the needs of her time.

Her keen interest in exploration and travel and her acknowledged partiality for the grizzled old—as well as the daring young—
sea dogs was another taste she shared with the citizens of her city.
This is clear from the tremendous number of travel books and
stories of heroic exploits and distant explorations carried on by
such curious and unconventional Englishmen as Sir Francis Drake
or Sir Walter Raleigh. These books seldom had much literary merit,
but they were a vital part of the exciting ferment of an age that
bred so great a literature. We must not forget Shakespeare's many
references to the "still-vext Bermoothes," the "Antipodes and men
whose heads beneath their shoulders grow," and the equally plausible "sea coast of Bohemia."

While the English Renaissance was thus fed by many other
streams beside the flow of literature from the ancient world, redis-
covered by fifteenth century European culture, it was, of course,
largely indebted to that source as well.

After the middle of the sixteenth century there was a flood of
translations of Greek and Latin classics, and of the fruits of the
earlier Italian and French Renaissance. It was in 1578 that George
Chapman published the translation of Homer which John Keats
has immortalized for us. Anyone taking the trouble to compare
Chapman's version with Pope's elegant and irrelevant eighteenth
century one will add a new respect for Elizabethan scholarship to
his admiration of Elizabethan poetry.

The great burst of lyric poetry by such sonneteers as Sir Philip
Sidney, Sir Thomas Wyatt, and the Earl of Surrey, and the richly
pictorial narrative poetry of the *Faerie Queene* by that poet's poet,
Edmund Spenser, are all well-known evidences of the Elizabethan
age's exuberant vitality.

Less interesting to us today, but also extremely important in
the development of our modern English, are the ornate and fantastic early prose narratives like John Lyly's *Euphues* and Sidney's
Arcadia. But such early literary criticism as Sidney's noble *Apologie
for Poetrie* in which he maintains the poet's dignity as the first
lawgiver of society, and its prophet, are still important for their
content as well as their style.

There are other less known theoretical works which are equally
valuable for those who wish fully to realize the meaning of humanism and its respect for man—an attitude absolutely fundamental to
any real understanding of Shakespeare's greatness. For example, we
may glance at *The Laws of Ecclesiastical Polity* by Richard Hooker,

which he had been working on for many years and which was published immediately after his death in 1600.

Hooker was the son of a poor man, destined for an apprenticeship, whose extraordinary brilliance attracted his schoolmaster's attention and won him a scholarship to Oxford. Graduated with high honors in the early seventies, he refused preferment and asked for a small country living where he might "behold God's blessings spring out of my mother earth and eat my own bread without oppositions."

There he devoted himself largely to the huge work he left unfinished at his death. Quiet and conservative in tone, it nevertheless shares the major attitude of his tumultuous and progressive age, its faith in active reason, in man's power to affect the world, and in his full responsibility for whatever he may choose to do or leave undone. A characteristic passage reads:

> Man in perfection of nature being made according to the likeness of his Maker resembleth Him also in the manner of working: so that whatsoever we work as men, the same we do wittingly work and freely; neither are we according to the manner of natural agents any way so tied but that it is in our power to leave done the things we do undone.

Another more obscure ecclesiastical writer, Thomas Starkey, also uses religious terminology to express his regard for the divinity of man's reason:

> Thus, if we with ourself reason, and consider the works of man here upon earth, we shall nothing doubt of his excellent dignity, but plainly affirm that he hath in him a sparkle of Divinity, and is surely of a celestial and divine nature, seeing that by memory and wit also he conceiveth the nature of all things. For there is nothing here in this world, neither in heaven above, nor in earth beneath, but he by his reason comprehendeth it. So that I think we may conclude that man by nature, in excellence and dignity, even so excelleth all other creatures here upon earth, as God exceedeth the nature of man.

These quotations are generally characteristic of Renaissance humanism, but the emphasis on society as an indivisible entity, which alone made it possible for men to realize their potentialities, is more specifically characteristic of the English culture of the period. Even in England there were many great men like Shakespeare's brilliant predecessor, Christopher Marlowe (1564-1593), who stressed the new freedom of individual development as opposed to the older sense of community, but the typical sixteenth century English thought is here better represented by such writers as Hooker, Starkey, and of course Shakespeare himself.

Starkey, for example, says:

> . . . we should have a multitude of people convenient to the place, flourishing with all good abundance of exterior things required to the bodily wealth of man, the which living together in civil life, governed by politic order and rule, should conspire together in amity and love, everyone glad to help another to his power, to the intent that the whole might attain to that perfection which is determined to the dignity of man's nature by the goodness of God, the which is the end of all laws and order, for which purpose they be writ and ordained.

And Hooker adds:

> . . . forasmuch as we are not by ourselves sufficient to furnish ourselves with a competent store of things needful for such a life as our nature doth desire, a life fit for the dignity of man; therefore to supply these defects and imperfections which are in us living single and solely by ourselves, we are naturally induced to seek communion and fellowship with others. This was the cause of men's uniting themselves at the first in politic societies, which societies could not be without government, nor government without a distinct kind of Law. Two foundations there are which bear up public societies; the one, a natural inclination whereby all men desire sociable life and fellowship; the other, an order expressly or secretly agreed upon touching the manner of their union in living together.

Yet for all the variety of Elizabethan literature, its great glory and supreme gift to the world was unquestionably its theatre—still the source of the greatest drama the English-speaking stage has ever known.

This theatre had, as we have seen, roots reaching back to the folk productions of the medieval morality plays, which had been presented by guilds in every sizable English town for centuries. But in its Elizabethan reincarnation this theatre was uniquely the product of late sixteenth century London, and so intimately affected by the queen and her court that we must consider a little more closely the position of the last of the Tudors and her relation to the people Shakespeare's theatre served.

Queen Elizabeth herself was an enlightened representative of her age and seemed surprisingly well aware of the contemporary movement of history. Absolute in power but flexible in policy, aware of the real importance of wealth and careless of military glory, personally interested in her country's welfare and indifferent in matters of religion, she deliberately appealed to widespread support among the common people and jealously repressed the rise of any powerful factions in the nobility. She served during the last third of the sixteenth century as a dramatic center and symbol for a rare—and brief—period in which the real interests of the most progressive class in the country were also the dominant ones of the country, and expressed themselves as those of the nation itself.

In 1608, five years after her death, that great thinker and shrewd observer, Francis Bacon, wrote some notes "On The Fortunate Memory of Elizabeth, Queen of England." These were presented to King James, a ruler under whom Bacon received the rewards and recognition Elizabeth never gave him, and a king who made barely a pretense of any respect or affection for his predecessor. He certainly was not to be favorably impressed by any praise bestowed upon her, and Bacon certainly knew it. We may, therefore, fairly accept what Bacon wrote in this brief essay as the honest and considered opinion of a competent judge who had had unusual opportunities for personal observation.

> Elizabeth both in her nature and her fortune was a wonderful person among women, a memorable person among princes. . . .
>
> The government of a woman has been a rare thing at all times; felicity in such government a rarer thing still; felicity and long continuance together the rarest thing of all. Yet this Queen reigned forty-four years, and did not outlive her felicity. . . .
>
> Observe too that this same humour of her people, over eager for war and impatient of peace, did not prevent her from cultivating and maintaining peace during the whole time of her reign. And this her desire of peace, together with the success of it, I count among her greatest praises; as a thing happy for her times, becoming to her sex, and salutary for her conscience. . . .
>
> Upon another account also this peace so cultivated and

maintained by Elizabeth is matter of admiration; namely, that it proceeded not from any inclination of the times to peace, but from her own prudence and good management. For in a kingdom laboring with intestine faction on account of religion, and standing as a shield and stronghold of defence against the then formidable and overbearing ambition of Spain, matter for war was nowise wanting; it was she who by her forces and her counsels combined kept it under; . . .

Nor was she less fortunate in escaping the treacherous attempts of conspirators than in defeating and repelling the forces of the enemy . . . and yet was not her life made thereby more alarmed or anxious; . . . but still secure and confident, and thinking more of the escape than of the danger, she held her wonted course. . . .

With regard to her moderation in religion there may seem to be a difficulty, on account of the severity of the laws made against popish subjects. But on this point I have some things to advance which I myself carefully observed and know to be true.

Her intention undoubtedly was, on the one hand not to force consciences, but on the other not to let the state, under pretence of conscience and religion, be brought in danger. . . . Not even when provoked by the excommunication pronounced against her by Pius Quintus, did she depart almost at all from this clemency, but perservered in the course which was agreeable to her own nature. For being both wise and of a high spirit, she was little moved with the sound of such terrors: knowing she could depend upon the loyalty and love of her own people, and upon the small power the popish party within the realm had to do harm, as long as they were not seconded by a foreign enemy. . . .

As for those lighter points of character,—as that she allowed herself to be wooed and courted, and even to have love made to her; and liked it; and continued it beyond the natural age for such vanities;—if any of the sadder sort of persons be disposed to make a great matter of this, it may be observed that there is something to admire in these very things, which ever way you take them. For if viewed indulgently, they are much like the accounts we find in romances, of the Queen in the blessed islands, and her court and institutions, who allows of amorous admiration but prohibits desire. But if you take them seriously, they challenge admiration of another kind and of a very high order; for certain it is that these dalliances detracted but little from her fame and nothing at all from her majesty, and neither weakened her power nor sensibly hindered her business:—whereas such things are not infrequently allowed to interfere with the public fortune. . . .

But the truth is that the only true commender of this lady is time, which, so long a course as it has run, has produced nothing in this sex like her, for the administration of civil affairs.

We have already noted the almost universal joy with which England greeted the beginning of Elizabeth's reign because it meant the end of religious persecution, of Spanish influence, and of the dangers of civil war.

For many years Elizabeth deliberately allowed Philip of Spain to think there was a chance of a marriage which would again bind England to a Spanish alliance and, in view of Spain's still greatly superior wealth and power, to Spanish domination. She realized that a test of strength with Spain was almost inevitable but hoped to postpone it as long as possible, partly because of her intense dislike of the waste and destruction war entailed, partly because England was daily becoming a more prosperous manufacturing nation, and every year made her better able to meet Spain's challenge.

Finally in 1587 Mary, Queen of Scots, and claimant to the English throne, was executed for complicity in a plot to assassinate Elizabeth. She bequeathed to Philip of Spain her claim, which was based on the grounds that Henry's non-Catholic marriage to Elizabeth's mother had been illegal, and that Elizabeth herself was therefore illegitimate.

Philip had by then long lost his faith in Elizabeth's susceptibility, and saw no reason for delaying an invasion. The awe-inspiring Armada was equipped and an uprising by the remaining Catholic nobility of the North, with whom he had for years been communicating through the Jesuits, was planned to coincide with the landing in London.

The enormous Spanish galleons were still organized essentially as ships for the transport of troops and, if forced to engage in naval battles, followed the time honored method of grappling with the enemy ship and boarding it, with as many men as possible, to fight on deck.

The lively little English ships, on the other hand, were built for maneuverability on the sea, had cannons fitted at every porthole as well as on deck, and literally sailed circles around the floating castles of Spain, pouring a steady fire of cannon balls which were made more terribly effective by the helplessly crowded Spanish decks.

In a very real sense the battle was a test of strength between the modern and the medieval world, and the rout of the latter was neither an accident nor a miracle but a predictable result.

The new national consciousness reached delirious heights of patriotism and self-confidence at the defeat of the imperial Spanish Armada by a fleet of small merchant ships whose captains and owners largely represented the most daring and representative members of the bourgeoisie.

The popularity of the queen, who had actively identified herself with the defense of London and its citizen-defenders, also reached new heights. Neither Elizabeth nor any other English sovereign was ever again to be so wonderful a symbol of national strength and unity.

Nowhere was this victory more resoundingly celebrated than in the London theatres.

Two parts of *Tamburlaine,* the first play by that extraordinary young Christopher Marlowe, appeared in 1587-88, and were rapidly followed by *The Tragical History* of *Doctor Faustus* in 1588 and *The Jew of Malta* in 1589.

In strange and terrible ways these are three variations on the soaring spirit of man, his eager curiosity, his towering pride, and his insatiable appetite for power whether that be won by military might, knowledge, or gold.

It is interesting to remember that Marlowe's spirit still had vitality enough to trouble a Congressional Committee in 1938 which, investigating the Federal Theatre, demanded, in reference to its production of *Doctor Faustus,* whether that author were "another party member."

But although he was the greatest of them, Marlowe, was only one of the impecunious university men whom the newly organized groups of professional London actors had begun to call on for assistance in supplying their growing public with up-to-date material. They paid writers little but provided a never glutted market, and many learned men condescended to write new plays or rewrite old ones for their vast new largely illiterate public.

The first permanent professional company had been organized in London in 1574 under the protection of the Earl of Leicester and two years later the first playhouse was built at Shoreditch just outside of London. A number of others rapidly followed, each technically of the household of some nobleman who gave them his protection and countenance, although their real economic dependence was then, as now, on the box office.

The queen herself frequently ordered command performance of new or markedly popular plays, and the members of her court followed her example.

Many noblemen themselves attended performances at the regular theatres as well, and the comparatively huge audiences presented an amazing cross section of London. Professor Alfred Harbage, in a carefully documented study of *Shakespeare's Audiences* has shown how representative an audience these plays appealed to, ranging from apprentices who paid tu'ppence for admission to gentlemen who had paid several pounds for a seat.

Legouis correctly relates this broad audience to the extraordinary power of the Elizabethan drama, saying:

> Rich as are all the manifestations of the English literature of the Renaissance, its highest glory and the most direct and original expression of the national genius are dramatic. Elsewhere imitation and artifice play a part; aristocratic sentiment or an ephemeral fashion is a check on spontaneity, ruling out whatever is of the people, . . .
>
> The theatre was open to all: the whole town was attracted by it and enthusiastic for it. It was truly national. For many it took the place of the church they neglected: to most, in this time of no newspapers and few and little-read novels, it was the only source of intellectual pleasure. A secular temple, it provided from time to time a communion of patriotism instead of the old communion of faith.
>
> . . . Never has any other audience been so stimulating to writers, who received their immediate reward in tears or laughter, noisy and multitudinous applause.

As we have already partially indicated, London had experienced an enormous influx of an active and alert but largely illiterate citizenry, keenly interested in matters of public concern, newly curious about the background of their so recently discovered "nation," and deeply stirred by England's sudden assumption of leadership in world affairs and London's growing cosmopolitanism. Their horizons were daily pushed further apart by returning travelers with tales of the antipodes, and stimulated by the talk filtering down to them of other travelers who had visited the starry regions and seen, in the mind's eye at least, the vistas of the ancient Roman world. This audience would in itself almost account for the spontaneous generation of an unequaled theatre.

It is a sad commentary on the distance which professional artists have traveled from the people when we find the last poet laureate of England blaming the "wretched beings" for whom Shakespeare was forced to write, for all the "faults" of his plays, and the sacrifice of an infinitely greater art!

But, of course, this theatre was no spontaneous generation. As we have seen, there was already in England a long and well-loved tradition of truly popular drama in the old miracle, mystery and morality plays, introduced by the Church and taken up and elaborated by the guilds in every sizable town of medieval England. This, together with the well-developed taste' for pageantry nourished first by the rich ritual of the Catholic Church and then by the numerous "royal progresses" or processions and frequent public masques and entertainments provide a legitimate ancestry and adequately account for the enormous popularity of the Elizabethan theatre.

There is also another more philosophical sense in which the drama was the logical expression of the Renaissance humanism of the Elizabethan Age. For the Elizabethan mind, man was, essentially, the hero of his own most dramatic story. And not a passive hero or a spectator but one who took it upon himself to change the map of the world and the shape of the heavens. Whether he was a king who redefined the channels through which God's rule might be exercised in England, a merchant adventurer who added a new dimension to the earth, or a lord chancellor who "took all knowledge to be his province," the representative Elizabethan man was an active and effective force in the world, which centered about him and his concerns. There was nothing he might not dare and little he could not do. And everything he dared or did affected the body politic itself, changing the lives of many of his fellows and making a difference to the whole universe. Macbeth's desire to be king does not merely lead to the early death of an old man and the subsequent remorse and sleeplessness of a younger one— Macbeth murdered sleep itself. He confounds the universal peace— the frame of things disjoints—both the worlds suffer until, with the help of the legitimate prince, those fighting against him succeed and give to their tables meat, sleep to their nights, free from their homes and banquets bloody knives, pay faithful homage and receive true honors; in other words, set the frame of things right again.

For such men, who were rooted in the real world, whose desires expressed themselves in practical action, and whose intentions had material results, drama was a natural form of expression and would no doubt have been important even if all rather than only some twenty or twenty-five percent of its audience had known how to read. As it was, it was supreme, and gives us in distillation whatever of woe and wonder occupied the mind of Elizabethan London —the heart of Renaissance England.

What this was we shall see in more detail when we turn to Shakespeare himself and the themes which absorbed the interest of his audiences, and his own interest. First, however, we must very briefly summarize the political movements of Elizabeth's last fifteen years, which were, roughly, also the first fifteen years of Shakespeare's writing career.

The jubilation of a united nation at the defeat of the Spanish Armada was not a triumphant fifth act curtain but only a dramatic second act climax.

The removal of an immediate external threat and the bourgeoisie's dawning realization of their great growing strength as a class made them begin to question the secondary role which was all they had, so far, aspired to play in national politics.

Meanwhile although the throne was no longer as seriously threatened by any revival of feudal power this was by no means an impossible fear. (See the discussion of Essex' rebellion on p. 88 ff.) There were also other ways in which the crown had to demand increased assistance from the commons.

Tudor government was by our standards extremely inexpensive, but compared to the altogether decentralized feudal system of medieval England it was very dear. Today England's national budget makes extravagant provision for a household and personal allowance to the sovereign, but in the sixteenth and seventeenth centuries it was the sovereign who had to provide a national budget out of his private estate.

It was therefore necessary for Elizabeth constantly to secure large sums of money. Many of these were provided by grants more or less voluntarily voted by a House of Commons and by wealthy

city councils, which generally approved the royal policy and took
a patriotic pride in the respect their queen's personal wit and learning and astute diplomacy won for England.

But there was always a deficit which she made up by granting
various noblemen "patents" or monopolies of such products as
wines, lace, and, too often, more necessary articles. These were
paid for either in lump sums of gold, or in services to the throne,
and amounted to a form of indirect taxation.

The growing independence of the large commercial interests
and the increasing burden of the longer and longer list of monopolies mounted steadily during the last years of her reign and
reached a climax in her last parliament, the year before her death.

The following incident is worth describing for the light it
throws on the genuine conflict her successor inherited, and on the
political tact with which she had kept it from breaking into open
opposition between the commons and the crown during her life.

Elizabeth was almost seventy, and had long been increasingly
imperious and notoriously quick tempered in her manner to the
court favorites and other members of the nobility. When she heard
of the unprecedented criticism which greeted the reading of the
long list of monopolies at the opening session of the House of
Commons, she immediately sent for the terrified Speaker. To his
overwhelming relief she was affability itself. She told him she had
just learned that "divers patents" she had granted "were grievous"
to her subjects and that this had occupied her thoughts "even in
the midst of . . . most great and weighty occasions," and that it
should be corrected with all convenient speed.

A delegation from the so recently disaffected Commons arrived,
knelt before her and said, in the words of the Speaker:

> In all duty and thankfulness, prostrate at your feet, we
> present our most loyal and thankful hearts, and the last spirit
> in our nostrils, to be poured out, to be breathed up, for your
> safety.

She answered:

> Mr. Speaker, we perceive your coming is to present thanks
> unto us; know I accept them with no less joy than your loves
> can have desired to offer such a present, and do more esteem
> it than any treasure or riches, for those we know how to prize,

> but loyalty, love and thanks I account them invaluable; and, though God hath raised me high, yet this I account the glory of my crown, that I have reigned with your loves.

Then, after telling the deputation to rise she continued, graciously and effectively, if disingenuously:

> When I heard it, I could give no rest unto to my thoughts until I had reformed it, and those varlets, lewd persons, abusers of my bounty, shall know I will not suffer it. And, Mr. Speaker, tell the House from me that I take it exceeding grateful that the knowledge of these things have come unto me from them.

She concluded, with substantially more honesty:

> Of myself, I must say this, I never was any greedy scraping grasper, nor a strict fast-holding prince, nor yet a waster; my heart was never set upon any worldly goods, but only for my subjects' good. . . .
> And, though you have had and may have many mightier and wiser princes sitting in this seat, yet you never had nor shall have any love you better.

In addition to this tension of class conflict beginning to appear during the last years of Elizabeth's reign, there was the continual threat of war through Spanish aggression, through England's commitments to the Protestant Netherlands in their fight for freedom, or through the pressure of the young lords of the powerful noble families, who still saw in military glory the main road to both prestige and wealth.

Most serious of all was the danger of a civil war which, many felt, would be precipitated by the queen's death since there was no natural heir to the throne.

These fears were kept alive by the innumerable plots for her assassination, the Catholic intrigues in Ireland made effective by the terrible oppression and justified grievances of that unhappy country—England's first colony—and the still fresh horrors of England's hundred and fifty year long war of the Roses, fought over a disputed succession.

It is this background of national growth, commercial expansion and political concern which gives us the key to the predominantly political drama that culminated in Shakespeare's great plays, where all the terrors of real life are faced and outfaced by an essentially sanguine and self-reliant humanity.

WILLIAM SHAKESPEARE

William Shakespeare was born in Stratford, a small but important market town, during the week of April 23, 1564, the third of a family of eight children. His father, John Shakespeare, was a well-to-do merchant and leading citizen in the town who had repeatedly served as a member of the town council and had held almost all the important town offices at one time or another.

Although there is no record of Shakespeare's education, Stratford is known to have possessed an excellent grammar school, taught by university graduates, and there is no reason to doubt that Shakespeare attended it.

In November, 1582, there is a record of a marriage between Shakespeare, then eighteen and a half, and the twenty-six year old daughter of a yeoman, Ann Hathaway. Since their first child, Susanna, was born less than five months later it is likely that the marriage was one of necessity. Their only remaining children, the twins Judith and Hamnet (who died at twelve), were born in February, 1585.

After this there is no further record of Shakespeare until we find him established as a rising young playwright in 1592. The likelihood is that he left Stratford for London and the theatre soon after the birth of the twins, and lived through the exciting years of the Spanish defeat in the capital.

There are legends of his having held horses outside the playhouses, and certainly he must have lived hard and undertaken many odd jobs before he succeeded in winning admission as a player of small parts and, soon, a refurbisher of old plays, to one of the several companies then using the three London houses.

But by 1592, when he was twenty-eight, his success was such that a contemporary, Robert Greene, one of the best known of the university men who somewhat patronizingly bestowed their talents on the theatre, wrote to his colleagues jealously denouncing the "upstart Crow, beautified with our feathers, that with his *Tiger's heart wrapt in a Player's hide*" (this parodies a line in *Henry VI* "O tiger's heart wrapt in a woman's hide") "supposes he is as well able to bombast out a blank verse as the best of you: and being an absolute Johannes fac totum [Jack of all trades] is in his own conceit the only Shake-scene in the country."

On April 18, 1593, there is an official record of the publication of Shakespeare's first known poem, the long narrative *Venus and Adonis,* which was dedicated to his patron, the Earl of Southampton, a friend and follower of Lord Essex. This poem was immediately popular and was reprinted eleven times in the next few years.

In May, 1594, Shakespeare's second nondramatic poem, *The Rape of Lucrece,* was published with a much warmer and more intimate dedication to the same patron.

That year the Lord Chamberlain's Company was formed. Shakespeare was from the beginning an important member of this leading theatrical company, and appears frequently in its business records from then on.

In 1598 a young scholar, Frances Meres, wrote *A Comparative Discourse of our English poets with the Greek, Latin and Italian poets.* In this he spoke warmly of Shakespeare as one by whom "the English tongue is mightily enriched, and gorgeously invested in rare ornaments and splendid habilments." He continued:

> As Plautus and Seneca are accounted the best for Comedy and Tragedy among the Latins: so Shakespeare among the English is the most excellent in both kinds for the stage. . . . so I say that the Muses would speak with Shakespeare's fine filed phrase if they would speak English.

Meres included in this article a list of the twelve principal plays which Shakespeare, was, so far, known to have written.

He also referred to the manuscript circulation of the sonnets, saying:

> the sweet witty soul of Ovid lives in mellifluous and honey-tongued Shakespeare, witness his *Venus and Adonis,* his Lucrece, his sugared sonnets among his private friends. . . .

In 1601 there developed a fierce rivalry between the "intellectuals" or classicists who wrote largely for the small aristocratic child-actor theatres, discussed at length in Professor Alfred Harbage's excellent *Shakespeare and the Rival Tradition*, and the less learned, more powerful, favorites of the popular audiences.

A topical satire of the time has an actor exclaim:

> Why, here's our fellow Shakespeare puts them all down; aye, and Ben Jonson too. O that Ben Jonson's a pestilent fellow; he brought up Horace giving the poets a pill, but our fellow Shakespeare hath given him a purge that made him bewray his credit.

Nine years later in an echo of this dispute a John Davies contrasted "W. S." with the bitter sneering favorites of the court coteries, saying:

> Some others rail, but rail as they think fit,
> Thou hast no railing but a reigning wit.

In 1612 a younger Jacobean dramatist, John Webster, author of *The White Devil* and *The Duchess of Malfi*, referred dutifully, but less enthusiastically, to Shakespeare's "right happy and copious industry."

In 1616, immediately after Shakespeare's death, an obscure contemporary poet, W. Basse, wrote charmingly, and on the whole prophetically:

> Renowned Spenser, lie a thought more nigh
> To learned Chaucer; and, rare Beaumont, lie
> A little nearer Spenser, to make room
> For Shakespeare in your threefold, fourfold tomb.
> To lodge all four in one bed make a shift,
> For until doomsday hardly will a fifth
> Betwixt this day and that by fate be slain
> For whom your curtains need be drawn again.

It is of course to this conceit that Ben Jonson is referring in the third, fourth and fifth lines of his tribute below. It was contributed to a formal memorial volume published in 1623, barely seven years after Shakespeare's death.

> . . . Soul of the age!
> The applause! delight! the wonder of our stage!
> My Shakespeare rise! I will not lodge thee by

> Chaucer, or Spenser, or bid Beaumont lie
> A little further off, to make thee room:
> Thou art a monument without a tomb,—
>
> .   .   .   .
>
> And tell how far thou didst our Lyly outshine
> Or sporting Kyd, or Marlowe's mighty line.
> And though thou hadst small Latin and less Greek
> From thence to honor thee, I will not seek
> For names: but call forth thundering Aeschylus,
> Euripides, and Sophocles to us, . . .
>
> .   .   .   .
>
> Triumph, my Britain, thou hast one to show,
> To whom all scenes of Europe homage owe.
> He was not for an age, but for all time!

In the face of all these and many other intimate contemporary references to Shakespeare's work, it is almost incomprehensible that so many men should have found the time, money, and energy to waste in writing, printing, buying, and reading books that "prove" Shakespeare's plays were written by the Baron of Verulam (better known as Francis Bacon); by Lord Rutland; by the Count of Derby; by the Earl of Oxford; or by a half dozen other invariably titled gentlemen.

That England's and, perhaps the world's, greatest poetry should have been written by "our fellow Shakespeare," a man with no title at all, who knew "little Latin and less Greek" has evidently presented insuperable difficulties to many. But, as Legouis says:

> Rather than be surprised that Shakespeare, like Moliere, was an actor and yet wrote plays which were masterpieces, we might well ask if it would have been possible for him to write them in any other walk of life.

However, true as this is, it is only part of the truth. Even after we have said that, if any man were to be able to write Shakespeare's plays he must have been a man of the working theatre, the major question still remains. Why should one human being tower so far above successive generations of his most magnificent fellows? How can one artist be unquestioned master in so rich a field of art as that which modern English literature presents to us?

This question, like so many others in the world of art, cannot be answered unless we see the artist as a part of the life by which he was formed, and which he himself helped to form. It is not the potential Shakespeare whom we have to consider as uniquely great —there may have been others, not many but a few, born with the same capacities—but the actual Shakespeare maturing in an age when the old social and economic order had been destroyed and a new world was coming to birth—and when his nation and indeed his city had taken a leading part in that destruction and that great new birth.

When we today think of a progressive artist it is almost impossible for us not, at the same time, to think of him as an "opposition" artist—as one who, with all his greatness, cannot speak in the tones of easy unself-conscious authority which a great writer, serving as the voice of his time and happily representing a comparatively unquestioned tradition, can use. It was Shakespeare's great good fortune—and ours—that brought him to birth at the brief period in which he could at one and the same time express his own deepest convictions and the central feeling of his age, analytically rather than argumentatively, to an audience which largely shared and embodied both. This period did not last out even his own time, but it sufficed for his formative years and the greater part of his writing life.

In these pages we cannot, of course, attempt anything like a real analysis of Shakespeare's thought. But, naming the plays roughly in the probable order of their appearance, we can glance at certain vital aspects of his political and social philosophy which they illustrate. If this running commentary suggests new questions for each reader's own attention as he returns to reconsider the plays it will be amply justified. This discursive chronological approach may also help us form a more concrete idea of the development of Shakespeare's political and social views in the course of his writing life.

That life began, as we have seen, some time in the late eighties. Before 1594 Shakespeare had written the trilogy of *Henry VI* (parts of which he may have preserved substantially unaltered from an older chronicle play in the possession of his company), *Richard III, Titus Andronicus* (almost certainly, and in much greater part, the work of a crude earlier hand), *Love's Labour Lost, The Two Gentlemen of Verona, The Comedy of Errors,* and *The Taming of the Shrew.*

Much of the mature Shakespeare is here already apparent, in subject matter more than in style, although in *Richard III* the language begins to be unmistakably that of Ben Jonson's "beloved master."

Four of the plays (the three parts of *Henry VI* and *Richard III*) deal concretely with then recent English history, stressing ideas of vital and controversial interest to Elizabethan audiences. Among these are, of course, the incomparable horrors of civil war and the necessity of national unity; the qualities and responsibilities of a real sovereign; the bearing of the personal relations and desires of important public figures on political events; the effect of the political climate of an age on private character; the essential irrelevance of religion to matters of state; and the importance of a legitimate and unquestioned succession to the throne.

This is far from an exhaustive list even of the most interesting general questions raised in these four plays, and there is much else of sheer dramatic and poetic excitement in *Richard III*. However even this brief reference should begin to show some of the major concerns which Shakespeare shared with his alert and politically minded audience.

Titus Andronicus, the poorest of Shakespeare's plays—it is only in very small part his play—deals with some of the same Elizabethan political problems, transposed in scene to Rome. It also has at least one passage of particular interest to modern readers, who know how soon and how far the bourgeoisie was to retreat, in racial terms, from any assertion of human equality.

The Roman empress, after an affair with Aaron, a Moor, gives birth to a black child which her two villainous older sons attempt to kill. Its father, almost equally wicked in other matters, defies them with:

> Stay, murderous villains! will you kill your brother?
> Now, by the burning tapers of the sky,
> That shone so brightly when this boy was got,
> He dies upon my scimitar's sharp point
> That touches this my first-born son and heir!
> I tell you, younglings, not Euceladus,
> With all his threat'ning band of Typhoon's brood,
> Nor great Alcides, nor the god of war,
> Shall seize this prey out of his father's hands.
> What, what, ye sanguine, shallow-hearted boys!
> Ye white-limed walls! ye alehouse painted signs!
> Coal-black is better than another hue;
> For all the water in the ocean
> Can never turn the swan's black legs to white,

> Although she lave them hourly in the flood.
> Tell the empress from me, I am of age
> To keep my own,—excuse it how she can.

The comedies are all amusing, as their frequent repetition for over three centuries has amply certified, and even the least known of them, *Two Gentlemen of Verona,* is precious for the many delightful passages between the poor servant, Launce, and the mongrel dog he treasures. We wait from scene to scene for a resumption of Launce's reproachful but forgiving talk of and to his beast, whom he loves far more than both gentlemen together do all their ladies.

In one such long-suffering monologue Launce begins plaintively to review the dog's misdeeds for the dog's own edification. Speaking in the third person that the lesson may be more impressive, he says:

> He thrusts me himself into the company of three or four gentleman—like dogs, under the duke s table: he had not been there (bless the mark!) a pissing while, but all the Chamber smelt him. "Out with the dog," says one; "What cur is that?" says another; "whip him out," says the third; "Hang him up," says the duke. I, having been acquainted with the smell before, knew it was Crab; and goes me to the fellow that whips the dogs: "Friend," quoth I, "you mean to whip the dog?" "Ay, marry, do I," quoth I, " 't was I did the thing you wot of." He makes me no more ado, but whips me out of the chamber. How many masters would do this for his servant? Nay, I'll be sworn, I have sat in the stock for puddings he hath stolen, otherwise he had been executed; I have stood in the pillory for geese he hath kill'd, otherwise he had suffer'd for 't.

Then in a grand climax of pathos Launce turns directly to his unrepentant hound and feelingly demands:

> Thou think'st not of this now! Nay, I remember the trick you served me when I took my leave of Madam Silvia; did not I bid thee still mark me, and do as I do? When didst thou see me heave up my leg, and make water against a gentlewoman's farthingale? didst thou ever see me do such a trick?

This is his last appearance, but only the first of a long series of increasingly important Shakespearian "clowns" whose simplicity is often shrewdly closer to the mark than all their masters' wisdom.

As T. A. Jackson, the provocative Irish literary critic and historian, says:

> the common people in Shakespeare . . . are more richly individual, more specifically "humorsome," and generally more human, than the lords and ladies who provide the decorative as distinct from the comic background to the plays. (In Hamlet, for instance, the grave digger has far more character than Horatio, or Rosencrantz and Guildenstern; while the most contemptible of the personages in the play is the courtly fop Osric.)

Love's Labour Lost, a far more lyrical comedy, has an interesting reversal of the conventional humorous situation in its mockery of three young aristocrats who proudly forswear love to devote themselves to deep studies, and are rapidly brought to their knees by the wit and beauty of three independent ladies. A comparison with Tennyson's insufferably patronizing *The Princess,* with its bland assumption that "man's love is of his life a thing apart; 'tis woman's whole existence," will show how far the position of women —in comedy as well as life—had deteriorated from Elizabeth to Victoria.

The next group of plays, probably written and produced between 1594 and 1597 were *Romeo and Juliet, A Midsummer Night's Dream, Richard II, King John* and *The Merchant of Venice.* Here there is no longer any question of the master's hand, and to ask which of these plays is best is only, as Keats said, to inquire in which mood you prefer the ocean.

Romeo and Juliet is one of Shakespeare's very few serious love plays, and again it is noteworthy that here, as later, we find an expression of his ungrudging, unreserved equalitarian attitude toward women. This attitude, too, was characteristic of the most progressive part of bourgeois thought in its revolutionary period.

The importance and dignity of Shakespeare's heroines, their frequent leadership in wit, courage, determination, honesty and resourcefulness, are all only one aspect of his thought on the question of woman's position in society. But so far as it goes, his attitude is as worthily represented by his picture of the fourteen-year old Juliet as it is later by his more mature heroines.

Again, just because it is clearly and avowedly a love play, *Romeo and Juliet* offers striking evidence of Shakespeare's consistent, often unconscious, interest in contemporary political and economic problems.

The play begins and ends with the theme of civil war—seen in miniature in Verona, this time. The Prologue opens:

> Two households, both alike in dignity,
> In Fair Verona, where we lay our scene,
> From ancient grudge break to new mutiny,
> Where civil blood makes civil hands unclean.

And in the closing scene the Prince declares:

> And I, for winking at your discords too,
> Have lost a brace of kinsmen: all are punisht.

We get an incidental but penetrating comment on the class nature of the law and the relation of the state to poverty at the very moment when Romeo, no political economist but a desperate and rash young lover, has just been (wrongly) informed that his bride is dead. He naturally wants to commit suicide upon her grave, needs poison, and begins to bethink himself where, in a strange city, he can purchase some.

> Romeo: Well, Juliet, I will lie with thee tonight.
> Let's see for means. O mischief, thou art swift
> To enter in the thoughts of desperate men!
> I do remember an apothecary,
> And hereabouts a' dwells, which late I noted
> In tatter'd weeds, with overwhelming brows,
> Culling of simples; meagre were his looks;
> Sharp misery had worn him to the bones;
>   .   .   .   .   .
> Noting this penury, to myself I said,
> "An if a man did need a poison now
> Whose sale is present death in Mantua,
> Here lives a caitiff wretch would sell it him."
>   .   .   .   .   .
> What, ho! apothecary!
> Apoth: Who calls so loud?
> Romeo: Come hither, man. I see that thou art poor;
> Hold, there is forty ducats: let me have
> A dram of poison; such soon-speeding gear
> As will disperse itself through all the veins,
> That the life-weary taker may fall dead,
>   .   .   .   .   .   .

> Apoth: Such mortal drugs I have; but Mantua's law
> Is death to any he that utters them.
> Romeo: Art thou so bare and full of wretchedness,
> And fear'st to die? famine is in thy cheeks,
> Need and oppression starveth in thy eyes,
> Contempt and beggary hangs upon thy back,
> The world is not thy friend, nor the world's law:
> The world affords no law to make thee rich;
> Then be not poor, but break it, and take this.
> Apoth: My poverty, but not my will, consents.
> Romeo: I pay thy poverty and not thy will.

Richard II, the first of Shakespeare's second series of history plays, is in some ways the most interesting of them all. In it Shakespeare goes back three generations before the outbreak of the civil wars to find their deep-rooted cause. He dramatically presents the contrast between a dying feudalism and the vigorous new bourgeois monarchy, and analyzes the concrete meaning of "the divine right" of kings by posing the question whether it is right to give allegiance to an irresponsible, weak, unjust but legitimate king rather than to replace him by a shrewd, politic and efficient one with no real legal claim to the throne.

The question thus schematically put gives no idea of the richness of its concrete representation in the play, or of the profound political understanding and amazing dramatic skill with which the balance is held.

There is little else in literature at once as subtle and as emphatic as the continual unresolved but uncontradictory distinction Shakespeare draws between the necessity of absolute royal power to end feudal conflicts, and the almost ridiculous arbitrariness of its personal use; between the need for adherence to the doctrine of divine right which insures a peaceful legitimate succession, and the preposterousness of a king's own literal belief in his divinity; between the sanctity of the sovereign's position, and the frequent futility of the individual sovereign.

John Palmer, in his indispensable book on *Political Characters of Shakespeare,* neatly summarizes this paradox in speaking of the "sentiment for royalty" which has survived "so many royal persons who left their country for their country's good."

All this is projected in the two brilliantly contrasted portraits of the immature, capricious, heartless witty and poetic Richard and his practical, self-controlled, reserved and forceful cousin Bolingbroke (later Henry IV).

At the very opening of the play, after a scene of glorious
medieval pageantry which Richard has engineered almost as a
practical joke, he banishes his cousin for ten years. Insincerely and
carelessly he reassures his aged uncle, who mourns that for him
this means a last farewell to his son: "Why uncle, thou hast many
years to live."

Old John of Gaunt—who has loyally refused to avenge his own
brother's murder because it was ordered by the king—retorts, both
admitting and setting the limits of royal power:

> But not a minute, king, that thou canst give:
> Shorten my days thou canst with sullen sorrow,
> And pluck nights from me, but not lend a morrow;

The power of life and death, too often confused, are here exactly distinguished:

> Thy word is current with [time] for my death,
> But dead, thy kingdom cannot buy my breath.

Richard presently concedes that his cousin may return from
exile in six years and Bolingbroke says bitterly, but seriously:

> Four lagging winters and four wanton springs
> End in a word: such is the breath of kings.

Later Richard describes Bolingbroke's departure. Like Hamlet,
he can often better understand what should be done than summon
the resolution to do it, and in this description he shrewdly summarizes much of the Tudor art of government without in the least
drawing a lesson from Bolingbroke's use of it.

> Richard II: He is our cousin, cousin; but 'tis doubt
> When time shall call him home from banishment,
> Whether our kinsman come to see his friends.
> Ourself and Bushy, Bagot here, and Green
> Observ'd his courtship to the common people;
> How he did seem to dive into their hearts
> With humble and familiar courtesy;
> What reverence he did throw away on slaves,
> Wooing poor craftsmen with the craft of smiles
> And patient underbearing of his fortune,
> As 'twere to banish their affects with him.

Off goes his bonnet to an oyster-wench;
A brace of draymen bid God speed him well
And had the tribute of his supple knee,
With "Thanks, my countrymen, my loving friends";
As were our England in reversion his,
And he our subjects' next degree in hope.

In little more than a hundred words Shakespeare here points the difference between the pre-Tudor feudal monarchs, first among their peers, and the new bourgeois monarchy which exalted the king to incomparable heights while paradoxically basing his absolute power on the tacit consent of the lower classes.

Still more sharply old John of Gaunt on his deathbed makes the same point in eight words when, concluding an indignant remonstrance at Richard's feudal use of his kingdom as a personal estate, he cries: "Landlord of England art thou now, not King."

Almost every scene combines the same richness of psychological insight, dramatic excitement and lyric beauty with a steady development of the underlying political theme.

Nowhere until *Hamlet,* for example, does Shakespeare again give us the clear, cold, biting sarcasm of Richard's great abdication scene, with its double irony at the unadmitted truth of the guilt he, in bitter mockery, assumes, and the overshadowing sense that his well-deserved inevitable fall is nevertheless as great a tragedy for England as he hints it will be.

God save the king! although I be not he;
And yet, amen; if heaven do think him me.

. . . . . .

Now mark me, how I will undo myself:—
I give this heavy weight from off my head,
And this unwieldy sceptre from my hand,
The pride of kingly sway from out my heart;
With mine own tears I wash away my balm,
With mine own hands I give away my crown,
With mine own tongue deny my sacred state,
With mine own breath release all duty's rites;

. . . . . .

God pardon all oaths that are broke to me!
God keep all vows unbroke that swear to thee!

. . . . . .

God save King Henry, unking'd Richard says,
And send him many years of sunshine days!

The other play of this period at which we must more particularly look has, partly for extraneous reasons, become one of the most controversial of Shakespeare's works.

The inaccurate but frequent use of the term "a Shylock" for an avaricious or heartless person, and the stereotype of a sadistic Jewish money lender are well known to many who have never read or seen *The Merchant of Venice*.

On the other hand, a long list of distinguished and progressive critics, including Heinrich Heine and William Hazlitt, have taken Shylock as the tragic hero of his own terrible story.

For our time the interpretation of this play in terms of the Jew's position is of such absorbing importance as to dwarf any other themes on which it may touch. This is certainly a valid emphasis, but we should note in passing that Shakespeare was also here concerned with the then new and important bourgeois concepts of laws guaranteeing at least commercial equality and protection to foreign traders, and the possible validity of unprecedented and perhaps antisocial contractual relationships. The idea of free enterprise had not yet in theory, and not wholly in practice, replaced the medieval guild concepts of a "just price" and other traditionally determined conditions.

The late Franklin D. Roosevelt wrote to a friend at the time of the early N.R.A. regulations: "I have just been re-reading a curious old play on the law of contracts. Perhaps you know it under the title of *The Merchant of Venice*."

But for us this is essentially a play on anti-semitism. What does it say about that matter?

The plot in its major outlines was an old one. In 1579 a play had been presented which "set forth the greediness of worldly choosers, and the bloody minds of usurers." In other words, the casket-plot and the pound of flesh motif were already combined in one play.

Marlowe's famous *Jew of Malta*, with its terrifying protagonist, had been enormously successful in the year 1589, and doubtless there had been many other now forgotten similar pieces.

Superficially Shakespeare's work seems to fit into the same genre. But at the very outset it poses a question which is inconceivable in terms of Marlowe's protagonist with his natural, uncaused, all-absorbing malevolence toward every Christian great or small.

Shakespeare, almost immediately at Shylock's first entrance, poses the question of why the Jew hates Antonio. And, in a few lines, he answers it by raising the more primary question as to how Antonio—a generous acquaintance, a magnanimous and loyal friend, a dignified and courteous gentleman—can treat another human being with the contempt and indignity he heaps on Shylock.

Shylock, for the first time able to speak to his old enemy, who has now approached him for a large loan, uses the opportunity to appeal to him on the basis of their common humanity—and their economic equality:

> Signior Antonio, many a time and oft
> In the Rialto you have rated me
> About my moneys and my usances
> Still have I borne it with a patient shrug;
> For sufferance is the badge of all our tribe.
> You call me misbeliever, cut-throat dog,
> And spit upon my Jewish gaberdine,
> And all for use of that which is mine own.
> Well then, it now appears, you need my help:
> Go to then; you come to me, and you say,
> "Shylock, we would have moneys," you say so;
> You, that did void your rheum upon my beard
> And foot me as you spurn a stranger cur
> Over your threshold: moneys is your suit.
> What should I say to you? Should I not say,
> "Hath a dog money? Is it possible,
> A cur can lend three thousand ducats?" or
> Shall I bend low, and in a bondman's key,
> With bated breath, and whispering humbleness,
> Say this:—
> "Fair sir, you spit on me on Wednesday last;
> You spurned me such a day; another time
> You called me dog; and for these courtesies
> I'll lend you thus much moneys!

Antonio, of course, coldly denies the existence of any such bond, replying:

> I am as like to call thee so again,
> To spit on thee again, to spurn thee too.
> If thou wilt lend this money, lend it not
> As to thy friends; for when did friendship take
> A breed of barren metal of his friend?
> But lend it rather to thine enemy;
> Who, if he break, thou may'st with better face
> Exact the penalty.

And Shylock promptly determines that Antonio will yet take him seriously as an enemy at least.

The further events of the money or Venice plot, such as Jessica's willing abduction by Antonio's friends, and her abuse of Shylock's trust which has made her the guardian of his coffers, are all contrived to keep Shylock's hatred at fever heat and intensify his desire for revenge.

Although the major part of the love plot is not here our concern, it is important to note Portia's attitude to the Prince of Morocco—an early sketch of "The Noble Moor"—and see what a deliberate contrast her prejudiced color consciousness affords to Desdemona's happy and candid exclamation, "He jealous? I think the sun where he was born sucked all such humours from him." Portia, on the contrary, at first hearing the Prince of Morocco named, declares: "If he have the condition of a saint, and the complexion of a devil, I had rather he should shrive me than wive me."

She remains unmoved when the Prince, clearly the most disinterested and loving of her suitors, pleads:

> Mislike me not for my complexion,
> The shadowed livery of the burnished sun
> To whom I am a neighbour and near bred.
> Bring me the fairest creature northward born,
> Where Phoebus' fire scarce thaws the icicles,
> And let us make incision for your love
> To prove whose blood is reddest, his or mine.
> .   .   .   .
> I would not change this hue,
> Except to steal your thoughts, my gentle queen.

Her attitude here is important, in view of her later attitude to Shylock, because it so clearly marks Shakespeare's astounding insight into the relatedness of all the prejudices which set barriers between human beings and deny the fundamental bond of their common humanity. We better understand Portia's insensitivity in the courtroom scene because we have here heard her: "Draw the curtains; go. Let all of his complexion choose me so."

Shylock's second passionate assertion of human equality is almost as well known as it deserves to be. Asked what good a pound of Antonio's flesh will do him, he replies:

> To bait fish withal; if it will feed nothing else, it will feed my revenge. He hath disgraced me, and hindered me half a mil-

lion, laughed at my losses, mocked at my gains, scorned my
nation, thwarted my bargains, cooled my friends, heated mine
enemies; and what's his reason? I am a Jew. Hath not a Jew
eyes? hath not a Jew hands, organs, dimensions, senses, affections, passions? fed with the same food, hurt with the same
weapons, subject to the same diseases, healed by the same
means, warmed and cooled by the same winter and summer
as a Christian is? If you prick us, do we not bleed? If you
tickle us, do we not laugh? If you poison us, do we not die?
and if you wrong us, shall we not revenge? If we are like you
in the rest, we will resemble you in that. If a Jew wrong a
Christian, what is his humility? revenge. If a Christian wrong
a Jew, what should his sufferance be by Christian example?
why, revenge. The villainy you teach me, I will execute, and
it shall go hard but I will better the instruction.

There is much that might relevantly be noted in almost every
succeeding scene but the final climax of the theme and the play
are, of course, found in the fourth act courtroom.

In opening his appeal to Shylock's "better nature" the Duke,
with some effort, uses his name, but before its conclusion he has
reverted to the direct address of "Jew"—and has, incidentally, urged
that Shylock not only forget the forfeit but that he also give
Antonio 1,500 ducats as a token of his sympathy!

Shylock's reply has long been recognized as a masterpiece of
rhetoric but it has a deeper logic than is generally realized. Twice
before, first in the powerful appeal to Antonio for recognition as a
human being and then, more formally, in his assertion of the Jew's
human identity, Shylock has given the reason for the lodged hate
and the certain loathing he bears Antonio. Now, when at last he
has a chance to act, he refuses to speak again for deaf ears. But
the specious logic of his analogy to a man who kills because he
cannot abide a gaping pig or a harmless necessary cat is specious
only because of the bond of a common humanity which forbids
man to treat his fellows as he may creatures of another species;
and Shylock is not the one who has first denied this bond or
broken the compact. He warned "Thou calledst me dog before
thou hadst a cause; but if I am a dog beware my fangs." Antonio,
who was as like to call him so again, has no right to refute the
reasoning by analogy.

This underlying justice is emphasized in the next long speech,
where after a few lines of witty fencing which demolish Bassanio's
verbal attack, Shylock reverts to this serious matter—the essential

theme of this play as well as *Othello*—the meaning of that basic prejudice which refuses to accept the bond of a fundamental identity between all human beings.

Choosing this time another form of oppression than the one from which his people had, generally, suffered, Shylock declares:

> You have among you many a purchased slave,
> Which, like your asses, and your dogs, and mules,
> You use in abject and in slavish parts
> Because you bought them:—shall I say to you,
> Let them be free; marry them to your heirs?
> Why sweat they under burdens? let their beds
> Be made as soft as yours, and let their palates
> Be seasoned with such viands? You will answer,
> The slaves are ours. So do I answer you:
> The pound of flesh which I demand of him
> Is dearly bought; 'tis mine, and I will have it.
> If you deny me, fie upon your law!
> There is no force in the decrees of Venice.
> I stand for judgment: answer; shall I have it?

It is easy, and meaningless, to point out earnestly that two wrongs do not make a right, as countless generations of Sunday School teachers have done. Shakespeare is not concerned with this kind of moral. He is again developing the deep significance of such a denial of humanity as slavery implies—a denial so blasphemous that the slaveholder forfeited all right to appeal to any man as one human being to another. There may perhaps be justification for killing a man. There can be no justification for enslaving him. It is, as Milton said a little later, "a sort of treason against the dignity of mankind," to think so.

A complete analysis of the play would provide much more material to this purpose, but it would also show a certain deliberate ambiguity in its presentation. A major example is the omission on the stage of Shylock's tragic homecoming. This is reported by unsympathetic witnesses whom each member of the audience is free to believe literally or to interpret as he chooses. Another evasion is, of course, the entire fifth act of moonlight, music and roses which enables us to forget Shylock's tragic exit, if we wish to do so.

It must be remembered that anti-Semitism was not a practical problem in sixteenth century England. While anti-Semitic expressions were very common and the Jew was a stock symbol for many unpleasant characteristics, there had been no significant number of Jews in England since the expulsion in 1290. The very few exceptions were one or two highly placed physicians attached to the court or to foreign, particularly Spanish, ambassadors' retinues. These were generally of Jewish origin, not Jews in religion or self-identification. Shakespeare, like the overwhelming majority of his countrymen, had in all probability never met a Jew.

But it is clear that Shakespeare, when in advance of a considerable part of his audience, felt no necessity to collide head-on with its prejudices, however clearly he might dissect and condemn them. This will become important in our consideration of his last ten years and his three final plays.

The busy years between 1597 and 1601 saw the production of *Henry IV* (Part I), and *Henry IV* (Part II), *Much Ado About Nothing, Merry Wives of Windsor* (at Queens Elizabeth's express request for more Falstaff), *As You Like It, Julius Caesar, Henry V,* and *Troilus and Cressida.*

The three English history plays complete the second series begun by *Richard II* which, in the chronology of its material, immediately precedes the four plays of the first series. (*King John,* written at about the same time as *Richard II,* dealt with a much earlier period and stands apart. Its general concern does not much differ from the rest of the series, but the construction and language relate rather to the earlier plays.)

The full century of English history thus consecutively dramatized is an amazing achievement. Legouis, discussing the history plays on that level alone, says:

> Nothing is more honourable to Elizabethan audiences than that they sought their amusement in the mere spectacle of great national events; . . . The simplicity and the greatness of conception found in the mysteries are repeated. . . . Country instead of faith is his theme. He imparts knowledge of history as those old poets taught religion: . . . all succeeded each other in the plays, painted almost impartially for a public enabled at once to marvel and to learn.

Jackson more analytically formulates the essence of the history plays, and indicates their importance in the body of Shakespeare's work and their relation to the plays of Roman history, the great tragedies, and even several of the comedies. He says:

> That his Chronicle-Histories deal nominally with feudal times is true. But if they be examined as to their dramatic

content it will be seen that never for a moment are they concerned with feudal issues. All of them turn upon themes then current:—upon the new anti-feudal sentiment of nationality (which Shakespeare voices); upon the perils on the one side of an unbridled tyranny, and on the other of an uncontrolled anarchy; above all on the danger to the State and all peace and harmony of a disturbed or usurped succession to the throne. This last, (with an application to the "popular" endorsement as well as the "legal" right of the Tudor dynasty and its legitimate successors) is the theme of the whole chronicle-history sequence which begins with Richard II, and ends with Henry VIII—nine plays in all. It is also directly and indirectly the theme too of Hamlet, Macbeth, Julius Caesar, and King Lear among the tragedies and As You Like It and the Tempest among the comedies. That is to say; it forms an ingredient, more or less primary, in fifteen out of the thirty-odd plays of Shakespeare. And their net political moral may be summed up in the conclusion that of all political calamities, submission to the clash of aristocratic and clerical ambitions, unrestrained by a wisely directed, and humane but unflinching, central rule, is the calamity most to be feared and most to be guarded against.

No words could better sum up the general opinion of the more thoughtful, and more progressive bourgeois in Shakespeare's own day—faced first with the prospect of the imminent death of the childless Elizabeth, and secondly with succession to the throne of the unpopular and alien but legitimate heir James, King of Scots.

One thing no man wanted—outside of the few cliques of court adventurers—and that was something all men feared: a reopening of the civil wars of the late feudal epoch by one or other of the gangs of the new . . . aristocracy. And this was all the more to be dreaded because already there were indications that the religious quarrels of the Reformation epoch might quite easily break out again in a new and more virulent form.

In the same article Jackson gives a detailed analysis of the way in which, in *Henry IV*, Falstaff and his familiars were, symbolically, developed out of the old "Devil" of the medieval mystery plays, and the "Vices" who were his somewhat degenerate successors in the later morality plays.

At the same time, as Jackson shows, Falstaff with his satellites was a perfectly realistic caricature of the groups of "professional soldiers" who were, between wars, "cut-purses, highway robbers, tavern-bullies, whores' protectors and general spongers." These were essentially composed of the large number of feudal retainers suddenly thrown on their own resources by the dissolution of feudal households under the Tudors. Jackson says, in part:

> In Falstaff and his crew the feudal-order, more than moribund,—decadent to putrescence—still cumbers the world-stage and makes its final grotesquely tragi-comic gesture of defiance in the face of its own inevitable extermination.
>
> The whole farce of the Falstaff scenes in *Henry IV* turns on this grotesque contrast between the feudal status as it was and that into which it has degenerated. The whole of the tragedy underlying the farce and giving it body and force, is the utter incompatibility between this status and relationship and the new bourgeois world which has come into being, throbbing with exuberant life, and finding fresh outlets for expansion every hour.
>
> [In one sense] Falstaff is startlingly "up-to-date" in a way Shakespeare could not have forseen. For instance: Falstaff leads the plunder raid upon the merchants on Gads-Hill with this slogan:—
>
> "Strike! Down with them! Cut the villains' throats! Ah! whoreson catterpillars! bacon-fed knaves! *they hate us youth!* Down with them! fleece them!"
>
> That Falstaff is in fact "some fifty years of age, or may be three-score" only makes this use of the term "youth" all the more startlingly "modern." Do we not know this "youth"? And also its *a-moralism*—its affectation of a super-Nietzschean "transvaluation" of Good and Evil?
>
> Along with this Shakespeare's genius shines out in that by a whole series of touches, we are made to see in Falstaff the other side to the fact that he is—
>
> "That trunk of humours, that bolting hutch of beastliness, that swollen parcel of dropsies, that huge bombard of sack, that stuffed cloak bag of guts, that roasted Manning tree ox with a pudding in his belly, that reverend Vice, that grey iniquity, that father ruffian, that vanity in years."
>
> All this is there: but there is also the memory of what he once was—a courtly page in the household of one of the highest nobles in the Kingdom, the Duke of Norfolk; a gallant soldier whose reputation as such is still so good that he is given a commission at once, as soon as a civil war breaks out; and so on.

Falstaff is also a real and humorous magnetic personality, but his role as tempter of the young prince, and his final rejection by the newly crowned king, cannot be understood in the purely personal terms used by most of the critics who have argued the matter.

As Jackson's interpretation indicates, Falstaff plays a role in *Henry IV* (Part II) which essentially, balances that of the romantic and gallant but equally reactionary Hotspur in Part I.

Hotspur is witty, he is charming, he is sincere and courageous, he has a perfectly well-justified grievance against *Henry IV* (Bolingbroke) whom he and his father did so much to seat on the throne. But he is as incapable of thinking of England as a nation, or of the king as a responsible sovereign with obligations to his people rather than to his friends, as any prehistoric monster would be.

Shakespeare underlines all this when Hotspur is planning the uprising with his two noble allies. Pointing to a map of England he complains of the proposed three-part division of the fruits of victory:

> Methinks my moiety, north from Burton here,
> In quantity equals not one of yours:
> See how this river comes me cranking in,
> And cuts me from the best of all my land
> A huge half-moon, a monstrous cantle out.
> I'll have the current in this place damn'd up;
> And here the smug and silver Trent shall run
> In a new channel, fair and evenly:
> It shall not wind with such a deep indent
> To rob me of so rich a bottom here.

One of his two confederates realizes that Hotspur is perfectly capable of forfeiting the whole uprising by fighting on this point, once he has made it a point of honor, and ends a delightful quarrel scene by saying: "Come, you shall have Trent turn'd."

Hotspur, as quickly and inconsequentially mollified as he was enraged, responds:

> I do not care: I'll give thrice so much land
> To any well-deserving friend;
> But in the way of bargain, mark ye me
> I'll cavil on the ninth part of a hair.

Shakespeare needs do no more to enlist us on the right side in the coming battle.

Similarly, the spirited old rascal, Falstaff, whom we can afford to enjoy as long as his depredations are limited to petty thievery, underlines by his own words the necessity of Henry V's complete rejection of the boon companion of his less responsible days.

On hearing that his Prince Hal is being crowned king, Falstaff exclaims to his band of petty ruffians and respectable gulls:

> Away, Bardolph! saddle my horse.—Master Robert Shallow, choose what office thou wilt; I am fortune's steward. Get on thy boots: we'll ride all night.—O sweet Pistol . . . devise something to do thyself good.—Boot, boot, Master Shallow! I know the young king is sick for me. Let us take any man's horses; the laws of England are at my commandment. Blessed are they that have been my friends; and woe to my lord chief justice!

Henry V has, on the whole, received less than justice from readers who conceive dramatic interest only in terms of psychological conflict. For in this play the interest is, more exclusively than usual, focused on the struggle between two worlds, and only the new one has a central personal representative.

For that reason Laurence Olivier's extraordinarily effective film was, actually, a far better presentation than any stage production. Shakespeare's equation between the decadent feudalism of sixteenth century Spain and fourteenth century France is brilliantly illuminated by the unwieldy armored French knights, lifted on to their horses by cumbersome machinery, who are helpless before the arrows of the lightly clad and agile English bowmen. The whole scene is, in the film, as it was for Shakespeare's time, a perfect translation of the Elizabethan battle between the heavy Spanish galleons and the agile English privateers.

Democratic language is, today, often an unattended platitude so that we must remind ourselves of the almost universal respect for "gentle blood" to understand the impact of Henry's appeal as a citizen king on a still largely feudal world. Almost two hundred years after Shakespeare, a member of the third estate in France declared "All Frenchmen are brothers of one blood," and was faced with a formal demand for an apology from the noblemen of the first estate! There is then a real sense of the new nationalism in Henry's declaration:

> . . . he to-day that sheds his blood with me
> Shall be my brother; be he ne'er so vile,
> This day shall gentle his condition:

Nor is it an accident that the three gunnery captains who play so staunch a part in England's victory are named Fluellen, Gower and MacMorris and so represent the whole of the British Isles.

The two romantic comedies and the satirical farce all show, in different ways, Shakespeare's respect for the wit, good sense, responsibility, and gallantry of women. In all three plays the absence of any masculine condescension is even more sharply marked by the portrayal of significant independent relationships between women. The friendship of men has been a favorite theme for storytellers ever since the days of Damon and Pythias, and, no doubt, long before. But very few writers have ever considered a relation between women of any importance except as it involved jealousy, generosity, or some other emotion on behalf of a husband, a lover, or a son.

Yet even in the most superficial of these three light-hearted comedies, the *Merry Wives of Windsor*, the very title hints the good-humored, matter-of-fact, practical friendship of Mistress Ford and Mistress Page. This alliance, incidentally, enables them to reverse the conventional intrigue of such a farce by exposing and triumphing over both the knight, who would be a seducer, and the suspicious husband he would cuckold.

In *Much Ado About Nothing* Beatrice is unquestionably the strongest as well as the gayest character, and much of the plot turns upon her firm faith in, and deep concern for, her cousin Hero.

The most important of the three plays, *As You Like it,* not only gives us two equally witty, charming and determined young women as heroines, but also shows us a warmth, loyalty and delight in their personal relations with each other which makes Rosalind's and Celia's friendship comparable to that of David and Jonathan. It is also noteworthy that in this play Rosalind dissects the aristocratic affectation of a cynical and misanthropic melancholy embodied in Jacques.

Julius Caesar, perhaps the most perfect of the Roman plays, must detain us a moment longer.

A large number of the political and social themes we have already noted, and of the subtle psychological development we have so far been constrained to ignore, are raised to new levels of intensity here.

For example, the humorous commoners of whom we have, as

yet, mentioned only a humble first example, appear in full force
in the opening scene where their rough wit easily gets the best of
a slanging match with their superiors.

> Flavius: Hence! home you idle creatures, get you home:
> Is this a holiday? what! know you not,
> Being mechanical, you ought not walk
> Upon a laboring day without the sign
> Of your profession? Speak, what trade art thou?
> 1st Commoner: Why, sir, a carpenter.
> Marullus: Where is thy leather apron and thy rule?
> What dost thou with thy best apparel on?
> You, sir, what trade are you?
> 2nd Commoner: Truly, sir, in respect of a fine workman, I
>   am but, as you would say, a cobbler.
> Marullus: But what trade art thou? answer me directly.
> 2nd Commoner: A trade, sir, that, I hope, I may use with a
>   safe conscience; which is indeed, sir, a mender of bad
>   soles.
> Marullus: What trade, thou knave? thou naughty knave, what
>   trade?
> 2nd Commoner: Nay, I beseech you, sir, be not out with me:
>   yet if you be out, sir, I can mend you.
> Marullus: What mean'st thou by that? mend me, thou saucy
>   fellow!
> 2nd Commoner: Why, sir, cobble you.
> Flavius: Thou art a cobbler, art thou?
> 2nd Commoner: Truly, sir, all that I live by is with the awl:
>   I meddle with no tradesman's matters, nor women's mat-
>   ters, but with awl. I am indeed, sir, a surgeon to old
>   shoes; when they are in great danger, I re-cover them.
>   As proper men as ever trod upon neats-leather have gone
>   upon my handiwork.
> Flavius: But wherefore are not in thy shop to-day? Why dost
>   thou lead men about the streets?
> 2nd Commoner: Truly, sir, to wear out their shoes, to get
>   myself into more work. But indeed, sir, we make holiday,
>   to see Caesar and to rejoice in his triumph.

There is also in this play a rather elaborate set piece of two
carefully arranged scenes which illuminate the contrast in character between imperial Caesar and republican Brutus by showing
us the sort of wife each one has chosen, and the nature of their
marriage. The deliberate parallel construction of these two short
scenes is obvious. In each the wife is concerned about her hus-

band, whom she loves and who loves her; in each she urges him
to do something which will, she is convinced, be for his own good;
in each she kneels to enforce her request; and in each her husband
accedes to it.

But within that framework of similarity the differences are
equally apparent and far more important. Brutus is truly shocked
at his wife's kneeling to him, and his quick "Kneel not, gentle
Portia" is not more conscious of the indignity than Portia's immediate "I should not need, if you were gentle Brutus." Caesar, on
the other hand, is so unconscious of any impropriety in his wife's
suppliant attitude that he not only makes no comment to her, but
later casually repeats to Decius, "Calpurnia here, my wife, stays
me at home: . . . and on her knee, Hath begged that I will stay at
home today."

Brutus responds with immediate emotion to Portia's first really
serious reproach. She asks:

> . . . Am I yourself
> But, as it were, in sort or limitation,
> To keep with you at meals, comfort your bed,
> And talk to you sometimes? Dwell I but in the suburbs
> Of your good pleasure? If it be no more,
> Portia is Brutus' harlot, not his wife.

And he exclaims: "You are my true and honorable wife, As dear
to me as are the ruddy drops that visit my sad heart."
He not only agrees to do what she asks because she has convinced
him he should, rather than as a favor, but offers an ardent apology
for having waited to be asked in his: "O ye gods, Render me
worthy of this noble wife."
Caesar treats Calpurnia's request as a childish whim—excusable
only in a woman—even when he agrees to grant it. Then, ignoring
his promise, he unhesitatingly and unapologetically breaks it when
Decius' threat that someone may ridicule him as a henpecked
husband changes his mind.

Nor is the contrast of the dictator and the republican any less
clear in terms of the kind of woman each has chosen to marry.
Portia stands on her dignity as an equal, and bases her right to
share her husband's responsibilities on the meaning of a real marriage, anticipating Desdemona's protest that, if she is not allowed
to go with Othello to his wars "The rites for which I loved him are
denied me." We may also remember Desdemona in the scene

where, urging Othello to reinstate Cassio as his lieutenant, she responded to his "I will deny thee nothing" with a proud: "Nay, this is not a boon, 'Tis as I should entreat you wear your gloves, Or feed on nourishing dishes, or keep you warm, Or sue to you to do a peculiar profit To your own person."

Portia similarly refuses to ask as a favor the knowledge "Which by the right and virtue of my place I ought to know of."

Calpurnia, on the other hand, begins with the mock-imperious command—meaningless since she has no power to enforce it, and excusable only in the unrealistic tone of a child's imperative "You shan't go!"—"What mean you Caesar? think you to walk forth? You *shall* not stir out of your house today."

She proceeds to coax—and flatter—her husband and at last diplomatically offers him the face-saving ". . . call it my fear that keeps you in the house and not your own. Let me upon my knee prevail in this."

She accepts unprotestingly Caesar's condescending "And for thy humor, I will stay at home," just as she later does his cavalier retraction "How foolish do your fears seem now, Calpurnia! I am ashamed that I did yield to them. Give me my robe, for I will go."

But this contrast shows only the best aspect of Brutus' character which, taken as a whole, is really the central pivot of the entire play.

In his *Political Characters of Shakespeare*, Palmer opens a masterly analysis of Brutus' inadequacy to the political action he undertakes by considering Brutus' first hundred and seventy line speech in detail:

> . . . Here, then, in one brief scene is an epitome of Brutus in six chapters. He is not gamesome and would leave Cassius to attend the festival alone. He had avoided the company of his friends to brood upon conceptions only proper to himself. He is vexed with passions of some difference, and is with himself at war. He shrinks from the dangers into which he may be led if he should look too deeply into his convictions and admit the necessity to act upon them. He, nevertheless, betrays involuntarily the secret that vexes him and is successfully brought to a full and frank confession by the skilful prompting of his future confederate. The instinctive reluctance of the political philosopher is not yet, however, overcome and he would not for this present be any further moved. He promises to consider what Cassius has said and concludes with a merely general assurance that Brutus would rather be a villager than accept the situation.

Palmer later comments similarly on Brutus' soliloquy before Caesar's assassination, emphasizing Shakespeare's political insight and the way in which it has baffled some of his best nonpolitical commentators:

> This soliloquy of Brutus, in which the dramatist exhibits a salient and abiding characteristic of the doctrinaire in politics, has been condemned by many commentators. Coleridge found the speech to be "singular" and frankly confessed that he did not understand it. How could Brutus, he asks, say that he had no cause to spurn at Caesar in his past conduct as a man? Had Caesar not crossed the Rubicon? Had he not entered Rome as a conqueror? Had he not placed his Gauls in the senate? Coleridge is even more disconcerted by the suggestion that Brutus would have had no objection to Caesar provided he remained as good a ruler as he had hitherto shown himself to be. This brilliant critic not only finds the speech "discordant," but accounts for his inability "to see into Shakespeare's motive" by quoting just those historical facts which give to the soliloquy its true significance. Brutus cannot see persons or events as they are. That is the essence of his character. Caesar has done all the things of which Coleridge reminds us. He is already a full-blown tyrant. But Brutus takes no account of these realities. He is obsessed by a pedantic horror of king-ship, by the republican traditions of his family and by the hypothetical evils which may follow upon the violation of a preconceived theory of government.

The wonderful psychological insight of the play, the unforseen but inevitable development of the contradictions in Brutus' character, and the way in which the reader, like Cassius, grows to love him more deeply while learning ever more sharply to condemn the ineptitude of his leadership, are remarkable. The intellectual intensity of the famous quarrel scene with its profound use of both conscious and unconscious personal and political emotions is seldom surpassed even in Shakespeare.

One is left breathless by the impact of such passages as Cassius' few lines describing how Rome had, like Nazi Germany, first to be enslaved herself in order that she might be fit to enslave the world.

> Those that with haste will make a mighty fire
> Begin it with weak straws; what trash is Rome,
> What rubbish and what offal, when it serves
> For the base matter to illuminate
> So vile a thing as Caesar! . . .

In the next five years the London theatres were several times closed by plague and we find only five Shakespearean plays produced: *Hamlet, Prince of Denmark, Twelfth Night, Measure for Measure, All's Well That Ends Well,* and *Othello, the Moor of Venice.*

It is significant that neither of the two most important plays here listed are ordinarily given their full titles. For if we remember, as no Elizabethan ever forgot, that Hamlet was Prince of Denmark and should have become king, we would be in less danger of reducing the dimensions of his world to those of the queen's bedroom. Not that that center and symbol of the court's corruption was unimportant, or that Hamlet's emotional impotence is unrelated to his political failure. But we should see Hamlet's psychological problems, as Shakespeare's audiences did, as part of a larger whole.

Coleridge, one of the earliest and best of Shakespeare's serious critics, has written a brilliant analysis of the former play's hero. But it is not complete until we add the insight gained by a study of Shakespeare's other plays about bad kings and good ones, about the duties and powers of princes and the needs of government. Specifically, we should ponder the elements of Hamlet's dilemma and character which Shakespeare experimented with in Richard II and Brutus if we wish to understand the play as he wrote it—the play of a prince too sensitive to ignore evil and too lacking in faith, in emotional health, effectively to fight it.

A political reading of the play not only restores the throne of Denmark to its central position but, as in *Othello,* also helps us to understand the psychological problems of its hero. We too often forget that the corruption of the court does not date merely from the late king's death and the queen's "o'er hasty marriage."

Polonius was chosen as prime minister by Hamlet's father, not his uncle; Rosencrantz and Guildenstern were chosen as his childhood companions by Hamlet's father, not his uncle; the queen herself was first chosen as wife by Hamlet's father, not his uncle. It was during his father's lifetime that Hamlet, like Prince Hal, chose to escape the duties and responsibilities of his position by studying philosophy in Wittenberg (rather than life at Eastcheap). And it is from his observation of his father's kingdom that Hamlet knows of:

> . . . the law's delay,
> The insolence of office, and the spurns
> That patient merit of the unworthy takes,

It is no wonder that he has so profound a distrust of the possibilities of good action, so coldly intellectual an admiration of the possibilities of goodness in man, combined with so deep a hatred and so concrete a knowledge of evil.

Our first glimpse of Hamlet shows us his verbal brilliance, the bitter effectiveness of his tongue, and above all the extraordinary quickness of his wit.

In reply to his uncle's dignified greeting: "But now, my cousin [nephew] Hamlet, and my son," he replies with ten swift words which express his utter distrust of the man and fury at the marriage, "A little more than kin and less than kind." And his contempt and anger for his mother's short-lived mourning is as swiftly and clearly stated:

> Seems, madam! nay, it is. I know not seems—
>
> .   .   .   .   .   .
> For I have that within which passeth show;
> These but the trappings and the suits of woe.

If we have not already sensed it in this first scene, the soliloquy which immediately follows shows us how little personal grief for his father, or any desire for his inheritance, account for Hamlet's bitterness. Hatred of his uncle, a burning jealous horror at his mother's remarriage, and hopeless disgust for a world in which such corruption flourishes and rules, are the only genuine emotions we find.

This is emphasized by the brief conversation with Horatio, who replies to the question, "And what make you from Wittenberg?", "My Lord, I came to see your father's funeral." Hamlet's bitter self-mockery flashes out:

> I pray thee, do not mock me, fellow-student;
> I think it was to see my mother's wedding.

Horatio reluctantly responds, "Indeed, my lord, it follow'd hard upon." And Hamlet, in perhaps the most searing reference any son ever made to his mother's body, replies:

> Thrift, thrift Horatio! the funeral baked meats
> Did coldly furnish forth the marriage table.

Then there is a complete drop in the emotional temperature as Horatio reveals the ghost's visit and Hamlet asks for details of his appearance.

After Hamlet's interview with the ghost and his oath to revenge the triple wrong of murder, usurpation and seduction, Shakespeare makes his "hero's" inability honestly to undertake action ironically explicit. He echoes the ghost's last words:

> —Remember thee!
> Yea, from the table of my memory
> I'll wipe away all trivial fond records,
> All saws of books, all forms, all pressures past,
> That youth and observation copied there;
> And thy commandment all alone shall live
> Within the book and volume of my brain
> Unmixt with baser matter: yes, by heaven!—

But in the very midst of this renunciation of words and self-dedication to action, Hamlet is struck by a phrase, "O villain, villain, smiling damned villain," and cries, "My tables, meet it is I set it down, That one may smile and smile, and be a villain." And after writing it down he concludes with satisfaction, "So, uncle, there you are."

The scene ends with his painful acceptance of an unwelcome but undisputed responsibility:

> The time is out of joint:—O cursed spite,
> That ever I was born to set it right!—

The arrival of the traveling players is, of course, most important for the plot but it is almost as important for the glimpse it gives us of Hamlet's self-knowledge and self-condemnation.

One of the players is carried away by his recitation of the fall of Troy, and Hamlet is stung to self-reproach by the glaring contrast between the actor's emotional responsiveness and his own real impotence of feeling:

> O, what a rogue and peasant slave am I!
> Is it not monstrous that this player here,
> But in a fiction, in a dream of passion,
> Could force his soul so to his own conceit,
> That, from her working, all his visage wann'd;
> Tears in his eyes, distraction in's aspect,
> A broken voice, and his whole function suiting
> With forms to his conceit? and all for nothing!
> For Hecuba!
> What's Hecuba to him, or he to Hecuba,
> That he should weep for her? What would he do,

> Had he the motive and the cue for passion
> That I have? He would drown the stage with tears,
> And cleave the general ear with horrid speech;
> Make mad the guilty, and appal the free,
> Confound the ignorant; and amaze, indeed,
> The very faculties of eyes and ears.
> Yet I,
> A dull and muddy-mettled rascal, peak,
> Like john-a-dreams, unpregnant of my cause,
> And can say nothing;—

After swearing at his uncle and himself for some dozen lines Hamlet cries out with disgust at this purely verbal assault:

> Why, what an ass am I! This is most brave,
> That I, the son of a dear father murder'd,
> Prompted to my revenge by heaven and hell,
> Must, like a whore, unpack my heart with words,
> And fall a-cursing, like a very drab,
> A scullion!
> Fie upon 't! foh!—

But what is to take the place of such ineffective speech? Action? No; not unless writing be an action. For his conclusion is that he will write a play! And then, if in watching it, the king's guilt (which neither Hamlet nor the audience has hitherto at all doubted), if, Hamlet says, the king's guilt appears—then he'll act.

As we know, the king's reaction to the play makes his guilt clear to the dullest, and Shakespeare obligingly provides Hamlet with an opportunity to act immediately thereafter. But since the king is at prayer Hamlet refuses to kill him, lest his soul go to heaven! The irony is underlined when Shakespeare has the king tell us, as he rises, that he had found himself altogether unable to pray. And Hamlet's inadequacy is recalled when in the next act Laertes, who by then also has a father to avenge, is asked, "what would you undertake To show yourself your father's son indeed More than in words?" He promptly answers that, as for his father's murderer, he would "cut his throat i' th' church," and is approved, "No place, indeed, should murder sanctuarize."

But first, of course, we have the famous scene in the queen's bedroom with Polonius hidden behind the arras. Here Hamlet shows no hesitation in driving his rapier through the curtains when he hears a voice, and we begin more fully to realize that what he shrinks from is neither the physical action nor its immediate personal danger, but the responsibility of a premeditated killing of a king—and its political result. This is emphasized by his prompt and unconcerned disposal of the dead body. And, again to anticipate, the same point is made in the fifth act when he tells how he has arranged for the execution of Rosencrantz and Guildenstern, and answers Horatio's rather shocked, "So Guildenstern and Rosencrantz go to't."

> Why, man, they did make love to this employment,
> They are not near my conscience; . . .

The third act ends with a repetition of Hamlet's self-reproach. This time he contrasts himself with the man of action, Fortinbras. In much the same way as he envied the player's power of feeling for Hecuba, he envies the general's power of fighting even "for a fantasy and trick of fame."

This soliliquy begins, very much like the earlier one:

> How all occasions do inform against me,
> And spur my dull revenge!
>
> . . . . . .
>   Now, whether it be
> Bestial oblivion, or some craven scruple
> Of thinking too precisely on th' event,—
> A thought which, quarter'd, hath but one part wisdom
> And ever three parts coward.—I do not know
> Why yet I live to say "This thing's to do;"
> Sith I have cause, and will, and strength, and means
> To do't. Examples, gross as earth, exhort me:
> Witness this army, of such mass and charge,
> Led by a delicate and tender prince;

It continues some lines later in a passage which deliberately echoes, "What would he do Had he the motive and the cue for passion That I have?:

> How stand I, then,
> That have a father kill'd, a mother stain'd,
> Excitements of my reason and my blood,
> And let all sleep?

Finally Hamlet again concludes:

> . . . O, from this time forth,
> My thoughts be bloody, or be nothing worth!

The last of these three parallel speeches comes in the fifth act. And just because it is the fifth act, there is here a significant difference.

Hamlet, as unable really to mourn Ophelia as he has been to weep for his father or fight for his kingdom, watches Laertes' frenzied expressions of grief at her grave. We must not forget that Laertes, like Fortinbras, has been specifically contrasted with Hamlet in several important respects. His whole-hearted desire to avenge his father's death has already been referred to. And in an earlier scene his recitation of his wrongs aroused the populace to cries of "Laertes shall be king, Laertes king!" This is, of course, an explicit demonstration of how much more easily Hamlet, the legitimate Prince of Denmark, who is "loved by the distracted multitude," could have undone the usurpation had he really wished to.

In this scene then, watching Laertes, Hamlet feels even more intensely his essential impotence. But he can no longer find relief in railing at himself for it and swearing to change. Because he can no longer believe in the possibility of such a change, he no longer dares admit to himself the present fact. So when his misery breaks into speech this time it is not in a self-critical soliloquy but in an angry rationalization attacking Laertes. He fantastically accuses Laertes of mourning Ophelia in order to insult Hamlet with "the bravery of his grief." "Dost thou come here to whine? To outface me with leaping in her grave?" And he too leaps into the grave.

Here again we realize that it is neither physical inhibition nor any fear of direct action which deters Hamlet from fulfilling the responsibility he has undertaken. This is further developed, and his practical abilities are stressed when, in the next scene, he tells Horatio of his adventure with the pirate ship, and of his strategy in disposing of Rosencrantz and Guildenstern. And even here, summarizing his wrongs to Horatio and repeating his determination to kill the king, he asks as though there were a real question:

> Does it not, thinks't thee, stand me now upon,—
> He that hath kill'd my king, and whored my mother;
> Popt in between th' election and my hopes;
> Thrown out his angle for my proper life,
> And with such cozenage,—is't not perfect conscience
> To quit him with this arm? and is't not to be damn'd
> To let this canker of our nature come
> In further evil?

Horatio, who was told two acts before, "Observe my uncle——
O Good Horatio, I'll take the Ghost's word for a thousand pound,"
has just been rebuked for speaking with some concern of the death
of Rosencrantz and Guildenstern. He does not even pretend to
take Hamlet's question seriously, but simply reminds his friend
that time is short. Hamlet replies, "a man's life's no more than to
say one," and reflects that he is sorry he attacked Laertes, "But
sure, the bravery of his grief did put me Into a towering passion."

The last scene of the play is, of course, that of Hamlet's fencing
match with Laertes. His courtesy in presenting his own weapon to
his disarmed opponent and his consequent unwitting use of the
secretly poisoned rapier, with which Laertes had already pricked
him, are well-known to everyone. But not everyone has noted that
Hamlet is even then able to kill the king only after Laertes, dying,
has cried out:

> . . . : Hamlet, thou art slain;
> No medicine in the world can do thee good,
> In thee there is not half an hour of life.

There is then no longer any need for delay, since the king's
death no longer means that the Prince of Denmark must succeed to
real responsibility. Hamlet himself is well aware of this. He uses
his last breath to say:

> But I do prophesy th' election lights
> On Fortinbras: he has my dying voice;

For Hamlet death is the escape from responsibility for the world—
or, at least, for Denmark—an escape which he was too honest to
take deliberately, but is weak enough to welcome. Yet, with all his
rationalizations and evasions, he has never denied his obligations
or doubted that Fortinbras' was the better part.

It may be no wonder that this prince of wits and of rationalizations should have been eagerly adopted as an alter ego and a
justification by generations of disinherited intellectuals, who plead
his failure as prima facie evidence of the impossibility of the
task he undertook, and so excuse themselves for not undertaking
any part in the real world. But we must not forget that Hamlet
did undertake such action, however reluctantly. And neither he
nor Shakespeare ever doubted that, when the times were out of
joint, man was, at whatever inconvenience, born to set them right.

A simple statement of the full title of *Othello, the Moor of Venice,* with its emphatic singular article and immediate emphasis on the hero's origin, centers attention on the still vital social problem of an interracial marriage.

The history of this play, like that of Hamlet, affords a singular illustration of the misinterpretation forced on over a hundred years of criticism by the bourgeois critics' unwillingness or inability to understand Shakespeare's progressive political viewpoint and concrete social interests.

From the beginning of the nineteenth century until its reinstatement by the magnificent production of Paul Robeson and Margaret Webster, *Othello* was one of the most completely misunderstood and, therefore, one of the least popular of Shakespeare's great tragedies. A bourgeois world, unable to countenance the reality of the intermarriage about which the play centers, replaced the Moor, as Margaret Webster says, by a series of "cultured gentlemen, reluctantly and faintly disguising from us their familiar features under a layer of becoming coffee-colored grease paint, rather as if they had recently returned from Palm Beach." But when the central problem of the play had been, thus rudely, thrust out of doors, even the same bourgeois audiences felt a lack of emotional reality in the terms of a conflict which made Othello pitiable, no doubt, but only as a dupe, the victim of an unreasonable, causeless jealousy which robbed him of all tragic stature, and which left the center of the stage to be filled by an Iago whose malignancy had, at the same time, lost the best part of its motivation. Margaret Webster, in her *Shakespeare Without Tears,* concludes:

> For the question of Othello's race is of paramount importance to the play. There has been much controversy as to Shakespeare's intention. It is improbable that he troubled himself greatly with ethnological exactness. The Moor, to an Elizabethan, was a blackamoor, an African, an Ethiopian. Shakespeare's other Moor, Aaron, in *Titus Andronicus,* is specifically black; he has thick lips and a fleece of woolly hair. The Prince of Morocco in *The Merchant of Venice* bears "the shadowed livery of the burnished sun" and even Portia recoils from his "complexion" which he himself is at great pains to excuse.
>
> Othello is repeatedly described, both by himself and others, as black; not pale beige, but black; and for a century and a half after the play's first presentation, he was so represented

on the stage. But after this the close consideration of nice
minds began to discern something not quite ladylike about
Desdemona's marrying a black man with thick lips. They cannot have been more horrified than Brabantio, her father, who
thought that only witchcraft could have caused "nature so
preposterously to err," or more convinced of the disastrous
outcome of such a match than Iago, who looked upon it as
nothing but a "frail vow between an erring Barbarian and a
super-subtle Venetian," and declared, with his invincible
cynicism, that "when she is sated with his body, she will find
the error of her choice: She must have change; she must!"

It is very apparent, and vital to the play, that Othello
himself was very conscious of these same considerations and
quiveringly aware of what the judgment of the world would
be upon his marriage. It is one of the most potent factors
in his acceptance of the possibility of Desdemona's infidelity.
And she herself loses much in the quality of her steadfastness
and courage if it be supposed that she simply married against
her father's wishes a man who chanced to be a little darker
than his fellows, instead of daring a marriage which would
cause universal condemnation among the ladies of polite society. To scamp this consideration in the play is to deprive
Othello of his greatest weakness, Desdemona of her highest
strength, Iago of his skill and judgment [and, we may add,
of much of his essential motive], Emilia of a powerful factor in
her behavior both to her master and her mistress, and Venice
itself of an arrogance in toleration which was one of the principal hall marks of its civilization—a civilization which frames,
first and last the soaring emotions of the play.

Once we realize, however, as Shakespeare did, that Othello is
a black man in a white society which then, as now, assumed its
racial superiority, we not only have a sufficient cause for an unconscious germ of self-doubt in the strongest hero, but have a clue to
help us trace its entirely logical development from the aloofness
and reserve overcome only by the surprise attack of Desdemona's
love—and in no other circumstances can we imagine a man as
warm as Othello waiting until "some nine moons wasted" to find
love, nor one as self-confident waiting until "she bade me, if I had
a friend that loved her, I should but teach him how to tell my
story, and that would woo her," to speak of it.

One of the most discerning of Shakespearian critics, Granville-
Barker, says in his famous preface to *Othello*:

This [Othello's prompt quelling of the midnight brawl in
Cyprus and his unforgettable "What, in a town of war—the

people's hearts brimful of fear—to manage private and domestic quarrel—'Tis monstrous . . . Cassio, I love thee, But never more be officer of mine.] is the last capital touch given to the picture of a still unscathed Othello. In retrospect we may recognize the danger that lay in a too inflexible perfection of poise; once upset, hard to regain.

It is the picture of a quite exceptional man; in high repute and conscious of his worth, yet not self-conscious; of a dignity which simplicity does not jeopardize; generous in praise of those who serve him; commanding respect without fear; frank and unsuspicious and ready to reciprocate affection. *Yet he has been a man apart, alone.* He is not young, has fought and adventured the world over, striking root nowhere. *And he is black.* The Venetians, truly, not only value his soldiership but Brabantio, as Othello says "loved me, oft invited me. . . ." They seemed to be treating him in everything as one of themselves. But to have him marry Desdemona! That would be quite another question. Neither he nor she was of the eloping kind; evidently no other way looked open to them . . . yet that the daughter of a Venetian Senator should "to incur a general mock, Run from her guardage to the sooty bosom" even of the renowned Othello . . . and should we, under the spell of his nobility be inclined to forget it—since Desdemona could!—reminder will not be lacking. For Iago's defiling eye sees only this, reads only foulness and perversity into such enfranchisement.

Only in the light of this central fact can we reconcile the course of the play with the proud self-assurance and firm dignity of Othello, as he reveals himself in his early scenes, ignoring all Iago's provocation to bluster or revenge with a quiet:

> . . . My demerits
> May speak unbonneted to as proud a fortune
> As this that I have reached: for know, Iago,
> But that I love the gentle Desdemona,
> I would not my unhoused free condition
> Put into circumscription and confine
> For the sea's worth. . . .
> . . . Not I: I must be found:
> My parts, my title and my perfect soul
> Shall manifest me rightly.

And again:

> . . . Keep up your bright swords
> For the dew will rust them. . . .

> . . . Hold your hands,
> Both you of my inclining, and the rest:
> Were it my cue to fight, I should have known it
> Without a prompter. . . .

Discussing the character changes Shakespeare made in adapting the story from which he took Othello's plot, Granville-Barker says:

> Again, while Desdemona in the story says to her husband
> ". . . you Moors are of so hot a nature that every little trifle
> moves you to anger and revenge," Shakespeare gives us an
> Othello calm beneath Brabantio's threats and abuse, in the
> matter of Cassio's brawl of iron self-control, and against that
> he sets the gadfly Iago, impatient from the first to be stinging.

The transparent complications of the handkerchief plot (which Shakespeare took almost unchanged from the contemporary story of "the unfaithfulness of husbands and wives" by Cinthio) have too long been used to overshadow the fact that in his insinuations to Othello Iago harps persistently on the two related strings of the unnaturalness of such a marriage as Desdemona's and of Othello's essential ignorance of what "our" women—Venetian women—think and feel.

> I know our country disposition well:
> In Venice they do let heaven see the pranks
> They dare not show their husbands;
>
>   .   .   .   .
>
> Ay, there's the point: as, to be bold with you,
> Not to affect many proposed matches
> Of her own clime, complexion and degree,
> Where to, we see, in all things nature tends;
> Fah! one may smell in such, a will most rank,
> Foul disproportion, thoughts unnatural—.

It is here that Othello is vulnerable. His suppressed consciousness of difference—his unadmitted doubts—are appallingly evidenced in such seemingly unrelated references to color as now begin to emerge in fragmentary images and exclamations.

> . . . Her name, that was as fresh
> As Dian's visage, is now begrimed and black
> As mine own face. . . .
> Arise, black vengeance, from thy hollow cell!

The most explicit of them, indeed, follows immediately upon
Iago's first hint, before the handkerchief has been lost or found
or mentioned. Iago has barely breathed his pretended suspicions
when Othello breaks out:

> Nor from mine own weak merits will I draw
> The smallest fear or doubt of her revolt;
> *For she had eyes,* and chose me. . . . [Italics added.]

and after Iago has concluded:

> . . . I do not in position
> Distinctly speak of her; though I may fear
> Her will, recoiling to her better judgment,
> May fall to match you with her country forms
> And happily repent. . . .

Othello, upon his exit, cries in pain:

> . . . If I do prove her haggard,
> Though that her jesses were my dear heart-strings,
> I'd whistle her off and let her down the wind,
> To prey at fortune. Haply, *for I am black* [italics added]
> And have not those soft parts of conversation
> That chamberers have, or for I'm declined
> Into the vale of years,—yet that's not much—
> She's gone. I am abused; and my relief
> Must be to loathe her. O curse of marriage,
> That we can call these delicate creatures ours
> And not their appetites! I had rather be a toad,
> And live upon the vapour of a dungeon,
> Than keep a corner in the thing I love
> For others' uses.

We see more clearly in every line that for Othello Desdemona's
supposed treachery means much more than the most terrible personal loss; it strikes at the very root of his manhood:

> . . . O, now for ever
> Farewell the tranquil mind! farewell content!
> Farewell the plumed troop and the big wars
> That make ambition virtue! O, farewell!
> Farewell the neighing steed and the shrill trump,
> The spirit-stirring drum, the ear-piercing fife,
> The royal banner, and all quality,
> Pride, pomp, and circumstance of glorious war
> Farewell! Othello's occupation's gone.

Finally after the scene in which Othello believes he has heard Cassio pile contempt on contempt—scorning as his strumpet Othello's wife—he bursts forth with what is, indeed, the deepest meaning of the betrayal, "Do you triumph, Roman? do you triumph?" After this we can not wonder at the death of Desdemona. Far more than his personal dignity depends upon it. His racial dignity, his very claim to human equality demand revenge. The same understanding of the play's central theme helps us understand how deeply caused Iago's seemingly whimsical malignity to Othello is. Iago's class position as an adventurer without background—a hired professional soldier at an aristocratic court—is in at least one respect, insofar as Othello is concerned, comparable to that of an overseer in the south who can advance as his major claim to respect his bond of color equality with his employers and who is therefore driven to a more apparent, more virulent, and more frequently expressed statement of hatred and contempt for—of difference from—the Negro than they themselves show.

Roderigo, a butt, and therefore to some extent also an inferior struggling for status among his betters, is the only other character in the play who refers disparagingly to Othello's physical characteristics in such remarks as "What a full fortune does the thick lips owe" and "To the gross clasps of a lascivious Moor" but he is then, of course, commenting directly on the marriage of his inamorata. Iago, however, refers bitterly and continually to the racial difference:

And I—God bless the mark—his Moorship's Ancient.

Even now, now, very now, an old black ram is tupping your white ewe.

You'll have your daughter covered with a Barbary horse;
You'll have your nephews neigh to you;
You'll have coursers for cousins and gennets for germans.

The devil will make a grandsire of you.

Her eye must be fed and what delight shall she have to look on the devil? . . . her delicate tenderness will find itself abused, begin to heave the gorge, disrelish and abhor the Moor; very nature will instruct her in it and compel her to some second choice.

Blessed fig's end! the wine she drinks is made of grapes. If she had been blessed, she would never have loved the Moor.

. . . and here without are a brace of Cyprus gallants who would fain have a measure to the health of black Othello.

A contemporary psychologist has suggested that we may, in a sense, consider Iago as the concentrated embodiment of all the spite, jealousy and ill will which would, in a literally realistic play on this theme, be focused upon the couple, and which might, in a less deliberate or dramatic manner, accomplish the same intentional destruction. This is, I think, a valid insight well worth our consideration. It calls up a picture very like the contemporary one Countee Cullen has given us in:

> Locked arm in arm they cross the road,
> The black boy and the white:—
> The golden splendor of the day,
> The sable pride of night.
> From lowered blinds the black folk stare
> And here the white folk talk—
> Indignant that the two should dare
> In unison to walk.
> Oblivious to word and look
> They pass, and see no wonder
> That lightning, brilliant as a sword,
> Should blaze the path of thunder!

We must not forget that the most friendly comment on the Moor made by Venetian society is the Duke, his patron's, casually contemptuous:

> If virtue no delighted beauty lack
> Your son-in-law is far more fair than black.

There is a further but not unrelated cause for Iago's directed enmity. Iago, by his own statement, has reached a certain degree of success only through using an active intelligence in flattery, trickery and fraud. He maintains his self-respect by asserting the half-truth that his superiors, if born with his nothing and left to their own resources, would have had to resort to similar measures with, in all probability, far less success. His entire philosophy is thus built on the postulate that the world is divided into cheats and their dupes and that the first class is, at least, superior to the second. Othello, then, by his very existence, challenges Iago's entire universe. "He has a daily beauty in his life that makes me ugly." Othello, beginning with far less than Iago's nothing—without the white skin which entitles Iago to speak of "*our* country disposition —*our* women"—has won a superlative degree of success, never condescending to flattery, trickery or fraud. Since Iago cannot think him a cheat, he must prove him a dupe if he is to keep from self-contempt. And, in fact, he repeatedly expresses this realization in such lines as:

> The Moor is of a free and open nature
> That thinks men honest who but seem to be so
> And will as tenderly be led by the nose
> As asses are.

and:

> Make the Moor thank me, love me, and reward me
> For making him egregiously an ass.

In achieving this purpose, as we have seen above, Iago is not only spurred on by his own resentment and bitterness but is also able to use the insight that hatred gives him into the failures and inadequacies of (interracial) human relationships in his—and our—society to attack the one vulnerable spot and destroy all.

This does not mean that he is conscious of all the strands in the intricately woven fabric of his hate, or could explicitly state the social implications he senses. The central point is underlined in the final scene of the play when *Othello* desperately cries out:

> Will you, I pray, demand that demi-devil
> Why he hath thus ensnared my soul and body?

The answer to that cannot be given on a personal level. It would demand a fully aware social consciousness impossible to Iago. And so there is no answer made. As Granville-Barker says:

> Does Iago even know the answer? "I hate the Moor," rabidly, senselessly, profitlessly; a search through the ruins of his tricks and lies would add nothing real to that. And in the light of the consequences—for him also—such an answer must seem almost less tragic than absurd. . . . "I hate the Moor"— there has been no more to the whole elaborately wicked business than that.

Finally, lest one mistake the matter and distort the argument of the play to conclude that such distrust, misunderstanding and eventual tragedy are the necessary or even natural consequences of an "unnatural" marriage, Shakespeare emphasizes the conclusion that it is intolerance, malice and distrust and not the simple human relationship which is unnatural. This is developed through the complete unconsciousness of Cassio, Cyprus in general, and, of course, the central figure of Desdemona herself. Perhaps of more weight than all her beautiful and passionate love speeches or her utter inability to imagine the cause of Othello's distemper, is the single jesting, altogether unemotional, reference to her husband's color and nativity which Desdemona makes. In response to a question of Emilia's "Is he not jealous?" she replies "Who! he? I think the sun where he was born drew all such humors from him."

This line alone, taken in context, is itself almost a sufficient indication of Shakespeare's complete unquestioning assumption of the irrelevance of the "color line." His almost invariable association of Negro skin pigmentation with the sun, evident in many other plays, in such lines as the Prince of Morocco's, "Mistake me not for my complexion—the shadowed livery of the burnished sun —to whom I am a neighbour and near bred," raises an interesting question. In discussing the common use of "dark" or "black" to connote evil, and its relation to color prejudice in the United States, a contemporary Negro novelist, Lloyd Brown, asks whether the evil or ominous connotations of black or darkness are not "a natural result of the conditions of life, the significance of the sun as the source of light, warmth and growth." If this is so, obviously the effect of Shakespeare's habit of explicitly relating dark skin pigmentation to the sun is, emotionally, to cancel such associations. The sun was, for Elizabethans, even a more potent affirmative symbol than it is for us, since it was a common metaphor for beneficent royalty, and for the principle of order or divinity in the universe.

Before leaving this play we should, perhaps, glance at one other aspect of Shakespeare's social attitude which it, in common with many others, illustrates. That is his remarkable understanding of the nature of a good relationship between men and women, an understanding which completely jumps the period of dawning protest that could create a Nora or a Hedda Gabler, and reaches into the heart of an altogether democratic, or socialist, society.

There are an extraordinary number of instances in which Shakespeare subtly uses a man's attitude toward women to give us a measure of the man himself. Perhaps the most elaborate and deliberate are the carefully contrasted parallel scenes between republican Brutus and his wife, and imperial Caesar and his. These two scenes were described in the discussion of *Julius Caesar* above, where we also cited Portia's statement, often quoted as the simplest and clearest explicit definition the plays afford of the meaning of a real marriage. A close second is certainly Desdemona's claim— indorsed by Othello—that marriage is a serious contract between two free agents, made because of a shared sense of values and community of interests, and gaining its validity from their respect for each other's essential nature and rights. It has, unfortunately, been obscured by the deplorable stage tradition of an ingénue Desdemona, but the briefest glance at the actual lines must dispel this convention.

With unconscious irony her father describes her as a maid "So opposite to marriage that she shunned the wealthy curled darlings of our nation." Not realizing he has answered his own question, he wonders how she could then have fallen in love with a *man* like Othello.

Othello (with some apparent naiveté) reports that on hearing the story of his heroic exploits, Desdemona, with no apparent diffidence:

> . . . wished she had not heard it, yet she wish'd
> That heaven had made her such a man; she thank'd me,
> And bade me, if I had a friend that lov'd her,
> I should but each him how to tell my story,
> And that would woo her.

Finally, Desdemona herself, just married, called in the middle of the night before a formal conclave of Duke and Senate, bitterly attacked by her father, speaks out not only about her love but about the essential meaning of her marriage:

> That I did love the Moor to live with him,
> My downright violence and storm of fortunes
> May trumpet to the world; my heart's subdued
> Even to the very quality of my lord;
> I saw Othello's visage in his mind,
> And to his honour and his valiant parts
> Did I my soul and fortune consecrate.

> So that, dear lords, *if I be left behind*
> A *moth of peace,* and he go to the war,
> *The rites for which I love him are denied me,*
> And I a heavy interim shall support
> By his dear absence. Let me go with him. [Italics added.]

Here we see the swiftly drawn portrait of a woman of energy, power and judgment, as well as emotion, who fell in love, not accidentally, with the man she would have wished to have been. To her marriage means, essentially, an active share in the responsibilities and accomplishments of her husband's life.

Nor is Othello less whole-hearted in his acceptance of this relationship. His immediate response is:

> Let her have your voices.
> Vouch with me, heaven, I therefore beg it not
> To please the palate of my appetite . . .
> But to be free and bounteous to her mind.

And his later spontaneous greeting at a moment of joyfully surprised reunion, "O, happy warrior," accepts Desdemona on her own terms of equality and partnership. Even when racked by agony, his parenthetical descriptive comments show the same equalitarian attitude.

> . . . 'Tis not to make me jealous
> To say my wife is fair, feeds well, loves company
> Is free of speech, sings, plays and dances well.
>
> A fine woman! A fair woman! A sweet woman!
> . . . O! the world hath not a sweeter creature;
> She might lie by an emperor's side and command him tasks
> . . . So delicate with her needle! An admirable musician!
> O, she will sing the savageness out of a bear.
> Of so high and plenteous wit and invention.

All these show how freely and ungrudgingly a man who is secure in his own manhood and strength can acknowledge the independent qualities of a woman—even of a wife!

The next five years saw the production of the last of Shakespeare's great tragedies, *Lear* and *Macbeth,* and the last two Roman plays, *Antony and Cleopatra,* and *Coriolanus,* as well as *Timon of Athens.*

In addition to its magnificent love story, *Antony and Cleopatra* unravels the logical conclusion of the triumvirate's unprincipled triumph in *Julius Caesar*. Again, as in the series of English history plays, we see in this later play a rich development of the subtle indications of character sometimes barely hinted in the earlier one. But we also find here, as in the far more bitter *Timon of Athens* (which may or may not be altogether Shakespeare's) a new note of cynicism. The infatuated Antony has, as one of his devoted followers, Scarus, says, lost "the greater cantle of the world . . . with very ignorance; . . . kist away kingdoms and provinces." His truest friend and adherent, Enobarbus, bitterly describes the general's ignominious desertion of his men in flight:

> Mine eyes did sicken at the sight, and could not
> Endure a further view.

And Scarus concludes:

> I never saw an action of such shame;
> Experience, manhood, honour, ne'er before
> Did violate so itself.

Important protagonists in other plays have been equally ignoble but always before there has been some character who asserted in his very being a kind of integrity. Here Octavius' cold-blooded lust for power is such that it goes far to reconcile us to Antony's warmer egotism. And as for the third of the triumvirate, Lepidus, he is carried off drunk from a meeting with his two peers and Enobarbus comments acidly, pointing to his bearer "There's a strong fellow, . . . 'A bears the third part of the world, man; see'st not?" There was no such sarcasm when Henry V was referred to as "England."

Finally even Enobarbus is driven to desert Antony, declaring "The loyalty well held to fools does make our faith mere folly." When he kills himself in remorse there is no one left alive who still knows the meaning of honor. Four years of James I, and the growing conflict between his interests and those of the nation have evidently had a large part in shaping this play.

Coriolanus too shows this influence but in a more hopeful way. Shakespeare does not quite envisage any alternative to monarchy—and, in fact, few in the early seventeenth century ever did—

but he is looking for an assertion of national values in new places. One of the early scenes in *Coriolanus* makes this quite clear:

First. Cit: Before we proceed any further, hear me speak.

All: Speak, speak.

First Cit: You are all resolved rather to die than to famish?

All: Resolved, resolved.

First Cit: First, you know Caius Marcius is chief enemy to the people.

All: We know't, we know't.

First Cit: Let us kill him, and we'll have corn at our own price. Is't a verdict?

All: No more talking on't; let it be done: away, away!

Sec. Cit: One word, good citizens.

First Cit: We are accounted poor citizens, the patricians good. What authority surfeits on would relieve us: if they would yield us but the superfluity, while it were wholesome, we might guess they relieved us humanely: but they think we are too dear: the leanness that afflicts us, the object of our misery, is as an inventory to particularize their abundance; our sufferance is a gain to them. Let us revenge this with our pikes, ere we become rakes; for the gods know I speak this in hunger for bread, not in thirst for revenge.

Sec. Cit: Would you proceed especially against Caius Marcius?

First Cit: Against him first: he's a very dog to the commonalty.

Sec. Cit: Consider you what services he has done for his country?

First Cit: Very well; and could be content to give him a good report for't, but that he pays himself with being proud.

Sec. Cit: Nay, but speak not maliciously.

First Cit: I say unto you, what he hath done famously, he did it to that end: though soft-conscienced men can be content to say it was for his country, he did it to please his mother, and to be partly proud; which he is, even to the altitude of his virtue.

Sec. Cit: What he cannot help in his nature, you account a vice in him. You must in no way say he is covetous.

First Cit: If I must not, I need not be barren of accusations; he hath faults, with surplus, to tire in repetition. (Shouts within.) What shouts are these? the other side o' the city is risen; why stay we prating here? to the Capitol!

All: Come, come.

First Cit: Soft! who comes here? (Enter Menenius Agrippa)

Sec. Cit: Worthy Menenius Agrippa; one that hath always loved the people.

First Cit: He's honest enough; would all the rest were so!

Menenius: What work's, my countrymen, in hand? where go
   you with bats and clubs? The matter? speak, I pray you.

First Cit: Our business is not unknown to the senate; they
   have had inkling this fortnight what we intend to do,
   which now we'll show 'em in deeds. They say poor suitors
   have strong breaths; they shall know we have strong arms
   too.

Menenius: Why, masters, my good friends, mine honest neighbours, Will you undo yourselves?

First Cit: We cannot, sir, we are undone already.

Menenius: I tell you, friends, most charitable care
Have the patricians of you. For your wants,
Your suffering in this dearth, you may as well
Strike at the heaven with your staves as lift them
Against the Roman state, whose course will on
The way it takes, cracking ten thousand curbs
Of more strong link asunder than can ever
Appear in your impediment. For the dearth,
The gods, not the patricians, make it, and
Your knees to them, not arms, must help. Alack!
You are transported by calamity
Thither where more attends you; and you slander
The helms o' the state, who care for you like fathers,
When you curse them as enemies.

First Cit: Care for us! True, indeed! They ne'er cared for us
   yet:— suffer us to famish, and their store-houses crammed
   with grain; make edicts for usury, to support usurers;
   repeal daily any wholesome act established against the
   rich, and provide more piercing statutes daily to chain up
   and restrain the poor. If the wars eat us not up, they will;
   and there's all the love they bear us.

The whole character of Coriolanus' aristocratic leadership also
emphasizes Shakespeare's realization that "noble" leadership was
no longer, in any sense, leadership in the interests of the people.
And here "noble" does not mean feudal as contrasted with truly
kingly. There is here a conscious exposition of the class interests
of the aristocracy represented both by the good-natured Menenius
and by the insufferable Coriolanus and his more insufferable
mother. The class interest of the common people is also represented not only by the rank and file citizens quoted above but
also by their chosen leaders.

Palmer summarizes this vital aspect of the play saying:

   For better or worse, these tribunes are Shakespeare's counterfeit presentment of two labor leaders. They are the natural

products of the class war in the commonwealth. They use their
wits to defend the interests of the popular party and to remove
from power a declared enemy of the people. They have neither
the wish, training nor ability to disguise the quality or intention of their activities. In working for their . . . [class] they
do not claim to be working disinterestedly for the nation. In
resorting to the lawful and customary tricks of the political
trade they neglect the noble postures and impressive mimicries
adopted by persons with a longer experience of public life and
of the deportment which public life requires. . . . But, essentially, the tribunes are right and they are giving proof of
precisely that "realism" and precisely that suspicion of their
political rulers which are characteristic of popular leaders in all
times and places. Tribunes of the people have notoriously little
respect for professions of altruism and of stainless regard for
the public welfare uttered by their social superiors. . . . These
tribunes are not concerned with the *motives* of Marcius [Corio-
lanus] in the particular case, but with the dangers inherent
in his character. They are diagnosing not the man but the
situation, and in their reading of the situation they are, as the
event will show, entirely right. They regard themselves as
watchdogs of the people, and Shakespeare, in this opening
scene, is at some pains to show that they are well-qualified for
their office and that they intend to be alert and vigorous in its
exercise.

Later Coriolanus, angered by the opposition of the citizens to
his election, defies the laws of Rome and is banished. He immediately offers his services to his country's foremost enemy and returns
leading an army pledged to the total destruction of Rome.

The frightened patricians blame the commoners—"O! you have
made good work! . . . you and your apron-men." But it is noteworthy that not one of them thinks of blaming Coriolanus for his
treachery. As Palmer says:

> That Marcius should be bringing up an army to burn
> Rome is, in fact, regarded by his friends as the perfectly
> natural gesture of an angry nobleman. . . . [All the patricians
> seem] equally unaware of the enormity of the situation.

It might have occasioned little more surprise at King James' court,
where almost every important figure, including some members of
the royal family itself, were in receipt of a pension from the King
of Spain.

Palmer concludes this analysis, "[The patricians merely think]
it hard lines that the nobility should have to suffer for the sins of

the Roman people . . . Only the tribunes plead for Rome, urging the senators to forget their feud and think of the common peril."

But while Shakespeare could envisage such tribunes in ancient Rome, they were still inconceivable in England. The two English plays, *King Lear* and *Macbeth,* which were, in all likelihood, written shortly after King James' accession, present for the last time Shakespeare's characteristic affirmation of national unity and royal responsibility as realistic possibilities.

Again in our consideration of Lear we are too apt to remember the father and forget the king. Mistaking two daughters' fulsome flatteries for sincere love, and the third's somewhat ungracious reserve for indifference, seem very trivial errors to precipitate the terrible action of the play. They are hardly the "tragic flaw" traditionally required to make the protagonist of such a play in some sort the logical cause of its catastrophe.

But we should remember old Gaunt's dying accusation "Landlord of England art thou now, not king" and Hotspur quarreling about his share in the prospective division of England, when we see Lear irresponsibly dividing up his kingdom.

Exposed to the pitiless storm, Lear does not express remorse for having misjudged his children, but compunction at having ignored the needs of his subjects:

> Poor naked wretches, wheresoe'er you are,
> That bide the pelting of this pitiless storm,
> How shall your houseless heads and unfed sides,
> Your loopt and window'd raggedness, defend you
> From seasons such as these? O, I have ta'en
> Too little care of this! Take physic, pomp;
> Expose thyself to feel what wretches feel,
> That thou mayst shake the superflux to them,
> And show the heavens more just.

Again, in his last madness his mind runs more on his kingdom's public corruption than on his private griefs:

> Thou rascal beadle, hold thy bloody hand!
> Why dost thou lash that whore? Strip thine own back;
> That hotly lusts to use her in that kind
> For which thou whipst her. The usurer hangs the cozener.
> Through tatter'd clothes small vices do appear;
> Robes and furr'd gowns hide all. Plate sin with gold,
> And the strong lance of justice hurtless breaks;
> Arm it in rags, a pigmy's straw doth pierce it.

When we turn to *Macbeth* we find one of the supreme illustrations of Shakespeare's assumption that man is essentially a political animal and that his proper sphere of being is action—action which invariably affects large numbers of his fellows.

At the opening of the play the great general, Macbeth, is a national hero who has won "Golden opinions from all sorts of people." Shakespeare's genuine respect for reputation here, as in *Othello* and many other plays, underlines his almost lifelong membership in a society whose major aims he could approve and whose progressive forces were, or seemed about to become, its dominant ones. When we approach the romantic writers two centuries later we realize how impossible this attitude is in a period of divisive protest at a dominant reaction. Then social reputation is bound to seem the hallmark of stupidity, dishonesty, or self-aggrandizement.

But Macbeth's overwhelming ambition does not permit him to wear these opinions "in their newest gloss." By his ambition he is driven to violate all the most fundamental ties of his society, murdering his guest, his kinsman, and his king.

I say driven because Macbeth is no naive murderer or political innocent. He knows that the real object of his desire—a dignified, respected, and assured sovereignty—is unattainable by such means.

Lady Macbeth is unimaginatively certain that the deed in which she helps him is one "Which shall to all our nights and days to come Give solely sovereign sway and masterdom." But Macbeth knows perfectly well that there is no need to await an after-life, which he's willing to chance, for judgment. No:

> . . . in these cases
> We still have judgment here; that we but teach
> Bloody instructions, which, being taught, return
> To plague the' inventor. . . .

And, as soon as he has murdered the peace and security of the land he knows that:

> . . . from this instant,
> There's nothing serious in mortality:
> All is but toys: renown and grace is dead;
> The wine of life is drawn, and the mere lees
> Is left this vault to brag of.

The logic of his position as a usurper who has violated his nation's most fundamental laws, and the constant justified fear that one or another of his peers has already learnt his "bloody instructions," drive Macbeth into more and more terrible deeds until he cries out:

> . . . : I am in blood
> Stept in so far, that, should I wade no more,
> Returning were as tedious as go o'er.

There is not one of his lords but in his house the tyrant keeps "a servant fee'd. The utmost horrors of life under fascism seem succinctly described by a political refugee from Scotland who exclaims:

> Alas! poor country;
> Almost afraid to know itself. It cannot
> Be call'd our mother, but our grave; where nothing
> But who knows nothing, is once seen to smile;
> Where sighs and groans and shrieks that rend the air
> Are made, not mark'd; where violent sorrow seems
> A modern ecstasy; the dead man's knell
> Is there scarce ask'd for who; and good men's lives
> Expire before the flowers in their caps,
> Dying or ere they sicken.

And the simple aims of a war of national liberation have seldom been as well summarized as they are in a plea to the legitimate Prince for his return:

> . . . your eye in Scotland
> Would create soldiers, make our women fight,
> To doff their dire distresses.
> . . . .
> That, by the help of these—with Him above
> To ratify the work—we may again
> Give to our tables meat, sleep to our nights;
> Free from our feasts and banquets bloody knives;
> Do faithful homage, and receive free honours;

A preceding scene gives, in a lighter tone, one of Shakespeare's most explicit statements as to the comparative importance of personal and political virtue in a public man.

In pursuance of a minor stratagem Malcolm, the legitimate heir to the throne, is bent on vilifying himself to test whether or not Macduff's anxiety to have him return to Scotland is based on a sincere wish that he assume the throne.

He begins to protest his unworthiness by accusing himself of voluptuousness and lust, "my desire all continent impediments would o'erbear that did oppose my will." Macduff calmly replies:

> Boundless intemperance in nature is a tyranny. . . .
> But fear not yet to take upon you what is yours;
>   .   .   .   .   .   .
> We have willing dames enough; there cannot be
> That vulture in you, to devour so many
> As will to greatness dedicate themselves,
> Finding it so inclined. . . .

Malcolm then continues to the more serious self-accusation of avarice which Macduff less confidently counters, "This avarice sticks deeper, grows with more pernicious root Than summer-seeming lust, . . . yet do not fear. . . ." Finally Malcolm concludes, "Nay, had I power, I should Uproar the universal peace, confound All unity on earth. . . . If such a one be fit to govern, speak." Macduff replies, "Fit to govern! No, not to live."

Both the arrangement of this series and the degree of response are amply definitive of the order of importance which Shakespeare attributed to lust, avarice and violence or tyranny. If we compare the number of sermons or even novels written about each of the three in the course of the last three centuries we understand more fully how far artists since Shakespeare have been forced to retreat to a standard of impotent personal morality far less socially conscious or progressive than was his.

As soon as the invading forces, led by the legitimate ruler, land:

> Both more and less have given him the revolt
> And none serve with him but constrained things,
> Whose hearts are absent too.

For Macbeth personally the attack is almost an anticlimax. He has already realized:

> . . . that which should accompany old age,
> As honour, love, obedience, troops of friends,
> I must not look to have; but in their stead,
> Curses not loud but deep, month-honour, breath,
> Which the poor heart would fain deny, and dare not. . . .

But tyranny dare not abdicate and the end of the play is a political, not a personal, one. Macbeth is killed in battle, where his own soldiers have joined the enemy ranks, and the true king has the last word:

> . . . What's more to do,
> Which would be planted newly with the time,—
> As calling home our exiled friends abroad,
> That fled the snares of watchful tyranny;
> Producing forth the cruel ministers
> Of this dead butcher and his fiend-like queen,—
> . . . ;—this, and what needful else
> That calls upon us, by the grace of Grace
> We will perform in measure, time and place.

Except for one dubious and at most only partially Shakespearian play, *Pericles*, which was not included in the first collected edition of his dramatic work in 1623, we have nothing new from Shakespeare's pen for almost four years.

Such an unprecedented silence from so prolific a writer, still only in his middle forties, technically at the height of his powers, with a continued practical interest in an active theatre, certainly demands an explanation. And the changing political climate about him clearly offers one.

By the time James I had been a few years on the throne it was apparent that the struggle for power in England would never again lie between the king and the nobility. The real challenge to the increasingly burdensome absolutism of the crown now came entirely from the bourgeoisie, represented by the House of Commons. The throne's most active and influential allies were the powerful bishops, seated in the House of Lords, as well as the important noblemen who held leading positions at court.

The center of this struggle was London, and the theatre was directly and forcibly affected by it in several ways.

Since the new aristocratic domestic policy of the Stuarts involved similar foreign alliances with Spain and other Catholic powers abroad it was essentially antinational and anti-Protestant as well as antipopular.

There was no longer any unanimity on matters of politics between the court and the people and the preponderant political emphasis of the Elizabethan theatre became most repugnant to the court. There were some new, and many newly enforced, censorship regulations to discourage the popular theatre, and there was also an unorganized but general withdrawal of court patronage from it.

We have already mentioned the small private theatres which charged far higher admissions, used expensive artificial lighting, and generally gave evening rather than afternoon performances. They catered to the fashionable hangers-on and devotees of the court, often law students or university men, as well as to the aristocracy, and jeered at the "greasy doublets" and "stinking breath" of the popular theatre's following. As early as *Hamlet* Shakespeare had referred to the companies of child actors, often with trained choir-boy voices, which presented the plays of the private theatres.

Their productions were naturally well adapted to the use of elaborate and elegant masques, often allegorical in nature, fantastic fairy tale material, and a realistic stylized satire. It is possible to imagine talented and precocious children presenting Ben Jonson's *Volpone.* It is not possible to imagine them presenting *Macbeth.*

Since these audiences were all attuned to the court and prided themselves on their knowledge of what went on behind the scenes, there were many veiled references to political events on the level of personal intrigue, but there was, of course, little or no serious consideration of fundamental political questions.

The defection of the aristocratic part of the great audiences might, in itself, have meant little to the dramatists who wrote for the popular theatre. But another more important and seemingly inconsistent antitheatre movement also began to gather momentum in this Jacobean period. That was the growing antagonism of the substantial middle class who had formed so large a part of late sixteenth century audiences.

As the struggle between the king, supported at home by bishops and lords and backed abroad by Rome and Spain, and the bourgeoisie, developed, the strong Protestant feeling which had inspired such early leaders as Wyclif and Tyndale revived. There was a well-known tradition of religious struggle already established in Europe and it was easy for the predominantly Protestant bourgeoisie to fall into this pattern. Attacking the Anglican Church was the most effective and, as yet, the most direct possible way of attacking, at his most vulnerable point, its head, the king.

But Protestantism had been traditionally opposed to the theatre ever since its adherents had criticized the medieval mystery plays as superstitious and mystical. Moreover, most sober hard-working thrifty Protestants were also constitutionally opposed to the theatre as a time-wasting, money-wasting indulgence which too often led to other even more reprehensible ones, like drinking parties and assignations.

All these motivations led to some withdrawal of patronage which was probably more important in terms of quality than quantity, but which was none the less keenly felt by serious dramatists.

Such dramatists, of whom Shakespeare was the preeminent example, were even more fundamentally affected by the apparently hopeless tenor of political events.

All the sixteenth century hardships and injustices, of which Shakespeare was well aware, could be accepted if they were part of a genuinely progressive national movement. But now it seemed as though the whole antifeudal struggle had created only a new, narrow tyranny of church and king, with public funds lavished on such "catterpillars of the commonwealth" as the homosexual favorites James created, like Robert Carr whom he made Viscount Rochester, and George Villiers, whom he named Duke of Buckingham. Here were "Bushy, Bagot, Greene"—the hated royal parasites Shakespeare had seen as so largely instrumental in Richard II's destruction—come to life again in a new and virulent form.

The positive aspect of the revolutionary civil war which was to break out in some thirty short years was not yet apparent. But all the negative conditions of increased dissension and oppression at home, dishonorable and reactionary alliances abroad, and the new ugliness of early seventeenth century imperialism in the Americas and the West Indies were only too evident.

A sadly bitter comment by two serving men in *Coriolanus* sharply points to the situation in Jacobean England. One says that peace "makes men hate one another." And his fellow replies, "Reason; because they then less need one another."

Shakespeare, as we have seen, was not even in his youth a poet of protest. His greatest plays are all plays of powerful clear-eyed affirmation. Later critics, who cannot conceive of an artist as an integrated part of his society, have made much of the obvious necessity a great dramatist feels adequately to present many opposed viewpoints and interests. They have distorted the plain evidence of each play's overall dramatic development to argue that Shakespeare believed all—or none—of the opinions expressed in its course. But, as Professor Harbage concludes his well-documented *Shakespeare and the Rival Tradition:*

> Shakespeare did not acquiesce in discrepancy. That we are forced to *prove* what we instinctively *know* (and what was once taken for granted) is the strange fruit of the art-for-art theorizing that has muddied critical thinking since the mid-nineteenth century. This movement has drawn all its strength from skepticism. As one loses faith in the power of his own age to discriminate between right and wrong, one loses faith in such power in any former age. The evidence of an artist's belief that he shared in this power in his age may be charitably ignored in view of the distinction of his technique. . . . If the symbols used—the characters, actions, the speeches—persist in obtruding ethical ideas, let these symbols be paired in such a way as to cancel each other out, or let them be attributed, like the bawdy jokes, to the demands of the groundlings.

Harbage continues more specifically to define Shakespeare's ethical outlook:

> He wrote for a theatre of a nation, not a theatre of the world, and for a society that was far from classless; yet he faced in the direction of what was in his day (and is in ours) the future, and in his conception of the community there is a breadth of sympathy unequalled among the writers for the theatre of the urban clique.

He concludes with some asperity and a tart but well-justified ad hominem aimed at one of Shakespeare's most fashionable contemporary misinterpreters:

> The statement that perhaps it was part of Shakespeare's "special eminence to have expressed an inferior philosophy in the greatest poetry" (T. S. Eliot) displays at least the virtue of a moment of candor. Provided one recognizes what Shakespeare's philosophy is, he has a right to express his own value judgment on it. More debatable is the right to assume that poetry can be better than its content. It can, of course, be worse.

But it was no longer possible for a great artist to affirm the values presented by the still dominant royal power of Shakespeare's last years. The best of the younger writers like John Ford, Philip Massinger, and John Webster wrote such bitter, impassioned and hopeless studies of corruption and despair as *'Tis Pity She's a Whore, A New Way to Pay Old Debts,* and *The Duchess of Malfi.* But as Shakespeare himself had said, he was:

> . . . too old to fawn upon a nurse,
> Too far in years to be a pupil now.

So while he continued active in the business of the theatre, for more than half of his last ten years we find him accepting a "speechless death," which robbed his pen "from breathing native breath."

Then we have the two coldly brilliant, cynical, most un-Shakespearian fairy tales of *Cymbeline* and *The Winter's Tale,* in which he showed the youngsters how easily he could have been master of the rival tradition as well, had he thought such mastery worth the winning. There is also the formal, only partly Shakespearian, *Henry VIII,* and finally, in the same year, the controversial *The Tempest.*

The strongest material in this play, important out of all proportion to the space it occupies, is that dealing with Caliban.

Recent scholarly research has presented more and more minute details to indicate how closely linked Prospero's island—and its "native"—were with the colonial explorations and conquests of the early seventeenth century.

The exciting and troubling news of these early imperialist adventures, and of the rebirth of slavery with which they were accompanied, are reflected in many other contemporary English writers. Francis Bacon, for example, who strongly favored colonies, begins his essay on the subject by recommending that they be "planted" on "pure," that is uninhabited grounds, as otherwise they may fairly be called extirpations of the native inhabitants rather than plantations.

The most casual reference to Shakespeare's introduction of Caliban shows how clearly colonization is the background of Shakespeare's thought as well.

Prospero, the civilized man who has taken over the island, says to his daughter:

> We'll visit Caliban, my slave, who never
> Yields us kind answer.

She objects:

> 'Tis a villain, sir,
> I do not love to look on.

To which he makes the simple and unanswerable reply:

> But, as 'tis,
> We cannot miss him: he does make our fire,
> Fetch in our wood, and serves in offices
> That profit us.

The rationale of "the white man's burden" was evidently not yet required. When Caliban, thus prepared for, enters he complains with evident justice:

> This island's mine, by Sycorax my mother,
> Which thou tak'st from me: when thou camest first
> Thou strok'st me, and made much of me, wouldst give me
> Water with berries in't, and teach me how
> To name the bigger light, and how the less,
> That burn by day and night: and then I loved thee,
> And showed thee all the qualities o' th' isle,
> The fresh springs, brine-pits, barren place and fertile.
> Cursed be I that did so! All the charms
> Of Sycorax, toads, beetles, bats, light on you!
> For I am all the subjects that you have,
> Which first was mine own king: and here you sty me
> In this hard rock, whiles you do keep from me
> The rest o' th' island.
> .   .   .   .
> You taught me language, and my profit on't
> Is, I know how to curse: the red plague rid you
> For learning me your language.

To this striking evaluation of the benefits of civilization Prospero can only respond:

> Hag-seed, hence
> .   .   .   .
> Fetch us in fuel, and be quick thou'rt best
> To answer other business: Shrug'st thou, malice?
> If thou neglect'st, or dost unwillingly
> What I command, I'll rack thee with old cramps,
> Fill all thy bones with aches, make thee roar
> That beasts shall tremble at thy din.

Nevertheless, no matter how strongly justice as well as generosity may range themselves on Caliban's side, he does not win his freedom. Furthermore we are clearly told that, if he did, he would people the isle with Calibans and bind himself to the first drunken sot he met, who would hold him in a more capricious and less fruitful servitude. Nor is there any promise, or hope, that he has a prospect of development toward freedom, or any chance of something better than a fairly well-behaved and less harsh slavery.

The same pessimism, amply warranted by those facts of the time apparent to Shakespeare, permeates every other theme developed in the play.

For example, let us glance at the relations of the evil brother and false friends—a subject treated with unmatched emotional depth and rich indignation in so many of the earlier plays. Here we have again three most unnatural villains—murderers and traitors in intention and attempt if not in act—but instead of a real horror or a real forgiveness we have here a cynically unmoved acceptance:

> You, brother mine, that entertained ambition,
> Expelled remorse, and nature—who, with Sebastian,
> Would here have killed your king—I do forgive thee,
> Unnatural though thou art
> . . . .
> But you, my brace of lords, were I so minded,
> I here could pluck his highness' frown upon you,
> And justify you traitors: at this time
> I will tell no tales.
> . . . . . .
> For you—most wicked sir—whom to call brother
> Would even infect my mouth, I do forgive
> Thy rankest faults—all of them; and require
> My dukedom of thee, which, perforce, I know,
> Thou must restore.

The cold contempt of this forgiveness is emphasized by Miranda's naive exclamation on seeing this band of traitors: "How many goodly creatures are there here! How beauteous mankind is! O brave new world, That has such people in 't!" And Prospero's condescending " 'tis new to thee."

The world of Shakespeare's youthful hopes and mature accomplishment seemed to have:

> . . . melted into air, thin air:
> And, like the baseless fabric of this vision
> The cloud-capp'd towers, the gorgeous palaces,
> The solemn temples, the great Globe itself
> Yea, all which it inherit, shall dissolve,

Nothing was left to do but break his staff and, "deeper than did ever plummet sound," to drown his book.

At the end of 1611 he retired to Stratford, which he had during the past twenty years only occasionally visited when the theatres were closed by plague, and died there on April 23, 1616.

There are some other trivial facts of his life, including the long series of detailed bequests in his will, available to the curious, but the vital facts for an understanding of his work are all to be found in the broad current of the political and social events of his time. It was the great time of the revolutionary bourgeoisie and to it we owe the greatest realistic literature of hope and affirmation which the bourgeois world has ever known.

FRANCIS BACON

Francis Bacon was born a commoner and died Baron of Verulam and Viscount of St. Albans (1561-1626). Educated to the law which occupied him for over forty years, he became the first "philosopher of industrial science." He sincerely professed himself to have "as vast contemplative ends, as I have moderate civil ends; for I have taken all knowledge to be my province," and picked his way through the intricacies of court politics to achieve the position of Lord Chancellor of England. He was one of the most competent and honest of judges but was correctly, if not quite fairly, impeached for bribery. He devoted the better part of his adult life to the zealous service of an undignified, corrupt and reactionary king but was after his death honored almost as a prophet by Goethe, Voltaire and Milton himself. He was the first great English prose writer, but translated all his important work into Latin so that it should not be wasted, writing:

> These modern languages will at one time or another play the bankrowt with books, and since I have lost much time with this age, I would be glad if God would give me leave to recover it with posterity.

For a farcical conclusion to this series of paradoxes, the one phenomenon he could not really understand was passion, and the one thing he could not write was poetry, but many who would never otherwise have heard his name, have heard vague rumors that he wrote all of Shakespeare's plays!

Bacon's first biographer, Dr. William Rawley, knew him intimately ten or fifteen years, was his chaplain while he was Lord Chancellor, and remained with him as literary secretary during the last five years of his life. In his memoirs written some thirty years later he tells us:

> His father was that famous counsellor to Queen Elizabeth, the second prop of the kingdom in his time, knight, lord-keeper of the great seal of England; a lord of known prudence, sufficiency, moderation and integrity. His mother was Anne, one of the daughters of Sir Anthony Cook; unto whom the erudition of King Edward the Sixth had been committed; a choice lady, and eminent for piety, virtue and learning; being exquisitely skilled, for a woman, in the Greek and Latin tongues.

These facts are, of course, a matter of record, together with many more details about both parents. His mother was ardently religious, an enthusiastic adherent of the extremely "protestant" wing of the Church of England, and actually translated and published several volumes of Calvinist controversy. Although she did her best to impress her views upon both Francis and his older brother neither of them seems to have been much affected.

Francis was persuaded to write a paper on *Controversies in the Church* and was later, for political reasons, much involved in helping to achieve the unification of the Established Church, but his mother could hardly have been much pleased by the mild tone of his early pronouncement:

> God grant that we may contend with other churches, as the vine with the olive, which beareth best fruit; and not as the brier with the thistle, which of us is most unprofitable.

She would have been even more displeased by such a fuller revelation of his mind on the subject as that expressed in a note to a Catholic friend some twenty years later:

> I myself am like the miller of Huntingdon, that was wont to pray for peace amongst the willows; for while the winds

blow, the wind-mills wrought, and the water-mill was less customed. So I see that controversies of religion must hinder the advancement of sciences.

His father was more successful in sharing his ideas with his brilliant youngest son. Mary Sturt, the best of Bacon's recent biographers, tells us that during Henry VIII's reign Nicholas Bacon

> presented a plan for the foundation of a great college to train statesmen. The students were to learn good Latin and French, public policy, domestic management and foreign negotiation. They were to make historical collections of systems of government, and they were to travel in the suites of the King's ministers. . . . The academy that he projected was to train his successors from the upper but not probably the noble classes. . . .

And Benjamin Farrington, in what is probably the best book on Bacon, *Francis Bacon, Philosopher of Industrial Science,* says

> Over the fireplace in the dining hall Nicholas, the improving landlord, had a painting executed showing the goddess Ceres introducing the sowing of grain. This concern of the father with the great invention on which civilization rests sank into the son's mind. The first revolution in man's earthly destiny brought about by the invention of agriculture became the symbol for him of the second revolution brought about by the application of science to industry. . . . In his father's hall the legend beneath the picture of Ceres was *Moniti Meliora* (Instruction brings Progress). The boy whose eyes had rested during dinner on the picture of Ceres became the man who justified his new philosophy of works by appeal to the agricultural revolution.

At the age of fourteen the precocious youngster entered Cambridge and within two years he had learned enough of the essentially medieval philosophy which still formed the staple of academic education to be convinced that he wanted no more. Rawley tells us,

> Whilst he was commorant in the university, about sixteen years of age, (as his lordship hath been pleased to impart unto myself), he first fell into the dislike of the philosophy of Aristotle; not for the worthlessness of the author, to whom he would ever ascribe all high attributes, but for the unfruitfulness of the way; being a philosophy (as his lordship used to

say) strong for disputations and contentions but barren of the production of works for the benefit of the life of man; in which mind he continued to his dying day.

We soon find Bacon's letters and unpublished writings as well as his more formal philosophical works sprinkled with such remarks as: "Will you tell any man's mind before you have conferred with him? So doth Aristotle in raising his axioms upon Nature's mind." And, "Plato corrupted natural philosophy by his theology as thoroughly as Aristotle by his logic."

There are also, of course, many fuller explanations of his "dislike of the philosophy" of the past, like those implied in the selections from the *Novum Organum* and in such passages of his unpublished works as this from the *Cogitata et Visa* which begins, 'Franciscus Baconus si cogitarit"—"Francis Bacon thought thus,"—and continues, speaking of himself in the third person throughout:

> In the mechanical arts and their history, especially when compared with philosophy, he (Francis Bacon) observed the following happy omens. The mechanical arts grow toward perfection every day, as if endowed with the spirit of life. Philosophy is like a statue. It draws crowds of admirers, but it cannot move. With their first authors the mechanical arts are crude, clumsy and cumbersome, but they go on to acquire new strength and capacities. Philosophy is most vigorous with its earliest author and exhibits a subsequent decline. The best explanation of these opposite fortunes is that in the mechanical arts the talents of many individuals combine to produce a single result, but in philosophy one individual talent destroys many. The many surrender themselves to the leadership of one, devote themselves to the slavish office of forming a bodyguard in his honour and become incapable of adding anything new. For when philosophy is severed from its roots in experience, whence it first sprouted and grew, it becomes a dead thing.

This criticism of the essential insignificance of the various "schools" of metaphysics, which devote themselves to obscuring with commentary the at least poetically meaningful insights of their founders, is a commonplace of philosophic criticism today. Bacon's sharp contrast of these barren philosophies with the fruitful development of the mechanical arts or, as· we call them, sciences, is also become a truism, although his parallel warnings against pragmatism and crude utilitarianism, at which we must glance later, are not yet either generally accepted or understood. But this opposition to metaphysics was a startling and almost unintelligible attitude for most of his contemporaries in sixteenth century England, and almost two centuries later the radical encyclopedists of France felt they were just beginning to develop his new way of thought.

After leaving Cambridge in disgust the seventeen-year-old spent two years studying and observing men and manners in France. He was recalled by his father's death which, coming rapidly as the result of a sudden chill, had prevented the completion of a special estate that had been planned for the youngster and left him only the very slight provision of a younger son.

Since a profession was now necessary, Bacon entered the Inns of Court in London as a law student, in chambers soon shared by his brother Anthony. His health was not at any time very good but he seems, nevertheless, to have accomplished an extraordinary amount, combining his official studies with much scientific reading and writing, some sustained but unsuccessful attempts at achieving a political position through the influence of his uncle, Lord Burghley, Lord Treasurer of England; and an amazingly ambitious and consistent plan of laying out huge gardens in the unused common ground belonging to Grays Inns. This last work survives not only in his many essays on landscape gardening, but in the actual appearance of the gardens still extant there.

A little pamphlet on the *State of Christendom,* in which he embodied the observations he had made during his stay in France, did not succeed in impressing Elizabeth sufficiently to give him a post in her service, but it helps us to understand his deep desire for a stable, united nation—attainable in England at the time only under the rule of a strong monarch. He says of France:

> The division in this country for matters of religion and state, through discontent of the nobility to see strangers advanced to the greatest charges of the realm, the offices of justice sold, the treasury wasted, the people polled, the country destroyed, hath bred great trouble and like to see more.

When he was twenty-four he was elected to the House of Commons despite the steady though unavowed opposition of his powerful uncle, who had a clever and ambitious son just a few months younger than Francis to provide for. His pen was occasionally employed by the queen in such honorable but unremunerated projects as a paper on *Controversies in the Church* in 1589, and in responding to a sharp Catholic attack on the English Church by a pamphlet called *Observations on a Libel* in 1594. Two years later he was appointed a member of the "Queen's Learned Counsel"—another dignified but unsalaried position.

Rawley summarizes Bacon's uncompensated services to the queen during the ten years with the discreet reflection that: "Nevertheless, though she cheered him much with the bounty of her countenance, yet she never cheered him with the bounty of her hand; . . ."

Ben Jonson, describing his conduct as a lawyer during this period tells us:

> There happened in my time one noble speaker who was full of gravity in his speaking. His language where he could spare or pass by a jest, was nobly censorious. No man ever spoke more neatly, more pressly, more weightily, or suffered less emptiness, less idleness in what he uttered. No member of his speech but consisted of his own graces. His hearers could not cough or look aside from him without loss. He commanded where he spoke, and had his judges angry and pleased at his devotion. No man had their affections more in his power. The fear of every man that heard him was lest he should make an end.

By 1594 when the post of Attorney-General fell vacant Francis and his brother Anthony—returned from a ten-year sojourn on the continent—were advisers to Lord Essex, the queen's favorite, who headed one of the three important factions in court. (The other two were those of their uncle, Lord Burghley and of Sir Walter Raleigh.) Lord Essex made a determined effort to get this appointment, or that of the lesser post of Solicitor General, for Bacon, but was unsuccessful. The cause may have been personal intrigue, but it is probable that the queen was still angry at the part which Bacon, as a member of the House of Commons, had played in the Long Parliament of 1593.

Certain new taxes had been suggested to raise additional revenue for the crown, and he had strongly opposed them, stating:

> The gentlemen must sell their plate, and the farmers their brass pots, ere this will be paid; and for us, we are here to search the wounds of the realm, and not to skim them over.

The dangers are these. First, we shall breed discontent and endanger her Majesty's safety, which must consist more in the love of the people than their wealth. Secondly, this being granted in this sort, other princes hereafter will look for the like; so that we shall put an evil precedent on ourselves and our posterity; and in histories it is to be observed, of all nations the English are not to be subject, base, or taxable.

Furthermore, he had been the only member of the House quick enough to see through a seemingly unobjectionable proposal that the House of Commons meet in a joint session wtih the House of Lords to discuss the matter. He had pointed out the great danger to the Commons' jealousy guarded prerogative of alone introducing financial proposals, and his motion had been almost unanimously carried. The queen might forgive such conduct since she was quite aware of Bacon's genuine devotion to the principles of sovereignty and his practical value to her counsels, but she was was unlikely to forget and much less likely to reward it.

Bacon was, however, sincerely anxious to do all he could for the power and prestige of the crown and, thus, as he saw it, for the stability, peace and prosperity of England. He had also serious hopes of inducing a learned and brilliant ruler to subsidize an ambitious program of scientific research—the first of its kind ever projected—on a scale that would then have been impossible for any other patron.

In 1592 he had had the opportunity to present this project in a speech, *Mr. Bacon in Praise of Learning,* which formed part of a masque presented by Lord Essex for the queen's birthday. It reads, in part:

Are we the richer by one poor invention by reason of all the learning that hath been these many hundred years? The industry of artificers maketh some small improvement of things invented; and chance sometimes in experimenting maketh us to stumble upon somewhat which is new; but all the disputation of the learned never brought to light one effect of nature before unknown.

All the philosophy of nature which is now received is either the philosophy of the Grecians or that other of the Alchemists. That of the Grecians hath the foundation in words, in ostentation, in confutation, in sects, in schools, in disputations. That of the Alchemists hath the foundation in imposture, in auricular tradion, and obscurity. The one never faileth to multiply words, and the other ever faileth to multiply gold.

He goes on to ask for royal support in substituting for these two false sciences true science which, he says, consists in:

> . . . the happy match between the mind of man and the nature of things. And what the posterity and issue of so honorable a match may be; it is not hard to consider. Printing, a gross invention; artillery, a thing that lay not far out of the way; the compass, a thing partly known before; what a change have these three made in the world in these times; the one in the state of learning, the other in the state of war; the third in the state of treasure, commodities and navigation. And those, I say, were but stumbled upon and lighted upon by chance. Therefore, no doubt the sovereignty of man lieth hid in knowledge; wherein many things are reserved, which kings with their treasure cannot buy, nor with their force command; their spials and intelligence can give no news of them, their seamen and discoverers cannot sail where they grow. Now we govern nature in opinions, but we are thrall unto her in necessity; but if we would be led by her in invention, we should command her in action.

Two years later Bacon wrote a similar masque to be presented as part of the Gray's Inn Christmas revels. Here a philosopher addresses to the king of a mythical kingdom concrete proposals similar to those Bacon had intimated to Queen Elizabeth, and was later, still hopefully, to present to King James. His protagonist says:

> I will wish unto your Highness the exercise of the best and purest part of the mind, and the most innocent and meriting conquest, being the conquest of the works of nature. And to this purpose I will commend to your Highness four principal works and monuments of yourself. First, the collecting of a most perfect and general library, wherein whatever the wit of man hath heretofore committed to books of worth, be they ancient or modern, printed or manuscript, European or of the other parts, of one or other language, may be made contributory to your wisdom.
>
> Next, a spacious, wonderful garden, wherein whatsoever plant the sun of divers climates, out of the earth of divers moulds, either wild or by the culture of man brought forth, may be with that care that appertaineth to the good prospering there of set and cherished. This garden to be built about with rooms to stable in all rare beasts and to cage in all rare birds; with two lakes adjoining, the one of fresh water, the other of salt, for like variety of fishes. And so you may have in small compass a model of universal nature made private.
>
> The third, a goodly huge cabinet, wherein whatsoever the

hand of man by exquisite art or engine hath made rare in stuff, form, or motion, whatsoever singularity change and the shuffle of things hath produced, whatsoever Nature hath wrought in things that want life and may be kept; shall be sorted and included.

The fourth such a still-house [laboratory] so furnished with mills, instruments, furnaces and vessels, as may be a place fit for a philosopher's stone.

About this time Lord Essex, who had failed in securing Bacon a political appointment, generously gave him an estate worth (in our money today) over $10,000. It must be remembered that regular remuneration for such work as both Francis and his brother were doing for Essex, in assembling news from foreign agents all over the continent, collating it, and advising policy on the results was not then paid for except through such preferments or gifts.

Anthony, a semi-invalid, was devoting his full time and a considerable part of his own small fortune to this work and it formed an essential part of the Earl of Essex' power and usefulness as a member of the queen's privy council.

Bacon's letter of thanks indicates that he was already troubled by a possible clash between the Earl's ambitions and the sovereignty of the queen. He writes:

> My Lord, I see I must be your homager, and hold land of your gift, but do you know the manner of doing homage in law? Always it is with a saving of his faith to the King and his other Lords, and therefore, my Lord, I can be no more yours than I was, and it must be with the ancient savings; and if I grow to be a rich man, you will give me leave to give it back to some of your unrewarded followers.

Four years later when, in 1599, Essex was setting off as Lord Deputy on the Irish campaign that did, indeed, prove to be the beginning of the romantic attempt at a palace revolution for which he was finally executed, Bacon again included in his letter of good wishes a more explicit warning:

> Therefore I will only add this wish—that your Lordship in this whole action, looking forward, would set down this position, that merit is worthier than fame, and looking back hither, would remember this text, that obedience is better than sacrifice.

In the meantime, in 1597, he had published his first famous series of ten short essays, dedicated to his brother. This small book included the essay "On Studies." The name "essay" was then unknown in England and was of course borrowed from Montaigne's recent description of his book of short prose pieces as attempts, *essais*, to express himself.

When Essex returned from Ireland in defiance of the queen's explicit commands, Bacon exerted himself to effect a reconciliation. The queen seemed not unwilling to envisage such a future result but insisted on a sort of special trial where the Queen's Learned Counsel (including Bacon) were to present the charges against Essex which he would admit, begging for pardon. The indeterminate and mild sentence, "that he should be suspended from the execution of his offices and continue in his own house until it should please Her Majesty to release both this and all the rest," was declared by the president of the privy council, as had, in fact, been arranged in advance, and it seemed possible that with patience Elizabeth's favorite might, in time, regain his offices as well as his freedom from this nominal arrest.

Patience, however, was not among his many gifts and Essex had not enough sense of history to realize that, popular as he undoubtedly was, the time when any part of England could be aroused to support a feudal adventure was long past. He attempted an absurdly ill-prepared and tragically improbable uprising, walking into the city with several hundred followers and calling upon the citizens of London to join him. It seems likely that he intended, as he later intimated, "only" to kill Lord Burghley and Sir Walter Raleigh and force his way to the Queen's presence to secure her promise of reinstatement in public office and, perhaps, in the long coveted position of prince consort.

In any event the scheme was so obviously fantastic that it seemed a sufficiently explicit confession and humble submission would win the royal pardon—as it did, after a comparatively short imprisonment, for his collaborator, the Earl of Southampton. There was no question of his guilt of treason, or of the sentence which would be pronounced; but there seemed to be almost as little question of its remission to nominal imprisonment and banishment from court.

Bacon was explicitly commanded to take part as one of the queen's counsel in the trial and did so. Although there has been considerable criticism of his "disloyalty" and "ingratitude" in accepting the position neither his contemporary biographers nor the best later ones—including the nineteenth century editor of the most complete and authoritative edition of his *Works, Life, and Letters,* James Spedding—feel that such attacks are at all justified.

Bacon was sincerely and correctly opposed to any revival of the feudal power of the nobility which had torn England apart during the Wars of the Roses and he had, as we have seen, warned Essex of the dangers of his attitude several times during the past six years. Essex' guilt was undisputed and the verdict was clear in advance. All intimacy between the two had terminated considerably before Essex' departure for Ireland; the few letters from 1596-1599 are friendly but increasingly formal and largely occupied with more specific advice and warning of the nature of those already quoted. It is true that Bacon would have been ruined and, perhaps, suspected of approval if not complicity had he refused to act, but there is no doubt that his deepest convictions and profound patriotism, as well as his interest, lay on the side of the queen. As Thomas Huxley, another scientific man of letters, a man of unquestioned integrity and disinterestedness, and a great admirer of Bacon's, said three centuries later: "A man ought to be ready to endure persecution for what he does hold; but it is hard to be persecuted for what you don't hold."

Essex' proud refusal to beg the queen for forgiveness, his dramatic execution, and the accession of King James who had always favored him and with whom, as probable successor to the throne, Essex had been illegally corresponding, combined to increase popular sympathy for him, and a corresponding criticism of his prosecutors. In 1604, the year after Elizabeth's death, Bacon felt himself compelled to write on the matter:

> My defence needeth to be but simple and brief: namely, that whatsoever I did concerning that action and proceeding, was done in my duty and service to the Queen and State; in which I would not show myself false-hearted nor faint-hearted for any man's sake living. For every honest man, that hath his heart well planted, will forsake his King rather than forsake God, and forsake his friend rather than forsake his King, and yet will forsake any earthly commodity, yea and his own life in some cases, rather than forsake his friend.

It is so difficult for us today to enter into the emotions of the Elizabethan for whom loyalty to the sovereign was, realistically, the only possible basis of peace and progress, that we can hardly understand the weight of such a statement unless we make a real effort at translating it into the concrete political terms of our own time. Such an effort is, of course, precisely the one we have already found necessary for a real understanding of Shakespeare's history plays and, to a lesser extent, of many of his other tragedies, and is all the more worth emphasizing on that account. Perhaps it will be easier to make it on Bacon's behalf if we keep in mind his notes "On The Fortunate Memory of Elizabeth, Queen of England" (see p. 11 ff.).

When James I succeeded to the throne in 1603, Bacon was already forty-three and although well-known as a lawyer, literary figure and statesman, had still never received a position or substantial income from the political activities which had engrossed so much of his time. His cousin, Robert Cecil, who had succeeded to the position held by Lord Burghley, was even more unfriendly to him than his uncle had been, and there seemed little likelihood of any real political advancement.

Nevertheless, James I had and treasured a reputation as a learned man and patron of philosophy, and Bacon hoped that he could induce him to undertake the project for a combined botanical and zoological garden, museum of arts and industries, and research laboratories, which he had outlined for Elizabeth ten years before. He made an early opportunity of attending court to see the new king—who knighted him together with some three hundred other commoners as a cheap reward for past service to the crown— and was evidently somewhat disappointed. He wrote privately to a friend, "I told your Lordship once before that (methought) his Majesty rather asked counsel of the time past than of the time to come. But it is early yet to ground any settled opinion."

Giving up, for the time, any hope of an official career Bacon evidently made a virtue of necessity, turning to the prospect of devoting his life to the scientific studies with which he was always profoundly if not exclusively concerned. In an unpublished fragment of biography written at this time (like most of his work, in Latin, and here translated by Spedding) he says, in part:

> Believing that I was born for the service of mankind, and regarding the care of the commonwealth as a kind of common property which like the air and the water belongs to everybody, I set myself to consider in what way mankind might

best be served, and what service I was myself by nature best
fitted to perform.

Now among all the benefits that could be conferred upon
mankind, I found none so great as the discovery of new arts,
endowments, and commodities for the bettering of man's life.
For I saw that among the rude people in the primitive times
the authors of rude inventions and discoveries were consecrated
and numbered among the Gods. And it was plain that the
good effects wrought by founders of cities, lawgivers, fathers
of the people, extirpaters of tyrants, and heroes of that class,
extend but over narrow spaces and last but for short times;
whereas the work of the Inventor, though a thing of less pomp
and show, is felt everywhere and lasts for ever.

But above all, if a man could succeed, not in striking out
some particular invention, however useful, but in kindling a
light in nature—a light which should in its very rising touch
and illuminate all the border-regions that confine upon the
circle of our present knowledge; and so spreading further and
further should presently disclose and bring into sight all that
is most hidden and secret in the world,—that man (I thought)
would be the benefactor indeed of the human race,—the propa-
gator of man's empire over the universe, the champion of
liberty, the conqueror and subduer of necessities.

For myself, I found that I was fitted for nothing so well
as for the study of Truth; as having a mind nimble and versa-
tile enough to catch the resemblance of things (which is the
chief point), and at the same time steady enough to fix and
distinguish their subtler differences; as being gifted by nature
with desire to seek, patience to doubt, fondness to meditate,
slowness to assert, readiness to reconsider, carefulness to dis-
pose and set in order; and as being a man that neither affects
what is new nor admires what is old, and that hates every
kind of imposture. So I thought my nature had a kind of
familiarity and relationship with Truth.

Nevertheless, because my birth and education had seasoned me in business of state; and because opinions (so young
as I was) would sometimes stagger me; and because I thought
that a man's own country has some special claims upon him
more than the rest of the world; and because I hoped that, if
I rose to any place of honour in the state, I should have a
larger command of industry and ability to help me in my
work;—for these reasons I both applied myself to acquire the
arts of civil life, and commended my service, so far as in
modesty and honesty I might, to the favour of such friends
as had any influence.

When I found however that my zeal was mistaken for ambition, and my life had already reached the turning-point, and
my breaking health reminded me how ill I could afford to be
slow, and I reflected moreover that in leaving undone that

good I could do by myself alone, and applying myself to that
which could not be done without the help and consent of
others, I was by no means discharging the duty that lay upon
me,—I put all those thoughts aside, and (in pursuance of my·
old determination) betook myself wholly to this work.

It is altogether characteristic of Bacon's consistent reserve that
neither in this solitary fragment of autobiography nor in any of his
letters then or later does he mention the recent death of the brother
who had been so close to him or his courtship of, and subsequent
marriage to, the young Alice Barnham, "an alderman's daughter, an
handsome maiden, to my liking."

However, he had been mistaken in his assumption that the new
regime meant the end of a public career and he was no doubt
pleased as well as surprised to find that King James immediately
gave him a small pension, some slight official position, and an
enormous amount of responsibility in the complicated negotiations
which, largely because of Bacon's work, brought about the immediate, peaceful and complete legal unification of England and
Scotland.

An unfinished essay, *The True Greatness of Britain,* written at
that time, describes the unified nation he wished to see under that
new—or, rather, renewed—title, as a nation not of great nobles and
peasants but one:

> whose wealth resteth in the hands of merchants, burghers,
> craftsmen, free holders, farmers in the country, and the like;
> whereof we have a most evident and present example before
> our eyes, in our neighbours of the Low Countries, who could
> never have endured and continued so inestimable and insup-
> portable charges [of the war with Spain], either by their
> natural frugality or by their mechanical industry, were it not
> also that their wealth was dispersed in many hands, and not
> ingrossed in few, and those hands were not so much of the
> nobility, but most generally of inferior condition.

The king's apparent friendliness revived Bacon's hopes for royal
support of science, and, in 1605, he published *The Advancement of
Learning,* dedicated to the king.

Bacon's practical purposes are immediately apparent in the
preface to the first book which skillfully mingles compliments to
the royal intellect, with appeals to the authority of Plato and the
Bible, that might influence one who "rather asked counsel of

the time past than of the time to come." After developing at some
length the value and beauty of true knowledge in the first book,
he begins the second with another dedicatory preface which, while
somewhat coldly paying its respects to Queen Elizabeth, contrasts
her state as a virgin with that of James, already sure of those who
would succeed him and, therefore, doubly concerned with improving the world in which they were to succeed.

This second introduction then proceeds with some anxious particularity to explain to the king just what it is that Bacon would
like to have him do.

> But to your Majesty, whom God hath already blessed with
> so much royal issue, worthy to continue and represent you for
> ever, and whose youthful and fruitful bed doth yet promise
> many the like renovations, it is proper and agreeable to be
> conversant not only in the transitory parts of good govern-
> ment, but in those acts also which are in their nature per-
> manent and perpetual. Amongst the which (if affection do not
> transport me) there is not any more worthy than the further
> endowment of the world with sound and fruitful knowledge;
> for why should a few received authors stand up like Hercules'
> columns, beyond which there should be no sailing or discover-
> ing, since we have so bright and benign a star as your majesty
> to conduct and prosper us?
>
> Let this ground therefore be laid, that all works are over-
> come by amplitude of reward, by soundness of direction, and
> by the conjunction of labours. The first multiplieth endeavor,
> the second preventeth error, and the third, supplieth the frailty
> of man. . . .

The work achieved no direct results but James was not displeased by it and continued to employ Bacon in his dealings with
Parliament, appointing him Solicitor-General in 1607.

The king's relations with the House of Commons were difficult
ones and Bacon's part in them was somewhat ambiguous.

The transition from feudalism to absolute monarchy which had
been completed by Henry VIII and stabilized by Elizabeth had,
naturally, entailed an enormous growth in the central government
with a corresponding increase of expense to which the normal royal
revenues, derived from the estate held by the family of the sovereign as by any other great family of nobles, was altogether
inadequate.

Henry VIII had solved this problem, along with many others,

by his confiscation of church lands. Elizabeth had met it by comparative economy—on a grand scale—by making various nobles
bear the expense for the lavish ceremonial which characterized her
court, by requesting frequent grants through special taxes or levies
which the commons were generally willing to raise since the class
they represented still depended on the queen and often benefited
by her policy, and by the use of "patents" or monopolies bestowed
on nobles important to the court. This last means was one increasingly resorted to and increasingly resented during the latter half of
Elizabeth's reign and, sensitive to public opinion and realistically
aware of the shifting relationship of class forces, she had promised
her last parliament in 1601 a virtual discontinuance of the practise.

In that same parliament Bacon had drawn a distinction between legitimate and illegitimate patents and monopolies, or
between what we would now call patents and what we would call
monopolies, defining the former to exist: "when any man by his
own charge, or by his own wit or invention doth bring any new
trade into the realm, or any engine tending to the furtherance of a
new trade that never was used before and that for the good of the
realm."

But James I, perpetually in need of money both for the necessarily increasing expenses of government and for the aggrandizement of the favorites he slobbered over and bestowed dukedoms
upon, was certainly not far-sighted enough voluntarily to give up
this power—or any other.

From the beginning to the end his relation with his parliaments
were a pattern of farcical futility.

They would be called into being to grant the king a sum of
money. They would refuse unless he in turn granted them the
redress of a long list of grievances, including repeal of special
patents. After long and undignified bargaining some sort of tentative agreement would be reached. The Commons would refuse to
hand over the money until they had received the promised redress.
The king, equally suspicious, or perhaps meditating a double-cross,
would refuse any action until he had received the money. The
long vacation might then intervene, and after consultation with
their constituents, the Commons would return to drive a harder
bargain or the king would in a temper dissolve Parliament with
nothing gained and all was to do again.

After such a dissolution in 1611, Bacon wrote the king one of many letters urging a complete change in tactics in his summoning the new parliament. He said, in part:

> My third proposition is that this Parliament may be a little reduced to the more ancient form which was to voice the Parliament to be for some other business of estate and not merely for money; but that to come in upon the bye, whatsoever the truth be. I mean it not in point of dissimulation but in point of majesty and honour; that the people may have somewhat else to talk of and not wholly of the King's estate, and that Parliament-men may not be wholly possessed of these thoughts. What shall be the causes of estate given forth ad populam, whether the opening and increase of trade, or whether the plantation of Ireland, or the reduction and recompiling of the laws, it may be left to further consideration. But I am settled in this, that somewhat be published beside the money matter, and that in this form there is much advantage.

This attempt to restore the royal prestige and unify the king and Commons was far from hypocrisy on Bacon's part, and his tactful understatement of the political role to be played by a genuine parliament was intended to conciliate James into giving the idea a trial.

For although the Elizabethan myth of national unity, which had already outlived its brief truth, was rapidly becoming too threadbare to deceive the most credulous, and the king's pro-Spanish policy and his wife's avowed conversion to Catholicism were destroying his credit with all but the most reactionary, yet Bacon still strove persistently to turn the king's policy into the path of true national interests, and, when he failed in a specific instance, continued, nevertheless, to support the measures actually undertaken by the crown. That is to say, of course, measures for the relief of pressing financial needs or assertion of the royal prerogative in internal affairs. Bacon never in any way furthered or even countenanced the undeclared attempts at rapprochement with Spain or the Vatican, and was practically the only man of his standing at Court never even offered a pension by the King of Spain.

The best explanation of Bacon's role in the reign of James is given by John Howard Lawson's discussion of seventeenth century England in *The Hidden Heritage*. He says, in part:

. . . Bacon was devoted to the principle of monarchial absolutism, but he differed from many of the crown's advisers in the quality of his intelligence as well as in his class interests. These were the factors which made Bacon invaluable to the government.

Since he did not suffer from the aristocratic astigmatism which afflicted most of the court circle, Bacon could see the problem of power as a national question rather than as a matter of arbitrary class domination. He wanted the king to assert his absolute authority, but he saw the royal will as a means of overcoming class antagonism and forcing the propertied classes to work together for their mutual advantage. . . . He had disapproved of the vulgar bargaining over the *Great Contract* because it exacerbated class differences and exposed the king's selfish aims. As an intellectual structure, Bacon's idea was impressive: James was to reassert his national leadership, balancing the interests of various propertied groups with such open-handed majesty that no one would dare to question his motives or oppose the subsidies which were necessary to maintain the state apparatus. . . .

But the grandeur of Bacon's plan—which doomed it to failure—lay in its abandonment of petty compromises, its large and unwarranted assumption that a unified national policy could be accepted and consistently followed.

One could formulate a policy for the advancement of industry, foreign commerce, territorial expansion and colonial aggrandizement. But such a policy demanded the elimination of monopolistic practices and feudal privileges; . . . it required the strengthening of England's economic and political influence in Europe, which could only be accomplished through opposition to the Hapsburgs and the papacy and an alliance with the Protestant forces on the continent.

All these things constituted the program of the bourgeoisie —which contravened the class interests of the crown and the court. Bacon's reconciliation of classes was an abstraction; it meant that absolutism would take over the program of the bourgeoisie and make it its own.

Nevertheless, for a time James did attempt to put some of Bacon's suggestions into effect, and in 1613 Bacon was made Attorney-General.

In the same year he published a second series of essays and their titles and content show how constantly and profoundly he was thinking of the major political problems of the time. For example, in "Of Plantations" (a name commonly used for colonies), he says first: "I like a plantation in a pure soil; that is, where people are not displanted to the end to plant in others. For else it is rather an extirpation than a plantation."

And again, later:

> Let there be freedom from custom [export duties], till the plantation be full of strength; and not only freedom from custom, but freedom to carry their commodities where they may make their best of them, except there be some special cause of caution.

In another essay "Of Nobility" we find Bacon first saying, as we might expect anyone in his time, place, and position to do:

> A *Monarchy*, where there is no *Nobility* at all, is ever a pure and absolute *Tyranny*; As that of the Turkes. For *Nobility* attempers *Soveraignty*, and drawes the Eyes of the People, somewhat aside from the *Line Royall*.

But he then rather surprisingly continues:

> But for *Democracies*, they need it not; And they are commonly, more quiet and lesse subject to Sedition, then where there are *Stirps* of *Nobles*. For Mens Eyes are upon the Businesse, and not upon the Persons; Or if upon the Persons, it is for the Businesse sake, as fittest, and not for Flags and Pedegree. Wee see the *Switzers* last well, notwithstanding their Diversitie of Religion, and of Cantons. For Utility is their Bond, and not Respects. The united Provinces of the Low Countries, in their Government, excell; For where there is an Equality, the Consultations are more indifferent, and the Payments and Tributes more cheerfull.

"Of Seditions and Troubles" begins:

> The *Matter* of *Seditions* is of two kindes; *Much Poverty*, and *Much Discontentment*. . . . And if this *Poverty*, and Broken Estate, in the better Sort, be joyned with a Want and Necessity, in the meane People, the danger is imminent, and great. For the Rebellions of the Belly are the worst.

The essay continues in shrewd detail:

> The *Causes* and *Motives* of *Seditions* are; *Innovation* in *Religion; Taxes; Alteration of Lawes and Customes; Breaking of Priviledges; General Oppression; Advancement of unworthy*

persons; Strangers; Dearths; Disbanded Souldiers; Factions growne desperate; And whatsoever in offending People, knotteth them, in a Common Cause.

Finally Bacon advises:

The first *Remedy* or prevention, is to remove by all meanes possible, that *materiall Cause of Sedition,* whereof we spake; which is *Want* and *Poverty* in the *Estate.* To which purpose serveth the Opening, and well Ballancing of Trade; The Cherishing of Manufactures; the Banishing of Idlenesse; the Repressing of waste and Excesse by Sumptuary Lawes; the Improvement and Husbanding of the Soyle; the Regulating of Prices of things vendible; the Moderating of Taxes and Tributes; And the like. Generally, it is to be foreseene, that the Population of a Kingdome, (especially if it be not mowen downe by warrs) does not exceed, the Stock of the Kingdome, which should maintaine them. Neither is the Population, to be reckoned onely by number; For a smaller Number, that spend more, and earne lesse, doe weare out an Estate, sooner then a greater Number, that live lower, and gather more. Therefore the Multiplying of Nobilitie, and other Degrees of Qualitie, in an over proportion, to the Common People, doth speedily bring a State to Necessitie: And so doth likewise an overgrowne Clergie; For they bring nothing to the Stocke; . . .

In another essay, "Of the true Greatnesse of Kingdomes and Estates," there is an extremely interesting discussion of man power and morale, beginning:

For *Solon* said well to *Croesus* (when in Ostentation he shewd him his Gold) *Sir, if any Other come, that hath better Iron then you, he will be Master of all this Gold.* Therefore let any Prince or State, thinke soberly of his Forces, except his *Militia* of Natives, be of good and Valiant Soldiers. . . . As for Mercenary Forces, (which is the Helpe in this Case) all Examples shew; That, whatsoever Estate or Prince doth rest upon them; *Hee may spread his Feathers for a time, but he will mew* them soone after.

The same essay continues to discuss means of holding as well as winning power, contrasting the Spartans who refused equal rights to aliens with the Romans, and drawing the appropriate moral.

Never any State was, in this Point, so open to receive *Strangers,* into their Body, as were the *Romans.* Therefore it sorted with them accordingly; For they grew to the greatest *Monarchy*. Their manner was, to grant Naturalization, (which they called *Jus Civitatis*) and to grant it in the highest Degree; That is, Not onely *Jus Commercij, Jus Connubij, Jus Haereditatis;* But also, *Jus Suffragij*, and *Jus Honorum*. And this, not to Singular Persons alone, but likewise to whole Families; yea to Cities, and sometimes to Nations. Adde to this, their Custome of *Plantation* of *Colonies*; whereby the Roman Plant was removed into the Soile, of other Nations. And putting both Constitutions together, you will say, that it was not the *Romans* that spred upon the *World*; But it was the *World* that spred upon the *Romans*; And that was the sure way of Greatnesse.

In addition to these and the many other specifically political topics, there are many illustrations drawn from the field of politics in the more general consideration of such subjects as, "Of Friendship," "Of Envy," "Of Counsell," and the like. A good example of these is the essay, "Of Wisdome for a Mans selfe," which begins:

An *Ant* is a *wise Creature* for it Selfe; But it is a shrewd Thing, in an Orchard, or Garden. And certainly, Men that are great *Lovers* of *Themselves*, waste the Publique. Divide with reason betweene *Selfe-love* and *Society*: And be so true to thy *Selfe*, as thou be not false to Others; Specially to thy King, and Country. . . . And certainly, it is the Nature of Extreme *Selfe-Lovers*; As they will set an House on Fire, and it were but to roast their Egges; . . .

There are also a few essays dealing explicitly with economic questions. Of these perhaps the most interesting to us is the one "of Usurie." Usury, it must be remembered, was still in early seventeenth century usage as it had been in Shakespeare's time, the correct name for any interest-bearing loan. The medieval prohibition of all interest charges had not yet been formally rescinded, although it was a regulation more honored in the breach than the observance.

Bacon, after summarizing the traditional religious arguments against charging interest, begins:

I say this onely, that *Usury* is a *Concessum propter Duritiem Cordis*: For since there must be Borrowing and Lending, and Men are so hard of Heart, as they will not lend freely, *Usury* must be permitted. . . . But few have spoken of *Usury* usefully. It is good to set before us, the *Incommodities*, and *Commodities* of *Usury*; . . .

It appeares by the Ballance, of *Commodities*, and *Discommodities* of *Usury*, Two Things are to be Reconciled. The one, that the *Tooth of Usurie* be grinded, that it bite not too much: The other, that there bee left open a Meanes, to invite Moneyed Men, to lend to the Merchants, for the Continuing and Quickning of Trade. This cannot be done, except you introduce two severall *Sorts* of *Usury*; A *Lesse*, and a *Greater*. For if you reduce *Usury* to one Low Rate, it will ease the common Borrower, but the Merchant will be to seeke for Money. And it is to be noted, that the Trade of Merchandize, being the most Lucrative, may beare *Usury* at a good Rate; other Contracts not so.

To serve both Intentions, the way would be briefly thus. That there be *Two Rates of Usury*, the one Free, and Generall for All; The other under *Licence* only, to *Certaine Persons*, and in *Certaine Places of Merchandizing*. First therefore, let *Usury, in generall, be reduced to Five in the Hundred*; And let that Rate be proclaimed to be Free and Current; And let the State shut it selfe out, to take any Penalty for the same. . . .

Finally, after further description of possible safeguards and means of lowering all interest rates, Bacon concludes with characteristic moderation and realism:

If it be Objected, that this doth, in a Sort, Authorize *Usury*, which before was, in some places, but Permissive: The Answer is; That it is better, to Mitigate *Usury* by *Declaration*, than to suffer it to Rage by *Connivence*.

Finally in 1616 Bacon succeeded to the office his father had held for twenty years, Lord Keeper of the Great Seal of England, and in 1617 he was, largely through the good offices of the king's then favorite, the Duke of Buckingham, appointed Lord Chancellor.

His predecessor had been ill for some time and there was even without such a delay, an enormous backlog of unheard cases in the ordinary course of events, so that Bacon inherited a court calendar almost two years in arrears. Yet three months after his appointment he was able to write triumphantly, to the Earl of Buckingham:

This day I have made even with the business of the kingdom for common justice. Not one case unheard. The lawyers drawn dry of all the motions they were wont to make. Not one petition unanswered, and this I think could not be said in our age before. This I speak not out of ostentation, but out of gladness, that I have done my duty. I know men think I cannot continue, if I should thus oppress myself with business. But that account is made. The duties of life are more than life. And if I die now I shall die before the world is weary of me, which in our times is somewhat rare.

Honors now crowded upon him. In 1618 he was named Baron Verulam and two years later Viscount St. Albans. He spent much time laying out extraordinary gardens about his father's old country house of Gorhamsbury and leased and completely redecorated and furnished York House in London where he had been born.

Nevertheless, he made time to draw up a detailed plan for his master work—*The Great Instauration*—and to complete the second of its six projected parts—*The Novum Organum*.

The work as Bacon envisaged it, was to consist of six independent but related parts. The first was to be called *The Division of the Sciences* and to contain a description of the various fields of natural knowledge with the kinds of activity or inquiry appropriate to each one. The second was *The Novum Organum* (completed in two books) or *Directions Concerning the Interpretation of Nature*. The third was to be what we should today call an Encyclopedia of Natural History and Scientific Experiments. Bacon called it *The Phenomena of the Universe,* or a *Natural and Experimental History for the Foundation of Philosophy.* The fourth section was to be called *The Ladder of the Intellect.* Bacon intended it to be an exposition of the way in which the scientific methods discussed in Part II should be applied to the essential facts or raw materials of science which would be recorded, when collected, in Part III. The fifth was to be *The Forerunners* or *Anticipations of the New Philosophy.* This would have been an illustrative account of various discoveries which had already been made more or less accidentally, and of the way in which man's life had been enriched by them. The last section was to be a summary of *The New Philosophy* or *Active Science.* In describing this sixth part Bacon says:

> The sixth part of my work (to which the rest is subservient and ministrant) discloses and sets forth that philosophy which by the legitimate, chaste, severe course of inquiry which I have explained and provided is at length developed

and established. The completion, however, of this last part is
a thing both above my strength and beyond my hopes. What
I have been able to do is to give it, as I hope, not a contemptible start. The fortune of the human race will give the
issue; such an issue, it may be, as in the present condition of
things and men's minds cannot easily be conceived or im-
agined. For what is at stake is not merely a mental satisfaction but the very reality of men's well being, and all his power
of action. Man is the helper and interpreter of Nature. He can
act and understand in so far as by working upon her or observing her he has come to perceive her order. Beyond this he
has neither knowledge or power. For there is no strength that
can break the causal chain: Nature cannot be conquered but
by obeying her. Accordingly these twin goals, human science
and human power, come in the end to one. To be ignorant
of causes is to be frustrated in action.

The Great Instauration in this fragmentary form was published
in 1620 and dedicated to King James in an introductory letter
which indicated Bacon's feeling that the work could not be completed by one man, and his persistent hope that the king, with his
comparatively unlimited resources, might be induced to undertake
it.

After the dedication to the king there is a preface addressed
to the reader. Bacon begins:

It seems to me that men do not rightly understand either
their store or their strength but overrate the one and under
rate the other. Hence it follows that either from an extravagant
estimate of the value of the arts which they possess, they seek
no further; or else from too mean an estimate of their own
powers they spend their strength in small matters and never
put it fairly to the trial in those which go to the main. These
are as the pillars of fate set in the path of knowledge; for men
have neither desire nor hope to encourage them to penetrate
further.

Near the conclusion he says:

Lastly, I would address one general admonition to all, that
they consider what are the true ends of knowledge, and that
they seek it not either for the pleasure of the mind, or for
contention, or for superiority to others, or for profit, or fame,
or power, or for any of these inferior things; but for the benefit
and use of life; and that they perfect and govern it in charity.
For it was from lust of power that the angels fell, from lust of

knowledge that man fell; but of charity there can be no excess, neither did angel or man ever come in danger by it.

The requests I have to make are these. Of myself I say nothing; but in behalf of the business which is in hand I entreat men to believe that *it is not an opinion to be held, but a work to be done*; and to be well assured that I am laboring to lay the foundation, not of any sect, or doctrine, but of human utility and power. Next I ask them to deal fairly by their own interests; and laying aside all emulations and prejudices in favour of this or that opinion, to join in consultation for the common good; and being now fixed and guarded by the securities and helps which I offer from the errors and impediments of the way, to come forward themselves and take part in that which remains to be done. Moreover, to be of good hope, nor to imagine that this Instauration of mine is a thing infinite and beyond the power of man, when it is in fact the true end and termination of error; and seeing also that it is by no means forgetful of the conditions of mortality and humanity, for it does not suppose that the work can be altogether completed within one generation, but provides for its being taken up by another; . . .

Suddenly in 1621, with no real warning, a cataclysm engulfed Bacon—or, at least, the Lord Chancellor.

Parliament convened in a mood of sullen anger at the king and his favorites. The immediate complaint was certain particularly oppressive patents granted to two creatures of Buckingham's and used by them with outrageous presumption, brazen dishonesty, and callous cruelty. The patents had, of course, been granted by the king who could not as yet be openly attacked, but had been legally certified by the Lord Chancellor and two other justices. There was an abortive attempt to take action against the three judges on those grounds, but the two patent holders were cheerfully sacrificed by the crown, and the matter seemed at an end. However, although the specific intrigues involved are still in dispute, it seems clear James learned that a more serious sacrifice was required—either his chief minister or his bedfellow, if not both.

Under the circumstances his choice was a foregone conclusion. Two plaintiffs who had appeared in suits before the Lord Chancellor testified that they had given him bribes which he had accepted—although both had lost their cases and in both instances Bacon's decision had been sustained on appeal.

Everyone available who had been a party to the more than

8,000 actions before Bacon was summoned, and some 28 were found who declared that they had sent him gifts, in most cases after the conclusion of their actions. It is significant that after the most searching investigation the courts failed then or later to reverse a single one of the decisions involved.

Bacon first prepared to make a vigorous defense, but after some communication with the king wrote a general admission of guilt, confessing that he had, as was then customary, taken gifts after the termination of suits and that in at least four cases he had not checked to find out whether the process had actually been terminated. He protested, what seems to have been true, that in no case was his judgment influenced by such gratuities, but submitted himself to the sentence of parliament.

Before the sentence had yet been considered he airily wrote the king:

> But because he that hath taken bribes is apt to give bribes, I will go farther and present your Majesty with a bribe. For if your Majesty give me peace and leisure and God give me life, I will present your Majesty with a good history of England and better digest of your laws.

The sentence, when rendered, read that he should be incapable of any office, place or employment in the State or Commonwealth; never be allowed to sit in Parliament or to come within the verge of the court, which at that time meant London; be imprisoned in the Tower during the King's pleasure; and be fined £40,000. The king's pleasure proved to be less than a week and the fine was transformed into a benefit since Bacon was then, as always, heavily in debt, and the (unpressed) crown lien on his income taking legal priority, prevented any other creditor from putting in a claim until it had been satisfied.

The banishment from London which meant, in this case, from libraries and research facilities, was not so easily overcome since Buckingham wanted the lease of York House and Bacon was unwilling to cede it. After six months exile and some threats of pressing the fine, Bacon gave in, received a limited pardon from the king, and found himself virtually free of penalties although in dishonorable retirement.

The dishonor seems even then to have been a matter of opinion since so censorious a contemporary critic of morals as Ben Jonson

—an acquaintance but by no means a close friend of Bacon's—wrote only a few years later:

> My conceit of his person was never increased toward him by his place or honours, but I have and do reverence him for the greatness that was only proper to himself: in that he seemed to me ever by his works one of the greatest men and most worthy of admiration that had been in many ages: in his adversity I ever prayed that God would give "him strength, for greatness he could not want." Neither could I condole in a word or syllable for him, knowing that no accident could do harm to virtue, but help to make it manifest.

With his usual amazing resilience Bacon spent the next four months writing an excellent history of Henry VII which he presented to the king in partial fulfillment of his promise, and settled down to complete as much as possible of the scientific writings outlined in *The Great Instauration*.

A comment to Rawley, who served as literary secretary for the remainder of Bacon's life, is as good an example of the judicial temperament as literature can afford. He said, after criticizing the custom by which judges were largely paid out of the fees of litigants, that he hoped his case would show the errors which persistence in such a custom could lead to, and concluded, "I was the justest judge that was in England this fifty years. But it was the justest censure of Parliament that was this two hundred years."

In 1622 he published two scientific treatises on *The Winds*, and *Life and Death* (medicine) and in 1623 his *De Augmentis Scientarium*, a greatly enlarged and improved Latin version of *The Advancement of Learning*.

In 1625 he published a revised edition of his Essays with a number of new ones including two cheerful analyses, "Of Judicature," and "Of Vicissitude of Things." Another very interesting new essay, "Of Greatness of Kingdoms and Estates," summarizes a viewpoint which Bacon had expressed at greater length in his survey of the rise of the Tudor absolutism in *The History of King Henry VII*. Its conclusions about small freeholders read remarkably like Thomas Jefferson's. Bacon says:

> Let states that aim at greatness, take heed how their nobility and gentlemen do multiply too fast. For that maketh the common subject grow to be a peasant and base swain, driven out of heart, and in effect but the gentleman's laborer.

Even as you may see in coppice woods; if you leave your
staddles too thick, you shall never have clean underwood, but
shrubs and bushes. So in countries, if the gentlemen be too
many, the commons will be base; . . . This which I speak
of hath been no where better seen than by comparing of England and France: whereof England, though far less in territory
and population, hath been nevertheless an over-match; in regard the middle people of England make good soldiers which
the peasants of France do not. And herein the devices of king
Henry the Seventh (whereof I have spoken largely in the
history of his life) was profound and admirable; in making
farms and houses of husbandry of a standard; that is, maintained with such a proportion of land unto them, as may breed
a subject to live in convenient plenty and no servile condition;
and to keep the plough in the hands of the owners, and not
mere hirelings.

That same March, on King James' death, Bacon gaily and
irreverently wrote to the new king, Charles I, that he hoped, as the
Father had been his Creator, the Son would be his Redeemer, and
in June he was summoned, as a Peer of the Realm, to the House
of Lords, although he was too ill that month to attend.

It is apparent that his temperament as well as his ideas justified
him in having said: "And it seemeth to me, that most of the doctrines of the philosophers are more fearful and cautionary than
the nature of things requireth."

At the beginning of April, 1626, seeing that the ground was
still covered with snow, it occurred to him that that would be a
good time to try whether flesh could not be preserved by cold as
well as salt. He got out of his carriage, bought a fowl from a cot-
tager, had it killed and cleaned, and then himself stuffed it with
snow. A letter he dictated from bed a few days later tells of the
conclusion of more than the experiment.

To the Earl of Arundel and Surrey.
My Very Good Lord:
   I was like to have had the fortune of Caius Plinius the
elder, who lost his life by trying an experiment or two touching the conservation and induration of bodies. As for the experiment itself, it succeeded excellently well; but in the journey
between London and Highgate I was taken with such a fit of
casting, as I knew not whether it were the stone, or some
surfeit, or a cold, or indeed a touch of them all three. But
when I came to your Lordship's house, I was not able to go
back, and therefore was forced to take up my lodging here,

where your housekeeper is very careful and diligent about me; which I assure myself your lordship will not only pardon towards him, but think the better of him for it. For indeed your Lordship's house was happy to me; and I kiss your noble hands for the welcome which I am sure you give me to it. . . .

Bronchitis rapidly developed and on April 9, 1626, he died and, as his will directed, was buried very quietly near his mother's grave. His wife, with whom he seems to have lived peacefully and pleasantly, although she apparently played no large share in his life, had probably left him shortly before his death. A codicil written that year canceled all bequests to her "for reasons she will understand," and she married a gentleman of her household a few months later. She was then of course still only in her middle thirties.

Today there is little need to urge recognition of scientific achievements. On the contrary, our respect for science is now so unquestioning that we can hardly appreciate Bacon's pioneer work in demanding it. But it is unquestionably true, as Goethe said, that: "The impact of Bacon's genius directed the mind of his age towards reality. This extraordinary man performed the inestimable service of calling attention to the whole field of natural science!"

But there is even more need now than there was four centuries ago to emphasize the other aspect of Bacon's thought which has, with the end of the bourgeois revolution, been forgotten by some of his most devout followers. Lord Macaulay, for example, the Whig historian who thought of himself as the statesman of industrialism, claimed the heritage of Bacon's philosophy for the Victorians, saying:

To make men perfect was no part of Bacon's plan. His humble aim was to make imperfect men comfortable. . . . In Plato's opinion man was made for philosophy; in Bacon's opinion philosophy was made for man; it was a means to an end; and that end was to increase the pleasures and to mitigate the pains of millions who are not and cannot be philosophers. . . .

To sum up the whole, we should say that the aim of the Platonic philosophy was to exalt man into a god. The aim of the Baconian philosophy was to provide man with what he requires while he continues to be man. The aim of the Platonic philosophy was to raise us far above vulgar wants. The aim of the Baconian philosophy was to supply our vulgar wants. The former aim was noble; but the latter was attainable.

Bacon himself would have indignantly refuted this interpretation. He says over and over again such things as:

> If there be any one on whose ear my frequent praise of practical activities has a harsh and unpleasing sound because he is wholly devoted to contemplative philosophy, let me assure him that he is the enemy of his own desires. In natural philosophy practical results are not only means to improve human well-being. They are also the guarantee of truth. There is a true rule in religion, that a man must show his faith by his works. The same rule holds good in philosophy. Science too must be known by its works. It is by the witness of works rather than by logic or even observation that truth is revealed and established. *It follows from this that the improvement of man's lot and the improvement of man's mind are one and the same thing.*

He asserts and reasserts that it is not merely inconvenient but morally wrong to despair of human powers or to suppose that man does not have the ability radically to alter nature.

> This philosophy, if it be carefully examined, will be found to advance certain points of view which are deliberately designed to cripple enterprise. Such points of view are the opinion that the heat of the sun is a different thing from the heat of fire; or that men can only juxtapose things while nature alone can make them act upon one another. The effect and intention of these arguments is to convince men that nothing really great, nothing by which nature can be commanded and subdued, is to be expected from human art and labour. Such teachings, if they be justly appraised, will be found to be nothing less than a wicked effort to curtail human power over nature, and to produce a deliberate and artificial despair. This despair in its turn confounds the promptings of hope, cuts the springs and sinews of industry, and makes men unwilling to put anything to the hazard of trial.

He promises that a true scientific history of inventions and their possibilities "will not only be of immediate benefit . . . but will give a more true and real illumination concerning the investigations of the causes of things and axioms of art than has hitherto shone upon mankind."

The true goal of science according to Bacon is not merely "to make imperfect men comfortable," although that may be a useful by-product, as Huxley explains in his essay, "On the Advisableness of Improving Natural Knowledge" (1866). "The true and lawful goal of science," Bacon says, "is the endowing of human life with new discoveries and powers. . . . For the world is not to be narrowed down till it will go into the understanding, which has been the practice hitherto, but the understanding must be stretched and expanded to take in the image of the world as it is discovered."

No, it is not the Whig Macaulay but rather a great radical contemporary of his who was the true heir to Bacon's philosophy. Bacon would have demolished Macaulay's smug dichotomy between the noble and unattainable objective of raising us above vulgar wants, and the ignoble and attainable one of supplying our vulgar wants. But he would have saluted as a logical next step Engels' conclusion that:

> . . . the final, essential distinction between man and other animals . . . the animal merely *uses* external nature, and brings about changes in it simply by his presence; man by his changes makes it serve his ends, *masters* it . . . all our mastery of it consists in the fact that we have the advantage over all other creatures of being able to know and correctly apply its laws.
> . . . by long and often cruel experience and by collecting and analyzing the historical material, we are gradually learning to get a clear view of the indirect, more remote, social effects of our productive activity, and so the possibility is afforded us of controlling and regulating these effects as well.

Almost four centuries ago Bacon could envision such a possibility for the future. In attempting to communicate this vision to his contemporaries he not only became the first "philosopher of industrial science," but also the first English writer of a flexible, varied, precise and colloquial prose.

An impersonal essayist, judicial and detached in tone, he has nevertheless established direct contact with readers' minds in over fifteen generations. For his thought is never an abstraction but always a concrete living thing. The few close-packed sentences of each essay expand and change visibly before our eyes whenever we read them with the attention they demand. And their inspired common sense still stands as one of the most enduring monuments

to the practical genius of modern man, which can change the world
by understanding it.

PURITANS AND CAVALIERS

If the defeat of the Spanish Armada in 1588 marks the culmina-
tion of the century-old alliance between the throne and the bourgeoisie in England, it no less truly marks the beginning of the
end of that alliance. Up to that point the middle class may be said
to have struggled for mere existence as a class; from that point on
its at first unrealized fight was, not for life, but for power.

The alliance disintegrated all the more suddenly because both
parties simultaneously felt ready for a test of strength. The still
powerful but rapidly declining remnants of the feudal nobility
were no longer a real threat to the throne and, with the accession
of James I in 1602, the king turned to consolidate relations with
them which would, he hoped, enable him successfully and completely to dominate the increasingly defiant House of Commons.
While James I's tactlessness, corrupt favorites, personal arrogance,
deep ignorance of English history, and unconcealed suspicion of
English institutions, undoubtedly accelerated the deterioration of
relations between the throne and parliament, and aggravated the
new unpopularity of the sovereign, the seeds of the violent struggle which culminated in civil war were inherent in the situation
itself, and it would probably have been impossible for the most
politic monarch to have avoided it.

The growing divergence between the court and the Commons
was soon reflected in the theatre. As early as 1594, Shakespeare
comments on the new artificial theatrical fashions which were
growing up in response to the demand of the more "precious"
aristocratic audience. This drama, presented in far more expensive
and exclusive "private theatres," relied heavily on masques, dances,
music, and elaborately learned witticisms or flowery conceits, and
shrank more and more from themes of serious concern or emotional
impact, turning to an unreal fairytale world distinguished only by
its verbal skill and pageantry. For such plays the clear cultivated
voices of young children and their immature unemotional grace

was well fitted—and the popularity of "child actors" (at which Shakespeare makes Hamlet exclaim) was a fad indicative of the real decadence of the drama.

Furthermore, the opposition to the king and court was expressed very largely in religious terms. It must not be forgotten that the king of England was head of church as well as of state, and that there was already a well-established form and tradition of religious struggle while there were not yet set ideological terms for a political struggle. The growing strength and anger of the bourgeoisie was therefore expressed as a renewed Puritan opposition to the Church of England. The Puritans had never been friendly to the theatre on moral and economic grounds, and its official position of existence by favor of, and under protection from, the court, or of individual great noblemen, gave a further edge to their displeasure.

Thus, less than a quarter of a century after it had reached unprecedented heights of almost universal popularity and significance, we find the drama as a great art form virtually disappearing. We must turn for the most important literature of the early seventeenth century to the lyrical poets of the court and to the great pamphleteers of the revolution—the greatest of whom, Milton, was also the single important epic poet whom English literature has, so far, produced.

The cavalier poets, Sir John Suckling, Richard Lovelace, Robert Herrick, whose very names seem set to music and fit burdens for old songs, inherited much of the grace, charm, verbal felicity and lyrical beauty which were the ornament of Elizabethan drama. Sometimes less fresh and spontaneous, often lightly cynical, always less convincing in their emotion, they limit their themes to the confines of an aristocratic court where lovemaking is the business of peace, and courage is shown by a gentleman's defending his king's honor in a war much as he would defend his lady's in a duel.

Oddly enough we find here that a concentration upon lovemaking does not help to create great love poetry—as we shall see with Wordsworth in the nineteenth century, it is impossible to write movingly even about daffodils if one thinks only of daffodils. So if we place some of the most delightful lines of the cavaliers side by side with those of their Elizabethan prototypes we may find that the best flowers of a court are not really as beautiful as those whose roots go deeper into the lives of their time.

Let us, for example, very briefly consider a comparison—and contrast—between the best known lyric by perhaps the most skillful cavalier poet, Robert Herrick (1591-1674), and an Elizabethan song on the same subject from *Twelfth Night*.

The first and last stanzas of Herrick's graceful exhortation "To the Virgins, To Make Much of Time," read:

> Gather ye rosebuds while ye may,
>   Old Time is still a-flying:
> And this same flower that smiles to-day,
>   Tomorrow will be dying.
>
> Then be not coy, but use your time,
>   And while ye may, go marry:
> For, having lost but once your prime
>   You may forever tarry.

Shakespeare seems, more warmly and personally, to urge much the same request in:

> O, Mistress mine, where are you roaming?
> O, stay and hear; your true love's coming,
>   That can sing both high and low.
> Trip no further, pretty sweeting,
> Journeys end in lovers meeting,
>   Every wise man's son doth know.
>
> What is love? 'tis not hereafter;
> Present mirth hath present laughter;
>   What's to come is still unsure.
> In delay there lies no plenty;
> Then come kiss me, sweet and twenty,
>   Youth's a stuff will not endure.

Yet when we come to examine the two poems at all closely we find that the greater emotional power, the sustained contemporary impact of the Elizabethan, is not due simply to a more musical note or more brilliant images. The whole tone of freedom and equality in which the young woman (her virginity is evidently for Shakespeare an irrelevant if not impertinent inquiry) is urged to fulfill herself by making love, as she laughs, at pleasure, with a young man whose voice is exerted to delight her, is sharply contrasted with the virgin whose function it is to please and whose beauty and virginity are perishable commodities to be sold while the market holds. We can be well assured that the latter's husband-to-be will offer nothing so insubstantial as a talent for part-singing, but will rather prove his worth by the tender of a well-filled rent roll.

It is no great step from this to the gay contempt shown by Sir John Suckling (1609-1642):

> Out upon it, I have loved
> Three whole days together!
> And am like to love three more
> If it prove fair weather.

or the pious platitude of Richard Lovelace (1618-1658) in his oft quoted:

> I could not love thee, dear, so much,
> Loved I not honor more.

The religious or "metaphysical" poets of the King and Church of England party have perhaps less to say to us today. Herbert, Crashaw, Vaughan and even the later Donne were turning to God rather to escape the struggle than to strengthen themselves in it, and the frequently contorted and mystical allegory, the involved conceits and the disguised platitudes of their verse are in sharp contrast with the heroic and powerful lines of Milton or the deeply felt, straightforward, and concrete allegory of a simpler nonconformist whom we shall meet a little later—John Bunyan. Even Milton's friend and sometime comrade, Andrew Marvell, lives for us rather in the single famous plea to his coy mistress than in his serious poetry, and for most modern readers it is the originality and, often, the bitterness of Donne's love poetry, with its frequent undertone of the cynicism of "Go and Catch a Falling Star," rather than any more devout emotion which carries conviction.

We may perhaps represent the course of English literature in the seventeenth century by some such image as that of a great and powerful current carrying with it all the rich hopes, accomplishments and aspirations of the Elizabethan age, which split on the rock of the growing national disunity and flowed for a while in two streams. One, the shallow pretty rivulet we have just glanced at; the other a narrow, deep and swift moving current which kept and even intensified some of the earlier emotional power, but had, at least temporarily, lost the tumultuous variety, the playfulness, the breadth and ease which were the particular glory of the parent river.

We have no time to pause with the many vital preachers and pamphleteers whose vocabulary is, sometimes, unfortunately, as foreign to us as their thought is, in many cases, contemporary. Certainly the democratic Levelers and their great spokesman, Lilburne, must be given some individual mention, however brief.

John Lilburne was the leader of the most progressive group which had any substantial following—a group essentially composed of independent farmers and small merchants including some shipowners and well-to-do craftsmen. They stood for individual liberty, absolute legal equality, abolition of all vested interests and most taxes, and complete free trade. Lilburne was jailed under Charles I for writing against the royal prerogative and his fight for a "trial by his peers" and not by the House of Lords or a picked "blue ribbon" jury is an important part of the history of the struggle for constitutional government in England.

When the Civil War actually began, Lilburne served devotedly in the parliamentary army and became a leading figure there. However, with victory, and especially after the decisive defeat of Charles I in 1646-47, the big bourgeoisie who dominated parliament began moving steadily to the right to consolidate their gains and prevent the revolution from going any further. Lilburne, as spokesman for the petty bourgeoisie who had, as yet, secured almost none of the fruits of victory, attacked parliament in a series of sharply worded pamphlets for which he was again jailed and threatened with execution.

This is an excerpt from *England's New Chaines for Old* published in defiance of the press censorship in 1649:

> . . . They have already lost the affections of all People, and are onely supported by their present strength; but when once those good men that hold them up, shall perceive how instrumentall they are made, contrary to their intentions, in advancing a few lofty and imperious mens designes; and how easy it is for them to convert their abilities and power to better, and more common, ends exprest in their former engagements, and with the complaints of the agrieved people, and their owne understandings can furnish them with all, they will then lament that they have so long been out of the way, and set themselves with the utmost courage and resolution to free their distressed country from the fears and captivity it now groans under. They may talk of freedom, but what freedom indeed is there, so long as they stop the Presse, which is indeed and hath been so accounted in all free nations, the most essentiall part thereof? . . .
>
> And as for the prosperity of the Nation; what one thing hath been done that tendeth to it? . . .

Nay, what sence of the heavy burdens of the people have they manifested of late, hath it not been by their procurement that the Judges their creatures have a thousand pound a yeer allow'd to every one of them above the ordinary fees? which were ever esteemed a heavy oppression in themselves; is there any abridgement of the charge, or length of time, in triall of causes? are the touch'd with the general burthen of Tithes, that canker of industry and tillage? or with that of Exize, which out of the bowells of labourers and other poor people enriches the usurers, and other caterpillars of the Commonwealth; or what have they done to free Trade from the intolerable burden of Customs? except the setting fresh hungry flyes, upon the old sores of the People? . . .

Far to the left even of this stand of the Levelers were the small and much persecuted group of Diggers, a curious early group of "premature communists" who felt, as their name implies, that man should live by the fruits of his own (primarily agrarian) labor and that no land should lie fallow and useless because of legal technicalities of ownership while there lived those able and willing to enrich it and with their labor.

Their courageous and vigorous leader, Gerrard Winstanley, wrote in 1647 a criticism of the fairly radical "Agreement of the People" proposed, after much discussion in Cromwell's New Model Army, as a minimum statement of the army's demands. This "agreement" provided for extreme toleration in religious terms and included much of the early political thinking of the Independents and more of even the Levelers, but completely ignored questions of economic oppression vital to the very poorest rural and city workers. Winstanley said:

A thing called An Agreement of the People . . . is too low and shallow to free us at all. . . . What stock . . . is provided for the *poor, fatherless, widows,* and *impoverished people?* and what advancement of encouragement for the labouring and industrious, as to take off their burthens, is there?

Although Winstanley supported to the full the middle-class struggle against Charles I and the "tything priests" of the established church, his consistent identification of kings, bishops and "rich men" and his persistent agitation on behalf of the poor agricultural workers was no more welcome to his middle-class allies than to the enemy.

In 1649 he issued the Diggers' Proclamation stating that: "the earth was not made purposely for you to be Lords of it, and we to be your Slaves, Servants and Beggars; but it was to be a common livelihood to all, without respect of persons."

And so as soon as the military victories of Cromwell's armies had culminated in Charles' execution, parliament turned to putting down at least the most extreme of the dissidents in the Commonwealth camp.

Winstanley responded in his last pamphlet; an appeal to Cromwell called *The Law of Freedom* published in November, 1650:

> No man can be rich but he must be rich either by his own labours or by the labours of other men helping him. If a man have no help from his neighbours he shall never gather an estate of hundreds and thousands a year. If other men help him to work then are those riches his neighbours' as well as his own. But all rich men live at ease, feeding and clothing themselves by the labours of other men, not by their own, which is their shame and not their nobility; for it is more blessed to give than to receive. But rich men receive all they have from the labourer's hand, and when they give they give away other men's labours, not their own.

This was so utopian in terms of the practical possibilities of the period that it seems to have been completely ignored, and Winstanley soon after disappears from view, leaving us for remembrance the moving motto he prefixed to his work:

> When these clay bodies are in grave, and children stand in
>   place,
> This shows we stood for truth and peace and freedom in our
>   days.

There was a much greater Puritan poet and pamphleteer, John Milton, England's single epic poet and one of her greatest political prose writers. His life was so intimately related to every stage of the revolution, the short-lived commonwealth and the restoration, that it is impossible to consider his work without, in effect, considering a summary history of England in the crucial years between 1640 and 1670.

We have already summarily examined the roots of the struggle which was basically carried on between bourgeois power fighting its way toward free trade and the rapid development of manufacture, and the royal prerogative using monopolies and other special privileges to maintain absolutism in a commercial society as, in fact, the French throne was to succeed in doing for over a century.

But as soon as this struggle approached an actual rupture, the bourgeoisie's public proclamation of its wrongs and demand for its rights stimulated similar demands on the part of the lower middle class and the poor. These cries for redress of grievances were all the more urgent because the miseries of both peasant and apprentice had been intensified by the rapid consolidation of bourgeois power, the enclosures of "modern" landlords, and the ruthless drive for more efficient large-scale methods of manufacture.

Furthermore, as soon as Civil War actually broke out, it became apparent, as Cromwell said, that you could not fight gentlemen trained in arms and confident of their cause, with hired or pressed starvelings or soft-living prosperous burghers.

The New Model Army which he recruited and organized was so far ahead of its time that it is one of the strangest phenomena in all history.

Composed largely of solid yeomen with a good sprinkling of devoted nonconformist skilled craftsmen, it included every shade of political opinion from the extreme democracy of the Anabaptists, through the large and important section of Levelers, merging into the left-of-center Independents, with whom Milton and Cromwell were most often identified, to the conservative Presbyterians—on the whole, a less conservative, more devoted group than their fellow religionists at home and in parliament. A contemporary writer, Joshua Sprigge, says of this New Model Army:

> The Army was, what by example and justice, kept in good order both respectively to itself and the country; there were many of them differing in opinion, yet not in action nor business: they all agreed to preserve the kingdom; they prospered in their diversity more than in uniformity.

The means by which this unity were achieved and the actual life and organization of the army were as extraordinary as the practical result.

In a time when literacy was still uncommon, the army constituted itself a school for all its members. Political as well as religious discussions of the most searching kind were regularly carried on in military units deliberately kept small for this—ordinarily—most unmilitary purpose. Each regiment had two enlisted men as well as its officers to represent it at the general army councils. The verbatim records kept of these meetings must be read to be believed.

In April, 1647, for example, when the parliamentary victories largely removed fear of any resurgence of royalist strength, there were proposals from parliament that the army be disbanded. Mess after mess refused, saying, in the words of one such resolution, that the army had to continue itself so that: "the poor commons may have a shelter and defence to secure them from oppression and violence." In June the army declared that it was determined: "to promote such an establishment of common and equal right and freedom to the whole, as all might equally partake of but those that do, by denying the same to others or otherwise, render themselves incapable of."

Jack Lindsay, the English literary historian, says in discussing this period of English history:

> The New Model Army that broke the King was an organization of tremendous historical significance. In it there was demonstrated for the first time that unity was possible as a popular construction on a grand scale, not only apart from feudal-religious or monarchial ideas, but in entire opposition to those ideas. Cromwell as the creator of this popular unity was the first great modern revolutionary leader.

He goes on to give us a rapid summary of the events of the next decade, which we will shortly follow in more detail through Milton's eyes:

> The Commonwealth had unshakeably consolidated the bourgeois position. At the same time . . . it aroused democratic hopes among the wider masses—hopes which the bourgeois solution could not satisfy. Cromwell was the leader of the more active sections of bourgeois and petty-bourgeois; he could not, of course, see the struggle in historical perspective; but he had a strong sense of the issues involved. Whenever he came up against one of the nodal points of class in the clashing forces of his day, he blazed out into mysticism. That was the only way he could overcome his sense of the contradictions involved.
>   . . . Emotionally there was much of him on the side of the Levellers. But he could not merely say to himself that he

rejected the Lilburnean programme as premature; to overcome the strong attraction he felt for it he had to hide in religious outbursts. The leadership of God that he intuited in those outbursts was the pressure of class-forces demanding so-far-and-no-further.

His dilemma was roughly this. He saw that if the Lilburnean plan was carried out while England was at such a low state of productivity, with organization so broken and localized, with literacy still confined to so few, the result would be, not to induce progress but to inhibit it. . . .

Both the Levellers and their opponents knew, and stated, that the achievment of political democracy would mean also an attempt to create economic equality. Such equality, in pre-industrial days, can only mean a sharing-out of the land. That is, a reversion to the ideal of medievalist self-sufficiency. And that would mean a crash of the political edifice, leading to full-blown feudalism. . . .

The difficulty that faced him was to find a way of establishing a collaboration between big and petty bourgeois, as he had established it during the Civil War. And the way was not evident; it was non-existent. What beat him was the deepening conflict between the small and the big land owners, the journeymen and their trade-masters, the small traders and the big companies. Everywhere the same division was showing up. The journeymen were making the last fight to control the masters within the guild organization; they were crushed. A more determined fight in the common council of London won a temporary democratic victory. But there was no means of welding all these forces in a national unity.

All this, however, was still in the undisclosed if imminent future when Milton, the great poet of the Commonwealth, was born a subject of James I in 1608, in circumstances which were peculiarly fortunate for English and, in fact, world literature.

John Milton's family background and education gave him knowledge of classical literature, drama, art, and especially, music, equaled by that of no other Puritan writer.

To this rich endowment and his own extraordinary gifts of sensitivity and expression, he added an understanding and power only to be learned through direct involvement in the sharpest, most important political struggles when their great demand meets, as it did in Milton, a great and willing response.

He himself believed that one rarely, in history, finds great deeds without finding great poets ready fittingly to sing them. Certainly it is then, fitting, that we should be able to survey one of the most heroic periods of English history through the work of the truly heroic poet whom many English critics consider second only to Shakespeare.

JOHN MILTON

Milton's father, disinherited by his father, a well-to-do Catholic yeoman of Oxfordshire, for too soon embracing Protestantism, migrated to London and apprenticed himself to a successful scrivener. The scrivener's profession or business was one which included many of the functions now performed by notaries, law writers, legal stationers or printers, debt collectors and, often, realty loan brokers. John Milton Sr. was evidently both competent and fortunate. Five years before the poet's birth in 1608 he had set up his own business and by 1621 he was employing four apprentices. Four years later he was elected steward of the Scrivener's Company and in 1634 was offered the presidency or mastership, which he declined.

His avocation, and perhaps the reason for that declination and for his comparatively early retirement during Milton's youth, was music. He was an accomplished organist and a composer of real talent, received wide recognition in Protestant circles—a number of hymns are still sung to tunes of his setting—and won a medal from a Polish prince of musical tastes.

He very early recognized his older son's exceptional abilities and encouraged them by providing an excellent day school education, additional private tutoring in Italian, French, music and other similar subjects, a leisurely college education and, more exceptionally, some five years of well-financed leisure for further self-directed study after graduation, climaxed by almost two years expensive travel in France, Switzerland and Italy.

Milton's school days were happy ones. He delighted in study; was fortunate in a courageous, independent and scholarly teacher; enjoyed the companionship of his younger sister and brother; and blossomed in the atmosphere of a sociable home full of music, charity, and respect for learning.

He read and admired Bacon and felt completely at one with his rationalist approach to the world and his emphasis on knowledge as a guide to power—on the necessary unity between fruitful thought and informed action.

For this reason his introduction to the still scholastic and essentially medieval curriculum at Cambridge was not a happy one, and while he rapidly attained a fair competence in the formal Latin disputations which occupied most of the students' hours, he never became reconciled to the waste of time and energy involved. His competence is attested by the fact that he was frequently chosen to deliver the "prolusion" or oration presented at set intervals before the faculty and student body of his own Christ's College and, occasionally, before the combined audience of several colleges.

An excerpt from one of these, translated from its original Latin, will show how strongly rebellious both thought and expression had already become in Milton's late teens.

After defining the true aim of knowledge in Baconian terms as "the enlarging of the bounds of human empire, to the effecting of all things possible," Milton proceeded to a detailed condemnation of the actual subjects and methods of study at the college and concluded his oration "Against the Scholastic Philosophy," by saying:

> Besides all this, it not infrequently happens that those who have entirely devoted and dedicated themselves to this blight of disputation lamentably display their ignorance and absurd childishness when faced with a new situation outside their usual idiotic occupation. Finally, the supreme result of all this earnest labour is to make you a more finished fool and cleverer contriver of conceits, and to endow you with a more expert ignorance; and no wonder, since all these problems at which you have been working in such torment and anxiety have no existence in reality at all, but like unreal ghosts and phantoms without substance obsess minds already disordered and empty of all true wisdom. . . .
>
> But how much better were it, gentlemen, and how much more consonant with your own dignity, now to let your eyes wander as it were over all the lands depicted on the map, . . . then to spy out the customs of mankind and those states which are well ordered; next to seek out and explore the nature of all living creatures, and after that to turn your attention to the secret virtues of stones and herbs. And do not shrink from taking your flight into the skies . . . ; yes, even follow close

upon the sun in all his journeys, and ask account of time itself and demand the reckoning of its eternal passage. . . .

So at length, gentlemen, when universal learning has once completed its cycle, the spirit of man, no longer confined within this dark prison house, will reach out far and wide, until it fills the whole world and the space far beyond with the expansion of its divine greatness. Then at last most of the chances of the world will be so quickly perceived that to him who holds this stronghold of wisdom hardly anything can happen in his life which is unforeseen or fortuitous. He will indeed seem to be one whose rule and dominion the stars obey, to whose command earth and sea hearken, and whom winds and tempests serve; to whom, lastly, Mother Nature herself has surrendered, as if indeed some god had abdicated the throne of the world and entrusted its rights, laws, and administration to him as governor.

Milton's early difficulties at college were not altogether with his teachers, nor were they all occasioned by such intellectual differences.

The medieval traditions of casual wenching and drinking were evidently also present, if not encouraged, and in one of his lighter holiday orations Milton, with the somewhat naive directness he was never to lose, characteristically mingled personal comment with his public address, referring for the first time to his college nickname of "The Lady of Christ's" and, not for the last time, to the chastity he thought more sinfully lost by man than by woman.

Some people have lately nicknamed me the Lady. But why do I seem to them too little of a man? I suppose because I have never had the strength to drink off a bottle like a prize fighter; or because my hand has never grown horny with holding a plough-share; or because I was not a farm-hand at seven, and so never took a midday nap in the sun—last perhaps I never showed my virility in the way these brothellers do. But I wish they could leave playing the ass as easily as I the woman.

His graduation took place in 1629, a year also marked by his first serious English poem, "On the Morning of Christ's Nativity," with its lovely unpuritanical hymn beginning:

It was the winter wild
While the Heaven-born child
    All meanly wrapped in the rude manger lies;
Nature in awe to him

> Has doffed her gaudy trim,
>   With her great Master so to sympathize;
> It was no season then for her
> To wanton with the sun, her lusty paramour.

Milton, as was then customary, continued a less consistent residence at Cambridge, interspersed with visits to London until he received his Master's degree in July 1632. He then retired to his father's country estate at Horton for almost six years of truly intensive independent study of ancient and modern history, mathematics, music, and the art of poetry.

During his last years at Cambridge he had written the amazing "apprentice works"—"L'Allegro" and "Il Penseroso," whose ease and lightness make them today perhaps the most generally read of his poems, and at Horton he wrote his deservedly famous sonnet "On Shakespeare."

Although his father had expected him to enter the Established Church, then the normal course for a young man intending to devote his life to serious literary pursuits, Milton could no longer accept the corrupt practises and superstitious beliefs he felt characterized the Church of England. As he said some years later:

> The Church, to whose service, by the intentions of my parents and friends, I was destined of a child, and in mine own resolutions: till coming to some maturity of years, and perceiving what tyranny had invaded the Church, that he who would take orders must subscribe slave and take an oath withal, which unless he took with a conscience that would retch he must either straight perjure or split his faith; I thought it better to prefer a blameless silence before the sacred office of speaking bought, and begun with servitude and for swearing.

A "Latin Epistle in Verse," written at about this time, expresses his appreciation for his father's forbearance in not urging him to enter the ministry against his conscience, or to attempt some such alternative profession as the law, which his brother Christopher was indeed to undertake, against his inclination. He says gratefully:

> You did not, Father, bid me go where a broad way lies open, where the opportunities for gain are easier, and the golden hope of amassing riches shines steadily. Nor do you force me to the civil code, and the ill-guarded principle of national justice, and thus condemn my ears to senseless clamor.

Later in the epistle he tactfully reminds his father that no one so devoted to the art of music can condemn his son's devotion to the sister art of poetry.

A letter written at the same period to an older man, perhaps a friend of his father's or a former tutor, who had evidently more earnestly raised with him the question of the choice of a profession, gives us a valuable revelation of Milton's more serious thoughts on the matter. He says in part:

> Sir,—Besides that in sundry respects I must acknowledge me to profit by you whenever we meet, you are often to me and were yesterday especially as a good watchman to admonish that the hours of the night pass on (for so I call my life, as yet obscure and unserviceable to mankind) and that the day with me is at hand wherein Christ commands us to labour while there is yet light.

He goes on to say that he is not given to overindulgence in useless learning:

> whereby a man cuts himself off from all action and becomes the most helpless, pusillanimous, and unweaponed creature in the world, the most unfit and unable to do that which all mortals must aspire to, either to be useful to his friends or to offend his enemies.

He then concludes:

> Yet, that you may see I am something suspicious of myself, and do take note of a certain belatedness in me, I am the bolder to send you some of my nightward thoughts sometime since.

The "nightward thoughts" inclosed are a copy of his charming sonnet, "On His Having Arrived at the Age of 23,"—which begins with one of the loveliest of sonnet openings:

> How soon hath Time, the subtle thief of youth,
> Stolen on his wing my three-and-twentieth year!
> My hasting days fly on with full career,
> But my late spring no bud or blossom shew'th.

Since Milton had at this time already completed the extraordinarily beautiful ode, "On the Morning of Christ's Nativity," as well as "L'Allegro" and "Il Penseroso," the fourth line might be considered an indication of extreme modesty, which is one of the virtues for which Milton has rarely been criticized, or an extreme stretch of poetic license. More probably, however, it means to state the simple truth, assuming what was in Milton's mind already long axiomatic, that real poetry is always an important public action. Just a few years later he was to write explicitly,

> These abilities [to write poetry] . . . are of power, beside the office of a pulpit, to imbreed and cherish in a great people the seeds of virtue and public civility, to allay the perturbations of the mind, and set the affections in right tune; . . .

and again:

> True poets are the object of my reverence and love and the constant sources of my delight.
> I know that the most of them from the earliest times have been the strenuous enemies of despotism, but these pedlars and milliners of verse who can bear?

Two years later at the request of an older friend, Henry Lawes, already probably the leading English musician of his time, Milton wrote the masque, *Comus,* to be set to music and performed at an important court celebration. It ends with the famous peroration:

> Mortals that would follow me,
> Love Virtue, she alone is free; . . .

This is consistent with Milton's lifelong emphasis on freedom from his invocation in "L'Allegro," to "The mountain nymph, sweet Liberty," to the end of his great tragedy, *Samson Agonistes,* completed over forty years later, but it must have fallen somewhat strangely on courtly ears. *Comus* was, however, well received, and Lawes won Milton's reluctant consent to an at first anonymous publication of it.

In 1637 a young minister, Edward King, who had been a classmate of Milton's at college and had shared—with a difference—his ambition to write poetry, was drowned at sea. The college decided on a memorial volume and Milton was solicited to contribute. His reply was "Lycidas" which has since shared honors with Shelley's "Adonais" as one of the two most famous English elegies.

Milton was far less personally affected by King's death than

Shelley was by that of Keats, and even more directly than the later poet, he turns his thoughts to a general consideration of the life of a young artist whose fate might well be his own. Since King had been about to enter seriously upon his life's work, Milton imagines his own case if an accidental death were now to come as anti-climax to his long and arduous preparation, and asks wistfully:

> Alas! what boots it with uncessant care
> To tend the homely slighted shepherd's trade,
> And strictly meditate the thankless muse?
> Were it not better done as others use,
> To sport with Amaryllis in the shade,
> Or with the tangles of Neaera's hair?
> Fame is the spur that the clear spirit doth raise
> (That last infirmity of noble mind)
> To scorn delight, and live laborious days;
> But the fair guerdon when we hope to find,
> And think to burst out into sudden blaze,
> Comes the blind fury with the abhorred shears,
> And slits the thin-spun life. . . .

Later, assuming that King like Milton himself, if he had continued with his clerical career, would have been a good and conscientious shepherd to his flock, Milton takes the occasion to attack the corrupt, ignorant, and worldly bishops by having St. Peter join in the mourning for his young minister, and say:

> How well could I have spared for thee, young swain,
> Enow of such as for their bellies' sake
> Creep and intrude and climb into the fold!
> Of other care they little reckoning make
> Than how to scramble at the shearers' feast,
> And shove away the worthy bidden guest.
> Blind mouths! that scarce themselves know how to hold
> A sheep-hook, or have learned aught else the least
> That to the faithful herdsman's art belongs!
> What recks it them? What need they? they are sped;
> And when they list, their lean and flashy songs
> Grate on their scrannel pipes of wretched straw;
> The hungry sheep look up and are not fed,
> But swoln with wind and the rank mist they draw,
> Rot inwardly, and foul contagion spread;
> Besides what the grim wolf with privy paw
> Daily devours apace, and nothing said;
> But that two-handed engine at the door
> Stands ready to smite once, and smite no more.

After these last ominous and prophetic two lines, Milton turns
to the gentler lamentations of the wild flowers and the welcome
no doubt prepared for Lycidas in heaven, and concludes, speaking
of himself as singer of the song:

> At last he rose, and twitched his mantle blue:
> Tomorrow to fresh woods, and pastures new.

His plans, probably crystallized by his mother's death and his
brother Christopher's marriage, which brought the young couple
to live at Horton, had been completed for two year's of foreign
travel.

He met and charmed all the leading intellectuals and artists in
the major Italian cities and was, in 1639, planning to extend his
journey but, as he later said:

> When I was preparing to pass over into Sicily and Greece,
> the melancholy intelligence which I received of the civil com-
> motions in England made me alter my purpose; for I thought it
> base to be travelling for amusement abroad, while my fellow-
> citizens were fighting for their liberty at home. . . .

His return coincided with an interval of uneasy truce between
the first overt actions of the civil war—two campaigns known as
"The Bishops' Wars."

Although the actual conflict was between the absolute power
claimed by the sovereign for his prerogative, and the rights of
parliament, the despotism of the Established Church was recognized, on both sides, as the real bulwark of the monarchy. A few
years later the famous *Eikon Basilike*, published by the royalists
after Charles I's execution as his work, says:

> I find it impossible for a Prince to preserve the State in
> quiet, unlesse he hath such an influence upon Church-men;
> and they such a dependance on Him, as may best restrain the
> seditions exorbitancies of Ministers tongues, . . .

One of the more moderate divines of the Church of England declared that it was: "natural and consonant that kings should defend
the rights of the church, and the church advance the honour of
kings."

And in 1641, just after Milton's return, Edmund Waller, speak-

ing in Parliament on the absolute necessity of maintaining the
established church, declared:

> I look upon episcopacy as a counterscarp, or outwork,
> which, if it be taken by this assault of the people, and withal,
> this mystery once revealed, "That we must deny them noth-
> ing when they ask it thus in troops," we may, in the next place
> have as hard a task to defend our property, as we have lately
> had to recover it from the [royal] Prerogative. If, by multiply-
> ing hands and petitions, they prevail for an equality in things
> ecclesiastical, the next demand perhaps may be Lex Agraria,
> equality in things temporal.

The church was thus not only the major defense of tyranny
but was also by far the largest single collector of taxes and compulsory fees from all, including the very poor, and a notoriously
greedy unimproving landlord of tremendous estates.

The defeat of the king in the first Bishops' War, undertaken
to impose the Episcopalian prayer book on Presbyterian Scotland,
was therefore the occasion for vigorous attacks on the Established
Church in England as well. When the Long Parliament met at the
end of 1640, after the brief and inglorious "Second Bishops' War,"
1,500 London citizens attended to present a petition signed by over
15,000, urging that the Episcopal Church government "with all its
dependencies, roots and branches, may be abolished."

Milton who had, on his return, taken a modest house in London and begun quietly to teach his sister's sons and several other
promising private pupils, was stirred to action by the controversy
and wrote three powerful pamphlets—*Of Reformation in England,
The Reason of Church Government Urged Against Prelaty*, and a
series of polemic tracts in defense of a nonconformist publication
called *Smectymnus*.

In the *Reason of Church Government* he describes his early life
and intimates, as he more explicitly said on a similar occasion later,
that his readers may well imagine:

> With what small willingness I endure to interrupt the pur-
> suit of no less hopes than these, and leave a calm and pleasing
> solitariness fed with cheerful and confident thoughts, to embark
> in a troubled sea of noise and hoarse disputes, put from be-
> holding the bright countenance of truth in the quiet and still
> air of delightful studies.

The "troubled sea" was, in truth, fraught with more dangers than Milton here implies. Three leading nonconformist ministers and many laymen of lesser note had only recently had their ears cut off; many more had been publicly whipped through the streets or set in the stocks; and several were indefinitely imprisoned in the tower "at the king's pleasure."

In this pamphlet Milton began, as so often in later ones, with a personal statement personifying religious freedom and dramatizing "her" demands on him.

> I forseee what stories I should hear within myself all my life after, of discourage and reproach: . . . when time was, thou couldst not find a syllable of all that thou hadst read, or studied, to utter in her behalf. Yet ease and leisure was given thee for thy retired thoughts out of the sweat of other men . . . but thou wert dumb as a beast; from hence forward be that which thine own brutish silence hath made thee.

He continued with a half apology for the prose form his present work necessarily had to take:

> Lastly, I should not choose this manner of writing, wherein, knowing myself inferior to myself, led by the genial power of nature to another task, I have the use, as I may account it, but of my left hand. . . . But were it the meanest under-service, if God by his secretary conscience enjoin it, it were sad for me if I should draw back; . . .

He urged the necessity of thorough reform and argued in a variety of ways against the idea of gradualism, concluding that section:

> Speedy and vehement were the reformations of all the good Kings of Judah, though the people had been muzzled in idolatry never so long before.
> And thus I have it as a declared truth, that neither the fear of sects, no, nor rebellion, can be a fit plea to stay reformation, but rather to push it forward with all possible diligence and speed.

Later he speaks with secular joy of "our time of parliament, the very jubilee and resurrection of the state."

In the controversial tracts of 1642 he again begins on a personal note but one of profound general relevance, saying:

> And because I observe that feare and dull disposition, luke-warenesse and sloth are not seldomer wont to cloak themselves under the affected name of moderation, then true and lively zeale is customably dispareg'd with the terme of indiscretion, bitternesse, and choler, I could not to my thinking honor a good cause more from the heart, than by defending it earnestly, as oft as I could judge it to behoove me, not withstanding any false name that could be invented to wrong, or under-value an honest meaning.

A chief defense advanced even by those moderately critical of the bishops was that at least an established church prevented all kinds of sects, errors, and schisms which would otherwise disrupt the kingdom. Milton made a direct attack upon this argument, often evaded by the nonconformists themselves, and said vehemently:

> If to bring a numb and chill stupidity of soul, an unactive blindness of mind, upon the people by their leaden doctrine or no doctrine at all is to keep away schism, they keep away schism indeed; . . . With as good a plea might the dead-palsy boast to a man. It is I that free you from stitches and pains, and the troublesome feeling of cold and heat, of wounds and strokes; if I were gone, all these would molest you. The winter might as well vaunt itself against the spring, I destroy all noisome and rank weeds, I keep down all pestilent vapours; yes, and all wholesome herbs, and all fresh dews, by your violent and hide-bound frost; but when the gentle west winds shall open the fruitful bosom of the earth, thus overguded by your imprisonment, then the flowers put forth and spring, and then the sun shall scatter the mists, and the manuring hand of the tiller shall root up all that burdens the soil without thanks to your bondage.

His appeal was addressed especially to the waverers and middle-of-the-roaders on his own side, whom he exhorted:

> Let us not make these things [sects and errors] an incumbrance or an excuse of any delay in reforming, which God sends us as an incitement to proceed with more honour and alacrity: for if there were no opposition, where were the trial

of an unfeigned goodness and magnananity? Virtue that wavers is not virtue, but vice revolted from itself, and after a while returning. The actions of just and pious men do not darken in their middle course; but Solomon tells us, they are as the shining light, that shineth more and more unto the perfect day.

Finally, after an impassioned description of the heroic work of Wyclif and other early pioneers and martyrs for religious freedom, he concludes lyrically:

> O if we freeze at noon after their early thaw, let us fear lest the sun forever hide himself, and turn his orient steps from our ungrateful Horizon, justly condemned to be eternally benighted. Which dreadful judgment, O thou the everbegotten Light and perfect Image of thy Father, intercede, may never come upon us. . . .

(When we remember his approaching blindness this and the many other radiant images of light which star Milton's pages have a special poignance for us, no matter what the context is.)

In this tract, bitter and controversial as is its public tone, we find, as in all of Milton, many delightful private passages such as the one in which he refers to his prose, explaining to God that after the final victory has been won:

> . . . he that now for haste snatches up a plain ungarnished present as a thank-offering to thee, which could not be deferred in regard of thy so many late deliverances wrought for us, one upon another, may then perhaps take up a harp and sing an elaborate Song to generations. . . .

The "elaborate song," a great epic Milton was already meditating, was to be postponed through many full and troubled years, but in 1642 he evidently thought that Parliament had both the will and the power to settle affairs with little further trouble. In fact, in the course of the same controversy he elsewhere remarks:

> And indeed if we consider the general concourse of suppliants, the free and ready admittance, the willing and speedy redress in what is possible it will seem not much otherwise than as if some divine compassion from heaven were descended to take into hearing and commiseration the long and remediless affliction of this kingdom.

Years later, when in pain and blindness he had begun more correctly to measure the cost of the struggle both to himself and the nation, he would still speak with satisfaction of his entry into political conflict:

> I saw that a way was opening for the establishment of real liberty; that the foundation was laying for the deliverance of man from the yoke of slavery and superstition; that the principles of religion, which were the first objects of our care, would exert a salutary influence on the manners and constitution of the republic; and as I had from my youth studied the distinctions between religious and civil rights, I perceived that if I ever wished to be of use, I ought not to be wanting to my country, to the Church and to so many of my fellow Christians, in a crisis of so much danger.

However, in 1642 public affairs seemed well on the way to a successful conclusion and Milton turned to think of private ones. He was then almost thirty-five, warmly responsive to all physical beauty, and romantically in love, not, unfortunately, with any particular lady, but with the idea of the joyous companionship of a happy marriage.

Whether there had been some previous tentative arrangement between his father and hers, or whether it was simply a matter of the time, the place and the girl, he rode into the country to collect a family debt of £500 from an extravagant royalist, a landed squire, near Oxford, and returned a month later without the money but with a bride of seventeen, Mary Powell.

The marriage was from the first an unhappy one. The Powell family was strongly royalist, indifferent in matters of religion or learning, and Mary who was altogether unable to share her husband's interests, may well also have been frightened by his intensity. She sadly missed the continual social life and careless easygoing hospitality of her father's home, and less than a month after the wedding she asked permission to pay her family a visit. Once home, she refused to return.

John Aubrey, Milton's contemporary biographer, gives great weight to her royalist beliefs, explaining the divorce by saying: "Two opinions agree not well on one boulster."

It is certainly true that her return home coincided with the early royalist military victories and that she later claimed her mother urged her, on those grounds, not to return to her anti-royalist husband.

Milton, who held a happy marriage one of the great joys of life, who was both sensitive and passionate, and whose morality and pride were equally revolted by the very idea of illicit or casual lovemaking, characteristically integrated his personal beliefs and public actions. He scandalized both his religious and irreligious compatriots by the publication in the next two years of four closely reasoned hard-hitting pamphlets in favor of what is still today an advanced idea, that incompatibility was sufficient cause, and should be made legal reason, for divorce!

While he is concerned almost entirely with the husband's problem and thinks of the need for such relief as almost invariably masculine, he does say explicitly:

> Not but that particular exceptions may have place, if she exceed her husband in prudence and dexterity, and he contentedly yield; for then a superior and more natural law comes in, that the wiser should govern the less wise, whether male or female.

Furthermore, his whole idea of a good marriage, eloquently urged in each of the pamphlets, indicates his high respect for woman as an intellectual companion and comrade, rather than as merely a housekeeper, childbearer and bedmate.

For example, he says in *The Doctrine and Discipline of Divorce*:

> As no man apprehends so well what vice is as he who is truly virtuous, no man knows Hell like him who converses most in Heaven; so there is none that can estimate the evil and affliction of a natural hatred in matrimony unless he have a soul gentle enough and spacious enough to contemplate what is true love. . . . This pure and more inbred desire of joining to itself in conjugal fellowship a fit conversing soul (which desire is properly called love) is stronger than death. . . .

Again in the last of the four pamphlets, *Tetrachordon*:

> . . . there is a peculiar comfort in the married state besides the genial bed, which no other society affords. . . . We cannot therefore always be contemplative, or pragmaticall abroad, but have need of some delightful intermissions, wherein the enlarg'd soul may leave off a while her severe schooling; and like a glad youth in wandring vacancy, may keep her

hollidaies to joy and harmless pastime: which as she cannot
well doe without company, so in no company so well as where
the different sexe in most resembling unlikeness, and most unlike resemblance cannot but please best and be pleas'd in the
aptitude of that variety.

As his custom is, he meets squarely the crucial question of a
man's responsibility for making so serious an error, and answers it,
with no fear of ridicule, showing concretely his own concern with
the situation and the reasons for his tragic mistake:

> The soberest and best governed men are least practised
> in these affairs; and who knows not that the bashful muteness
> of a virgin may ofttimes hide all the unliveliness and natural
> sloth which is really unfit for conversation? Nor is there that
> freedom of access granted or presumed, as may suffice to a
> perfect discerning till too late; and where any indisposition is
> suspected, what more usual than the persuasion of friends, that
> acquaintance, as it increases, will amend all? And lastly it is
> not strange though many, who have spent their youth chastely,
> are in some things not so quick-sighted, while they haste too
> eagerly to light the nuptial torch; nor is it, therefore, that
> for a modest error a man should forfeit so great a happiness,
> and no charitable means to release him, since they who have
> lived most loosely, by reason of their bold accustoming, prove
> most successful in their matches, because their wild affections
> unsettling at will, have been as so many divorces to teach them
> experience. Whenas the sober man honouring the appearance
> of modesty, and hoping well of every social virtue under the
> veil, may easily chance to meet, if not with a body impene-
> trable, yet often with a mind to all other due conversation in-
> accessible, and to all the more estimable and superior purposes
> of matrimony useless and almost lifeless; and what a solace,
> what a fit help such a consort would be through the whole life
> of a man, is less pain to conjecture than to have experience.

Far from seeking to disguise his personal need for relief, he
generalizes from the pain which did not create, but which made
him conscious of, a wrong, saying:

> Indeed man's disposition though prone to search after vain
> curiosities, yet when points of difficulty are to be discusst, ap-
> pertaining to the removal of unreasonable wrong and burden
> from the perplext life of our brother, it is incredible how cold,
> how dull, and fane from all fellow feeling we are, without the
> spur of self-concernment.

Although the basis of his argument is an appeal to reason and human kindliness the fashion of the time led him to quote scriptural authority after arguing each point. Thus, for example, referring to Adam's biblically asserted need of congenial companionship, he concludes:

> . . . ; the desire and longing to put off an unkindly solitariness by uniting another body, but not without a fit soul to his, in the cheerful society of wedlock? Which if it were so needful before the fall, when man was much more perfect in himself, how much more is it needful now against all the sorrows and casualties of this life, to have an intimate and speaking help, a ready and reviving associate in marriage? Whereof who misses, by chancing on a mute and spiritless mate, remains more alone than before, and in a burning less to be contained than that which is fleshly, and more to be considered; as being more deeply rooted even in the faultless innocence of nature.

The Protestant Churches did all admit the possibility of divorce for adultery and Milton reasonably protests that:

> The very cause that renders the pollution of the marriage-bed so heavy a calamity is that in its consequences it interrupts peace and affection; much more, therefore, must the perpetual interruption of peace and affection by mutual differences and unkindness be a sufficient reason for granting liberty of divorce.

Similarly, beginning with the Catholic admission of annulment for an unconsummated marriage, he argues:

> that indisposition, unfitness, or contrariety of mind, arising from a cause in nature unchangeable, hindering and ever likely to hinder the main benefits of conjugal society, which are solace and peace, is a greater reason of divorce than natural frigidity, especially if there be no children, and that there be mutual consent.

It is easy to ridicule the naivete and simplicity of Milton's public protest against a private grief, but while he made no pretense about the intensely personal nature of the trouble which had first turned his attention to the problem, that does not gainsay the justice of his position. One of his best nineteenth century critics, a later Sir Walter Raleigh, has summarized the matter with unusual insight.

> . . . ; he was a citizen first and a poet and an unhappy man afterwards. He directed his energies to proving, not that he should be exempted from the operations of the law, but that the law itself should be changed. . . . Thus even in this most personal matter he pleads, not for himself, but for the commonweal. He cannot conceive of happiness as of a private possession, to be secretly enjoyed; it stands rooted, like justice, in the wise and equal ordinances of the State; and the only freedom that he values is freedom under the law.

Of course parliament did not pass the law Milton indignantly demanded, and in 1645, after the decisive defeat of the royalist army, Mary's family decided that a Puritan son-in-law could be an important asset. They arranged matters so that Mary, surprising him at a relative's home, successfully begged for a reconciliation.

Her family as well as his own father, who had been living with the royalist son, Christopher, soon took refuge with Milton. While Mary bore him four children in the next seven years—she died soon after the birth of the last in 1652—there was evidently no joy in the marriage.

A letter to an Italian friend written soon after his own loved father's death in 1647 gives us a sad picture of his domestic life:

> It is often a matter of sorrowful reflection to me that those with whom I have been linked by chance or the law, by propinquity or some connection of no real meaning, are continually at hand to infest my home, to stun me with their noise and wear out my temper, whilst those who are endeared to me by the closest sympathy of tastes and pursuits are almost all denied me either by death or by an insuperable distance of place.

During the stirring early years of the parliamentary victories Milton had not, of course, confined his interests or activities to the discussions on divorce.

He had increased the number of promising students he accepted for instruction and had, in 1644, printed a short account of his system *Of Education*. In this he said: "I call therefore a complete and generous education that which fits a man to perform justly, skilfully and magnanimously all the offices both private and publick of Peace and War."

He felt that pupils should study: "the beginning, end, and reasons of Political Societies; that they may not in a dangerous fit of the Common-wealth be such poor, shaken, uncertain Reeds, of such a tottering Conscience, as many of our great Counsellors have lately shewn themselves, but stedfast pillars of the State."

He emphasized his belief that pupils should be: "stirr'd up with high hopes of living to be brave men, and worthy Patriots, dear to God, and famous to all ages."

While he describes what seems to us an extraordinarily demanding program wherein "they may have easily learnt at any odd hour the Italian Tongue," Milton relaxes into the conclusion:

> In those vernal seasons of the year when the air is calm and pleasant, it were an injury and sullenness against nature not to go out and see her riches, and partake in her rejoicing with heaven and earth . . . to ride out in companies with prudent and staid guides, to all the quarters of the land; learning and observing all places of strength, all commodities of building and of soil, for towns and tillage, harbors and ports for trade. Sometimes taking sea as far as to our navy, to learn there also what they can in the practical knowledge of sailing and of sea-fight.

On the whole, however, his system at best requires Miltons both as instructors and as students, and may be fairly enough characterized by his own summary:

> Only I believe that this is not a Bow for every man to shoot in that counts himself a Teacher; but will require sinews almost equal to those which Homer gave Ulysses; yet I am withall persuaded that it may prove much more easie in the assay, then it now seems at distance, and much more illustrious; . . .

In the same year, 1644, Milton wrote in protest against a parliamentary decree reinstating complete censorship of the press, his best known prose work, *Areopagitica*.

Aereopagitica—A Speech for the Liberty of Unlicensed Printing was dedicated "To the Parlament of England" with a freely translated motto from Euripides:

> This is true Liberty, when freeborn men
> Having to advise the public, may speak free,
> Which he who can, and will, deserves high praise,
> Who neither can nor will, may hold his peace;
> What can be juster in a state than this?

It summarizes Milton's belief in political action, struggle, and fearless inquiry, and his contempt for those who fear error or change more than they love truth.

It is starred with such memorable images as: "Truth is compared in Scripture to a streaming fountain; if her waters flow not in a perpetual progression, they sicken into a muddy pool of conformity." There are also powerful plain statements of direct experience like: "Where there is much desire to learn, there of necessity will be much arguing, much writing, many opinions; for opinion in good men is but knowledge in the making." And there is much biting contempt for bigotry: "Yet when the new light which we beg for shines in upon us, there be who envy and oppose, if it come not first in at their casements."

This magnificent plea for the freedom of the press includes the justly famous statement in which Milton forever rebukes all ivory tower artists and sheltered intellectuals:

> I cannot praise a fugitive and cloistered virtue unexercised and unbreathed, that never sallies out and seeks her adversary, but slinks out of the race, where that immortal garland is to be run for, not without dust and heat. Assuredly we bring not innocence into the world, we bring impurity much rather; that which purifies us is trial, and trial is by what is contrary. That virtue which is but a youngling in the contemplation of evil, and knows not the utmost that vice promises to her followers, and rejects it, is but a blank virtue, not a pure, her whiteness is but an excremental whiteness.

Throughout we feel the same deep personal concern in this pamphlet as in his arguments on divorce. As one of the best historians of English literature—The Frenchman, Taine—said a hundred years ago: "he spoke as a man who is wounded and oppressed, for whom a public prohibition is a personal outrage, who is himself fettered by the fetters of the nation."

On the three hundredth anniversary of Milton's birth, December 9, 1908, an interesting note appeared in the London *Daily News*. It said, referring to the abortive 1905 revolution in Russia:

> At the first sign of the stirring of a new life in Russia, translations of Areopagitica made their appearance, and hawkers sold them for a few kopeks to defy the censor in Nijni Novgorod. When a press was devised at Simla it was on the eternal reasonings of Aeropagitica that Mr. Gokhale based his opinions.

In 1788, the year before the French Revolution, Mirabeau published an article *"Sur la liberte de la presse, imité de l'Anglais de Milton."* The entire edition was immediately exhausted, as were subsequent editions in 1789 and 1792.

In 1646, two years after *Aeropagitica,* Milton was deeply angered and concerned by the attempt of the conservative Presbyterian majority in Parliament to impose an Established Church of their own on the nation. Using his right hand this time, he wrote a sonnet "On the New Forcers of Conscience under the Long Parliament":

> Because you have thrown off your Prelate Lord,
> And with stiff Vowes renounc'd his Liturgie
> To seize the widowed whore Pluralitie
> From them whose sin ye envi'd, not ahhor'd,
> Dare ye for this adjure the Civil Sword
> To force our Consciences that Christ set free?
> .   .   .   .
> When they shall read this clearly in your charge
> New Presbyter is but Old Priest writ Large.

That year, 1646, he also began work on his *History of Britain* which would, he thought, be a practical contribution to statecraft:

> For if it be a high point of wisdom in every private man, much more is it in a Nation to know itself; rather than puft up with vulgar flatteries, and encomiums, for want of self knowledge, to enterprise rashly and come off miserably in great undertakings.

Although he watched the course of public events and the consistent left pressure of Cromwell's New Model on parliament with keen interest during the next two years, the only public statement we find is another sonnet, addressed to one of the great army leaders, Lord Fairfax. This shows Milton's growing awareness of the essentially self-seeking and corrupt policies of the upper middle-class bloc in Parliament, who became less willing to make concessions to their poorer allies as they saw military victory more fully within their grasp:

> Fairfax, whose name in arms through Europe rings,
>   Filling each mouth with envy or with praise,
>   And all her jealous monarchs with amaze,
>   And rumors loud that daunt remotest kings,
> Thy firm unshaken virtue ever brings
>   Victory home, though new rebellions raise
>   Their Hydra heads, and the false North displays
>   Her broken league to imp their serpent wings.
> O yet a nobler task awaits thy hand
>   (For what can war but endless war still breed?)
>   Till truth and right from violence be freed,
> And public faith cleared from the shameful brand
>   Of public fraud. In vain doth Valor bleed,
>   While Avarice and Rapine share the land.

In January, 1649, it had become clear that no firm peace could be made with Charles I, since it was impossible to rely upon his promises and there was ample evidence that he was attempting to secure the intervention of foreign armies to restore his sovereignty. The left and center sections of the parliamentary forces, dominated largely by Cromwell and his New Model Army, therefore determined to execute the king. The right wing were terrified at the audacity of, as Cromwell said, "cutting off his head with the crown on it," and attempted even at the last moment to achieve a compromise.

Even among those really convinced of the necessity of the execution there were many in Parliament who shrank from the direct personal responsibility of so unprecedented a regicide, one, moreover, which would surely be terribly avenged should any turn of fortune restore monarchy to England.

Milton, however, felt no such hesitation and immediately after the sentence had been pronounced began work on *The Tenure of Kings and Magistrates,* a powerful and effective justification of the impending event which was published only a few days after the execution. The argument he presents anticipated in extraordinary detail the basic reasoning of our own Declaration of Independence, and Jefferson may well have used it in some sort as a partial source of that manifesto.

The entire work expresses the most profound admiration of man's dignity and shows almost a solemn joy in the English people's daring so radically to assert it. It begins:

> It being manifest, that the power of kings and magistrates is nothing else but what is only derivative, transferred, and committed to them in trust from the people to the common good of them all, in whom the power yet remains fundamentally, and cannot be taken from them, without a violation of their natural birthright . . . it follows from necessary causes that the titles of sovereign lord, natural lord, and the like are either arrogancies or flatteries.
>
> . . . unless the people must be thought to be created all for him, he not for them, and they all in one body inferior to him single; which were a kind of treason against the dignity of mankind to affirm.

and that section concludes:

> . . . it follows, lastly, that since the king or magistrate holds his authority of the people both originally and naturally for their good, in the first place, and not his own, then may the people, as oft as they shall judge it for the best, either choose him or reject him, retain him or depose him, though no tyrant, merely by the liberty and right of freeborn men to be governed as seems to them best. . . .

There is, later, some discussion of those afraid to realize their own strength and righteousness:

> . . . who coming in the course of these affairs to have their share in great actions above the form of law or custom, at least to give their voice and approbation, begin to swerve and almost shiver at the majesty and grandeur of some noble deed, as if they were newly entered into a great sin.

A more bitter attack on the feigned kindliness of the upper bourgeoisie, the Presbyterians, concludes:

> If we consider, who and what they are, on a sudden grown so pitiful, we may conclude their pity can be no true and christian commiseration, but either levity and shallowness of mind, or else a carnal admiring of that worldly pomp and

greatness, from whence they see him fallen; or rather, lastly, a dissembled and seditious pity, feigned of industry to get new discord.

The voluntary publication of this work allied Milton more closely than anyone else outside the sixty members of Parliament supposed to act as judges—actually only some forty served—with the full responsibilities of the revolution. Its effectiveness led the Council of State—a smaller and more militant body than Parliament, with more substantial New Model Army representation—to offer Milton the position of Latin Secretary or Secretary for Foreign Tongues. This position he accepted in the spring of 1650, and, on the minutes of the Council, we find the many duties of correspondence, research and pamphleteering which he was assigned.

It is pleasant to record that the only one he did not fulfill was that of writing an answer to Lilburne's *New Chains for Old*, which sharply attacked many of the parliamentary abuses, of which Milton himself was critical. He was enough of a practical politician to realize, or at least accept, a compromise necessitated by the broad coalition of forces which had effected the revolution, but he never neglected an opportunity to press to the left, and he evidently found himself unable or unwilling personally to defend actions he personally condemned.

However, he soon had more serious business on hand.

Immediately after Charles' execution, the royalists had widely published an effectively sentimental religious little book with a frontispiece which pictured the king kneeling in prayer shortly before his death.

This book, which was falsely supposed to have been written by the king himself, purported to give an account of his meditations during the last months of his life. It had a tremendous popular appeal and was widely circulated. Milton was directed to write an answer to *Eikon Basilike*—the King's Book—which he did in *Eikonoklastes*—the King Breaker.

While the conventional form he followed, confuting paragraph by paragraph, makes this less representative than most of Milton's prose, we find every now and then such deeply characteristic thoughts flash out as:

> Truth is but justice in our knowledge and justice is but truth in our practice. . . . Truth is properly no more than contemplation; and her utmost efficiency is but teaching; but

justice in her very essence is all strength and activity . . .
and hath a sword put into her hand, to use against all violence
and oppression on the earth. . . . She is the strength, the
kingdom, the power, and the majesty of all ages.

The completion of this task led to a far more important one. A
famous Latin scholar, Salmasius, had been hired by Charles II's
friends abroad to write a book in Latin, entitled *Defensio Regia
pro Carolo I.* This *Defense of the King* was a strong and comprehensive attack containing in its most damaging form the whole case
against the commonwealth. It was widely circulated on the continent, where English was still considered a somewhat barbarous
language, and English envoys sent word home from every court in
Europe deploring its effect on England's prestige abroad. Milton
was assigned to answer it.

He began his task with great enthusiasm but was soon compelled to heed the increasing deterioration of his always weak
eyesight. Physicians warned him that the sight of one eye was
already hopelessly destroyed and that only a complete respite from
all such close application could save even partial sight in the other.
His decision may be given in his own words:

My resolution was unshaken, though the alternative was
either the loss of my sight or the desertion of my duty.
I considered that many had purchased a less good by a
greater evil, the meed of glory by the loss of life; but that I
might procure great good by little suffering, that though I am
blind I might still discharge the most honourable duties, the
performance of which, as it is something more durable than a
glory, ought to be an object of superior admiration and esteem.
I resolved therefore to make the short interval of sight which
was left me to enjoy, as beneficial as possible to the public
interest.

His completed work proudly entitled *A Defense of the English
People by John Milton, Englishman* was published with enormous
acclaim in 1651.

There was a great deal of personal invective against Salmasius'
character and scholarship, which the controversial conventions of
the time demanded, and which no more than matched the similar
attacks Salmasius had already made on Milton. But the heart of the
argument merits the dignity of the title.

Milton summarizes the people's case in many such succinct passages as:

> A most potent king, after he had trampled upon the laws of the nation, and given a shock to its religion, and begun to rule at his own will and pleasure, was at last subdued in the field by his own subjects, who had undergone a long slavery under him; . . . afterwards he was cast into prison, and when he gave no ground, either by words or actions, to hope better things of him, was finally by the supreme council of the kingdom condemned to die, and beheaded before the very gates of the royal palace. . . . For what king's majesty sitting upon an exalted throne, ever shone so brightly, as that of the people of England then did, when, shaking off the old superstition, which had prevailed a long time, they gave judgment upon the king himself, or rather upon an enemy who had been their king. . . . By his [God's] manifest impulse being set on work to recover our almost lost liberty, following him as our guide, and adoring the impresses of his divine power manifested upon all occasions, we went on in no obscure but an illustrious passage, pointed out and made plain by God himself.

In terms which recall Shelley's reminder, "the sacred Milton was, let it ever be remembered, a republican and a bold inquirer into morals and religion." Milton celebrates the worth of his countrymen:

> . . . that with so great a resolution, as we hardly find the like recorded in any history, having struggled with, and overcome, not only their enemies in the field, but the superstitious persuasions of the common people, have purchased to themselves in general amongst all posterity the name of deliverers: the body of the people having undertook and performed an enterprise which in other nations is thought to proceed only from a magnanimity that is peculiar to heroes.

Finally Milton restates the argument developed in *The Tenure of Kings and Magistrates*:

> So that wise and prudent men are to consider and to see what is profitable and fit for the people in general, for it is very certain that the same form of government is not equally convenient for all nations, nor for the same nation at all times; but sometimes one, sometimes another, may be more proper,

according as the industry and valour of the people may increase or decay. But if you deprive the people of this liberty
of setting up what government they like best among themselves, you take that from them in which the life of all civil
liberty consists.

The *Defense* was published in 1651 and by the beginning of
1652 Milton had become totally blind.

The death of his infant son and of his wife that spring seem
to have occasioned no interruption in the performance of his duties,
assigned or self-assigned, for in addition to his official work we
find a sonnet written that May, with an impassioned appeal to
Cromwell to prevent the renewed (and, soon, partially successful)
attempt of the strong right-wing Presbyterian group to set up their
own compulsory established church. It is interesting to note that
from the tenth and eleventh lines of this sonnet the late President
Franklin D. Roosevelt borrowed the text for one of his most profound and prophetic speeches.

To *Oliver Cromwell*

Cromwell our Chief of Men, that through a Croud,
   Not of War only, but distractions rude;
   Guided by Faith, and Matchless Fortitude:
   To Peace and Truth, thy Glorious way hast Plough'd,
And on the neck of crowned Fortune proud
   Hast rear'd God's Trophies, and his Work pursu'd,
   While *Darwent* Streams with Blood of *Scots* imbru'd;
   And *Dunbarfield* resound thy Praises loud,
And *Worcester's* Laureat Wreath; yet much remains
   To Conquer still; Peace hath her Victories
   No less than those of War; new Foes arise
Threatning to bind our Souls in secular Chains,
   Help us to save Free Conscience from the paw
   Of Hireling Wolves, whose Gospel is their Maw.

The conservative parliamentarians were, of course, neither
unaware of, nor indifferent to, Milton's attitude, and they showed
their hostility in many petty ways hoping, perhaps, to force a resignation which Cromwell would not permit them to demand.

Milton's request for the appointment of Andrew Marvell as
assistant secretary to perform those duties his total blindness rendered impossible was refused, and he was grudgingly granted the
help of another official not actually under his direction and, probably, unsympathetic to him. He was forced to surrender his official

residence to a younger government employee of superior status and may, perhaps, have known of a semipublic apology made to a foreign ambassador for intrusting the translation of some important document to a "blind old man."

These slights must have been particularly painful to a man of the rather touchy personal pride and, indeed, vanity we often see in Milton. Nevertheless, he continued at his post, and at his self-appointed task of helping to keep Cromwell and his Council aware of the support and demands from the left.

In 1653 Cromwell was finally forced to take the drastic step of dissolving parliament, and assumed the title of Lord Protector.

This was, in effect, a virtual dictatorship but as Milton was perhaps even then writing of parliament in his still uncompleted and unpublished *History of Britain*:

> The votes and ordinances which men look'd should have contain'd the repealing of bad laws and the immediate constitution of better, resounded with nothing else but new impositions, taxes, excises, yearly, monthly, weekly, not to reckon the offices, gifts and preferments bestow'd and shar'd among themselves.

A year later we find in his *Second Defense of the People of England* a similar description addressed to Cromwell himself:

> But when you saw that the business was artfully procrastinated, that everyone was more intent on his own selfish interest than the public good, that the people complained of the disappointments which they had experienced, and the fallacious promises by which they had been gulled, that they were the dupes of a few overbearing individuals, you put an end to their domination. . . . In this state of desolation you, O Cromwell! alone remained to conduct the government and to save the country.

There is evident also in that work something of an apology for the necessity under which Milton finds himself, of accepting, temporarily, even a progressive sort of dictatorship:

> The circumstances of the country, which has been so convulsed by the storms of faction, which are yet hardly still, do not permit us to adopt a more perfect or desirable form of government.

The bulk of the *Defensio Secundo,* although it is ostensibly written in reply to an attack on Milton himself and on the argument of the first defense, is an amazingly outspoken warning to Cromwell on the dangers of dictatorship, and an appeal to him for the continued preservation of England's liberty.

After opening with a brief autobiographical sketch in defense against the personal slanders contained in this second royalist attack, Milton continues with extraordinary nobility:

> A grateful recollection of the divine goodness is the first of human obligations; and extraordinary favors demand more solemn and devout acknowledgments: with such acknowledgments I feel it my duty to begin this work. First, because I was born at a time when the virtue of my fellow citizens . . . in greatness of soul and vigour of enterprise . . . has succeeded in delivering the commonwealth from the most grievous tyranny. . . . And next because . . . I . . . was particularly selected . . . openly to vindicate the rights of the English nation, and consequently of liberty itself. Lastly, because in a matter of such moment, and which excited such ardent expectations, I did not disappoint the hopes nor the opinions of my fellow citizens; . . . For who is there, who does not identify the honour of his country with his own? And what can conduce more to the beauty or glory of one's country than the recovery, not only of its civil but its religious liberty? And what nation or state ever obtained both by more successful or more valorous exertion.

He described the acclaim with which the victory of English freedom and his own account of it had been greeted throughout Europe:

> I seem to survey as from a towering height, the far extended tracts of sea and land, and innumerable crowds of spectators, betraying in their looks the liveliest interest, and sensations the most congenial with my own. Here I behold the stout and manly prowess of the Germans disdaining servitude; there the generous and lively impetuosity of the French; on this side the calm and stately valour of the Spaniard; on that, the composed and wary magnanimity of the Italian. Of all the lovers of liberty and virtue, the magnanimous and the wise, in whatsoever quarter they may be found, some secretly favour, others openly approve; some greet me with congratulations and applause; others, who had long been proof against conviction, at last yield themselves captive to the force of truth. Surrounded by congregated multitudes, I now imagine

that, from the columns of Hercules to the Indian Ocean, I
behold the nations of the earth recovering that liberty which
they so long had lost. . . .

Then he turned to thank—and advise—Cromwell directly:

> For you our country owes its liberties, nor can you sustain
> a character more momentous and more august than that of the
> author, the guardian and the preserver of our liberties, and
> hence you have not only eclipsed the achievements of all our
> kings, but even those which have been fabled of our heroes.
>
> Often reflect what a dear pledge the beloved land of your
> nativity has entrusted to your care, and that liberty which she
> once expected only from the chosen flower of her talents and
> her virtues, she now expects from you only, and by you only
> hopes to obtain.
>
> You cannot be truly free unless we are free too, for such
> is the nature of things that he who entrenches on the liberty
> of others is the first to lose his own and become a slave.

This exhortation he concluded:

> Revere also the opinions and the hopes which foreign na-
> tions entertain concerning us, who promise to themselves so
> many advantages from that liberty which we have so bravely
> acquired, from the establishment of that new government
> which has begun to shed its splendour on the world, and
> which, if it be suffered to vanish like a dream, would involve
> us in the deepest abyss of shame; and lastly, revere yourself;
> and, after having endured so many sufferings and encountered
> so many perils for the sake of liberty, do not suffer it, now it
> is obtained, either to be violated by yourself, or in any one
> instance impaired by others.

In another section, addressed more generally to the leaders of
the English people, he said:

> War had made many great whom peace makes small. If
> after being released from the toils of war, you neglect the arts
> of peace, if your peace and your liberty be a state of warfare;
> if war be your only virtue, the summit of your praise, you will,
> believe me, soon find peace adverse to your interests. Your
> peace will be only a more distressing war; and that which you
> imagined liberty will prove the worst of slavery. . . .
>
> If you think that it is a more grand, a more beautiful, or a
> more wise policy, to invent subtle expedients for increasing the
> revenue, to multiply our naval and military force, to rival in

craft the ambassadors of foreign states, to form skillful treaties and allegiances, than to administer unpolluted justice to the people, to redress the injured, and to succour the distressed, and speedily to restore to everyone his own, you are involved in a cloud of error.

And he added advice which foreshadows Jefferson's "Educate and inform the whole mass of the people. They are the only sure reliance for the preservation of our liberty." His conclusion was an urgent request for the promotion of "education . . . the only genuine source of political and individual liberty, the only true safeguard of states. . . ."

In 1655 Milton was, voluntarily or involuntarily, relieved of most of the duties of his Secretaryship and granted a reduced salary for life—in actuality most likely a pension.

The sonnet "To Mr. Cyriak Skinner Upon His Blindness" (1655) gives a beautifully simple statement of Milton's feelings, his regretful love for the objects of sight, his harmless vanity which clings to the idea that he is at least not disfigured, and his serious consoling pride in the consciousness that his great sacrifice has accomplished its object, and is known to have done so!

> To Mr. *Cyriac Skinner*. Upon his Blindness
> Cyriac this Three years day, these Eyes though clear
>   To outward view of blemish or of Spot,
>   Bereft of Sight, their Seeing have forgot:
>   Nor to their idle Orbs doth day appear,
> Or Sun, or Moon, or Star, throughout the Year;
>   Or Man, or Woman; yet I argue not
>   Against Heaven's Hand, or Will, nor bate one jot
>   Of Heart or Hope; but still bear up, and steer
> Right onward. What supports me, dost thou ask?
>   The Conscience, Friend, to have lost them over ply'd
>   In Liberties Defence, my noble task;
> Of which all *Europe* rings from side to side.
>   This thought might lead me through this World's vain mask
>   Content, though blind, had I no other Guide.

This is at least as moving as the better known sonnet written three years before:

> When I consider how my light is spent
> Ere half my days in this dark world and wide
> And that one talent which is death to hide
> Lodged with me useless. . . .

and is far more characteristic. Passive standing and waiting was
never, for Milton, a congenial pose.

That year probably saw the beginning of his epic poem, *Paradise
Lost,* to whose composition Milton had looked forward some twenty
years before, when he wrote:

> I was confirmed in this opinion, that he who would not be
> frustrated of his hope to write well of hereafter in laudable
> things, ought himself to be a true poem; that is, a composition
> and pattern of the best and honorablest things; not presuming
> to sing high praises of heroic men, or famous cities, unless he
> have in himself the experience and the practice of all that
> which is praiseworthy.

He had set up equally demanding conditions for the prose historian, saying:

> One who would be a worthy historian of worthy deeds
> must possess as noble a spirit and as much practical experience
> as the hero of the action himself, in order that he may be able
> to comprehend and measure even the greatest of these actions
> on equal terms.

But he had already proved himself able to fulfill those, for as
he wrote in the *Second Defense*:

> I have delivered my testimony, I would almost say have
> erected a monument that will not readily be destroyed, to the
> reality of those singular and mighty achievments which were
> above all praise.

Nor was this all merely self-praise. Milton's high regard for
himself was largely the counterpart of his deep respect for mankind. Saurat, one of his most important contemporary critics, says:
"His high opinion of himself is also a high opinion of man! It is
also a high opinion of life as it might be lived on earth."

And in one of Milton's first published works we find:

> But he that holds himself in reverence and due esteem,
> both for the dignity of God's image upon him, and for the
> price of his redemption, which he thinks is visibly marked
> upon his forehead, accounts himself a fit person to do the
> noblest and godliest deeds. . . .

Nor does this faith in man's potentialities waver through all the bitter disappointments and disillusionments of his life.

It is pleasant here to remember that the virtual end of his public career found him enjoying a brief interlude of the kind of happiness he had never known.

In the end of 1656 he married the twenty-eight year old Katherine Woodcock. They seem to have been well suited and deeply devoted to each other and when, in February 1658, she and her infant daughter both died, Milton wrote for the wife he had never seen his only real love poem, the sonnet beginning:

> Methought I saw my late espoused saint.

That September there was another loss whose consequences to England, and perhaps even to Milton himself, were more far-reaching and catastrophic.

As we have seen, the bourgeoisie, having clearly won its struggle for power against the throne, had now little to fear from the monarchy and was, on the other hand, extremely afraid of any increase in strength for the lower classes whom they themselves had had to mobilize, as later in the French Revolution and ours, to help win their own victory. Even during Cromwell's lifetime there were many Presbyterian royalists who wished to reinstate the king, Charles II, now that he had, presumably, learned to know his place. It would then, they felt, no longer be necessary to keep the radical New Model Army in existence, or to fear the anger of the lower classes.

Cromwell's death in the fall of 1658 left the opposition to this bourgeois royalism leaderless; several generals of the New Model Army attempted to use their commands to bolster their personal seizures of power, and the left elements of the coalition both in the army and the nation had long been increasingly disorganized and officially voiceless with, as yet, no really solid class power to back up their demands.

Under the circumstances the weak attempt of Cromwell's peace-loving son to step into his father's shoes was foredoomed to failure, and the resurrection of the remnants of the old Rump Parliament, dissolved by Cromwell in 1653, was obviously also at best a temporary expedient.

Milton, who had been somewhat isolated in his blindness, semi-retirement, and growing disquiet at Cromwell's increasing concessions to the Presbyterians, had evidently no suspicion of the treacherous counter-revolution for which negotiations were already under way. With renewed hopefulness, in February 1659, he addressed *A Treatise of Civil Power in Ecclesiastical Causes* to the old Republican army leaders, urging the end of the established church which Cromwell had given state tax support, though no coercive powers. In May, the reestablishment of the Rump Parliament was greeted by another advisory pamphlet whose message is explicit in the title, *Considerations Touching the likliest means to remove Hirelings from the Church.*

By the end of that year it was, however, apparent that the coalition of former Presbyterians and Royalists was to be established on Parliament's terms, and that the complete Restoration of monarchy was only a matter of months.

At this point Milton stood, as his hero, blind Samson was later to do, sole champion of the liberty of his country.

Almost alone he raised his voice boldly against the imminent reinstatement of the monarchy. He spoke out first in a published letter to General Monk—who had, ironically, just completed negotiations with Charles II. Then he published an enlarged letter or appeal addressed to the new parliament, which had just been called into being to vote approval for the Restoration.

Finally, only a few weeks before Charles II actually landed in England, when practically every republican of note was fleeing the country or frantically attempting to obliterate the record of his past rebellion, Milton published a powerful pamphlet of remonstrance addressed to the last court of appeal—the English people themselves. This was a clarion call for continued resistance to tyranny and devotion to freedom.

The Readie and Easie Way to establish a free Commonwealth describes the sacrifices already made for freedom and decries the shame:

> . . . if by our ingrateful backsliding we make these fruitless; . . . making vain and viler than dirt the blood of so many thousand faithful and valiant Englishmen, who left us in this liberty, bought with their lives;

Again he reverts to this theme and passionately demands:

> Are the lives of so many good and faithful men, that died for the freedom of their country, to be so slighted, as to be forgotten in a stupid reconcilement without justice done them.

With no false self-consciousness he cites his own heroic example in speaking out for "that which is not call'd amiss The good Old Cause," and concludes with a desperate appeal:

> That a Nation should be so valorous and courageous to win their Liberty in the Field, and when they have won it, should be so heartless and unwise in the Councils, as not to know how to use it, value it, what to do with it, or with themselves; but . . . basely and besottedly to run their Necks again into the yoke which they have broken, and prostrate all the fruits of their Victory for naught at the feet of the vanquished . . . will be an ignominy if it befal us, that never yet befel any Nation possess'd of their Liberty; worthy indeed themselves, whatsoever they be, to be forever slaves; but that part of the Nation which consents not with them, as I perswade me, of a great number, far worthier than by their means to be brought into the same Bondage. . . .
>
> What I have spoken, is the Language of that which is not call'd amiss "The good Old Cause": if it seem strange to any, it will not seem more strange, I hope, than convincing to Backsliders. Thus much I should perhaps have said, though I were sure I should have spoken only to Trees and Stones; and had none to cry to, but with the Prophet, "O Earth, Earth, Earth!" to tell the very Soil itself, what her perverse Inhabitants are deaf to. Nay, though what I have spoke, should happ'n . . . to be the last words of an expiring Liberty. But I trust I shall have spoken Persuasion to abundance of sensible and ingenuous men; to some perhaps whom God may raise of these Stones to become Children of reviving Liberty; . . .

God made no sign, and on May 29, 1660, Charles II entered London to receive the homage of his faithful subjects.

Milton spent some months in hiding and was then, briefly, placed under arrest. His £2,000 in government funds—a major part of his estate—was confiscated and various other fines and special charges were imposed which, with the accidental destruction of his house by fire some years later, reduced his income to less than £100 a year. This made it impossible for him to command the secretarial assistance with which he had been composing *Paradise Lost* and completing his *History of Britain*, but considering his voluntary and avowed association with the execution of Charles I, the course the government followed was certainly a lenient one.

Charles II himself was a reasonable and unrevengeful man with a sound instinct against making famous martyrs. For reasons we must examine more closely in our discussion of the restoration in the next section, his course was one of great moderation. The few actual "regicides" left in England, who were barbarously tortured and killed, fell a victim to the animosity of their erstwhile colleagues in parliament—the conservative Presbyterians—who evidently could not rest until they had succeeded in physically destroying all the real republican leaders.

Milton's position was by no means secure. For some time he feared legal penalties, and for a much longer time received threats of assassination which must have been particularly distressing to a blind man. Although it was impossible for him to take any political action, he made no secret of his unchanged opinions. Taine summarizes his situation:

> Milton himself had been constrained to hide; his books had been burned by the hand of the hangman; even after the general act of indemnity he was imprisoned; when set at liberty, he lived in the expectation of being assassinated, for private fanaticism might seize the weapon relinquished by public revenge. Other smaller misfortunes came to aggravate by their stings the great wounds which afflicted him. Confiscation, a bankruptcy, finally the great fire of London, had robbed him of three fourths of his fortune; his daughters neither esteemed nor respected him; he sold his books, knowing that his family could not profit by them after his death; and amid so many private and public miseries he continued calm. Instead of repudiating what he had done, he gloried in it.

The rest of Milton's story is a great one, but soon told. Until 1663 his household consisted of his three daughters, the two elder of whom, then in their late teens, had been brought up largely by Mary Powell's royalist mother. She had expressed bitter animosity to Milton almost from the day of her daughter's marriage, and this had been intensified by his divorce pamphlets and the humiliation she felt when forced to urge her daughter to plead a reconciliation. Although Mrs. Powell and her whole family had been materially indebted to Milton during the years of the commonwealth, she persisted in claiming and, no doubt believing, that he could, somehow, have prevented the fines imposed upon her husband's estate as the penalty of his royalist political activities.

The two daughters were naturally affected by their grandmother's hostility to their father, and must have deeply resented it when the curtailment of his income forced their return to his austere and unhappy home.

His blindness combined with poverty forced him to depend on them not only for some degree of physical care but also for an enforced and uninterested assistance with his writing. There is some contemporary evidence for the story that they read aloud to him in languages they could only pronounce, but none for the idea that it was his wish rather than theirs that kept them in ignorance of all but the minimum accomplishment.

One of the young men who volunteered to read to him daily for some time wrote later:

> He, on the other hand, perceiving with what earnest desire I pursued learning, gave me not only all the encouragement, but all the help, he could. For, having a curious ear, he understood by my tone, when I understood what I read and when I did not, and accordingly would stop me, examine me, and open the most difficult passages to me.

The youngest daughter Deborah, born in 1650 or 1651, had evidently remained at home during Milton's brief second marriage and still spoke with warm affection of her father many years after his death.

We may feel deep sympathy for the unhappy young girls who conspired with the servant to sell their blind father's books, to buy small comforts he could not, or, they thought, would not, afford. But we must spare at least as much for the unhappy patriot living among his enemies, and for the poet who dictated his great epic, ten or twenty lines at a time, to "whatever hand came next"—many of them, as the manuscript shows, almost illiterate hands!

The older of the two nephews he had educated came as often as he could to correct punctuation and spelling, and Milton continued doggedly with his determined effort to "justify the ways of God to man." This objective is stated in the opening lines of *Paradise Lost*:

> Of Mans First Disobedience, and the Fruit
> Of that Forbidden Tree, whose mortal tast
> Brought Death into the World, and all our woe,
> With loss of *Eden*, till one greater Man
> Restore us, and regain the blissful Seat,
> Sing Heav'nly Muse. . . .

> . . . . . .
> . . . What in me is dark
> Illumin, what is low raise and support;
> That to the highth of this great Argument
> I may assert Eternal Providence,
> And justifie the wayes of God to men.

There were still several close friends who visited him at frequent intervals and one of those, his doctor, did much to remedy his domestic discomfort by introducing a young woman of twenty-four, probably a distant relative of his own, whom Milton married in 1663.

Her education and previous station were humble, and to us the disparity of age seems very great, but the marriage was evidently a happy one. The two elder daughters left home to learn the then very fashionable trade of gold lace making, and we have evidence from Milton's contemporary biographer, Aubrey, his nephew Edward Phillips, and others, that his home life soon settled into a comfortable routine. Two or three hours a day were devoted to singing; time was spent sitting out of doors whenever sun was available; and, of course, study and dictation continued daily under no matter what difficulties.

There are very few letters and almost no other directly autobiographical notes from these last fourteen years, but so personal a poet as Milton has left many revealing glimpses of himself throughout his tremendous epics—*Paradise Lost* and *Paradise Regained*—and his last great work, the triumphant tragedy of *Samson Agonistes* is in a sense pure autobiography throughout.

This is not the place to attempt the difficult and lengthy task of analyzing the still controversial *Paradise Lost*. E. M. W. Tillyard, probably the greatest living Milton scholar, and, more briefly, the novelist Rex Warner, in his excellent short biography of Milton, have written the most interesting recent interpretations of this great and, for modern readers, sometimes forbidding, poem.

Tillyard says in a general discussion of the biblical mythology which so puzzles many contemporary readers, but which obviously had a deep emotional connotation for Milton:

> Largely because of the power he felt in his own mind, Milton believed in the almost boundless possibilities of Man; in the Bible he found this expressed in the statement that God

made Man in his own image. But he sees also, has had it forced upon him by his experience, that actually there is a perverseness in men that brings them to failure without there being any absolute need of their failing. The Fall is a myth at once recounting the perverse nature of men and attaching to them the responsibility. This perverseness is common to all men: through Adam all have fallen. But there is still that in the human mind which can live down this perverseness and lead on to these possibilities: a few take advantage of this possible good. This idea is expressed in Scripture by the possibility of regeneration in Christ.

Rex Warner summarizes his interpretation of the poem by saying:

> Like Lycidas, the poem closes in perfection, but as one looks back over its great events one cannot help feeling that the loss of Heaven for Satan and of Paradise for Adam and Eve symbolise something even greater and wider than what they are intended to do in the successful scheme of the justification of God's ways. Revolt is in the nature of things and so is the violence and enchantment of sexual feeling. Both may lead to disaster, as Milton well knew, yet both are so strong elements in his own character that they command, even against his better judgment, his respect. True, that Satan, whose pride turns to malignity, is lost beyond redemption; yet the original pride was splendid. True, that Adam was more moved by feeling than by the strict injunctions of authority; yet his unhesitating acceptance of death rather than to desert his love has its own nobility. There is a sense in which here, as in all Milton's work, it is man rather than God who is justified. The loss of Paradise gives scope certainly for a greater exercise of God's love, but also for a fuller dignity in man. Such qualities as fortitude and endurance were scarcely required in a life devoted to gardening and love-making. Now they are required in a world "to good malignant, to bad men benigne." Also and even more are necessary those original sins in which Milton so profoundly believed and which can now take on the form of virtue—revolt against unjust authority, and the shared love which can both delight and console.

There are a few passages among the many in the epic carrying special biographical interest which we may stop to note. For example, the beautiful invocation at the opening of the third book, probably still written in the comparative contentment of his semi-retirement, 1655-1658, gives us a restrained but moving statement

of what blindness meant to Milton even then, successful, respected
and secure in a state he had helped build.

> Thus with the year
> Seasons return, but not to me returns
> Day, or the sweet approach of Ev'n or Morn,
> Or sight of vernal bloom, or Summers Rose,
> Or flocks, or herds, or human face divine;
> But cloud instead, and ever-during dark
> Surrounds me, from the chearful wayes of men
> Cut off, and for the Book of knowledg fair
> Presented with a Universal blanc
> Of Natures works to me expung'd and ras'd,
> And wisdome at one entrance quite shut out.
> So much the rather thou Celestial light
> Shine inward, and the mind through all her powers
> Irradiate, there plant eyes, all mist from thence
> Purge and disperse, that I may see and tell
> Of things invisible to mortal sight.

No one at all familiar with Milton's work can ever be unmind-
ful of the constant loving references to the sun, the stars, and light
itself, from his very earliest college poems until the end of his life.

In Book VII, written during his doubly dark days of exile, we
find another more bitter reference to the now threatening dark:

> . . . though fall'n on evil dayes,
> On evil dayes though fall'n, and evil tongues;
> In darkness, and with dangers compast round,
> And solitude; yet not alone, while thou
> Visit'st my slumbers nightly, or when Morn
> Purples the East.

The growing dissensions of the commonwealth council were
obviously judged with unsparing rigor by their Latin Secretary,
who, in Book II, commented on the well-ordered plans of Satan's
legions:

> O shame to men! Devil with Devil damn'd
> Firm concord holds, men onely disagree
> Of Creatures rational, though under hope
> Of heavenly Grace; and God proclaiming peace,
> Yet live in hatred, enmitie, and strife
> Among themselves, and levie cruel warre,

Wasting the Earth, each other to destroy:
As if (which might induce us to accord)
Man had not hellish foes anow besides,
That day and night for his destruction waite.

Yet although Blake, and Shelley after him, felt that as a true
poet Milton was "of the devil's party without knowing it," Satan
is by no means his hero. The later poets found themselves in a
world they never made where the only attitude to be sustained
with integrity was that of rebellion. For Milton this was not yet
true. He had done as much as any man to make his world; it had
been unmade by what he felt to be an accidental not an inevitable
failure; and he identified freedom with the just law and order of an
improved commonwealth, and not with the violence of a counter-
revolutionary rebellion.

His identification with the one great angel, Abdiel, who refuses
to fall with Satan but remains firm in his loyalty and faith makes
it very clear that Milton was still emotionally far closer to feeling
like an honored artist of the republic than an outlaw.

God, welcoming Abdiel, is evidently speaking to the still republican Milton when he says:

Servant of God, well hast thou fought
The better fight, who single hast maintained
Against revolted multitudes the Cause
Of Truth, in word mightier than they in Armes;
And for the testimonie of Truth has born
Universal reproach, far worse to beare
Than violence; for this was all thy care
To stand approv'd in sight of God.

Before completing *Paradise Regained,* in 1671, Milton published
the *History of Britain* on which he had been working so many
years before. It is interesting to note that in this first edition he
omitted the strong criticisms of the Long Parliament which we
have noted above. He had not come to doubt its justice—the passage was preserved for insertion in later editions—but he saw no
reason to give the worse hated monarchy a stick with which to
belabor its defeated opponents.

The work is of interest not only for its historical material but
also for many shrewd psychological and sociological observations
like:

> It is a fond conceit in many great ones, and pernicious in
> the end, to cease from no violence till they have attain'd the
> utmost of their ambitions and desires; then to think God
> appeas'd by their seeking to bribe him with a share however
> large of their ill-gott'n spoils, and then lastly to grow zealous
> of doing right, when they have no longer need to do wrong.

Milton's continued defiance of tyranny, and irrepressible tendency to advise men for their own good, are evidenced by a sentence he added, just before publication in 1670, to his discussion
of the ease with which Romans, Danes and Normans had all, in
former times, conquered England because of its internal divisions
and injustice. He concludes with a stern warning:

> If these were the Causes of such misery and thraldom to
> those our ancestors, with what better close can be concluded,
> then here in fit season to remember this Age in the midst of
> her security, to fear from like Vices without amendment the
> Revolutions of like Calamities.

Paradise Regained, written in 1671, devotes its four books to a
description of Christ's temptations in the desert. There is evidently
much that is part of Milton's autobiography in Christ's description
of his childhood studies and youthful ambitions, and there may
well be a topical reference in its opening lines:

> I who e're while the happy Garden sung,
> By one man's disobedience lost, now sing
> Recover'd Paradise to all mankind,
> By one man's firm obedience fully tri'd
> Through all temptation, and the Tempter foil'd
> In all his wiles, defeated and repuls't,
> And Eden rais'd in the vast Wilderness.

But the great creation of Milton's old age was a far different
poem—the only true "Greek Tragedy" in English, written about a
hero of the Old Testament—*Samson Agonistes.* This must be read
as a whole and is far easier for the average reader than any of
Milton's other major work.

Samson who had first been betrayed by his cowardly countrymen when he stood as their champion fighting for the freedom of
Israel, and who had then been more irremediably betrayed by his
own besotted love for Delilah which enabled her to deliver him,
weak and helpless, to the Philistines, is, of course, Milton from

beginning to end. His miserable blind servitude among his enemies, his agonized longing for sight and freedom, everything except the last terrible triumph of his death is Milton. And the triumph itself is so imaginatively realized we are forced to share Milton's fierce longing that he too could bring destruction down upon the enemy at the negligible cost of his own unhappy life. We also share his tremendous sense of release in the imaginary accomplishment and must hope Milton himself was far-sighted enough to realize that with less than his two bare hands—with no weapon but his poetic imagination—he had created an engine which would help avenge his defeat long after his death. He would have rejoiced to know, for example, that in 1788, the year before the French Revolution, there were twenty-one editions of his great epic published in France!

He lived only three years longer and died peacefully in 1674, leaving all his small property to the wife who had cherished and comforted his old age.

Since in this brief account of Milton's work and life we have been forced almost altogether to ignore the many gentler qualities which so enriched them, we should perhaps include in this story of the patriot poet Rex Warner's reminder:

> Yet, if his great work is, as he wished it to be, "doctrinal to a nation," it is also in itself delightful. . . . One's enjoyment will almost certainly be marred if one thinks of him too exclusively as the blind and defeated patriot, the unflagging scholar, the austere educationist, the anti-clerical, the prophet of a creed of freedom. One should think too of the brilliant young man who astonished Italy with his wit and learning, of the poet who of all others, with the possible exception of Shakespeare, has written most beautifully of flowers and of everything that strikes the sense in an English landscape, of the vigorous believer in the possible goodness of life, who, so far from denying or belittling pleasure, made angels lovers and included in the wholesome delights of Paradise a "sweet reluctant amorous delay."

Although we may be sure Milton would have approved our thinking of "the brilliant young man" with a taste for all the delicate joys of life, he would have been both puzzled and indignant at any hint of a dichotemy that somehow set these qualities in opposition to those of the scholar-patriot fighting for freedom.

Milton did not write beautifully of flowers and friendship *in spite of,* or even in addition to, his militant struggles and heroic self-devotion. He wrote movingly of life *because* he loved it enough to fight for it; he fought for freedom because anything less betrayed the possibilities of human beauty and happiness.

Milton was a whole man, integrated in both his art and his life, and political in the highest sense in both. It is no wonder that every great progressive English poet since his day has claimed his inspiration.

THE RESTORATION

Although the House of Stuarts were installed on the throne in 1660 it was clear to Charles II as well as to his erstwhile opponents that essentially he ruled by the grace of Parliament and not by the divine right of kings.

All the points which had been at issue between his father and the bourgeoisie were explicitly or tacitly ceded by him, and while the Church of England was restored we have seen that the leading Presbyterians themselves (who now found it easy to reconcile their consciences to a friendly Episcopalianism) had already realized the need of an established church to support their state power. They were far more concerned about the dangerous agitation of unlicensed preachers and the subversive activities of nonconformist congregations than they were about the precise ritual of church service—or even about the appointment of bishops by a king, once he himself was, in a sense, their own appointee.

The reality of the situation was so apparent that the French ambassador wrote in a private report to Louis XIV "They think, because there is now a king, that this is a monarchy, but it isn't one." Charles himself, when his less astute brother urged him to punish their father's enemies, reclaim the estates lost by the royalists and, in general, "act like a king," replied succinctly, "I have no wish to start again on my travels."

He made the best of a hard bargain by getting as much money as he could to spend on his titled mistresses and illegitimate children, and assuaged his pride by flaunting an aristocratic debauchery and noble bastards in the face of outraged bourgeois morality.

His court was composed largely of those who had spent idle and dissolute years in exile with him, and of others who had similar reasons for spite against the solid bourgeoisie, and who gratified that spite as well as their tastes in doing all they could to mock and destroy the remnants of Puritanism represented by its personal morality.

The extravagance, intrigue and licentiousness of the court were truly indescribable. J. H. Wilson, a by no means unfriendly or censorious commentator, writes in his book on *The Court Wits of the Restoration Period* that, although contrasted with the general aristocrat and courtier of the time who "with almost complete immunity committed assault, theft, rape, or even murder," the wits were comparatively moral, yet:

> They all wore swords and occasionally used them. They all kept mistresses—ladies of fashion, actresses, miscellaneous willing wenches. Occasionally they drank too much, scoured the town, broke windows, and fought with the watch. They lived in a Godless world [perhaps even more important, in a functionless one as well] and sought their pleasure where it was to be found, certain of being able to "jump the life to come." Nor were they fearful of "judgement here"; their master, the King, was indulgent to their follies and sure to remit their fines. . . . Francis Math, Lord Guilford, a sober lawyer was seriously advised to "keep a whore" because he was ill looked upon at Court for want of doing so!

There are innumerable less authenticated incidents of the same nature as the one which legal records tell us caused Sir Charles Sedley, a leading court figure, to be fined and sentenced to a week's imprisonment. He had appeared naked on a balcony with two noble companions after a drinking bout at Covent Gardens, insulting passers-by with obscene language, and throwing wine bottles at the crowd which then gathered. The records do not verify what popular contemporary anecdote adds, that one of the noble companions, Lord Dickhurst, a member of Parliament, concluded the episode by saying loudly, "Come now, let us go make laws for the nation."

Nor were the ladies of the Court behind the gentlemen. Pepys casually comments in his diary: "Lady Shrewsbury . . . is at this time and hath for a great while been, a whore to the Duke of Buckingham," and there are a tiresome number of far less delicate comments on similar matters in the squibs, epigrams and lampoons with which the court was delighted. The "hero" of Congreve's play, *Way of the World,* wishing to please a lady, gets "a friend to put her into a lampoon and compliment her with the imputation of an affair with a young fellow."

It is not without reason that Wycherly (except for Dryden, perhaps the only other Restoration dramatist of any importance) intimates in his *Plain Dealer* that his heroine's impudence which could "put a court out of countenance" would "debauch a stews."

As we should expect, the only literature which came out of this background, beside a large number of more or less pungent lampoons or epigrams, and a few highly praised formal odes, was that of the licentious comedy of the Restoration theatre—a theatre set up as a part of the Court, officially ruled over by Charles' "Master of Revels," and having no further purpose than any other form of aristocratic dissipation. A gentleman of fashion in the theatre was privileged to cry aloud "Damnme, Jack, 'tis a confounded Play, let's to a Whore and spend our time better," and the playwrights, many of whom were themselves gentlemen of fashion, strove to use their wit and impudence as far as possible (and impudence alone beyond that point) so to amuse the Court audience and its hangers-on as to avoid such an unfavorable comparison.

The two most considerable achievements of the theatre were the plays of Congreve and Wycherly and, partly for their real wit and partly as a mirror of the age, it may be worth one's time to read Wycherly's *The Country Wife* and *The Plain Dealer,* and Congreve's later and more restrained *Love for Love, Double Dealer,* or *Way of the World.* Perhaps also the more typical plays of Etheridge, *She Would if She Could* or *The Man of Mode,* would serve to round out the picture for readers especially interested in drama.

If the froth of the aristocracy could provide no better soil for literature, the dominant bulk of the solid bourgeoisie were still less to the purpose. They maintained the pretence of a religion whose real emotion had been spent, continued to use the terms of a hypocritical and meaningless morality, and accepted for their own purposes the rule of a king of whom one of his own favorites unrebuked wrote:

> Restless he rolls about from Whore to Whore,
> A Merry Monarch, Scandalous and Poor.

A better known epigram was posted outside the bedroom door of one of the ladies of the court when Charles II was favoring her with his company:

> Here lies a pretty, witty King,
> Whose word no man relies on,
> Who never said a foolish thing
> Nor ever did a wise one.

For this the Earl of Rochester was publicly thanked by the king, who said that his words were his own but his acts those of his ministers!

The sons and grandsons of Milton's "slaughtered saints" could inded offer no inspiration to art.

It is, therefore, not surprising that the single great work of the period is that of a poor nonconformist tinker and unlicensed minister, three times jailed because he refused to stop preaching the truth as he saw it, and equally opposed to the dissolute extravagance of the Court and the worldly prudence of the bourgeoisie.

Although Bunyan was, in literary terms, by far the greatest of the seventeenth century "mechanick preachers" he was, of course, not a unique phenomenon but part of a deeply rooted and flourishing tradition whose essence his own personal genius enabled him to crystallize in the imperishable form of *Pilgrim's Progress*.

Jack Lindsay, in his excellent biographical study, *John Bunyan —Maker of Myths*, describes in general terms the development of this tradition.

> In England the first great bourgeois wave was at every point vivified by the Protestant idiom; and this unity proceeded up to the Civil War. After that war the inner rifts in the bourgeoisie, the increasing pressure of a dispossessed proletariat, destroyed the vital coherence of the Protestant movement; only with the lower classes did Protestantism remain a living force, compacting their resistance and submission till the day when they could begin to organize for a juster society. . . .

> We have seen how in 1649 there occurred the first grand division in the Protestant movement in England. The bourgeois, having won to power, renounced everything in Protestantism that savored of insurgency. . . .

Cromwell and Lilburne on the side of political action, Milton and Bunyan on the side of literary expression, were the four great figures embodying at highest tension the drama and meaning of the seventeenth century revolution. Bunyan gave voice to all the popular feelings of derelict despair, the general stupefaction and suspension that followed the failure of Lilburne, even among those who had not consciously identified themselves with the Lilburnean cause. He, more than any other man, transmuted the cloudy frustration into an ideological weapon of hope which served the masses well in the difficult century and a half awaiting them.

In these comments Lindsay evidently sees, as we have done, that the Restoration was only the logical conclusion to the reactionary course which the major part of the bourgeoisie had followed since the very moment of the king's decisive defeat. To understand the radical religious groups which Bunyan represented we must look back, briefly, to their formation under the commonwealth, precipitated by the revolutionary activities of the early forties, stimulated by the unredressed and, sometimes, increased grievances of the next decade, and protected by Cromwell's sympathetic policy of toleration until his death.

The preaching laymen who led the various groups of working-class dissenters were almost all essentially agitators speaking and, indeed, thinking, in the religious idiom of their time but directing their attacks against social abuses and the oppressors of the poor.

In *John Bunyan, Mechanick Preacher,* W. Y. Tindale, speaking of Bunyan's contemporaries and immediate predecessors, says: "In pulpit or market place they directed and inflamed the passions of the discontented, revealed the corruption of church, society and state, and extended to the vulgar the hope of justice or of baptism." He continues:

But those saints whose troubles were social and economic as well as religious generally found their way to the company of the radicals, Quakers, Baptists, Fifth Monarchists or Ranters who promised a new society. Though for example the Baptists and even the Quakers secured the loyalty of some polite and eminent men, they claimed the adherence of innumerable laborers, small farmers, shop keepers, and artisans. It is improper, therefore, to ignore the social character of the radical sects or to treat purely as a religious and political revolt that which was also social and economic. The rise of the radical sects . . . gave expression and the hope of relief to men of

all classes, but especially to those whose difficulties were social
or economic. The sorrow of the lower orders, which finds expression today in the secular creed of Marxism, embraced in
the 17th century the comforts of radical Christianity, whose
banners had sanctified the insurrections of the peasants and
the revolts of the masses under John of Leyden at Munster.

This study which combines the too infrequently united virtues
of scholarship and wit, proceeds to illustrate by an enormous number of lively quotations the fact that both the Presbyterian and
Episcopalian attacks on these sects, and the retorts of their far
from masochistic adherents, clearly recognized the class basis of
the opposition. A judge trying itinerant preachers as vagabonds
would declare, "this fellow would have Ministers to be . . . Tay-
lors, Pedlars, and Tinkers, such Fellows as he is." And a lay
preacher—who died in jail—would protest indignantly that Christ
was a carpenter and Peter a Fisherman "But you cry out that we
send . . . Weavers, Smiths, Cappers, Soldiers."

A Presbyterian minister in 1651, one of many harassed by the
increasing swarm of articulate workingmen, preached angrily in his
church: "Superiors must govern; Inferiors Obey, and be governed;
Ministers must study and Preach; People must hear and obey. . . .
Baking and Preaching, Nailing and Preaching, Patching and Preaching . . . will not hold." And a gifted cobbler retorted at an open
air meeting: "If a Man have the Spirit of God, though he be a
Pedler, Tinker, Chimney-sweeper, or Cobbler, he may by the helpe
of God's Spirit give a more publique interpretation, than they all."

Attacks on the Ranters in the fifties spoke, truly or falsely, of
their sexual orgies, but concluded with a more heartfelt if less
picturesque indignation: "They taught that it was quite contrary
to the end of the Creation, to Appropriate any thing to any Man
or Woman; but that there ought to be a Community of all things."

And a Ranter, later forced to recant by a year's imprisonment
in Newgate, justified this accusation by declaring: "Howl, howl, ye
nobles, howl honourable, howl ye rich men . . . bow downe, bow
downe . . . before those poore, nasty, lousie, ragged wretches . . .
you have feared sword-levelling and man-levelling but now you
will be levelled by me, the Lord, the real Leveller."

The Leveler leader, Lilburne, ended his life a Quaker, and
Quaker preachers by the hundreds during the last years of the
Commonwealth took as their texts economic equality and the spe-
cific oppression of rack-rent landlords in such sermons as:

> Against all those who lay heavie burthens upon the poor
> by deceipt and oppression, and against all who live in pride
> and idlenesse, and fulnesse of bread, by whom the creation is
> devoured, and many made poor by your meanes, and you who
> are rich, who live at ease, and in pleasure, you live upon the
> labours of the poor, and lay heavy burthens upon them grievous
> to be born. . . .

> Was the creature made for that end, to set your hearts
> upon them: to heape together, out of the reach of the poore
> and needy; and he who can get the greatest share, should
> become the greatest man; and all that have little, shall bow
> downe and worship him. . . .

> Woe, woe, woe, to the oppressors of the Earth, who grind
> the faces of the poor, who rack and stretch out their Rents,
> till the poor with all the sweat of their brows and hard labour
> can scarce get Bread to eat, and Raiment to put on. . . .

It is not surprising that the Quaker preacher, in the words of
one such who also died in jail, was considered: "a sower of Sedition, a subverter of the Laws, or turner of the World up-side down,
a pestilent fellow."

A contemporary wit summarized the matter—as the universities
saw it—:

> A Preachers work is not to gelde a Sowe,
> Unseemly 'tis a Judge should milk a Cowe:
> A Cobler to a Pulpit should not mount,
> Nor can an Asse cast up a true account.
>
> .   .   .   .   .   .
> Let tradesmen use their trades, let all men be
> Employ'd in what is fitting their degree.

And an eighteenth century satirist reviewed the troublesome
period:

> When tinkers bawl'd aloud to settle
> Church discipline, for patching kettle;
> No sow-gelder did blow his horn
> To geld a cat, but cry'd Reform.

The Fifth Monarchy Men shared with Bunyan's Baptist brethren
the seditious belief in the millennium—that is, in Christ's coming,
at least in spirit, to rule on earth for a thousand years *before* the
end of the world; and unlike the Baptists, they felt that his way

should be prepared by the propaganda of the sword as well as that of the word.

In 1661 the general confusion seemed to indicate a favorable opportunity for ending his unaccountable delay and smoothing his path by removing the wicked. A small group of enthusiasts in London went armed to St. Paul's, asked those there whom they were for and, on the reply "King Charles," shot one in the name of "King Jesus."

This hopeless riot was all too easily and bloodily suppressed, but although Bunyan and his colleagues honestly expressed their condemnation of such procedure it was as indicative of the basic social unrest and rebellion they represented as were the actions of the anti-Czarist nihilists, who used a different idiom but the same weapons, two centuries later.

Although even Cromwell had been forced to suppress the proponents of such direct action on a similar occasion years before, Lindsay is undoubtedly correct when he says:

> But meanwhile, in 1660, what the bourgeoisie wanted above all things was to have a sympathetically oppressive state which would allow them to make the fullest use of the Civil War gains and to crush the democratic manifestations which Cromwell tolerated and in so many ways encouraged.

He, more specifically, concludes, "Among the many reasons, the bourgeoisie wanted the King back so that they might put such men as John Bunyan in prison."

Paradoxically enough, then, we must look for the major literature of the Restoration in the work of those for whose suppression it was invoked, just as almost the only surviving literature of our own slave-holding South is still to be found in the magnificent songs of those on whose oppression it was built.

JOHN BUNYAN

John Bunyan was born at the end of November 1628, the son and the grandson of a tinker with, apparently, no specific knowledge of his more remote ancestry. His family has now, however, been traced back for over four hundred years, and it is clear that in

the fifteenth and sixteenth century they were among the small independent farmers or yeomen who lost their land in the first
enclosures and were forced lower in the world with each successive
generation.

Both Bunyan's father and grandfather were named Thomas
and there is a record of a Thomas Bunyan innkeeper in the same
small village in 1547. However slight Bunyan's knowledge of his
forebears he must certainly have known that they had once had,
as their birthright, some portion of England's green and pleasant
land.

His later repeated use in sermons of this symbol of the land
as a precious birthright of which he and his people had been
fraudulently deprived is, of course, based on the general practise
of the time. Such admonitions as this from his *Heavenly Footman*
are ostensibly directed only to the salvation of the soul and are
part of the ordinary nonconformist pulpit usage:

> What is before you is worth striving for. As the men of
> Dan said to their brethren after they had seen the goodness of
> the land of Canaan, "Arise, for we have seen the land, and
> behold it is very good. Be not slothful to go and possess the
> land." . . .

But that usage was, in turn, based on the fact that the congregations were composed of innumerable poor rural laborers and
village artisans, as well as of many city apprentices and "mechanicks" (working men) who had also been similarly dispossessed
in the transition to a capitalist society.

As early as 1645 Lilburne had used what was evidently already
a familiar term, in the title of his pamphlet: "England's Birth-right
justified against all arbitrary usurpation, whether regal or parliamentary, or under what rigor soever."

Gerrard Winstanley, when arrested for his attempt to start a
colony on the basis of a primitive agricultural communism, had
declared:

> And is this not slavery, say the people, that though there
> be land enough in England to maintain ten times as many
> people as are in it, yet some must beg of their brethren, or
> work in hard drudgery for day wages for them, or starve, or
> steal, and so be hanged out of the way as men not fit to live
> on the earth?
> Before they are suffered to plant the waste land for a liv-

lihood, they must pay rent to their brethren for it. Well, this is the burden the Creation groans under; and the subjects (so-called) have not their Birthright Freedom granted them from their brethren who hold it from them by club law, but not by righteousness.

In the next century, as we shall see below Swift also used the same term in a similar appeal for the plundered and dispossessed of Ireland. And at the end of the nineteenth century Ruskin was still able to demand:

> Trade Unions of England—Trade Armies of Christendom, what's the roll call of you, and what part or lot have you, hitherto, in this Holy Christian Land of your Fathers?
> Is not that heritage to be claimed, and the Birth Right of it no less than the Death Right?

Of his immediate family background and education Bunyan says in his autobiographical *Grace Abounding*:

> For my Descent then, it was, as is well known by many, of a low and inconsiderable generation; my father's house being of that rank that is meanest, and most despised of all the families in the Land. . . .
> But yet, notwithstanding the meanness and inconsiderableness of my Parents, it pleased God to put it into their hearts, to put me to School, to learn both to read and write; the which I also attained, according to the rate of other poor men's children; though to my shame, I confess, I did soon lose that little I learnt, even almost utterly, and that long before the Lord did work his gracious work of Conversion upon my Soul.

Many of his generous biographers have claimed that Bunyan here modestly exaggerated his lack of social standing, but a less generous contemporary minister in 1659 attacked him as a "Wandering preaching Tinker . . . the meanest of all the vulgar in the Country," so that his description seems to have been reasonably accurate.

There seems to have been some early friction between Bunyan, who was an extremely robust, energetic, and self-willed youngster, and his father, and we learn that he was considered a reckless, vaguely rebellious youth, a ringleader in his companions' more dangerous exploits, given especially to extraordinarily foul and blasphemous language.

In 1642 both his mother and his only sister suddenly took ill and died, and when, barely two months later, his father remarried, Bunyan, not yet sixteen, joined the Parliamentary Army.

The fact that his half-brother, born the next year, was named Charles, leads us to suspect that the friction with his father may have been related, whether as cause or effect, to political as well as other differences.

After reenlisting twice Bunyan was, in 1647, honorably discharged and returned home, a nineteen-year old with a wife of whom we know little except his own statement:

> Presently after this, I changed my condition into a married state; and my mercy was, to light upon a wife, whose father was counted godly: This woman and I, though we came together as poor as poor might be, (not having so much household-stuff as a dish or spoon betwixt us both) yet this she had for her part, *The Plain Man's Path-way to Heaven,* and *The Practice of Piety,* which her father had left her, when he died. In these two books I would sometimes read with her, wherein I also found some things that were somewhat pleasing to me; (but all this while I met with no conviction). She also would be often telling of me, *what a godly man her father was, and how he would reprove and correct vice, both in his house, and amongst his neighbours: what a strict and holy life he lived in his day, both in word and deed.*

Although he was reconciled to his father, who helped him get the tools necessary to set up as a tinker on his own, neither his work nor his happy marriage enabled Bunyan to accept emotionally the world in which he found himself. We feel in his many accounts of his search for God during the next few years a search for the sense of vital purpose, fellowship and direction which he had briefly enjoyed in the army of "the good old cause."

He later wrote in his spiritual autobiography, *Grace Abounding*:

> Wherefore these books, with this relation, though they did not reach my heart, to awaken it about my sad and sinful state, yet they did beget within me some desires to Religion: So that, because I knew no better, I fell in very eagerly with the Religion of the times; to wit, to go to Church twice a day, and that too with the foremost; and there should very devoutly, both say and sing as others did, yet retaining my wicked life: But withal, I was so over-run with the spirit of Superstition, that I adored, and that with great devotion, even all things (both the High-place Priest, Clerk, Vestments, Service, and

what else) belonging to the Church; counting all things holy, that were therein contained; and especially, the Priest and Clerk most happy, and without doubt, greatly blessed, because they were the Servants, as I then thought, of God; and were principal in the holy Temple, to do his work therein.

This conceit grew so strong, in little time, upon my spirit, that had I but seen a Priest (though never so sordid and debauched in his life) I should find my spirit fall under him, reverence him, and knit unto him; yea, I thought, for the love I did bear unto them (supposing they were the Ministers of God) I could have lain down at their feet, and have been trampled upon by them; their Name, their Garb, and Work did so intoxicate and bewitch me.

After I had been thus for some considerable time, another thought came in my mind; and that was, Whether *we* were of the *Israelites*, or no? For finding in the Scriptures, that they were once the peculiar people of God, thought I, If I were once of this race, my Soul must needs be happy. Now again I found within me a great longing to be resolved about this Question, but could not tell how I should: At last, I asked my father of it; who told me, *No, we were not*. Wherefore then I fell in my spirit, as to the hopes of that, and so remained.

Seeking for a more purposeful and dedicated way of life, and no doubt strongly influenced by memories of the army in which nonconformist, lay preachers of all kinds abounded and spoke as the spirit moved them, Bunyan began a two-and-a-half year internal struggle "for grace."

This army was probably the only one in the world where a near-riot was ever started—as it was in Bunyan's regiment—by a sermon preached on Infant Baptism, An official of the town in which it was stationed explained to a gentleman who protested against such unlicensed preaching by soldiers: "Sir, I assure you, if they have not leave to preach they will not fight; and if they fight not, we must all fly the land and be gone."

Bunyan may have heard, and certainly knew prototypes of, the Colonel who declared at an army council: "The poorest he that is in England hath a life to live as the greatest he. . . . Everyman that is to live under a Government ought first by his own consent to put himself under that government."

It is not surprising that in the years immediately after his return to the narrow, remote village life, he felt, as he tells us, utterly lost, cast away, in short, "damned." Looking for the guilt which had called down this judgment, he found it in such irrelevancies as playing one-a-cat with other young men of the village, dancing, and even bell-ringing for the church.

This last seemingly harmless indulgence was one he found it particularly difficult to give up, and we might well account his agonies about that generally approved amusement as a purely personal idiosyncrasy if it were not for such passages as this; which we find in the journals of his contemporary, the great Quaker leader, George Fox, and others:

> The black earthly spirit of the priests wounded my life; and when I heard the bell toll to call people together to the steeple-house, it struck at my life; for it was just a market-bell, to gather people together that the priest might set forth his wares to sale. Oh! the vast sums of money that are gotten by the trade they make of selling the Scriptures; and by their preaching, from the highest bishop to the lowest priest. . . .

In July 1650, his wife gave birth to a blind baby whom Bunyan had christened Mary and whom, as we shall see, he loved with extraordinary tenderness. Shortly thereafter he experienced, in his own terms, an even more significant birth, or, rather, rebirth. He tells us:

> But upon a day, the good Providence of God did cast me to *Bedford*, to work on my Calling; and in one of the streets of that Town, I came where there were three or four poor women sitting at a door, in the Sun, talking about the things of God; and being now willing to hear them discourse, I drew near to hear what they said, for I was now a brisk Talker also myself, in the matters of Religion: But I may say, *I heard, but I understood not*; for they were far above, out of my reach: . . .
>
> And me-thought they spake, as if joy did make them speak; they spake with such pleasantness of Scripture-language, and with such appearance of Grace in all they said, that they were to me, as if they had found a new world, as if they were *people that dwelt alone, and were not to be reckoned amongst their Neighbours*. Numb. 23.9. . . .
>
> Therefore I should often make it my business to be going again and again into the company of these poor people, for I could not stay away; and the more I went amongst them, the more I did question my condition; and, as I still do remember, presently I found two things within me, at which I did sometimes marvel. . . .

His mental struggles continued for another year or two, but sometime in 1653 he found himself—and was found—fit to join the fellowship of the small Baptist church, and after the birth of his second daughter, Elizabeth, in 1654, he moved his family into Bedford to live as fully as possible with the group of which he had become part.

Such small nonconformist groups formed actual communities rather than mere church congregations, as any study of the minute books in which they recorded the work of their meetings shows us. The relation of their members to each other and the completely democratic community of which they formed a part resembled the life of such utopian nineteenth century colonies as Alcott's Brook Farm and Owen's New Harmony, rather than that of any purely religious group we know. They were, however, composed almost entirely of working people rather than intellectuals, were far more practically rooted in the economic life of their place and time, and carried on a militant and realistic though losing propaganda fight against its values.

Lindsay in his analysis of *Pilgrim's Progress* speaks of Bunyan's relation to this "fellowship," as he himself repeatedly called it, when he says:

> The Celestial City is the dream of all England, all the world, united in Fellowship. Meanwhile there was, for Bunyan, the little congregation of Bedford who were doing their best in a world of distorting pressures.
>
> They [the Independent churches] were, so to speak, constructions *outside society* of what the people felt that society lacked and must continue to lack while operated on a class basis.
>
> It was in this atmosphere of democratic activity that Bunyan wrote his third book—*A Few Sighs from Hell.* It is lurid with hell-terror—and that is the expression of the sense of dissatisfaction and instability, of ceaseless crisis, resulting from the fact that the democratization was based on an outside—society formulation, not on a concrete social order. But it is also a healthy warning to the wealthy classes, the cause of the instability. It is built on the parable of Lazarus and Dives, the poor man who goes to heaven and the heart-less rich man who goes to hell. For if the upper classes were watching with fear masked as scorn the irruption of mechanics into places reserved for their betters, the lower classes were retorting distrust for distrust.

The next few years for Bunyan were strenuous but happy ones. He rapidly became an extremely active and much respected member of the group, discovered a gift for preaching which was recognized and admired by his brethren, and even developed a certain facility with his pen in the course of a number of satisfactorily violent controversies with more educated ministers who were "angry with the Tinker, because he strives to mend Souls as well as Kettles and Pans."

These attacks on lay preachers represented much more than personal jealousy. As Lindsay says:

> The insistence of the masses on their right to think and preach their own religion was an essential part of the revolutionary movement. For such a claim undermined the whole ideology of absolutism. Nothing astonished and outraged the reactionaries so much as the spectacle of a working-man in the pulpit. . . . [A contemporary Restoration historian] never loses a chance to mention the appearance of a weaver, tapster, pedlar, mason, or such as a preacher.

And Bunyan loses no opportunity to vaunt his class consciousness in attacking the learned ministers' addiction to classical quotations and aristocratic manners whereas Christ, he insists, "was born in a stable, laid in a manger, earned his bread with his labour, being by trade a carpenter."

A landed proprietor who, as Parliamentary Chaplain in 1640, had then joined the fight against the bishops, sadly remarked: "We intended not to dig down the banks, or pull up the hedge and lay all waste and common when we desired the prelate's tyranny might cease," and later added, more bitterly, "If any would raise an army to extirpate knowledge and religion the Tinkers and Sowgarters and crate carryers and beggars and bargemen and all the rabble that cannot reade . . . will be the forwardest to come to such a militia."

In 1659, after the birth of two sons, Bunyan's wife died and he, left with four young children, remarried a year later. His choice was again a happy one. Elizabeth, although then only a girl in her teens, soon proved herself a woman of extraordinary spirit and devotion and played a part not less heroic than Bunyan's own in the difficult years upon which they were entering.

In May, 1660, Charles II had been restored to the throne, having first made a general promise of political amnesty and religious toleration. He was willing enough to keep both promises as long as they cost him nothing, but the Presbyterians who were, as we have seen, unable to feel safe until they had secured the death of the few remaining revolutionary leaders, were also most anxious to use the reestablished church as a means for silencing the criticism of the poor, and buttressing the position of the wealthy.

To Charles' mild reminder that he had promised "no forcing of tender consciences," Parliament replied brusquely that "a schismatical conscience was not a tender conscience," and went to work with a will.

Bunyan had the honor not only of being one of the first sufferers under the new law forbidding unlicensed preaching, but of suffering from it before it was actually passed!

His preaching from 1658-1660 had aroused increasing attention from the authorities in his neighborhood and one of the sermons which was published under the title of *The Rich Man and Lazarus* survives to show us why. It is easy to imagine the attitude a magistrate who was also a large landlord would take to such passages as this one, preached in the year of Cromwell's death:

> Oh, what red lines will there be against all those rich ungodly landlords that so keep under their poor tenants that they dare not go out to hear the word for fear that their rent should be raised or they turned out of their houses. Think on this, you drunken rich, and scornful landlords; think on this, you mad brained blasphemous husbands, that are against the godly and chaste conversation of your wives; also you that hold your servants so hard to it that you will not spare them time to hear the Word, unless it will be where and when your lusts will let you . . . the rich man cries to "scrubbed beggarly Lazarus": "What shall I dishonor my fair sumptuous and gay house with such a creephedge as he?" The Lazaruses are not allowed to warn them of the wrath to come, because they are not gentlemen, because they cannot with Pontius Pilate speak Hebrew, Greek and Latin. Nay, they must not, shall not, speak to them, and all because of this.

Before Parliament had actually passed any law against unlicensed preachers, although they had already ordered the compulsory use of the established Common Prayer Book in all regular church services, and were obviously intending to forbid any irregular ones, the neighborhood magistrate had issued a warrant for the arrest of "One Bunyan of Bedford, tinker."

On November 12, 1660, when he arrived at a friend's farmhouse where he had promised to preach, Bunyan's host warned him of the warrant, and urged him to dismiss the meeting being, as Bunyan said, "more afraid of me, than of himself, for he knew better than I what spirit they [the magistrates] were of, living by them."

Bunyan goes on to say:

> After I walked into the close, where I somewhat seriously considering the matter, this came into my mind: That I had shewed myself hearty and couragious in my preaching, and had, blessed be Grace, made it my business to encourage others; therefore thought I, if I should now run, and make an escape, it will be of a very ill savour in the country. For what will my weak and newly converted brethren think of it? But that I was not so strong in deed, as I was in word. Also I feared that if I should run now there was a warrant out for me, I might by so doing make them afraid to stand, when great words only should be spoken to them. Besides I thought, that seeing God of his mercy should chuse me to go upon the forlorn hope in this country; that is, to be the first, that should be opposed, for the Gospel; if I should fly, it might be a discouragement to the whole body that might follow after. And further, I thought the world thereby would take occasion at my cowardliness, to have blasphemed the Gospel, and to have had some ground to suspect worse of me and my profession, than I deserved. These things, with others considered by me, I came in again to the house, with a full resolution to keep the meeting, and not to go away, though I could have been gone about an hour before the officer apprehended me; but I would not; for I was resolved to see the utmost of what they could say or do unto me: For blessed be the Lord, I knew of no evil that I had said or done. And so, as aforesaid, I begun the meeting: But being prevented by the constable's coming in with his warrant to take me, I could not proceed: But before I went away, I spake some few words of counsel and encouragement to the people, declaring to them, that they see we was prevented of our opportunity to speak and hear the word of God, and was like to suffer for the same: desiring them that they should not be discouraged. . . .

Arrested, he was brought before the magistrate who had, perhaps, some qualms at the legality of his action since he arranged for a number of people, including a lawyer and a clergyman, to argue with Bunyan in an attempt to secure his promise that if released he would not again attempt to preach.

Bunyan naturally refused to make such a promise, and entered on several interesting debates, of which he wrote a detailed account in his *Relation of Imprisonment*.

Although, as he correctly indicates, he won the debates, he lost the argument, being remanded to jail for seven weeks until the next quarter session meeting of the county court.

At the trial he continued the argument with the members of the bench who finally declared that by arguing, he had confessed his guilt, and sentenced him to three months imprisonment; after this, if there were another similar offense, he would be banished and, if again found in the realm, hanged.

The illegality of his trial was compounded when at the end of three months, on his refusal to promise that he would, if released, refrain from preaching, he was simply kept in jail with no opportunity to commit a second offense, until such time as he might change his mind!

Although he knew nothing of his legal rights and had no way to enforce them, he directed a number of energetic attempts, carried out with extraordinary courage and spirit by his young wife, to secure a hearing. His own relation gives us a remarkably objective account of her final attempt.

> Now at that assizes, because I would not leave any possible means unattempted that might be lawful; I did, by my wife, present a petition to the Judges three times, that I might be heard, and that they would impartially take my case into consideration.
>
> The first time my wife went, she presented it to Judge *Hales,* who very mildly received it at her hand, telling her that he would do her and me the best good he could; but he feared, he said, he could do none. The next day again, least they should, through the multitude of business forget me, we did throw another petition into the coach to Judge *Twisdon;* who, when he had seen it, snapt her up, and angrily told her that I was a convicted person, and could not be released, unless I would promise to preach no more, etc.
>
> Well, after this, she yet again presented another to Judge *Hales* as he sate on the bench, who, as it seemed, was willing to give her audience. Only Justice *Chester* being present, stept up and said, that I was convicted in the court, and that I was a hot spirited fellow (or words to that purpose) whereat

he waved it, and did not meddle therewith. But yet, my wife being encouraged by the High Sheriff, did venture once more into their presence (as the poor widow did to the unjust Judge) to try what she could do with them for my liberty, before they went forth of the town. The place where she went to them, was to the *Swan Chamber*, where the two Judges, and many Justices and Gentry of the country, was in company together. She then coming into the chamber with a bashed face, and a trembling heart, began her errand to them in this manner.

Woman. My Lord, (directing herself to Judge *Hales*) I make bold to come once again to your Lordship to know what may be done with my husband.

Judge Hales. To whom he said, Woman, I told thee before I could do thee no good; because they have taken that for a conviction which thy husband spoke at the sessions: And unless there be something done to undo that, I can do thee no good.

Woman. My Lord, said she, he is kept unlawfully in prison, they clap'd him up before there were any proclamation against the meetings; the indictment also is false: Besides, they never asked him whether he was guilty or no; neither did he confess the indictment.

One of the Justices. Then one of the Justices that stood by, whom she knew not, said, My Lord, he was lawfully convicted.

Wom. It is false, said she; for when they said to him, do you confess the indictment? He said only this, that he had been at several meetings, both where there was preaching the word, and prayer, and that they had God's presence among them.

Judge Twisdon. Whereat Judge *Twisdon* answered very angrily, saying, what you think we can do what we list; your husband is a breaker of the peace, and is convicted by the law, etc. Whereupon Judges *Hales* called for the Statute Book.

Wom. But said she, my Lord, he was not lawfully convicted.

Chester. Then Justice *Chester* said, my Lord, he was lawfully convicted.

Wom. It is false, said she; it was but a word of discourse that they took for a conviction (as you heard before.)

Chester. But it is recorded, woman, it is recorded, said Justice *Chester*. As if it must be of necessity true because it was recorded. With which words he often endeavoured to stop her mouth, having no other argument to convince her, but it is recorded, it is recorded.

Wom. My Lord, said she, I was a-while since at *London*, to see if I could get my husband's liberty, and there I spoke with my Lord Barkwood, one of the house of Lords, to whom

I delivered a petition, who took it of me and presented to some of the rest of the house of Lords, for my husband's releasement; who, when they had seen it, they said, that they could not release him, but had committed his releasement to the Judges, at the next assizes. This he told me; and now I come to you to see if any thing may be done in this business, and you give neither releasement nor relief. To which they gave her no answer, but made as if they heard her not.

Chest. Only Justice *Chester* was often up with this, He is convicted, and it is recorded.

Woman. If it be, it is false, said she.

Chest. My Lord, said Justice *Chester*, he is a pestilent fellow, there is not such a fellow in the country again.

Twis. What, will your husband leave preaching? If he will do so, then send for him.

Wom. My Lord, said she, he dares not leave preaching, as long as he can speak.

Twis. See here, what should we talk any more about such a fellow? Must he do what he lists? He is a breaker of the peace.

Wom. She told him again, that he desired to live peaceably, and to follow his calling, that his family might be maintained; and moreover said, my Lord, I have four small children, that cannot help themselves, of which one is blind, and have nothing to live upon, but the charity of good people.

Hales. Hast thou four children? said Judge Hales; thou art but a young woman to have four children.

Wom. My Lord, said she, I am but mother-in-law to them, having not been married to him yet full two years. Indeed I was with child when my husband was first apprehended: But being young and unaccustomed to such things, said she, I being smayed at the news, fell into labour, and so continued for eight days, and then was delivered, but my child died.

Hales. Whereat, he looking very soberly on the matter said, Alas poor woman!

Twis. But Judge *Twisdon* told her, that she made poverty her cloak; and said, moreover, that he understood, I was maintained better by running up and down a preaching, than by following my calling.

Hales. What is his calling? said Judge *Hales.*

Answer. Then some of the company that stood by, said, A Tinker, my Lord.

Wom. Yes, said she, and because he is a Tinker, and a poor man; therefore he is despised, and cannot have justice.

Hales. Then Judges *Hales* answered, very mildly, saying, I tell thee, woman, seeing it is so, that they have taken what thy husband spake, for a conviction; thou must either apply thyself to the King, or sue out his pardon, or get a writ of error.

Chest. But when Justice *Chester* heard him give her this

counsel; and especially (as she supposed) because he spoke of a writ of error, he chaffed, and seemed to be very much offended; saying, my Lord, he will preach and do what he lists.

Wom. He preacheth nothing but the word of God, said she.

Twis. He preach the word of God! said *Twisdon* (and withal, she thought he would have struck her) he runneth up and down, and doth harm.

Wom. No, my Lord, said she, it's not so, God hath owned him, and done much good by him.

Twis. God! said he, his doctrine is the doctrine of the Devil.

Wom. My Lord, said she, when the righteous judge shall appear, it will be known, that his doctrine is not the doctrine of the Devil.

Twis. My Lord, said he, to Judge *Hales*, do not mind her, but send her away.

Hales. Then said Judge *Hales*, I am sorry, woman, that I can do thee no good; thou must do one of these three things aforesaid, namely: either to apply thyself to the King, or sue out his pardon, or get a writ of error; but a writ of error will be cheapest.

Wom. At which *Chester* again seemed to be in a chaffe, and put off his hat, and as she thought, scratched his head for anger: But when I saw, said she, that there was no prevailing to have my husband sent for, though I often desired them that they would send for him, that he might speak for himself, telling them, that he could give them better satisfaction than I could, in what they demanded of him; with several other things, which now I forget; only this I remember, that though I was somewhat timerous at my first entrance into the chamber, yet before I went out, I could not but break forth into tears, not so much because they were so hard-hearted against me, and my husband, but to think what a sad account such poor creatures will have to give at the coming of the Lord, when they shall there answer for all things whatsoever they have done in the body, whether it be good, or whether it be bad.

So, when I departed from them, the book of Statute was brought, but what they said of it, I know nothing at all, neither did I hear any more from them.

On these grounds Bunyan was kept in jail for the next six years, knowing that he could at any time secure freedom by giving up his stand for free speech. He said that the parting from his wife and children:

hath often been to me in this place, as the pulling the Flesh from my Bones; and that not only because I am somewhat

too too fond of these great Mercies, but also because I should
have often brought to my mind the many hardships, miseries
and wants that my poor Family was like to meet with, should
I be taken from them, *especially my poor blind Child*, who
lay nearer my heart then all I had besides; O the thoughts of
the hardship I thought my blind one might go under, would
break my heart to pieces.

Poor Child! thought I, what sorrow art thou like to have
for thy Portion in this World? Thou must be beaten, must
beg, suffer hunger, cold, nakedness, and a thousand Calamities,
though I cannot now endure the Wind should blow upon thee:
But yet recalling my self, thought I, I must venture you all
with God, though it goeth to the quick to leave you; O, I saw
in this condition, I was as a man who was pulling down his
House upon the head of his Wife and Children; yet thought I,
I must do it, I must do it: . . .

His ignorance of the law and, indeed, the authorities' indifference to it, also made him fear at first that if wearied by his ob-
duracy they might release him by way of the scaffold. He describes
these not unreasonable fears:

I will tell you of a pretty business; I was once above all
the rest, in a very sad and low Condition for many Weeks, at
which time also I being a young Prisoner, and not acquainted
with the Laws, had this lay much upon my Spirit, That my
Imprisonment might end at the Gallows for ought that I could
tell; now therefore Satan laid hard at me to beat me out of
heart, by suggesting thus unto me; But how if when you come
indeed to die you should be in this Condition; that is, as not
to savour the things of God, nor to have any evidence upon
your Soul for a better state hereafter? (for indeed at that time
all the things of God were hid from my Soul.)

Wherefore when I at first began to think of this, it was a
great trouble to me: for I thought with my self, that in the
Condition I now was in, I was not fit to die, neither indeed
did think I could if I should be called to it: Besides, I thought
with my self, if I should make a scrambling shift to clamber
up the Ladder, yet I should either with quaking or other
symptoms of fainting, give occasion to the Enemy to reproach
the Way of God and his People, for their Timorousness. This
therefore lay with great trouble upon me, for methought I was
ashamed to die with a pale Face, and tottering Knees, for such
a Cause as this.

Wherefore I pray'd to God that he would comfort me, and
give me strength to do and suffer what he should call me to;
yet no comfort appear'd, but all continued hid: I was also at
this time so really possessed with the thought of death, that

oft I was as if I was on the Ladder with the Rope about my
Neck; only this was some Encouragement to me, I thought I
might now have an opportunity to speak my last words to a
Multitude which I thought would come to see me die; and
thought I, if it must be, if God will but convert one Soul by
my very last words, I shall not count my Life thrown away,
nor lost.

But however short life might be, it was necessary to sustain it,
and Bunyan soon found a way to contribute to the support of his
family by learning to make shoe laces. Although the physical condition of the jail was bad, the routine was, according to our notions,
an informal one. Often as many as thirty-five or forty dissenters
were housed there, as well as more ordinary felons and, in private
rooms above, a number of debtors. Bunyan immediately resumed
his unlicensed preaching and soon hit on a way of earning money
for his family by writing and publishing his sermons, or the more
elaborate religious pamphlets which grew out of them.

In 1661 his first such publication, a book of verse called *Prison
Meditations,* appeared. Bunyan is a real poet only in prose, but
his words were always direct and forceful and often arresting by
the very boldness and simplicity of their images. For example:

> The Truth and I, were both here cast
> Together, and we do
> Lie arm in arm, and so hold fast
> Each other; this is true.

In 1662 the second, *Praying in the Spirit,* and in 1663 the third,
Christian Behaviour, both sermons in prose, contained many such
charming and unself-conscious illustrations as:

> True Christians are like the several flowers in a garden,
> that have upon each of them the dew of heaven, which, being
> shaken with the wind, they let fall their dew at each others
> roots, whereby they are jointly nourished, and become nour-
> ishers of each other.

This plague of militant religious tracts by Bunyan and many
like him led the Restoration's chief licenser, Roger L'Estrange, to
urge in 1663 that all censors carefully examine and if possible
destroy the works of these "great masters of the Popular Stile"
which "strike home to the capacity and Humour of the Multitude."

In 1664 Bunyan published two books, *One Thing Needful,* and

The Blessing and the Curse, and in 1665 the better known *Holy City* and *The Resurrection of the Dead.*

In 1666 we have the now classic, spiritual autobiography, quoted above, *Grace Abounding,* which concludes in its first edition: "I was had home to prison again, where I have now lain above five years and a quarter, waiting to see what God will suffer these men to do with me."

In 1666 the disorganization of the prisons due to the great plague forced the discharge of many prisoners whose sentences had not yet expired, and also released Bunyan who was not really under sentence at all.

However, he immediately accepted an invitation to address his brethren, and six months later was again arrested and, this time legally, returned to jail.

The sixth edition of *Grace Abounding,* has a slightly altered conclusion which states that he has "lain now complete twelve years waiting to see what God will suffer these men to do with me."

Either physical illness or discouragement kept Bunyan from much writing during the next six years, and he published only *A Confession of Faith* and *A Defense of the Doctrine of Justification by Faith* during that entire period.

In 1672 Charles II issued a Declaration of Indulgence since, as he truly said, "the sad experience of twelve years—showed . . . very little fruit . . . of the forceable courses." A further reason was that, as he did not say, he had just concluded a secret treaty with Louis XIV binding himself to announce his conversion to Catholicism as soon as practicable, and was therefore anxious to undermine the monopoly of the Church of England.

Bunyan was, immediately upon his release, chosen pastor of his fellowship which had maintained itself, often in hiding, and had met with surprising regularity in secret, during the years of persecution.

When, that May 1672, lay preachers were admitted to license, Bunyan applied for such a license not only for himself and the large barn his congregation had managed to purchase, but for twenty-four other lay preachers and thirty other similar buildings which it was, thenceforward, evidently a part of his duty to supervise.

During the next three years he and Elizabeth had two children. His older sons by his first wife were now assisting him as "braziers" and he continues to sign himself so, although he probably spent little time personally at the forge. In addition to preaching and church organization, he published three more religious works, one of them an attempt to eliminate nonessentials and reconcile the different Baptist sects by proving *Differences in Judgment about Water Baptism No Bar to Communion.*

In 1675 the temporary revocation of licenses and a renewed attempt to silence the nonconformists again led Bunyan to jail, and there he began a parable for the religious instruction of simple folk—a book called *The Pilgrim's Progress.*

This begins conventionally enough as a dream in which the narrator tells us he "saw a man clothed with rags, standing in a certain place, with his face from his own house, a book in his hand, and a great burden upon his back. I looked, and saw him open the book and read therein; and, as he read, he wept, and trembled; and not being able longer to contain, he brake out with a lamentable cry, saying 'What shall I do?'"

The man is, of course, the Pilgrim; his book is the Bible; and the burden on his back is the weight of worldly cares and concerns. (Not, in the ordinary sense of the word, sins. Thrift and ambition are as likely to find a place therein as profligacy or dissipation.)

The formal pattern of the allegory that is to follow is already clearly implied. Aroused to the evils of the world in which he lives, Christian attempts to convince his wife, children and neighbors of the dangers which threaten them, and to enlist their companionship in his search for salvation.

> O my dear wife, said he, and you the children of my bowels, I, your dear friend, am in myself undone by reason of a burden that lieth hard upon me; moreover, I am for certain informed that this our city will be burned with fire from heaven, in which fearful overthrow both myself, with thee my wife, and you my sweet babes, shall miserably come to ruin, except (the which yet I see not) some way of escape can be found, whereby we may be delivered. At this his relations were sore amazed; not for that they believed that what he had said to them was true, but because they thought that some frenzy distemper had got into his head; therefore, it drawing towards night, and they hoping that sleep might settle his brains, with all haste they got him to bed. But the night was as troublesome to him as the day; wherefore, instead of sleeping, he spent it in sighs and tears. So, when the morning was come, they would know how he did. He told them, Worse and worse: he also set to talking to them again: but they began to be hardened. They also thought to drive away his distemper by

harsh and surly carriages to him; sometimes they would deride, sometimes they would chide, and sometimes they would quite neglect him.

Finally he decides to start out alone but at the last minute a friend, Pliable, is so impressed by the strength of his conviction that he offers to go with him. They soon stumble and fall into the slough of Despond, at which Pliable is discouraged and turns back. Christian bravely struggles on but is persuaded to turn off from the right path by Mr. Worldly Wiseman who assures him that a Mr. Legality nearby can show him a much easier way to get rid of his burden. By the help of Mr. Evangelist he eventually gets back to the main road, and is overtaken by a neighbor, Faithful, who had set out later but had made better progress. The two continue together through many adventures, including the great struggle with Apollyon, ruler of this world, who claims them as his subjects and refuses to accept their allegiance to God.

After many other experiences they try to pass through Vanity Fair where both are arrested as foreign agitators. Brought to trial before a lord of the fair, Judge Hate-Good, Faithful is condemned and tortured to death. Christian, however, escapes and continues on his way, assisted by a new friend, Hopeful, who has been converted by Faithful's martyrdom. Although the book should be read as a whole, this chapter alone gives an excellent idea of the amazing contemporary quality it still holds for us today.

They hold to the high road despite many difficulties and dangers but finally, their feet being weary and the road growing hourly more hard and rocky, they are tempted to take a by-path through a pleasant meadow which seems to follow the same general route. It soon diverges, however, and they are warned barely in time by the fate of Mr. Vain-Confidence who, rushing ahead, falls into a deep pit and is dashed to pieces.

Unable to win back to the right road before nightfall, they are captured by Giant Despair and thrown into the dungeon of Doubting Castle. Here they are almost driven to suicide, but again escape and go on their way, posting a warning to help other pilgrims avoid their mistakes. At last they reach the Celestial City, which they enter to enjoy eternal life in the fellowship of the blessed.

Only a small part of the book's real value lies in this familiar framework, although it is extraordinary how much the very fabric of our daily speech has been affected by the language and incidents of Bunyan's classic pilgrimage. But the great literary interest of *Pilgrim's Progress*, the most important forerunner of the English novel, lies in its rich variety of concrete situations, living characters, and vital experiences. The profound psychological insight with which many of the minor characters as well as the hero himself are realized is truly extraordinary. This is all the more amazing when one considers the rapidity of the narrative and the specific allegory it maintains throughout.

For while its central symbol of life as a pilgrimage and man as a pilgrim gives the story much of its emotional power and universality, it also creates certain special problems, and a fundamental contradiction which Bunyan triumphantly ignores, and thus overcomes, without solving it. Superficially the book accepts the idea that this world is merely an ante-chamber through which the soul must pass on the way to everlasting bliss or damnation. Actually it brings us just the opposite message. As Lindsay says:

> The impression conveyed by the allegory is the exact opposite of what it literally professes. The phantasms of good and evil become the real world; and in encountering them the Pilgrim lives through the life that Bunyan had known in definite place and time. The pattern of his experience, the fall and the resolute rising-up, the loss and the finding, the resistance and the overcoming, the despair and the joy, the dark moaning valleys and the singing in the places of the flowers— it is the pattern of Bunyan's strenuous life. There are comrades and enemies, stout-hearts and cravens, men who care only for the good of fellowship and men of greed and fear; and they are the men of contemporary England.

Such a chapter as the trial at "Vanity Fair" will give some idea of the contemporary impact of Bunyan's experiences and of the vivid racy narrative style he had developed, but, like a novel, the book must be read as a whole to be fully appreciated.

It was immediately successful, selling three editions in less than a year and over 100,000 copies before Bunyan's death! It has since been translated into more than 120 languages and has certainly been read by more people than any other single book except the Bible.

But although its popular success and circulation among the bakers, weavers, cobblers, tailors, tinkers, shepherds, ploughmen, dairy maids, seamstresses, and servant girls was immediate, its critical reputation and academic acclaim are much more recent.

In the eighteenth century Dean Swift and Dr. Johnson were, significantly, the only men of any note who had a good word to say for it. Swift wrote that he had been more confirmed and entertained by a few pages in the *Pilgrim's Progress* than by a long discussion upon the will and the intellect, and Johnson compared passages in it to Spenser and Dante, and told Boswell it was one of the only three books which readers wished longer.

But Addison cited Bunyan to prove that even the most despicable of writers had their admirers; the sympathetic Cowper at the end of the eighteenth century hinted a personal liking for the Pilgrim he had met in his childhood but concluded:

> I name thee not, lest so despised a name
> Should move a sneer at thy deserved fame

and Burke spoke of "degrading a book to the style of Pilgrim's Progress."

On the other hand Burns and Blake were both intimately acquainted with this "prose epic of puritanism" and Blake often borrows its very phraseology in his attacks on the Law as opposed to the free grace of the spirit, vouchsafed to those who belong to a true fellowship. Fielding betrays his knowledge of it in more than one passage, and Dickens openly revels in its rich physical detail and high-hearted conflict.

The best of the later academic critics have a sensitive perception of one part of its appeal, its psychological truth and ethical realism, while they ignore or distort its more fundamental impact.

For example the nineteenth century French critic, Taine, says:

> Protestantism . . . could not sing the battles and works of God, but the temptations and salvation of the soul. At the time of Christ came the poems of cosmogony; at the time of Milton, the confessions of psychology. At the time of Christ, each imagination produced a hierarchy of supernatural beings, and a history of the world; at the time of Milton, every heart recorded the series of its upliftings, and the history of grace. Learning and reflection led Milton to a metaphysical poem which was not the natural offspring of the age, whilst inspiration and ignorance revealed to Bunyan the psychological narrative which suited the age, and the great man's genius was feebler than the tinker's simplicity.

This analysis, perceptive as it is in incidentals, ignores both the very substantial difference in class position between Milton and

Bunyan and the small but significant lapse of time between the conception and actual beginning of *Paradise Lost* in the middle fifties, and the creation of the *Pilgrim's Progress* a full generation later.

Milton was, as we have seen, a leading member of that class which was actually responsible for the revolution, and despite his personal disappointment there was nothing at all unreasonable in his envisioning the re-creation of heaven and earth with the assurance of one who has played an active and effective part in such an undertaking.

Bunyan, on the contrary, was a dispossessed member of the lower class whose hopes had been aroused and whose energies had been used in the course of a revolution which, as yet, had only increased the hardships and miseries of their lot.

And although there may have been in his case, as of course there was, to a much greater extent in Milton's, some glimpse of the more profound eventual significance of the bourgeois revolution which England was the first nation in the modern world to complete, yet Bunyan came to full maturity only after the seemingly final defeat of those hopes.

The enormous emotional force of his great work in its very opening scene is derived not simply as Taine implies, from his psychological insight or even his ethical concern, but depends largely on his ability to convey the heart sickness of an enthusiast in an altogether conventional society—the burning indignation of a man who hears the words which are the breath of life not merely denied but, even worse, mouthed and ignored by those whose superficial acceptance is a mockery of the truth.

Bernard Shaw has keenly observed what generations of religious teachers have apparently overlooked when he says of *Pilgrim's Progress*:

> Bunyan's perception that righteousness is filthy rags, his scorn for Mr. Legality in the village of Morality, his defiance of the Church as the supplanter of religion, his insistence on courage as the virtue of virtues, his estimate of the career of the conventionally respectable and sensible Worldly Wiseman as no better at bottom than the life and death of Mr. Badman: all this is expressed by Bunyan in the terms of a tinker's theology. . . . Bunyan makes no attempt to present his pilgrims as more sensible or better conducted than Mr. Worldly Wiseman. Mr. W. W.'s worst enemies, as Mr. Embezzler, Mr. Never-go-to-Church-on-Sunday, Mr. Bad Form, Mr. Murderer, Mr. Burglar, Mr. Co-respondent, Mr. Blackmailer, Mr. Cad,

Mr. Drunkard, Mr. Labour Agitator, and so forth, can read the Pilgrim's Progress without finding a word said against them: whereas the respectable people who snub them and put them in prison, such as Mr. W. W. himself and his young friend Civility; Formalist and Hypocrisy; Wildhead, Inconsiderate and Pragmatick (who were clearly young university men of good family and high feeding); that brisk lad Ignorance, Talkative, By-Ends of Fairspeech and his mother-in-law Lady Feigning, and other reputable gentlemen and citizens, catch it very severely. Even Little Faith, though he gets to heaven at last, is given to understand that it served him right to be mobbed by the brothers Faint Heart, Mistrust and Guilt, all three recognized members of respectable society and veritable pillars of the law. The whole allegory is a consistent attack on morality and respectability, without a word that one can remember against vice and crime.

Bunyan was so concerned about the wickedness of the lawmakers and so unconcerned about the wickedness of the lawbreakers because he realized that the laws themselves are grounded in undemocratic power and sanctify oppression, and that by far the greater social evil is the work of those who live on them rather than that of those who die under them.

This is the measure of Bunyan's greatness and the secret of his appeal to generations of less religious fighters for freedom. He knew that the power of the class state was the power of the oppressor, and that there was no essential merit in obeying its laws even when they were called the ten commandments.

Bunyan would have spoken with more indignation and less cynicism but he was in full accord with the anonymous satirist who said, of the enclosures:

> The law locks up the man or woman
> Who steals the goose from off the common;
> But leaves the man or woman loose
> Who steals the common from the goose.

He does say in a hundred different passionate ways what the realistic and dispassionate dissenter Defoe announced a century later:

> Knowledge of things would teach them every hour
> That Law is but a heathen word for Power.

But unlike his gifted contemporary, the Quaker leader, George Fox, who wandered staring and rapt about the countryside, Bunyan was not, at heart, an anarchist or even an individualist.

During the worst of his early mental struggles he never lost his practical sense of the necessities of life, carried on his daily tinker's work and maintained his family. His search for a meaningful and dedicated way of life was also a search for an organized community with which to share it, and nothing is more common in his writing than such an emphasis on earthly companionship as: "Yea, I could be content to live and die with those people that have the grace of God in their souls."

One of the most moving of his vivid allegories is the dream he relates in *Grace Abounding*:

> About this time, the state and happiness of these poor people at *Bedford* was thus, *in a kind of Vision*, presented to me: I saw, as if they were set on the Sunny-side of some high Mountain, there refreshing themselves with the pleasant beams of the Sun, while I was shivering and shrinking in the Cold, afflicted with Frost, Snow and dark Clouds: Methought also, betwixt me and them, I saw a Wall that did compass about this Mountain; now through this Wall my Soul did greatly desire to pass; concluding, that if I could, I would go even into the very midst of them, and there also comfort my self with the heat of their Sun.

This realistic unmystical consciousness of other people is, as we have noted, one of the reasons for the tremendous appeal of *Pilgrim's Progress* which, using the traditional parable form, brings it so much closer to reality that it trembles on the verge of fiction.

After the publication of several further religious pamphlets, Bunyan in 1680, wrote another story *The Life and Death of Mr. Badman*. The title indicates the book's intention but belies its interest. Again we have real characters sketched in with quick incisive strokes, and recognize a far from conventional or superficial observation. The growing degradation of women in the fashionable literature of the period is highlighted by the wealthy widower's refusal to consider remarriage for: "Who would keep a cow of his own that can have a quart of milk for a penny?"

Bunyan's own idea of woman's position, like Milton's, accepts the general religious assumption of her probable inferiority, but also like Milton's, allows for exceptions. For example, Mr. Badman's good wife, when he tries to influence her conduct and undermine her convictions, says:

> I have a husband, but also a God; my God has commanded me, and that upon pain of damnation, to be a continual wor-

shipper of him, and that in the way of my own appointments. I have a husband but also a soul, and my soul ought to be more unto me than all the world besides.

And, far from the hypocritical denial of sex we associate with a later Victorian "puritanism," Bunyan tolerantly remarks of her error in having accepted Mr. Badman's courtship:

> As to his person, there she was fittest to judge, because she was to be the person pleased, but as to his godliness, there the Word was the fittest judge, and they that could best understand it, because God was therein to be pleased.

Another more conscious and complete opposition between the views of Bunyan and his class-conscious brethren, and those of more respectable Protestant ministers was their attitude to worldly success. In what was to become the accepted Protestant view the Lord, far from chastising those whom he loveth, signifies his love by gifts and favors so that temporal success may be taken as an almost infallible sign of eternal election. Respectable Protestantism held that the poor probably deserve damnation in this world because, whether by predestination or thriftlessness, they are bound to it in the next.

Bunyan, on the other hand, felt that while some of the wealthy might be converted, yet on the whole the accumulation of money was ordinarily accomplished: "by hook and by crook, as we say, by swearing lying, cozening, stealing, covetousness, extortion."

In Mr. Badman he arraigns the wickedness of those who take advantage of the poor, overcharging them because they cannot travel to market or buy in large quantities, as well as of those who hoard grain, and so raise its price.

He consistently contradicts such typical pronouncements from contemporary pulpits as: "Grace in a poor man is grace, and 'tis beautiful, but grace in a rich man is more conspicuous, more useful," and "Faith is a successful grace and hath a promise of prospering."

For example, in one of his later printed sermons, *The Greatness of the Soul* (1682), he builds on a text from Mark:

> For following of me is not like following of some other masters. The wind sits always on my face, and the foaming rage of the sea of this world, and the proud and lofty waves

thereof do continually beat upon the sides of the bark or ship
that myself, my cause, and followers are in; he therefore that
will not run hazards, and that is afraid to venture a drowning,
let him not set foot into this vessel.

And in another, *The Jerusalem Sinner Saved*, which appeared
in the year of his death, he asks emphatically about Christ:

> Why should he so easily take a denial of the great ones
> that were the grandeur of the world, and struggle so hard for
> hedge-creepers and highway men . . . ?

Again, while he necessarily accepted the idea of a frugal hard
working life it was never, for him, precisely the ideal which the
preachers from above tried to make it. In a posthumous publication
Paul's Departure and Crown, he says:

> A horse that is loaded with gold and pearls all day may yet
> have a foul stable and a galled back at night. And woe be to
> him that increaseth that which is not his, and that ladeth him-
> self with thick clay.

And in his description of *The House of God* in 1688, he says that
all must work there but:

> The work is short, the wages last forever,
> The work like us, the wages like the giver.

To return, however, to *Mr. Badman* there is one kind of sinner
whom he there vituperates more severely than any other, and that,
interestingly enough, is a latter day saint, the government spy or
informer.

Five years later in *The Pharisee and the Publican* he remarks:

> . . . the Publican was counted vile and base and reck-
> oned among the worst of men, even as our informers and bum-
> baliffs are with us at this day.

And here, in 1680, he gives at full length two "true stories" of the
deservedly horrible fate which was visited on wretches who surpassed even the villainous Mr. Badmen in the evil he did not dare
to do.

In our town there was one W. S. a man of a very wicked life; and he, when there seemed to be countenance given to it, would needs turn informer. Well, so he did, and was as diligent in his business as most of them could be; he would watch of nights, climb trees, and range the woods of days, if possible, to find out the meeters, for then they were forced to meet in the fields. . . . Well, after he had gone on like a bedlam in his course awhile, and had done some mischiefs to the people, he was stricken by the hand of God, and that in this manner: (1) . . . (2) . . . (3) . . . (4) . . . In that posture . . . half a year or thereabouts. . . . But after that he also walked about until God had made a sufficient spectacle of his judgment for his sin, and then on a sudden he was stricken and died miserably; and so there was an end of him and his doings.

I will tell you of another. About four miles from St. Neots there was a gentleman had a man, and he would needs be an informer, and a lusty young man he was. Well, an informer he was and did much distress some people, and had perfected his informations so effectually against some, that there was nothing further to do but for the constables to make distress on the people, that he might have the money or goods, and, as I heard, he hastened them to do it. Now while he was in the heat of his work . . . a dog, some say his own dog, took distaste at something, and bit his master by the leg . . . that wound was his death and that a dreadful one too. . . .

But what need I instance in particular persons, when the judgment of God against this kind of people was made manifest, I think I may say, if not in all, yet in most of the counties in England where such poor creatures were? But I would if it had been the will of God, that neither I nor anybody else could tell you more of these stories; true stories that are neither lie nor romance.

In 1680 occurred a flurry of exciting political events—intrigues stemming from a number of indirectly related causes. Among these were Parliament's attempt to prevent the Catholic James' being named as eventual successor to his brother, the fraudulent discovery of a "Popish Plot" to murder the king and restore the Catholic Church, and Charles II's conclusion of a secret treaty with the king of France, which guaranteed him a sufficient income to make him, personally, independent of Parliament. These all culminated in Charles' largely successful attempts to cancel the charters of such municipal corporations as Bedfordshire, replacing them by others which gave the throne virtual control of the county councils.

Those events shaped Bunyan's next book—a long and ambitious project, published in 1682—which he himself probably considered his major work.

The Holy War, like Pilgrim's Progress, begins with a well-established religious "similitude" or allegory. The city of Mansoul, built by Shaddai (a Hebrew name often used to indicate God), is attacked by the Diabolonians, briefly conquered by entrances forced at the city gates—Eye Gate, Ear Gate, and so forth—and rescued by the leadership of Emanuel (a name which the Fifth Monarchy Men and others often used to denote Jesus in his role as ruler of *earth* during the millenium).

In strictly Calvinist or Baptist terms this would be the end of the story but it is only the beginning of Bunyan's Holy War. For here too the embodiment of the myth becomes intrinsically important, and altogether alters its original significance.

Through the growing indifference of the prosperous godly, and through secret Diabolonians or half-Diabolonians left as citizens of the city, a new conquest, engineered from within, is achieved, which follows very closely the story of the internal defeat of the commonwealth. The major events of *The Holy War* deal with the eventual extirpation of these evil forces, the defense against future assaults, and the firm establishment of Emmanuel's kingdom on earth.

We have already mentioned Bunyan's unadvertised belief in some period—presumably the conventional thousand years—of millennial organization on earth. While there are few explicit statements on the matter, there are many such earlier references as those in *Prison Meditations*:

> Just thus it is, we suffer here
>   For him a little pain,
> Who, when he doth again appear,
>   Will with him let us reign.

In *The Holy City*, written in 1665, which somewhat anticipates the general outline of *The Holy War*, Bunyan said:

> For observe it, Christ hath not only obtained the kingdom of heaven for these that are his, when this world is ended, but hath also, as a reward for his sufferings, the whole world given into his hand; wherefore, as all the kings, and princes, and powers of this world have had their time to reign, and have glory in this world in the face of all, so Christ will have his time, at this day, to show who is "the only Potentate and Lord of Lords" 1.Ti:VI 15. At which day he will not only set up his kingdom in the midst of their kingdoms, as he doth now, but will set it up even upon the top of their kingdoms;

at which day there will not be a nation in the world but must bow to Jerusalem or perish.

In that work, too, as we have seen, he stressed the material nature of this ideal social establishment by denying that Christ would personally rule it, his spirit in the elect brethren being taken to represent him, and by even more strongly contradicting the belief that the new order would be of merely momentary or symbolic duration.

The charter granted by Emmanuel to Mansoul further emphasizes this anticipation of a physically based heaven on earth:

> I do give, grant and bestow upon them freely the world, and what is therein for their good, and they shall have that power over them as shall stand with the honour of my Father, my glory, and their comfort, yea I grant them the benefits of life and death and of things present and things to come.

The overwhelming success of *The Pilgrim's Progress* led Bunyan in 1684 to attempt a second part, popular enough in its time but not comparable to the original.

It deals with the pilgrimage of Christian's widow, children and neighbors, inspired by his example, and is chiefly interesting for the portrait of Roundhead warriors whom he must have known in his army service, like Mr. Greatheart, and Mr. Valiant who says after his last fight:

> My sword I give to him that shall succeed me in my pilgrimage, and my courage and skill to him that can get it. My marks and scars I carry with me, to be a witness for me, that I have fought his battles, who now shall be my rewarder.

It is interesting to note that Mr. Valiant's parents were evidently conventional Protestants who knew the duty of success and warned him not only that the way of the pilgrim was "a dangerous way, yea, the most dangerous way in the World," but also that "it was an idle Life, and if I myself were not inclined to Sloath and Laziness, I would never countenance a Pilgrim's condition."

It is also noteworthy that Bunyan here explicitly and prophetically denies the entire individualistic ethic of a competitive society since Mr. Greatheart and Mr. Valiant slow their pace to accommodate not only women and children but also especially

weak or timorous brethren, who have been outstripped by former
pilgrims and left to make their difficult way unassisted.

When the cavalcade finally arrives at the Delectable Mountains
the good Shepherds give them a particularly warm welcome,
saying:

> This is a comfortable Company, you are welcome to us,
> for we care for the *Feeble*, as for the *Strong*: our Prince has
> an Eye to what is done to the least of these. Therefore In-
> firmity must not be a block to our Entertainment. So they
> had them to the Palace Door, and then said unto them, Come
> in Mr. *Feeble-mind*, come in Mr. *Ready-to-halt*, come in Mr.
> *Despondency*, and Mrs. *Much-afraid* [his daughter]. *These* Mr.
> *Great-heart*, said the Shepherds to the Guide, we call in by
> Name, for that they are most subject to draw back; but as
> for you, and the rest that are *strong*, we leave you to your
> wonted Liberty. Then said Mr. *Great-heart*, This day I see
> that Grace doth shine in your Faces, and that you are my
> Lords Shepherds indeed; for that you have not *pushed* these
> Diseased neither with Side nor Shoulder, but have rather
> strewed their way into the Palace with Flowers, as you should.
> So the Feeble and Weak went in, and Mr. *Great-heart*,
> and the rest did follow. When they were also set down, the
> Shepherds said to those of the weakest sort, what is it that you
> would have? For said they, all things must be managed here,
> to the supporting of the weak, as well as to the warning of the
> Unruly.

A later nonconformist who was perhaps the most courageous
fighter for freedom on the English literary scene more than a century later, adopted as his motto poor Mr. Feeble's resolution:

> Other Brunts I also look for, but this I have resolved on,
> to wit, to *run* when I can, to *go* when I cannot *run*, and to
> *creep* when I cannot *go*.

All those who love Hazlitt must treasure the second part of *Pilgrim's Progress*, if for that quotation alone.

The next year, 1685, James II's accession to the throne caused
a renewed fear of prison sentences and heavy fines. Bunyan who
was now well-known not only in Bedfordshire but also in London,
where he frequently preached as the guest of some independent
congregation, was advised that it might be well, for his children's
sake if not his own, to be cautious. He replied that "their Heavenly

Father will provide what is necessary, and what is more than necessary is hurtful." His faith, however, was of that practical turn which had led Cromwell's army to "trust in God and keep their powder dry," and Bunyan assisted his children's heavenly father to keep them from want by executing a deed of gift, proof against fines, if not imprisonment, to his wife.

Fortunately James II, himself a Catholic, was set on securing general indulgence for Catholicism as a first step to reestablish the Catholic Church in England, and made no effort to enforce religious conformity.

The next year Bunyan wrote his most successful book in verse, *Country Rhimes for Children*, which contained seventy-four "similitudes." Two of the best are:

"The Hypocrite"

The Frog by nature is but damp and cold,
Her mouth is large, her belly much will hold,
She sits somewhat ascending, loves to be
Croaking in gardens, though unpleasantly.

The hypocrite is like unto this Frog,
And like as is the puppy to the dog.
He is of nature cold, his mouth is wide
To prate, and at true goodness to deride.
And though this world is that which he doth love,
He mounts his head as if he lived above,
And though he seeks in Churches for to croak,
He neither seeketh Jesus nor His Yoke.

"The Formalist"

Thou booby, says't thou nothing but Cuckoo?
The robin and the wren can that out do.
They to us play thorough their little throats
Not one, but sundry pretty tuneful notes.
But thou hast fellows, some like thee can do
Little but suck our eggs, and sing cuckoo.
. . . .
Since Cuckoos forward not our early spring
Nor help with notes to bring our harvest in,
And since while here, she only makes a noise
So pleasing unto none as girls and boys,
The Formalist we may compare her to,
For he doth suck our eggs and sing Cuckoo.

In 1687 political events took a peculiar turn. James II, finding the wealthy ministers and members of the Established Church altogether unwilling to consider any approach toward Catholicism, decided to enlist the aid of the heretofore persecuted dissenters in his campaign for a return to Rome and absolute monarchy.

He proclaimed a Declaration of Indulgence which went much further than Charles II's Declaration of 1672, since it not only suspended all penalties for nonconformity but also abolished religious "tests" or oaths for those appointed to political office.

He also made personal overtures to such leading nonconformists as Bunyan, hoping he could enlist their influence in the election of a parliament pledged to confirm these measures and any further ones he might propose.

Although Bunyan had suffered so seriously from the religious penal laws and had every reason to hate the Established Church and welcome its discomfiture, he saw with extraordinary clarity the whole import of these maneuvers, and subordinated his personal interests and even the immediate interests of his fellowship to defeat their more fundamentally reactionary opponent. An anonymous contemporary biographer, writing in 1692, gives us his first-hand account:

> During these things there were Regulations sent in to all Cities and Towns corporate, to new model the Government in the Magistracy, etc. by turning out some, and putting others; against this, Mr. Bunyan expressed his zeal with some wariness, as foreseeing the bad consequence that would attend it, and laboured with his Congregation to prevent their being imposed on in this kind, and when a great man in those days coming to Bedford, upon some such Errand, sent for him, as 'tis supposed to give him a place of publick trust, he would by no means come to him, but sent his Excuse.

While Bunyan's published work contains the required formal asserverations of loyalty toward the king, he was very strongly opposed to absolute monarchy and perhaps to all monarchy. There is the signature of a John Bunyan on a petition signed by a number of his coreligionists in Bedfordshire in 1653 asking Cromwell *not* to assume the crown.

In an *Exposition of the First Ten Chapters of Genesis* which was, perhaps deliberately, not published until after his death, he says: "It is the lot of Cain's brood, to be lords and rulers first, while Abel and his generation have their necks under persecution."

Again in reference to Nimrod in the same work we find:

> I am apt to think he was the first that in this new world
> sought after absolute monarchy . . . through the pride of his
> countenance he did scorn that others, or any, should be his
> equal: nay, could not be content till all made obeisance to
> him. He therefore would needs be the author and master of
> what religion he pleased; and would also subject the rest
> of his brethren thereto, by what ways his lusts thought best.
> Wherefore he began a fresh persecution.

Readers of *Pilgrim's Progress* will remember the attack of
Apollyon, who bears a certain family resemblance to the Stuarts,
on those who proclaimed their adherence to a heavenly rather than
an earthly ruler, and the pilgrim's assertion that he could not be
considered a traitor since his true allegiance was prior to any loyalty
oaths. In the later unpublished commentary on Genesis, Bunyan
more explicitly defends the seeming disingenuousness of holy men
in difficult political situations:

> Hence note, that a man is not to be counted an offender,
> how contrary soever he lieth, either in doctrine or practice,
> to men, if both [doctrine and practice] have the command of
> God. . . . This made Jeremiah, though he preached, That
> the city of Jerusalem should be burnt with fire, the king and
> people should go into captivity; yet stand upon his own vin-
> dication before his enemies, and plead his innocency against
> them that persecuted him. . . . Daniel also, though he did
> openly break the king's decree, and refused to stoop to his
> idolations and devilish demand; yet purged himself of both
> treason and sedition, and justifies his act as innocent and harm-
> less even in the sight of God.

A colleague of Bunyan's, had even more forthrightly defended
his speaking in parables, clear only to the initiated, by demanding:
"Must we counterfeit with you? . . . must we either speak in
Tropes and Figures? or else in Ropes and Faggots? or imprison-
ment at least?"
Tindall summarizes this attitude saying:

> That Bunyan cherished a deep and natural hatred of both
> king and government, like any normal Baptist of the time, is
> apparent from remarks scattered throughout his tracts, often
> next to professions of loyalty, which served to hide his real
> opinions from all but the elect and the inquisitive. . . . His
> hope of the conversion of some kings did not lessen his belief

in their present wickedness: he saw and detested the injustice of laws, jails, magistrates, and governors, between whom and the saints was a perpetual war. His denial of sedition was a denial of violence, not of propaganda against the government.

This is borne out by another posthumously published work, *Of Anti Christ, and of the Slaying of the Witnesses,* in which Bunyan even more explicitly indicates his belief, already glanced at in our discussion of *The Holy War,* that some kind of millennium will be established *on earth* when, for the last thousand years of the world's history, things will be rightly ordered here as well as in heaven. In this later unpublished work he seems even to intimate a hope that that millennial period of justice may arrive within an ordinary lifetime:

> God will have his primitive Church state set up in the world (even where Antichrist has set up his), wherefore, in order to do this, Antichrist must be pulled down, stick and stone; and then they that live to see it, will behold the new Jerusalem come down from heaven, as a bride adorned for her husband.

In 1688, just a few months before the then still unexpected "bloodless revolution" which forced James II to abdicate, and made William and Mary rulers of a constitutional monarchy, Bunyan died. He had caught a bad chill riding through forty miles of rain to London, and though he preached the sermon he had planned he died ten or twelve days later, at the end of August 1688.

His first biographer, Charles Doe, was a comb maker who had become acquainted with him some three years before his death and who a year later became a bookseller and finally a publisher because, as he tells us:

> In March, 1686, as I was reading Mr. Bunyan's Book "Saved by Grace," I thought certainly this is the best Book that was ever writ, or I read except the Bible, and then I remembered I had received a great deal of comfort in all of his Books. Some time after my assurance, and being under the sense of the peculiar Love of God, it came into my mind as I was upon my Stair-head what work I should do for God, and about the middle of the Stair I reckoned that to sell books was the best I could do, and by that time I came to the bottom I concluded to sell Mr. Bunyan's and so I began to sell Books

and have sold about 3,000 of Mr. Bunyan's, and also have been concerned in printing the following Books: The Works of Mr. John Bunyan in folio, and the "Heavenly Footman" by John Bunyan.

Elizabeth outlived him for only a year and a half, but all his children except the blind daughter, Mary, whose death had preceded his, survived for many years.

The enormous popularity of his books, or, rather, of his major book, we have already discussed, but its long critical depreciation and sudden glorification in the respectable nineteenth century merits a word of explanation. This has been best given by Lindsay, who concludes his analysis of Bunyan's reputation by saying:

> All that was most vital in the English masses was linked up with the dissenting struggle. Bunyan entered deep into the consciousness of the masses. They were all his Pilgrims accepting the toil and the trial because of the warm light of fellowship on the mountains of the future. They were building a house of fellowship, and Bunyan abode with them as the password of the faithful in a world of environing malignants. The glow in their hearts and the courage of their resistance they felt were owed to him more than to any other one man.

However, his acceptance by the upper classes:

> came at the moment when the class-struggle had sharpened to the point where *any* writer with religious professions became respectable; for the proletarian forces were steadily moving away from the religious formulation, being able to let their sense of unity flow into trade-unions and political agitation. Then was the ripe moment for discovering that the Bedford Tinker was a genius.

Bunyan's position in English literature has survived both denigration and sanctification. Unlike such more sophisticated allegories as *Don Quixote* and *Gulliver's Travels,* children, in enjoying the *Pilgrim's Progress,* appreciate the essential theme as well as the story. And adults, engaged in the same progress, find a more profound relevance in its pages as often as they return to it with a richer experience of life.

It is unfortunately true that today, among the growing number of young people who have not read *Pilgrim's Progress* in their childhood, there is often an impression that he is "old-fashioned religious stuff." But it takes hardly more than a paragraph of direct personal acquaintance with Bunyan to make us realize that his enemies are our enemies, his fight our fight, and his emotional fortitude a source of strength we cannot afford to ignore.

The Age of Reason

THE AUGUSTANS

The pleasures of dissipation are perhaps more limited than has sometimes been supposed, and "épater le bourgeoisie" can be an engrossing objective to writers, artists, or even wits, only in default of any vital alternative possibility. The healthy, rapidly expanding economy of late seventeenth century mercantile England had essentially too much to offer for the mores of the restoration to last long, even at court, and there were already many signs of a growing respectability and decorum even during the lifetime of the returned émigrés and their king.

The immorality of the stage had begun to shock many who could by no stretch of the imagination be called puritans, and the justice of their attacks was tacitly acknowledged by such leading playwrights as John Dryden and William Congreve. Dryden had stopped writing anything but translations long before his death in 1700, and Congreve, who lived until 1729, wrote practically nothing during the last twenty-five years of his life.

Although Dryden's name bulks large in many histories of English literature, his work is of little interest to most twentieth century readers.

His long so-called satirical poems—actually not satires but personal attacks of a burlesque or caricature nature on political opponents and literary rivals—and his frigid plays, of which the best known *All for Love* was hailed by his contemporaries and successors of the eighteenth century as a vastly improved and more civilized version of Shakespeare's *Antony and Cleopatra*, are today practically unread and, for most people, unreadable. Nevertheless, his unquestioned leadership of his own age, the great re-

spect of succeeding generations and his genuine, if limited, abilities
as a literary critic and as the originator of a clear forceful prose
make his name one that even a casual student of English literature
should know. His versatility in style, and convictions, are illustrated
by his famous elegy for Cromwell's death in 1659, his ode of
rejoicing at the restoration of Cromwell's old enemies, the Stuarts,
in 1660, his arguments (in verse) for the Church of England during
Charles II's reign, and his prompt celebration in the long poem,
The Hind and the Panther, of his conversion to Catholicism when
James II ascended the throne.

Hazlitt analyzed the essential difference between Dryden and
his follower, Pope, on the one hand, and the great poets whom we
have so far considered, on the other, in his *Lectures on the English
Poets* in 1818. He then said, in part:

> Dryden and Pope are the great masters of the artificial
> style of poetry in our language as . . . Chaucer, Spenser,
> Shakespeare and Milton were of the natural; and though this
> artificial style is generally and very justly acknowledged to be
> inferior to the other, yet those who stand at the head of that
> class, ought, perhaps, to rank higher than those who occupy
> an inferior place in a superior class . . . for it should be recol-
> lected, that there may be readers (as well as poets) not of the
> highest class, though very good sort of people, and not alto-
> gether to be despised. . . . The capacious soul of Shakespeare
> had an intuitive and mighty sympathy with whatever could
> enter into the heart of man in all possible circumstances; Pope
> had an exact knowledge of all that he himself loved or hated,
> loathed or wanted. Milton has winged his daring flight from
> heaven to earth, through Chaos and old Night. Pope's Muse
> never wandered with safety, but from his library to his grotto,
> or from his grotto into his library back again. . . . He lived in
> the smiles of fortune and basked in the favor of the great.

In 1685, as we have seen, Charles' death brought his brother,
James, Duke of York, to the throne. James II was an avowed
Catholic who had married a Catholic princess, Mary of Modena,
and who was obviously intent not only on restoring Catholicism
as the state religion but also, by the help of the Pope and the
Catholic monarchs of Europe, on restoring absolute power to the
throne of England. For three years there was, as has been noted in
the discussion of Bunyan's life, an increasing tension and jockeying
for power between the crown on one hand, and a combination of
the landed gentry (who would have been represented by Parlia-

ment had James not illegally dismissed it) and the powerful dignitaries of the Anglican Church, on the other hand. It was widely
believed that James' early dissipations had left him incapable of
begetting a son, and if he had died without one his daughter, Mary,
then the Protestant queen of Holland, would have been heir to the
throne. Therefore matters did not come to a head until 1688. Then,
as we saw above, his forcing through of an Act of Indulgence and
the announced birth of a son (commonly rumored to have been
smuggled into the palace in a warming pan) precipitated a crisis.
In this several leaders of the Tory party and the church joined
with the leading Whigs to invite William of Orange, Mary's husband and the recognized head of the Protestant powers in Europe,
to land in England with an armed force and to ascend the throne.

James II fled to France and the revolution of 1688 was pain-
lessly accomplished. English historians are fond of referring to this
as the "glorious" or "bloodless" revolution, in contrast with the
more violent revolutions suffered by less fortunate and well-
deserving lands. The fact is, of course, that this was merely a
postscript to, or reaffirmation of, the prolonged and serious struggle
led by Cromwell forty years earlier, and that only the blood then
spilled made it unnecessary to spill any more later. The substantial
transfer of power to the bourgeoisie had already taken place in
1649 and was, as we have seen, not fundamentally disturbed in
1660. Practically, it mattered only to James II himself that he had
delusions of grandeur and thought he was king by divine right.
After 1688 not even a king could any longer doubt that he ruled
by courtesy of his subjects, and that the throne as well as the
church was now an asset of the upper bourgeoisie (which, practically speaking, already included the peerage).

The Augustan Age or "The Age of Enlightenment," as eighteenth
century literary England was fond of calling itself, began, and
ended, some ten or twenty years before the eighteenth century
itself, and what we are to say of it is essentially said of the hundred years from 1688 to 1789—that is, from the "Glorious or Bloodless Revolution" (whose blood had been spilled forty years before),
to the "French Revolution" (most of whose bloodshed was necessitated by the long subsequent, and still unfinished, struggle against
reaction).

The Augustan Age was, as the name implies, very pleased with
itself. The name was chosen by neoclassicist admiration for the
culture of Rome under the Emperor Augustus, in the belief that

that greatest height of all preceding civilizations had now found a worthy and comparable successor. Alternatively its fortunate citizens referred to their period as "The Age of Reason" or "The Golden Age."

First Addison, and then Pope, were acknowledged arbiters of the polite letters of the age until their respective deaths in 1713 and 1739. Many literary historians still refer to this half century as the Age of Pope, and Pope was, indeed, an extraordinarily good representative of the time, giving us in brief quotable form a real understanding of its values, objectives, limitations and accomplishments.

If the *Tatler* and *Spectator* papers of Addison and Steele are, in bulk, more readable for us than Pope's work, it is perhaps largely because we are today less impatient of uninspired prose than of uninspired poetry, and expect the emotion which the eighteenth century so conspicuously and contentedly lacked more consistently from a versifier than from an essayist.

But we must remember that poetry was still the dominant form of polite literature at the beginning of that century (though it was no longer so by its end) and that prose was, for an educated man, a far more unconventional medium than verse.

However, in everything but the nonessential matter of rhyme and meter, we find complete agreement among the early eighteenth century literary leaders of society. Addison may speak a trifle more gently, Steele a little more warmly, Pope a great deal more sharply, but all use an elegant and well-turned phrase, a graceful classical allusion, a playful acknowledgment of the detailed realistic surface of contemporary upper-class life, and a generalized stingless satire designed to flatter rather than embarrass readers who would usually have a comfortable assurance of its being aimed only at their neighbors. There were, of course, enough and more than enough stinging insults in such verses as Pope's famous attack on Addison (see p. 223) and others, but these are simply sarcastic personal comments and should not be confused with satire which critically portrays general characteristics or foibles.

Pope, who excels at polishing a platitude, has wrapped up for us in an incomparably neat and portable package the general theme of this select chorus:

All Nature is but Art unknown to thee;
All chance direction, which thou canst not see;

All discord, harmony not understood;
All partial evil, universal good:
And spite of Pride, in erring Reason's spite,
One truth is clear, *Whatever is, is right.*

Of course, this comfortable assurance refers only to funda-
mentals. In detail Pope, as well as Addison, Lord Chesterfield,
Steele, and a whole host of lesser figures knew well enough that
there was much to be corrected. Indeed, the entire polite literature
of the time is deliberately designed to pare off excrescences, tone
down extremes, elaborate impeccable standards of taste, and punish
with mockery any deviations from propriety and elegance in sentiment or expression.

From the essayists we learn that some ladies were too promiscu-
ous and others too prudish; that some ambitious literary men forgot their old friends when promoted to high places; that there
were still aristocrats who thought ignorance fashionable or who
were overly contemptuous of new titles; and that there was already
a little too much pushing vulgarity on the part of substantial new
fortunes whose owners did not wish to wait for a generation or
two of landed proprietorship, or for a noble son-in-law, to sweeten
the odor of trade and fit them for the company of their betters.
But these were all clearly removable blemishes. The faults were
on the surface; the core of England was sound.

It is true that Pope is at his rudest in attacking those luckless
denizens of "Grub Street" who have the temerity to write for a
bare living without having enough of a gentleman's education to
supply either correct Latin mottoes or an intimate knowledge of
court intrigues; and the courteous Addison (who later succeeded
in marrying a Duchess) is almost sharp about those wretched retail
tradesmen, like Defoe, who neglect their shop to take an interest
in political news and foreign affairs. But even those regrettable
types seemed trivial enough to be laughed out of sight—and forgotten.

Fundamentally the world, or at least England, was a good place,
needing just that degree of guidance and polish which its witty
and elegant writers were so well equipped to give it—not, indeed,
to be much changed, which was both unnecessary and impossible—
but to shine eternally refulgent with its virtue all apparent and
undimmed. And fundamentally, from the viewpoint of their own
class, the fashionable writers were correct.

The bourgeoisie was an expanding class, expanding in both directions. New fortunes were being made in trade almost daily by "nobodies" rising from below and, as Addison said:

> It is the happiness of a trading nation like ours, that the younger sons, though incapable of any liberal art or profession may be placed in such a way of life, as may perhaps enable them to vie with the best of their family: accordingly, we find several citizens that were launched into the world with narrow fortunes, rising by an honest industry to greater estates than those of their elder brothers.

Its members were not only increasing but, on the whole, becoming individually wealthier, more powerful and better educated. England's world power and prestige were rising steadily; the long inconclusive series of wars on the continent were comfortably removed, in terms of danger or observable bloodshed; and they provided an unprecedented demand for the products of a vastly improved and more efficient form of agriculture, and for the beginnings of a "mass production" of such manufactured goods as uniforms and weapons. The possibility of religious persecution seemed at an end and a universal toleration, generally credited to the new enlightenment of mankind rather than to skepticism or indifference, was one of the distinguishing marks of the happy island. Newton had opened the door into a world of scientific understanding which Pope complacently hailed with: "Nature and Nature's laws lay hid in Night: God said, *Let* Newton *be!* and all was Light." And, in general, the eighteenth century's pleased description of itself as "The Age of Enlightenment" was, from the point of view of articulate upper middle-class England, not too unrealistic.

What then of inarticulate England? What of the nobodies who remained nobodies? What of the small farmers dispossessed because they lacked the capital necessary for the new agricultural methods? What of the thousands forced into jail, beggary, servitude or emigration by the new Acts of Inclosure, those thousands of whom Morton, in his *People's History of England,* says:

> In other parts of England those of the smaller farmers who were tenants were gradually evicted or were ruined by rents four, five and even ten times as high as had been customary. Land farmed on the new methods could be made to pay these increased rents but this was no help to men whose farms and capital were too small to adopt them successfully. Many of the

small freeholders were also forced to sell out by the impossibility of competing with the up-to-date methods of their richer neighbours. The sums received under conditions amounting virtually to a forced sale were usually too small to be employed successfully in any other business even if the farmer had known how to make good use of them. A few, especially in Lancashire and Yorkshire, became successful manufacturers, but the vast majority spent their money quickly and then sank to the position of wage labourers whether on the land or in the new industrial towns.

A third class, the cottagers, found their rights even more ruthlessly violated. Few were able to establish any legal grounds for the customary rights over the village commons and fewer still received any adequate compensation for the loss of these rights. A whole class that had lived by a combination of domestic industry, the keeping of a few beasts or some poultry and regular or occasional work for wages, now found itself thrown back entirely on the last of these resources, since the period of enclosures was also the period in which domestic industry was being destroyed by the competition of the new factories. Lord Ernle fills nearly three pages of his English Farming Past and Present with a list of local and domestic industries which perished at this time.

From about the middle of the Eighteenth Century the improvement in agricultural technique began to make it possible to economise in labour. Wages fell rapidly in relation to prices: in many parts cottages were destroyed or allowed to become ruinous and there was both a decrease in numbers and a decline in the standards of life of the majority throughout the greater part of rural England. In the later part of the century there was not only an increase in the total population but a marked shifting of population from one part of the country to another. No reliable figures are available, but it is at least probable that the increase was smaller and the shifting greater than was at one time supposed.

The revolution in agriculture had three results which went far beyond the limits of agriculture itself. First it increased the productivity of the land and so made possible the feeding of the great industrial population in the new towns.

Second, it created a reserve army of wage earners, now "freed" completely from any connection with the soil, men without ties of place or property.

Third, there was the creation of a vastly increased internal market for manufactured goods. The subsistence farmer, with his domestic industry and his isolation from the outside world, might consume a good deal and yet buy very little. The labourer into whom he had now evolved was usually compelled to consume a great deal less but everything he consumed had to be bought. And it was only on the firm basis of

a substantial home market that a great exporting industry could
be built up.

It was his awareness of this vast submerged beggared peasantry
and ex-peasantry upon whose misery so much of the prosperity of
eighteenth century England was erected, and at whose expense the
bourgeoisie conducted its remarkably swift and easy consolidation
of power, that gave the greatest writer of the early eighteenth century, Jonathan Swift, the emotional force to create works of universal significance out of the polished periods and satirical wit
which are the hallmarks of his time.

Before we turn to consider his towering figure, however, let us,
if only for the sake of contrast and a proper perspective, look a
little more closely at his contemporaries.

In 1709 Richard Steele sensed the possibilities of a growing
fashionable public, wealthy, literate and with some pretensions to
education, but without the serious university training which would
make it possible for them to read the classics, then almost the only
belles lettres in an age which found Shakespeare uncouth, Milton
uncomfortable, and Bunyan absurd. Steele published the first English literary periodical, *The Tatler,* which is the ancestor of such
widely different contemporary magazines as *The Atlantic Monthly,*
The Saturday Review of Literature, the *Sunday Times* or *Tribune
Book Review,* and *Magazine Sections,* and *The New Yorker.*

The opening number announced Steele's intention to print a
paper every Tuesday, Thursday and Saturday:

> Where politic persons, who are so public-spirited as to
> neglect their own affairs to look into transactions of state . . .
> may be instructed, after their reading, what to think . . .
> also to have something which may be of entertainment to the
> fair sex, in honour of whom (is) invented the title of this
> paper . . . all accounts of gallantry, pleasure, and entertain-
> ment shall be under the article of White's Chocolate-house;
> poetry, under that of Will's Coffee-house; learning, under the
> title of the Grecian; foreign and domestic news, you will hear
> from Saint James's Coffee-house. . . .

Joseph Addison, a more consistent, prolific, and serious writer,
if less quick and imaginative, was soon called on for help and for
two years the paper appeared, with remarkable regularity, for the
edification of an increasing number of ladies and gentlemen. It
offered sketches or "short short stories" with emphasis on character

and manner rather than on plot, occasional literary and art criticism of a topical nature, and sprightly satirical comment on such extravagant or crude fads and conventions as duelling, drinking bouts, and exaggerated styles of dress or flirtation. When it was ended in 1711, because of some too indiscreet political reflections and gossip, it was soon replaced by the *Spectator*, under Addison's editorship, which opened with a fictitious picture of the anonymous editor and his declaration:

> Thus I live in the world rather as a Spectator of mankind than as one of the species; by which means I have made myself a speculative statesman, soldier, merchant and artisan without ever meddling with any practical part in my life. I am very well versed in the theory of a husband or a father and can discern the errors in the economy, business and diversion of others, better than those who are engaged in them. . . . I never espoused any part with violence, and am resolved to observe an exact neutrality between the Whigs and Tories, unless I shall be forced to declare myself by the hostilities of either side. [Addison himself was an active and leading Whig and was, in fact, four years later promoted to the position of Secretary of State.]
>
> I have often been told by my friends, that it is pity so many useful discoveries which I have made should be in the possession of a silent man. For this reason, therefore, I shall publish a sheet-full of thoughts every morning for the benefit of my contemporaries; and if I can any way contribute to the diversion or improvement of the country in which I live, I shall leave it, when I am summoned out of it, with the secret satisfaction of thinking that I have not lived in vain.

Although Addison considered himself, and was considered, an unusually religious man, the depth of religious feeling of the period may be judged from his comments in any number of papers, particularly in the famous *Sir Roger de Coverley* series:

> I no sooner saw this venerable [clergy] man in the pulpit, but I very much approved of my friend's insisting upon the qualifications of a good aspect and a clear voice; for I was so charmed with the gracefulness of his figure and delivery, as well as the discourses he pronounced, that I think I never passed time more to my satisfaction. A sermon repeated after this manner is like the composition of a poet in the mouth of a graceful actor.
>
> I could heartily wish that more of our country clergy would follow this example, and, instead of wasting their spirits in

laborious compositions of their own, would endeavor after a
handsome elocution, and all those other talents that are proper
to enforce what has been penned by greater masters. This
would not only be more easy to themselves, but more edifying
to the people.

And again:

I am always well pleased with a country Sunday; and
think, if keeping holy the seventh day were only a human
institution, it would be the best method that could have been
thought of for the polishing and civilizing of mankind. It is
certain the country-people would soon degenerate into a kind
of savages and barbarians, were there not such frequent returns of a stated time, in which the whole village meet together
with their best faces, and in their cleanliest habits, to converse
with one another upon indifferent subjects, *hear their duties
explained to them*, [italics added] and join together in adora-
tion of the Supreme Being.

While the general belief of the early eighteenth century man-of-
the-world was a genteel deism or rationalism which would not have
been unacceptable to Rousseau or Voltaire, his attitude toward
religion was not the Frenchmen's bitter enmity toward a church
with power to persecute, but rather tolerant support for a church
which was a harmless and necessary part of the existing order. As
thorough-going a sceptic as David Hume could advise a clergyman
friend to preach the ordinary doctrines, because it was paying far
too great a compliment to the vulgar to be punctilious about speaking the truth to them; Hume's political attitude appears more explicitly in his regret that the events of the revolution and subsequent
Commonwealth period had changed the English "from a tranquil
and submissive people" to a "restless, fanatic and rebellious"; Edward Gibbon could, a little later, more frankly point out that to
the statesman a creed may be equally useful, whether it is true
or false; and Horace Walpole perfectly expressed the dominant
attitude of the educated classes in a letter from Paris saying that
he would not allow guests of his to talk of the Old Testament as
his French philosophe hosts talked before their servants "if a single
footman were in the room."

Addison, however, whether from a more timid and conventional
temperament, or a more perspicacious sense of social responsibility,
himself held mild religious convictions and pointed out in one of

his essays that ordinary people: "who are so used to be dazzled
with riches, that they pay as much deference to the understanding
of a man of an estate, as of a man of learning . . . are very hardly
brought to regard any truth, how important so ever it may be,
that is preached to them when they know there are several men
of five hundred pounds a year who do not believe it."

Before turning to Addison's friend—and rival—Pope, we may
pause a moment to remark on the general upper-class attitude toward women which Addison, in a friendlier but equally unmistakable way, expressed.

The position of woman had indeed deteriorated rapidly since
the age when Chaucer's Wife of Bath and his Prioress could, in
their own different ways, maintain their independence, fulfill their
varying economic functions, and even travel, uncriticized, without
masculine guardianship. Women in eighteenth century society
(that is, essentially, of course, upper middle-class women—not servants, the rapidly disappearing peasant wives, or the newly appearing group of wives of petty tradesmen) had now become essentially
sexual objects. The fashionable literature of the time tells us that
the enjoyment of her body by rape or seduction, and the enjoyment
of her fortune by marriage, were the only contexts in which it was
possible for a man to consider a woman; and she herself seemed
but infrequently to consider herself in any other light. Her chastity,
or at least her reputation for chastity, is of vital importance before
marriage, to enable her to make the best possible bargain; afterwards also she must avoid indiscretion lest she be held too cheap;
but the whole business of her life is to arouse and glamorize those
appetites from which she derives her importance and for whose
satisfaction she may, if skillful, be well paid. Defoe's inimitable
Moll Flanders says very sensibly:

> How necessary it is for all Women who expect anything
> in the World to preserve the character of their Virtue, even
> when perhaps they may have sacrificed the thing itself.

And Richardson's too often imitated Pamela preserves her "virtue"
through three volumes of attack and is, at the end of the prolonged
and earnest if involuntary "strip-tease," rewarded by marriage to
her would-be ravisher—and by a permanent share in his country
house and coach and six.

Addison is unfortunately even further removed from the frank insight of Defoe (of whom we must speak in more detail a little later) than he is from the unmitigated sentimentality of Richardson. He says repeatedly

> I consider woman as a beautiful romantic animal, that may be adorned with furs and feathers, pearls and diamonds, ores and silks. One of the fathers, if I am rightly informed, has defined a woman to be "An animal that delights in finery." . . . This observation is so very notorious, that when in ordinary discourse we say a man has a fine head, a long head or a good head, we express ourselves metaphorically, and speak in relation to his understanding; whereas when we say of a woman, she has a fine, a long or a good head, we speak only in relation to her commode [head dress].
>
> The toilet is their great scene of business, and the right adjustment of their hair the principal employment of their lives. The sorting of a suit of ribands is considered a very good morning's work; and if they make an excursion to a mercer's or a toy-shop, so great a fatigue makes them unfit for anything else all the day after. Their more serious occupations are sewing and embroidering and their greatest drudgery the preparation of jellies and sweetmeats.

More seriously, he says in another essay:

> As our English women excel those of all nations in beauty, they should endeavor to outshine them in all other accomplishments proper to the sex, and to distinguish themselves as tender mothers and faithful wives. . . . Female virtues are of a domestic turn. The family is the proper province for *private* women to shine in. . . . After having addressed himself to the several ranks and orders of his countrymen, and shown them how they should behave themselves in the public cause he [Pericles] turns to the female part of his audience, "And as for you" says he, "I shall advise you in very few words: aspire only to those virtues that are peculiar to your sex; follow your natural modesty, and think it your greatest commendation not to be talked of one way or other."

That a very considerable part of Addison's readers were women shows their own acceptance of their degradation. The saving word "private" preserves Addison from presuming to criticize Queen Anne and, perhaps, such bedchamber politicians as the Duchess of Marlborough. But we are already more than halfway from Elizabeth's un-sex-conscious rebuke to Lord Burghley: "Little man, little man, 'must' is not a word to use to princes" to Victoria's comment (on refusing to consider a petition against the fourteen-hour factory workday for children), "This is a political question and on such questions the queen, being a woman, cannot presume to hold an opinion."

Even the gentle Edward Young wrote:

> Ladies supreme among amusements reign
> By nature born to soothe and entertain.
> Their prudence in a share of folly lies;
> Why will they be so weak as to be wise?

And Thomas Rymer, among the other absurd rules he promulgated to restore classical correctness to the drama, decreed:

> In poetry no woman is to kill a man except her quality gives her the advantage above him. Poetical decency will not suffer death to be dealt to each other by such persons whom the laws of duel allow not to enter the lists together.

When we hear Pope we find, as we should expect, a more brutal directness whose personal spite and occasional violence is, however, perhaps less intolerable than Addison's amiable condescension. He makes a summary statement:

> Nothing so true as what you once let fall;
> "Most women have no character at all,"
> Matter too soft a lasting mark to bear
> And best distinguished by black, brown or fair.

After this it is almost anticlimactic to turn to such other authorities as Lord Chesterfield who said, in a letter of advice to his son:

> A man of sense only trifles with them [women], humours and flatters them as he does with a sprightly, forward child; but he neither consults them about, nor trusts them with, serious matters, though he often makes them believe that he does both, which is the thing in the world that they are proud of. . . . No flattery is either too high or too low for them. They will greedily swallow the highest and gratefully accept of the lowest.

However, it is not only, or even chiefly, in his attitude toward women that Pope best represents his age. We find Pope the epitome of his period whether we accept Carlyle's unkind description of

"The withered unbelieving eighteenth Century," or Austin Dobson's homage:

> So I that love the old Augustan days
> Of formal Courtesies and formal Phrase
> That like, along the finished line to feel
> The Ruffles flutter and the flash of steel
> That like my Couplet as compact as clear,
> That like my Satire sparkling tho severe
> Unmixed with Bathos and unmarr'd by Trope,
> I fling my Cap for Polish—and for Pope.

Pope's choice of the mock heroic *Rape of the Lock* and the sententious *Essay on Man* as titles for two of his major works; his sensible superficial psychology; his correct and uninspired comments on the art of poetry and of life; his pose of fashionable cynicism, and his genuine unashamed egotism; these are all clearly apparent from the beginning to the end of his work, and can be adequately indicated by the briefest of quotations from one poem after the other.

In the *Essay On Criticism,* for example, written in 1709 when Pope was just twenty years old, he begins so deftly and prosaicly that it is easy to see why a later critic exclaimed, "No great poet *would* write like Pope—but no other *could*":

> 'Tis hard to say if greater want of skill
> Appear in writing or in judging ill;
> But of the two less dangerous is th' offence
> To tire our patience than mislead our sense:
> Some few in that, but numbers err in this;
> Ten censure wrong for one who writes amiss;
> A fool might once himself alone expose;
> Now one in verse makes many more in prose.
> 'Tis with our judgments as our watches, none
> Go just alike, yet each believes his own.

The poem continues effortlessly through hundreds of lines as well turned and snobbish as the famous:

> A little learning is a dangerous thing;
> Drink deep or taste not the Pierian spring:
> There shallow draughts intoxicate the brain
> And drinking largely sobers us again;

and through innumerable half-truths as correct and misleading as:

> True wit is Nature to advantage dress'd,
> What oft was thought, but ne'er so well express'd;

or as practical and patronizing as:

> True ease in writing comes from Art, not chance,
> As those move easiest who have learned to dance;

and:

> Men must be taught as if you taught them not
> And things unknown proposed as things forgot.

Pope's next major effort, *The Rape of the Lock*, written about two years later is a mock-epic or, as he calls it, "An Heroi-Comical Poem," on the unauthorized theft of a Lady's lock of hair by an enamored young lord, and on the consequent furor. It is tricked out in pseudohomeric style with an elaborate mythology of fairies, elves, and guardian spirits invented for the occasion, and built on much sharply detailed description of dressing table, ball gown, card-playing mothers and dancing daughters. The confusion of values which equates such possible catastrophes as a seduction and a ruined dress is, of course, deliberately used for humor. But Pope's avowedly moral essays come, as we shall see, so close to the same attitude that we cannot help feeling his parody involved less exaggeration than he supposed.

The poem begins with his heroine preparing for the ball, assisted by her maid Betty and by the invisible Sylphs who wait on beauty. The unself-conscious awareness of colonial commerce in the ninth to the sixteenth lines are as characteristic as the self-conscious classicism of the verses as a whole.

> And now, unveil'd, the toilet stands display'd,
> Each silver vase in mystic order laid.
> First, robed in white, the nymph intent adores,
> With head uncover'd, the Cosmetic powers.
> A heav'nly image in the glass appears;
> To that she bends, to that her eyes she rears.
> Th' inferior priestess, at her altar's side,
> Trembling begins the sacred rites of Pride.

Unnumber'd treasures ope at once, and here
The various off'rings of the world appear;
From each she nicely culls with curious toil,
And decks the Goddess with the glittering spoil.
This casket India's glowing gems unlocks
And all Arabia breathes from yonder box.
The tortoise here and elephant unite,
Transform'd to combs, the speckled, and the white.
Here files of pins extend their shining rows,
Puffs, powders, patches, trifles, billet-doux.
Now awful beauty puts on all its arms;
The Fair each moment rises in her charms,
Repairs her smiles, awakens every grace,
And calls forth all the wonders of her face;
Sees by degrees a purer blush arise,
And keener lightnings quicken in her eyes
The busy Sylphs surround their darling care,
These set the head, and those divide the hair,
Some fold the sleeve, while others plait the gown;
And Betty's praised for labours not her own.

Belinda's attendant spirits have an uneasy foreboding of catastrophe:

This day black omens threat the brightest Fair
That e'er deserv'd a watchful spirit's care;
Some dire disaster, or by force or slight;
But what or where, the Fates have wrapt in night.
Whether the nymph shall break Diana's law,
Or some frail China Jar receive a flaw;
Or stain her honour, or her new brocade,
Forget her prayers, or miss a masquerade,
Or lose her heart, or necklace, at a ball;

Meanwhile we see the arbiters of social life:

Hither the Heroes and the Nymphs resort,
To taste awhile the pleasures of a court;
In various talk the instructive hours they past,
Who gave the ball, or paid the visit last;
One speaks the glory of the British Queen,
And one describes a charming Indian screen;
A third interprets motions, looks, and sighs;
At every word a reputation dies.

Then suddenly, in the midst of the idyllic scene, the Baron flashes
a pair of scissors and:

> The meeting points the sacred hair dissever
> From the fair head, for ever, and for ever!
> Then flash'd the living lightning from her eyes,
> And screams of horror rend th' affrighted skies.
> Not louder shrieks to pitying Heav'n are cast,
> When husbands, or when lapdogs breathe their last;
> Or when rich China vessels, fall'n from high
> In glitt'ring dust and painted fragments lie!

This is excellent foolery, although perhaps too long drawn for modern taste, but in Pope's major philosophical work, the *Essay on Man*, written in 1732-33, we find him concluding, in all seriousness, with a somewhat similar catalogue of human values and their comparative importance, or, rather, unimportance:

> Behold the child, by Nature's kindly law,
> Pleas'd with a rattle, tickled with a straw;
> Some livelier plaything gives his youth delight,
> A little louder, but as empty quite:
> Scarfs, garters, gold, amuse his riper stage,
> And beads and prayer-books are the toys of age:
> Pleas'd with this bauble still, as that before,
> Till tired he sleeps and life's poor play is o'er.

Milton would certainly have been all the more outraged by this view of human life because Pope presumes to open his "essay" by deliberately borrowing the line in which his great predecessor announced the epic purpose of *Paradise Lost*—"to justify the ways of God to man!" Pope declares that the poet's true purpose is to:

> Eye Nature's walks, shoot folly as it flies,
> And catch the manners living as they rise;
> Laugh where we must, be candid where we can,
> But vindicate the ways of God to man.

After a number of such quotable and overquoted pseudoprofundities as:

> Hope springs eternal in the human breast:
> Man never is, but always to be, blest.

Pope completes his vindication and summarizes his philosophy in the famous lines:

> All Nature is but Art unknown to thee;
> All chance direction which thou canst not see;
> All discord harmony not understood;
> All partial evil, universal good:
> And spite of Pride in erring Reason's spite,
> One truth is clear, *Whatever is, is right*.

Art has perhaps never more explicitly spoken in the service of the status quo, although Pope himself has often approximated this explicitness in such less solemn recommendations as:

> Be not the first by whom the new is tried
> Nor yet the last to lay the old aside.

Finally, in this same work, Pope anticipates the bourgeois political philosophy of "laissez-faire" and the ethics of "enlightened self-interest":

> For forms of government let fools contest;
> Whate'er is best administered is best;
> For Wit's false mirror hold up Nature's light,
> Show'd erring pride, *Whatever is, is right*;
> That Reason, Passion, answer one great aim;
> That true Self-love and Social are the same;
> That Virtue only makes our bliss below,
> And all our knowledge is, *ourselves to know*.

After this it is, perhaps, anticlimactic to quote anything further, but in justice to Pope's happiest vein of satire we must conclude on a more congenial note with his delightful "Epigram Engraved on the Collar of a Dog Which I Gave to His Royal Highness":

> I am his Highness' dog at Kew;
> Pray tell me, Sir, whose dog are you?

And the even sharper sting that describes his friend, and rival, Addison:

> Peace to all such! but were there one whose fires
> True Genius kindles; and fair Fame inspires,
> Bless'd with each talent and each art to please,
> And born to write, converse, and live with ease;
> Should such a man, too fond to rule alone,
> Bear, like the Turk, no brother near the throne;

View him with scornful, yet with jealous eyes
And hate for arts that caus'd himself to rise;
Damn with faint praise, assent with civil leer,
And without sneering teach the rest to sneer;
Willing to wound, and yet afraid to strike,
Just hint a fault, and hesitate dislike;
Alike reserved to blame or to commend,
A tim'rous foe, and a suspicious friend;
Dreading ev'n fools; by flatterers besieged,
And so obliging that he ne'er obliged;
Like Cato give his little Senate laws,
And sit attentive to his own applause:
While Wits and Templars ev'ry sentence raise,
And wonder with a foolish face of praise—
Who but must laugh if such a man there be?
Who would not weep, if Atticus were he?

What Pope says of Addison is perhaps reasonably true; if Addison had said it of Pope it would certainly have been even truer; and we might with no great loss here leave the Augustans to each other's company if it were not for Jonathan Swift, the giant who was caught among these Lilliputians.

JONATHAN SWIFT

Jonathan Swift, known throughout the world as the author of *Gulliver's Travels*, and to students of literature as the writer of the most savage, bitter and utterly damning satire ever written in English—*A Modest Proposal*—is still loved and honored all over Ireland as one of the first and greatest of the fighters for Irish freedom.

Some forty years after his death Henry Grattan, securing the adoption of the Declaration of Irish Independence in the Irish House of Commons, cried out, "Spirit of Swift! your genius has prevailed. Ireland is now a nation!' and today, more than two hundred years later, the Drapier's Head still gives its name to scores of Irish inns and taverns, commemorating Swift's series of great political pamphlets published under the title of *The Drapier's Letters*.

Although Swift was born in Dublin his parents were both English, connected with several important families but themselves possessed of little or no financial resources. His father had followed three successful lawyer brothers to Ireland a few years before, but died at twenty-five with his fortune still unmade and his son still unborn. Swift himself entered the world on November 30, 1667, some six months after his father's death. His oldest uncle, Godwin Swift, undertook the expense of his upbringing and education, but in so grudging and "charitable" a fashion that, as Swift said, he "never loved his Uncle Godwin, nor the remembrance of his Uncle to the hour of his death." After attending Trinity College with little satisfaction to either himself or the authorities, he later wrote in a characteristically third person fragment of autobiography:

> By the ill treatment of his nearest relations, he was so discouraged and sunk in his spirits that he too much neglected his academic studies, for some parts of which [notably philosophy and theology, then a very important part of the college curriculum] he had no relish by nature, and turned himself to reading history and poetry.

Later he was to declare, to the scandal of his learned colleagues:

> I have been better entertained, and more informed, by a chapter in the "Pilgrim's Progress" than by a long discourse on the will, and the intellect, and simple and complex ideas.

He reiterated in this and other arguments: "Style? Here's a fine pother about nothing; proper words in proper places make a true definition of a style."

Swift was graduated without honors in 1688. Through family connections a place in England was secured for him as secretary to Sir William Temple, formerly an important English statesman and diplomat, and in 1688 still famous, active, and much visited by leading writers and politicians in his retirement at Moor Park.

This was an interesting position for a novice of twenty-one, which afforded him unusual chances of meeting important men; but it was also in many respects a humiliating one, as Swift's later comments in his private journal make clear. He learned much of the behind-scenes of politics, and the pettiness and dishonesty of successful politicians, and he so bitterly resented the patronage and cavalier treatment with which he met (even family chaplains were still treated rather as upper servants or very poor relations), that twice in the ten years he spent with Temple, he broke away to try his fortune elsewhere. He found no real opening, although he took orders on the promise of a church vacancy by King William III, to whom Temple had recommended him, and he remained at Moor Park in growing discontent until he was thirty-two.

During this time he filled some of his long empty hours by teaching the housekeeper's young daughter Stella, who became his intimate friend and was his close companion for the rest of her life. He also made a bid for fame by writing much utterly valueless poetry on the pompous Augustan model, and, finally, his first two real works—a satirical dialogue *The Battle of the Books,* and a sharp travesty on religious disputes, *The Tale of A Tub.* The latter was not published until 1705, when it was issued anonymously. Swift claimed that this parodied only the Roman Catholic and Dissenting Churches and that it was really a defense of the Episcopalian Church, in which he was seeking preferment; but Queen Anne, who later refused him a bishopric as its author, evidently felt it was essentially an attack on the established church as well. Most modern readers would certainly agree with her.

At Temple's death in 1699 Swift, failing to secure any other appointment, accepted the position of chaplain to the Earl of Berkeley who soon gave him a small living, the vicarage of Laracour in Ireland. From 1701 Swift visited much in London political circles and wrote one or two unimportant political pamphlets mildly defending certain personalities of the Whig ministry then in power. However, the alliance was lukewarm on his part and when it became, or remained, disappointingly cold and unappreciative on the part of the ministers, he returned to Ireland. There he spent most of his time in the duties and pleasures of his country vicarage and in the companionship of Stella, whom he had advised to settle in nearby Dublin under the chaperonage of a distant relative.

In 1707 he undertook a visit to London on behalf of the Irish Church, in hopes of persuading the Queen to give up her claim to an annual tax on that Church's income as she had already given up her claim to any part of the income of the Church of England. Here he entered into long drawn out and, finally, fruitless negotiations on his mission, but meanwhile rapidly made friends of Addison, Steele, Pope, Gay, and almost all the other leading writers of the time. Addison, then already very well known, presented a book to him with the inscription, "To Dr. Jonathan Swift, the most agreeable companion, the truest friend, and the greatest genius of the age," and published a number of his papers and verse in the *Tatler* and *Spectator*. Swift also found time to write a serious attack on contemporary morality in public and private life in his *Project for the Advancement of Religion and Reformation of Manners* which was printed in 1709, just before his return to Ireland.

His unhypocritical but non-religious attitude toward his sacred profession, and the sincere practical support he gave the Church that employed him, are well illustrated in his notebook of private meditations, published after his death. Here, under "Thoughts on Religion" he mused:

> The want of belief is a defect that ought to be concealed, when it cannot be overcome. . . . I look upon myself, in the capacity of a clergyman, to be one appointed by Providence for defending a post assigned to me, and for gaining over as many enemies as I can.

In 1710 political events which threatened the fall of the Whig ministry made Swift hurry back to London. There, partly because of his annoyance with the Whig minister's continued refusal to grant the request of the Irish Church for equal treatment, partly because of his personal liking for the incoming Tory prime minister who made extremely courteous—and witty—overtures to him, and partly because of his genuine lifelong hatred of war (the Whig party and its famous general, the Duke of Marlborough, were pressing for a continuance of the now almost thirty-year old "War of the Protestant Succession"), Swift joined the Tory party.

His first service to the party was a powerful antiwar pamphlet, *The Conduct of the Allies*, which, as a nineteenth century historian said, "knocked Marlborough's sword out of his hand." Dr. Johnson was not fond of Swift and felt that too much fuss had been made about this pamphlet, which, according to him, simply put "all the facts plain." Nevertheless, Johnson said almost half a century later:

> Swift must be confessed to have dictated for a time the political opinions of the English nation. In the succeeding reign he delivered Ireland from plunder and oppression; and shewed that wit confederated with truth, had such force as authority was unable to resist.

Several comments in Swift's private journal to Stella, written shortly before the publication of the pamphlet which made him famous, give an interesting glimpse of his own attitude:

October 23, 1711: I was today in the city concerning something with a printer, and am tomorrow all day busy with Mr. Secretary about the same. I won't tell you now, but the ministers reckon it will do an abundance of good, and open the eyes of the nation, who are half bewitched against a Peace. Few of this generation can remember anything but war and taxes, and they think it is as it should be; whereas 'tis certain we are the most undone people in Europe, as I am afraid I shall make appear beyond all contradiction.

On another occasion, a few months before, Swift had written in his confidential notes to Stella that Marlborough: "is as covetous as Hell, and ambitious as the Prince of it; he would fain have been general for life, and has broken all endeavors for Peace, to keep his greatness and money. . . ."

After the publication of the pamphlet and the termination of the war Swift was probably the most powerful and courted private citizen in England, and with memories of the many snubs and humiliations he had earlier received, amused himself by forcing lords and cabinet ministers to dance attendance on him and put up with his shocking disregard for titles and court etiquette.

Again we find his personal attitude frankly set down in the secret, day-by-day journal he faithfully kept to send Stella whenever he was away from her:

February 12, 1711: I dined today with Mr. Sec. St. John: I went to the Court of Requests at noon, and sent Mr. Harley into the House to call the Secretary, to let him know I would not dine with him if he dined late.

February 17: I took some good walks in the Park today, and then went to Mr. Harley. Lord Rivers was got there before me, and I chid him for presuming to come on a day when only Lord-Keeper and the Secretary and I were to be there.

February 25: I dined today with Mr. Sec. St. John, on condition that I might choose my company.

April 4: Don't you remember how I used to be in pain when Sir Wm. Temple would look cold and out of humour for three or four days, and I used to suspect a hundred reasons? I have plucked up my spirits since then, faith; he spoiled a fine-gentleman.

April 5: I have been used barbarously by the late ministry; I am a little piqued in honour to let people see I am not to be despised.

May 19: Mr. Secretary told me the Duke of Buckingham had been talking to him about me, and desired my acquaint-

ance. I answered, it could not be, for he had not made sufficient advances. Then the Duke of Shrewsbury said he thought
the Duke was not used to make advances. I said I could not
help that; for I always expected advances in proportion to
men's quality, and more from a Duke than other men.

October 7: . . . Lady Oglethorpe brought me and the
Duchess of Hamilton together today in the drawing-room, and
I have given her some encouragement, but not much.

During these few fashionable London years Swift became
friendly with an unpretentious though wealthy widow, Mrs. Van-
homrigh, and her daughter, Vanessa. The daughter's youth made him
feel that it was safe to play the "guide, philosopher and friend,"
direct her education and, after her mother's death, advise her on
her business problems. Although she declared herself in love with
him he evidently took the affair as a conventional flirtation, and
wrote a long formal poem, *Cadenus and Vanessa,* full of elaborate
mythological compliments to the lady and much more genuine
touches of satire about himself, such as:

> 'Tis an old maxim in the schools,
> That flattery's the food of fools;
> Yet now and then your men of wit
> Will condescend to take a bit.

He told her of Stella and wrote Stella all about her, but Vanessa
seems to have been genuinely in love with him, and when he returned to Ireland she followed him to an estate she owned there,
still passionately urging marriage.

He was furious both at her insistence and at Stella's uneasiness
and refused ever to see Vanessa again during her tragically brief life
—she died just two years later. According to some accounts he also,
at that time, acceded to Stella's request for a secret and platonic
marriage.

There was clearly a pathological element in his insuperable
aversion to any sexual relations—a theme developed in Gulliver's
return from the Land of Houyhnhnms—and there are many ama-
teur psychologists who have erected tomes over these scanty facts.
But Swift's vitally important and well-documented public life and
its effect on his work have been largely ignored, and to this we
must return.

There seemed no position Swift could not get for his friends—
and he got many for the Whig writers he had known. with most

of whom he remained very friendly—but his irreverent wit and, perhaps, his pride, barred the way to preferment in the Church, while his being in orders closed the door to any official non-clerical appointment out of it. Finally he accepted the Deanery of St. Patrick's, Dublin, although he had strongly protested against exile from England and bitterly opposed the prospect of more or less permanent banishment to a poverty stricken and subject country. His reluctance seems to have been reciprocated by his congregation and on the day of his installation someone posted a long poem on the door of the Cathedral, beginning:

> This Place He got by Wit and Rhyme
> And many ways most odd;
> And might a Bishop be in time
> Did he believe in God.

it ended:

> Look down, St. Patrick, look, we pray
> On thine own Church and Steeple;
> Convert the Dean on this Great Day;
> Or else, God help the people.

Whether it was St. Patrick's doing or not, the Dean, who never ceased to inveigh against having to live in Ireland, nevertheless soon threw himself heart and soul into the struggles of the nation against its English oppressors:

In 1699 Ireland's flourishing wool industry had been killed by an English law forbidding the exportation of woolen goods and when some of the thousands abruptly thrown out of employment turned to the manufacture of linen, similar laws were passed against the exportation of this and, in fact, all other manufactured goods and even cattle! The bitter struggle for land by a population forced to depend entirely on agricultural pursuits intensified the hardships of an incredibly barbaric system of land tenure, with its heavy drain of enormous profits for absentee landlords. Swift wrote bitterly during his first few months as Dean of St. Patrick's:

> I confess myself to be touched with a very sensitive pleas-
> ure when I hear of a mortality in any country parish or village,
> where the wretches are forced to pay for a filthy cabin and
> two ridges of potatoes treble their worth; brought up to steal
> or beg for want of work; to whom death would be the best

thing to be wished for on account both of themselves and the public.

When, in 1719, an Act was passed in England robbing the Irish Parliament and Courts of their last shreds of independence and reaffirming all the general restrictions which had been enacted since 1495, Swift was driven into public action. In 1720 he published his powerful pamphlet, *A Proposal for the Universal Use of Irish Manufacture*, which proposed a virtual boycott of English goods, and an economic declaration of independence for Ireland, with the slogan "Burn everything that comes from England except the coal." This attack was so sharp and stinging that the government brought the printer up for trial as "seditious," since the author was, formally, unknown, although most of Dublin knew perfectly well who he was. Despite the judge's explicit charge the jury refused to convict the printer—they were sent out of court nine times to change their verdict and threatened with prosecution themselves if they did not!—and Swift became the hero of Dublin. One of the sentiments often quoted from this pamphlet by Irish "agitators" for the next hundred years was the characteristic comment:

> The Scripture tells us "oppression makes a wise man mad." Therefore, consequently speaking, the reason why some men are not mad, is because they are not wise: However, it were to be wished that oppression would, in time, teach a little wisdom to fools.

Two years later a particularly obvious "job" (the eighteenth century synonym of our "racket") gave Swift the opportunity he had been waiting for.

One of the King's mistresses, who was already drawing an annual pension of £3,000 from the Irish establishment had, for favors received, been given a "patent" to supply copper coins to Ireland. She arranged with a Mr. William Wood of Birmingham to coin £100,800 worth of coins out of £60,000 worth of metal, and to divide the profits by giving her £10,000 and the King £14,000.

This would have worked some genuine hardship in Ireland by its cheapening of the minor currency but, more important, it was a blatant reminder of Ireland's helpless state of subjection and the callous indifference to her welfare or opinion which permeated the attitude of the English government. Swift realized that this was an issue immediate, concrete and dramatic enough to arouse and unite all classes and religions—he said that "even goslings know enough to huddle together when a kite pauses overhead"—and used it as a springboard for his plunge into serious anti-English agitation. Under the title of *The Drapier's Letters* he issued the first of a series of some of the most effective propaganda leaflets ever written. The first letter is addressed "to the tradesmen, shop keepers, farmers and country people in general of the Kingdom of Ireland," and begins:

> What I intend now to say to you, is, next to your duty to God, and the care of your salvation, of the greatest concern to yourselves, and your children; your bread and clothing, and every common necessary of life, entirely depend on it. Therefore I do most earnestly exhort you as men, as Christians, as parents, and as lovers of your country, to read this paper with the utmost attention, or get it read to you by others, which that you may do at the less expense, I have ordered the printer to sell it at the lowest rate. . . .

The response to this first letter was so overwhelming that a compromise was suggested restricting Wood's coinage to £40,000 worth, and restricting its use to no more than five pence in any one transaction. This brought forth a second letter denouncing the "job" anew, and attacking Wood with every species of ridicule and contumely: "It is no loss of honour to submit to the lion, but who, with the figure of a man, can think with patience of being devoured by a rat?" It called on the people to maintain and increase their resistance. A third letter to the same effect was next addressed "to the nobility and gentry of the Kingdom of Ireland." Public enthusiasm mounted so sharply that there seemed danger of a general uprising, and the Lord Lieutenant wrote to Prime Minister Walpole that it was "impossible to stop the torrent" unless Wood's grant were canceled. Walpole removed him from office and sent over a new Lord Lieutenant. A few days before this dignitary's arrival the fourth and perhaps the greatest of the letters appeared addressed "to the whole people of Ireland." A brief quotation from this will show how important a structure Swift had erected upon the simple foundation of popular opposition to the debased English coinage. Remember that the date is 1724 and anticipates Thomas Paine by almost half a century!

For, *in reason,* all government without the consent of the governed, is the very definition of slavery; but, *in fact,* eleven men well armed will certainly subdue one single man in his shirt. . . . A people long used to hardships lose by degrees the very notions of liberty; they look upon themselves as creatures at mercy, and that all impositions laid on them by a stronger hand are, in the phrase of the report, legal and obligatory. Hence proceed that poverty and lowness of spirit, to which a kingdom may be subject, as well as a particular person. And when Esau came fainting from the field at point to die, it is no wonder that he sold his birthright for a mess of pottage.

The new Lord Lieutenant's first official act was to offer a reward of £300 (subsequently increased) for the name of the author —which was an open secret to every Irishman—and to arrest the printer. However, as Swift later said in his own "Verses on the Death of Dr. Swift":

> Ne'er a traitor could be found
> To sell him for six hundred pound.

The grand jury, every member of which had mysteriously received an "anonymous" leaflet, "Seasonable Advice to the Grand Jury," refused to indict the printer; so did a second grand jury illegally impaneled by the same Lord Chief Justice who had had such troubles trying to get a sentence of guilty for the earlier printer!

Swift's well-founded trust in the people of Dublin is illustrated by the fact that on the day after the announcement of the reward he publicly attended the new Lord-Lieutenant's reception, strode up to him, and said, in a voice which filled the ballroom: "So, my lord, this is a glorious exploit you performed yesterday, in suffering a proclamation against a poor shopkeeper, whose only crime is an honest endeavor to save his country from ruin."

Wood's patent was revoked (he was consoled with £24,000 paid from the English treasury, of which no doubt the Duchess got her fair share) and in all Ireland, as Johnson later said:

> The Drapier was a sign; the Drapier was a health; and which way so ever the eye or the ear was turned, some tokens were found of the nation's gratitude to the Drapier.

Swift made this the occasion for one of his rare sermons—he himself said, "I never preached but twice in my life, and they were not sermons but pamphlets"—and announced as his subject, "Doing Good." The sermon reads in part:

> . . . But, besides this love we owe to every man in his particular capacity, under the title of our neighbour, there is yet a duty of a more large extensive nature incumbent on us; which is, our love to our neighbour in his public capacity, as he is a member of that great body the commonwealth, under the same government with ourselves; and this is usually called love of the public, and is a duty to which we are more strictly obliged than even that of loving ourselves; because therein ourselves are also contained, as well as all our neighbours, in one great body. This love of the public, or of the commonwealth, or love of our country, was in ancient times properly known by the name of virtue, because it was the greatest of all virtues and was supposed to contain all virtues in it; . . .
>
> But here I would not be misunderstood: by the love of our country, I do not mean loyalty to our king, for that is a duty of another nature; and a man may be very loyal, in the common sense of the word, without one grain of public good at his heart. Witness this very kingdom we live in [Ireland] I verily believe, that since the beginning of the world, no nation upon earth ever showed (all circumstances considered) such high constant marks of loyalty, in all their actions and behaviours as we have done: and at the same time, no people ever appeared more utterly void of what is called a public spirit. When I say the people, I mean the bulk or mass of the people; for I have nothing to do with those in power. . . .
>
> Perhaps it may be thought by some, that this way of discoursing is not so proper from the pulpit. But surely, when an open attempt is made, and far carried on, to make a great kingdom a poorhouse, to deprive us of all means to exercise hospitality or charity, to turn our cities and churches into ruins, to make the country a desert for wild beasts and robbers, to destroy all arts and sciences, all trades and manufactures, and the very tillage of the ground, only to enrich one obscure ill—designing proprietor and his followers; it is time for the pastor to cry out "that the wolf is getting into his flock," and to warn them to stand together and all to consult the common safety. And God be praised for his infinite goodness in raising such a spirit of union among us, at least in this point, in the midst of all our former divisions; which union, if it continue, will in all probability defeat the pernicious design of this pestilent enemy to the nation!
>
> . . . I am sensible that what I have now said will not go very far, being confined to this assembly: but I hope it may

stir up others of my brethren to exhort their several congregations, after a more effectual manner, to show their love for their country on this important occasion. And this, I am sure, cannot be called meddling in affairs of state.

The years 1720-1725 which were so busy politically also saw the completion of Swift's best known and most ambitious literary work, *Gulliver's Travels*. This had been begun in jest while Swift was meeting Pope, Gay and other wits at the Scriblerus Club in London, and probably the greater part or all of the "Voyage to Lilliput" had been written there. The touches of personal satire on Walpole and other ministers, and the comparative light-heartedness change rapidly as Swift became more and more immersed in Irish affairs, although even in the first two voyages his deep hatred of war and overwhelming contempt for corrupt politicians are apparent. But the final chapters, culminating in the unforgettable attack on social evils interwoven with the descriptions of the Yahoos, are in another tone altogether and echo the fury of notes like this one, written from Ireland:

> There are thousands of poor wretches who think themselves blessed if they can obtain a hut worse than a squire's dog-kennel, and an acre of ground for a potatoe plantation, on condition of being as very slaves as any in America. What can be more deplorable than to behold wretches starving in the midst of plenty?

The hero of Swift's best known work is one Lemuel Gulliver, a plainspoken simple straightforward man with some education both as a navigator and a doctor. Unable to build a medical practise which will adequately support his wife and young children, he reluctantly accepts an offer to go back to sea as a ship's surgeon and sets sail from Bristol on the first of his now famous voyages, May 4, 1699.

After a successful six months trading cruise in the East Indies they are driven out of their way by a storm and shipwrecked in a strange region northwest of Van Dieman's land.

Gulliver, separated from his companions, is cast up on the shore of what he later discovers to be Lilliput. While asleep he is captured and bound by some thousands of the six-inch tall inhabitants.

His adventures among the Lilliputians have been read in emasulated nursery editions by most children, who enjoy without fully understanding the satire involved in such descriptions as that of the Emperor, "taller by almost the Breadth of my Nail, than any of his Court, which alone is enough to strike an Awe into the Beholders."

There are, of course, many far more elaborate passages which, for Swift's contemporaries, unmistakably indicated current figures of state. And we need no such special knowledge to appreciate their more fundamental satirical attack upon political and court intrigues in general. A well-known illustration opens the third chapter.

Other unmistakable references to the religious wars show how well justified Queen Anne was in her suspicion that Swift's earlier ridicule had been meant impartially to embrace all sects.

After many amusing and some hazardous experiences Gulliver succeeds in returning to England where he makes a small fortune by exhibiting and selling a number of the Lilliputian sheep, cows and other livestock which he had taken with him on his departure.

Two months later, on June 20, 1702, he again goes to sea. The ship is almost immediately driven out of its course by a storm and when the wind subsides several members of the crew row to a strange shore to get drinking water. While Gulliver wanders a little way inland the others are terrified by the approach of one of the gigantic inhabitants and escape, leaving Gulliver alone.

He is soon picked up between thumb and forefinger by one of the sixty-foot tall natives, and naturally gives himself up for lost. "For, as human Creatures are observed to be more Savage and cruel in proportion to their Bulk; what could I expect but to be a Morsel in the Mouth of the first among these enormous Barbarians who should happen to seize me?"

However the Brobdingnagans (as he later learns to call them) prove to be superior to mankind in wisdom and humanity as well as stature. The satire of western civilization is here developed more directly by statement of differences rather than by observation of similarities.

For example, when, after many adventures, Gulliver is purchased by the Queen and becomes something of a court pet the King "desired I would give him as exact an account of the Government of England as I possibly could; because, as fond as Princes commonly are of their own Customs (for so he conjectured of other Monarchs by my former Discourses) he should be glad to hear of anything that might deserve imitation." But the result was disconcerting.

In an effort more favorably to impress the king, Gulliver offers to teach him the arts of war, since the Brobdingnagans have never discovered or invented such things as gunpowder.

> The King was struck with horror at the description I had given of those terrible engines, and the proposal I had made. He was amazed how so impotent and grovelling an insect as I (these were his expressions) could entertain such inhuman ideas, and in so familiar a manner as to appear wholly unmoved at all the scenes of blood and desolation, which I had painted as the common effects of those destructive machines, whereof he said some evil genius, enemy to mankind, must have been the first contriver. As for himself, he protested that although few things delighted him so much as new discoveries in art or in nature, yet he would rather lose half his kingdom than be privy to such a secret, which he commanded me, as I valued my life, never to mention any more.
>
> A strange effect of narrow principles and short views! that a prince possessed of every quality which procures veneration, love, and esteem; of strong parts, great wisdom, and profound learning, endued with admirable talents for government, and almost adored by his subjects, should from a nice unnecessary scruple, whereof in Europe we can have no conception, let slip an opportunity put into his hands, that would have made him absolute master of the lives, the liberties, and the fortunes of his people.

Finally by a strange series of accidents Gulliver is carried out to sea, rescued by an English ship, and returns home.

The third voyage, undertaken a few months later, is the least interesting whether as story or as satire.

Captured by pirates and set adrift in a small boat, Gulliver manages to reach an uninhabited island from which he is rescued by the people of a sort of floating island called Laputa. They are a caste of absent-minded astronomers who rule a small continent, over which they can make their floating island move at will, and who care for nothing but mathematics and music. Despite this promising beginning Gulliver meets with no really exciting adventures here and none of the individuals come alive for us as did many of the persons he met in Lilliput and Brobdingnag.

The object of Swift's satire here is apparently the arid rationalism and formal metaphysical discussions of many eighteenth century literati, but he himself is evidently not clear as to the practical possibilities of scientific investigation, and there seems to be little coherence or discrimination in his attacks on a number of disparate experiments and innovations.

The only detail of this third voyage which strikes the imagination is Gulliver's description of the few individuals in each generation who are, in this region, born immortal.

When he first hears of these Struldbruggs, as they are called, he ecstatically envisions the wisdom, benevolence and happiness which such fortunate beings must achieve, but is rapidly disillusioned. His informant tells him:

> They were not only opinionative, peevish, covetous, morose, vain, talkative, but uncapable of friendship, and dead to all natural affection, which never descended below their grandchildren. Envy and impotent desires are their prevailing passions. . . . The least miserable among them appear to be those who turn to dotage, and entirely lose their memories; these meet with more pity and assistance, because they want many bad qualities which abound in others.

After an absence of five and a half years, Gulliver finally returns to England. "I continued at home with my Wife and Children about five Months in a very happy Condition, if I could have learned the lesson of knowing when I was well. I left my poor Wife big with Child; and accepted an advantageous offer made me to be Captain of the Adventure, a stout Merchantman of 350 Tuns."

Forced to replace a number of his crew by strangers at the Barbadoes, Captain Gulliver learns too late that most of the new recruits had been buccaneers. They seize the ship to use as a pirate vessel, and maroon the captain on a strange shore which, as he later finds out, is the land of the Houyhnhnms. These are rational horses, and the name is intended to be an approximation of a horse's neighing.

The story here loses the close attention to realistic detail which characterises the account of the first two travels, but it is still absorbing and the satire becomes far sharper and more biting.

Among the wild animals in this country are the Yahoos, a vile species which Gulliver, to his infinite horror, finally recognizes as genus Homo. The direct physical elements of his description of these hairy, naked and wild Yahoos becomes amazing when we realize that it was written more than a century before there was

any tentative suggestion of evolution or any notion of a link between Man and the Ape.

Gulliver is soon taken into the household of a dapple-gray steed,
a Houyhnhnm of quality, and shows the same aptitude in learning
the language there as he has displayed in the course of his previous
travels. "The Curiosity and Impatience of my Master were so great,
that he spent many Hours of his Leisure to instruct me. He was
convinced (as he afterwards told me) that I must be a Yahoo, but
my teachableness, civility and cleanliness astonished him; which
were Qualities altogether so opposite to those Animals."

Requested to tell the history of his country Gulliver does so,
dwelling upon the many wars, both domestic and foreign.

> What you have told me (said my master) upon the sub-
> ject of war, does indeed discover most admirably the effects
> of that reason you pretend to: however, it is happy that the
> shame is greater than the danger; and that nature hath left
> you utterly uncapable of doing much mischief.
>
> For your mouths lying flat with your faces, you can hardly
> bite each other to any purpose, unless by consent. Then as
> to the claws upon your feet before and behind, they are so
> short and tender, that one of our Yahoos would drive a dozen
> of yours before him. And therefore in recounting the numbers
> of those who have been killed in battle, I cannot but think
> that you have *said the thing which is not.*
>
> I could not forbear shaking my head and smiling a little
> at his ignorance. And being no stranger to the art of war, I
> gave him a description of cannons, culverins, muskets, cara-
> bines, pistols, bullets, powder, swords, bayonets, battles, sieges,
> retreats, attacks, undermines, countermines, bombardments,
> sea fights; ships sunk with a thousand men, twenty thousand
> killed on each side; dying groans, limbs flying in the air,
> smoke, noise, confusion, trampling to death under horses' feet;
> flight, pursuit, victory; fields strewed with carcasses left for
> food to dogs, and wolves, and birds of prey; plundering, strip-
> ping, ravishing, burning, and destroying. And to set forth the
> valour of my own dear countrymen, I assured him that I had
> seen them blow up a hundred enemies at once in a siege, and
> as many in a ship, and beheld the dead bodies come down in
> pieces from the clouds, to the great diversion of the spectators.
>
> I was going on to more particulars, when my master com-
> manded me silence. He said whoever understood the nature
> of Yahoos might easily believe it possible for so vile an animal
> to be capable of every action I had named, if their strength
> and cunning equalled their malice. But as my discourse had
> increased his abhorrence of the whole species, so he found it

gave him a disturbance in his mind, to which he was wholly
a stranger before. He thought his ears being used to such
abominable words, might by degrees admit them with less
detestation. That although he hated the Yahoos of this country,
yet he no more blamed them for their odious qualities, than
he did a *gnnayh* (a bird of prey) for its cruelty, or a sharp
stone for cutting his hoof. But when a creature pretending to
reason could be capable of such enormities, he dreaded lest
the corruption of that faculty might be worse than brutality
itself. He seemed therefore confident, that instead of reason,
we were only possessed of some quality fitted to increase our
natural vices; as the reflection from a troubled stream returns
the image of an ill-shapen body not only larger, but more
distorted.

Gulliver then turned to describe his people's civil rather than
their military accomplishments.

Whereupon I was at much pains to describe to him the use
of money, the materials it was made of, and the value of the
metals; that when a Yahoo had got a great store of this precious substance, he was able to purchase whatever he had a
mind to; the finest clothing, the noblest houses, great tracts
of land, the most costly meats and drinks, and have his choice
of the most beautiful females. Therefore since money alone
was able to perform all these feats, our Yahoos thought they
could never have enough of it to spend or save, as they found
themselves inclined from their natural bent either to profusion
or avarice. That the rich man enjoyed the fruit of the poor
man's labour, and the latter were a thousand to one in proportion to the former. That the bulk of our people were forced
to live miserably, by labouring every day for small wages to
make a few live plentifully. I enlarged myself much on these
and many other particulars to the same purpose; but his Honour
was still to seek; for he went upon a supposition that all animals had a title to their share in the productions of the earth,
and especially those who presided over the rest. Therefore he
desired I would let him know what these costly meats were,
and how any of us happened to want them. Whereupon I
enumerated as many sorts as came into my head, with the
various methods of dressing them, which could not be done
without sending vessels by sea to every part of the world, as
well for liquors to drink, as for sauces, and innumerable other
conveniences. I assured him that this whole globe of earth must
be at least three times gone round, before one of our better female Yahoos could get her breakfast or a cup to put it in. He
said that must needs be a miserable country which cannot
furnish food for its own inhabitants.

Finally Gulliver completely realized the superiority of the Houyhnhnms and happily settled down to live among them and learn from them.

> When I thought of my family, my friends, my country-men, or human race in general, I considered them as they really were, Yahoos in shape and disposition, perhaps a little more civilized, and qualified with the gift of speech, but making no other use of reason than to improve and multiply those vices whereof their brethren in this country had only the share that nature allotted them. When I happened to behold the reflection of my own form in a lake or fountain, I turned away my face in horror and detestation of myself, and could better endure the sight of a common Yahoo than of my own person.

Unfortunately the Houyhnhnm Supreme Council was unwilling to allow even a superior Yahoo to remain among them permanently, and decreed his banishment. He was overcome with grief but submitted; contrived to make a boat, and sailed to an uninhabited island. A ship's crew of European Yahoos discovered him there, and despite his urgent remonstrance insisted on taking him back to civilization.

The book, *Travels into Several Remote Nations of the World by Lemuel Gulliver,* was first published anonymously in 1726. It was immediately reprinted in a large number of unauthorized editions. In 1727 a new authorized edition included a letter from Lemuel Gulliver to his cousin, Richard Sympson, who had ostensibly first published the work. There was also an explanatory preface by Richard Sympson himself.

The emphasis in Captain Gulliver's letter makes it very clear that by the time Swift had finished writing the book it was its fourth part which expressed his unqualified condemnation of the world in which he lived.

In 1728 Swift wrote *A Short View of the State of Ireland* which deals trenchantly with absentee landlordism and the deliberate murder of Irish manufacture and commerce by the mercantile interests of England. That same year he wrote in a letter to Pope and Bolingbroke:

> I do profess without affectation, that your kind opinion of me as a patriot, since you call it so, is what I do not deserve; because what I do is owing to perfect rage and resent-

ment, and the mortifying sight of slavery, folly, and baseness about me, among which I am forced to live.

And in a note to an Irish friend he demanded:

Does not corruption of men in high places eat into your heart and exhaust your spirits?

In 1730 he published a brief—and savage—satire on an unofficial suggestion that the French king be allowed to recruit soldiers in Ireland to help relieve the growing "overpopulation" and unemployment in that unhappy island.

This suggestion and similar ones for the emigration of young people as indentured servants to Australia, which were put forth by humane church dignitaries and other public spirited citizens were also, in 1730, responsible for Swift's last political pamphlet, *The Modest Proposal*, which remains the most heart-breaking piece of sarcasm that savage indignation has yet given birth to.

A MODEST PROPOSAL: FOR PREVENTING THE CHILDREN OF POOR PEOPLE IN IRELAND FROM BEING A BURTHEN TO THEIR PARENTS OR COUNTRY, AND FOR MAKING THEM BENEFICIAL TO THE PUBLIC.

It is a melancholy object to those who walk through this great town or travel in the country, when they see the streets, the roads, and cabin doors, crowded with beggars of the female sex, followed by three, four, or six children, all in rags and importuning every passenger for an alms. These mothers, instead of being able to work for their honest livelihood, are forced to employ all their time in strolling to beg sustenance for their helpless infants: who as they grow up either turn thieves for want of work, or leave their dear native country to fight for the pretender in Spain, or sell themselves to the Barbadoes.

I think it is agreed by all parties that this prodigious number of children in the arms, or on the backs, or at the heels of their mothers, and frequently of their fathers, is in the present deplorable state of the kingdom a very great additional grievance; and, therefore, whoever could find out a fair, cheap, and easy method of making these children sound, useful members of the commonwealth, would deserve so well of the public as to have his statue set up for a preserver of the nation.

But my intention is very far from being confined to provide only for the children of professed beggars; it is of a much greater extent, and shall take in the whole number of

infants at a certain age who are born of parents in effect as
little able to support them as those who demand our charity
in the streets.

As to my own part, having turned my thoughts for many
years upon this important subject, and maturely weighed the
several schemes of our projectors, I have always found them
grossly mistaken in their computation. It is true, a child just
dropped from its dam may be supported by her milk for a solar
year, with little other nourishment; at most not above the
value of 2s., which the mother may certainly get, or the value
in scraps, by her lawful occupation of begging; and it is exactly at one year old that I propose to provide for them in
such a manner as instead of being a charge upon their parents
or the parish, or wanting food and raiment for the rest of their
lives, they shall on the contrary contribute to the feeding, and
partly to the clothing, of many thousands.

There is likewise another great advantage in my scheme,
that it will prevent those voluntary abortions, and that horrid
practice of women murdering their bastard children, alas! too
frequent among us! sacrificing the poor innocent babes I doubt
more to avoid the expense than the shame, which would move
tears and pity in the most savage and inhuman breast.

The number of souls in this kingdom being usually reckoned one million and a half, of these I calculate there may be
about 200,000 couple whose wives are breeders; from which
number I subtract 30,000 couple who are able to maintain
their own children (although I apprehend there cannot be so
many, under the present distresses of the kingdom); but this
being granted, there will remain 170,000 breeders. I again
subtract 50,000 for those women who miscarry, or whose children die by accident or disease within the year. There only
remains 120,000 children of poor parents annually born. The
question therefore is, how this number shall be reared and
provided for? which, as I have already said, under the present
situation of affairs, is utterly impossible by all the methods
hitherto proposed. For we can neither employ them in handi-
craft or agriculture; we neither build houses (I mean in the
country) nor cultivate land; they can very seldom pick up a
livelihood by stealing, till they arrive at six years old, except
where they are of towardly parts; although I confess they
learn the rudiments much earlier; during which time, they
can however be properly looked upon only as probationers;
as I have been informed by a principal gentleman in the
county of Cavan, who protested to me that he never knew
above one or two instances under the age of six, even in a
part of the kingdom so renowned for the quickest proficiency
in that art.

I am assured by our merchants, that a boy or a girl before
twelve years old is no saleable commodity; and even when

they come to this age they will not yield above 3l. or 3l.2s.6d. at most on the exchange; which cannot turn to account either to the parents or kingdom, the charge of nutriment and rags having been at least four times that value.

I shall now therefore humbly propose my own thoughts, which I hope will not be liable to the least objection.

I have been assured by a very knowing American of my acquaintance in London, that a young healthy child well nursed is at a year old a most delicious, nourishing, and wholesome food, whether stewed, roasted, baked, or boiled; and I make no doubt that it will equally serve in a fricassee or a ragout. I do therefore humbly offer it to public consideration that of the 120,000 children already computed, 20,000 may be reserved for breed, whereof only one-fourth part to be males; which is more than we allow to sheep, black cattle or swine; and my reason is, that these children are seldom the fruits of marriage, a circumstance not much regarded by our savages, therefore one male will be sufficient to serve four females. That the remaining 100,000 may, at a year old, be offered in sale to the persons of quality and fortune through the kingdom; always advising the mother to let them suck plentifully in the last month, so as to render them plump and fat for a good table.

A child will make two dishes at an entertainment of friends; and when the family dines alone, the fore or hind quarter will make a reasonable dish, and seasoned with a little pepper or salt will be very good boiled on the fourth day, especially in winter.

I have reckoned upon a medium that a child just born will weight 12 pounds, and in a solar year, if tolerably nursed, will increase to 28 pounds.

I grant this food will be somewhat dear, and therefore very proper for landlords, who, as they have already devoured most of the parents, seem to have the best title to the children.

Infant's flesh will be in season throughout the year, but more plentifully in March, and a little before and after: for we are told by a grave author, an eminent French physician, that fish being a prolific diet, there are more children born in Roman Catholic countries about nine months after Lent than at any other season; therefore, reckoning a year after Lent, the markets will be more glutted than usual, because the number of popish infants is at least three to one in this kingdom: and therefore it will have one other collateral advantage, by lessening the number of papists among us.

I have already computed the charge of nursing a beggar's child (in which list I reckon all cottagers, labourers, and four-fifths of the farmers) to be about 2s. per annum, rags included; and I believe no gentleman would repine to give 10s. for the carcass of a good fat child, which, as I have said, will make four dishes of excellent nurtitive meat, when he has only some particular friend or his own family to dine with him. Thus the squire will learn to be a good landlord, and grow popular among the tenants; the mother will have 8s. net profit, and be fit for work till she produces another child.

Those who are more thrifty (as I must confess the times require) may flay the carcass; the skin of which artificially dressed will make admirable gloves for ladies, and summer boots for fine gentlemen.

As to our city of Dublin, shambles may be appointed for this purpose in the most convenient parts of it, and butchers we may be assured will not be wanting; although I rather recommend buying the children alive than dressing them hot from the knife as we do roasting pigs. . . .

. . . Some persons of a desponding spirit are in great concern about that vast number of poor people, who are aged, diseased, or maimed, and I have been desired to employ my thoughts what course may be taken to ease the nation of so grievous an encumbrance. But I am not in the least pain upon that matter, because it is very well known that they are every day dying and rotting by cold and famine, and filth and vermin, as fast as can be reasonably expected. And as to the young labourers, they are now in as hopeful a condition; they cannot get work, and consequently pine away for want of nourishment, to a degree that if at any time they are accidentally hired for common labour, they have not strength to perform it; and thus the country and themselves are happily delivered from the evils to come. I have too long digressed, and therefore shall return to my subject. I think the advantages by the proposal which I have made are obvious and many, as well as of the highest importance.

For first, as I have already observed, it would greatly lessen the number of papists, with whom we are yearly overrun, being the principal breeders of the nation. . . .

. . . Secondly, The poor tenants will have something valuable of their own, which by law may be made liable to distress and help to pay their landlord's rent, their corn and cattle being already seized, and money a thing unknown.

Thirdly, Whereas the maintenance of 100,000 children, from two years old and upward, cannot be computed at less than 10s. a-piece per annum, the nation's stock will be thereby increased £50,000 per annum, beside the profit of a new dish introduced to the tables of all gentlemen of fortune in the kingdom who have any refinement in taste. And the money will circulate among ourselves, the goods being entirely of our own growth and manufacture.

Fourthly, The constant breeders, beside the gain of 8s. sterling per annum by the sale of their children, will be rid of the charge of maintaining them after the first year.

Fifthly, This food would likewise bring great custom to taverns; where the vintners will certainly be so prudent as to procure the best receipts for dressing it to perfection, and consequently have their houses frequented by all the fine gentlemen, who justly value themselves upon their knowledge in good eating: and a skilful cook, who understands how to oblige his guests, will contrive to make it as expensive as they please.

Sixthly, This would be a great inducement to marriage, which all wise nations have either encouraged by rewards or enforced by laws and penalties.

It would increase the care and tenderness of mothers toward their children, when they were sure of a settlement for life to the poor babes, provided in some sort by the public, to their annual profit or expense. We should see an honest emulation among the married women, which of them could bring the fattest child to the market. Men would become as fond of their wives during the time of their pregnancy as they are now of their mares in foal, their cows in calf, their sows when they are ready to farrow; nor offer to beat or kick them (as is too frequent a practice) for fear of a miscarriage. . . .

. . . I can think of not one objection that will possibly be raised against this proposal, unless it should be urged that the number of people will be thereby much lessened in the kingdom. This I freely own, and it was indeed one principal design in offering it to the world. I desire the reader will observe, that I calculate my remedy for this one individual kingdom of Ireland and for no other that ever was, is, or I think ever can be upon earth. Therefore let no man talk to me of other expedients: of taxing our absentees at 5s. a pound: of using neither clothes nor household furniture except what is of our own growth and manufacture: of utterly rejecting the materials and instruments that promote foreign luxury. . . .

. . . Supposing that 1000 families in this city would be constant customers for infants' flesh, beside others who might have it at merry-meetings, particularly at weddings and christenings, I compute that Dublin would take off annually about 20,000 carcasses; and the rest of the kingdom (where probably they will be sold somewhat cheaper) the remaining 80,000. . . .

. . . I profess, in the sincerity of my heart, that I have not the least personal interest in endeavouring to promote this necessary work, having no other motive than the public good of my country, by advancing our trade, providing for infants, relieving the poor, and giving some pleasure to the rich. I have no children by which I can propose to get a single penny; the youngest being nine years old, and my wife past child-bearing.

In 1733 he received a letter from Pope, congratulating him because his seventieth birthday had been celebrated throughout
Ireland with bells, bonfires, and toasts of "Long life to the Drapier,
Prosperity to poor Ireland, and the liberty of the press!" He wrote
in response:

> My popularity that you mention is wholly confined to the
> common people, who are more constant than those we miscall
> their betters. I walk the streets, and so do my lower friends,
> from whom, and from whom alone, I have a thousand hats
> and blessings upon old scores [the fight for Irish rights] which
> those we call the gentry have forgot. But I have not the love,
> or hardly the civility of any one man in power or station. . . .
> What has sunk my spirits more than even years and sickness
> is, reflecting on the most execrable corruptions that run
> through every branch of public management.

Although his popularity in Ireland never waned, the next ten
years were spent in growing loneliness (Stella had died in 1728)
and a suppressed hopeless fury at the misery all around him which
made him feel, as he said in more than one letter, that he was
dying in a trap, poisoned with his own venom. In practical terms
he did much, devoting the greater part of his income to such immediate social services as innumerable noninterest-bearing loans of
£50 to £100 to set small tradesmen and craftsmen up in business;
reductions in the rent and improvements on the farm property his
church living controlled; and the more conventional charity demanded to preserve from literal starvation some part of the swarm-
ing slum population of Dublin. But he was too clear-sighted to
think that any or all of these measures were effective even as an
amelioration of conditions, and his growing desperation vented itself in increased irritability, varied by indulgence in all kinds of
intellectual, and physical, horseplay with forced, almost hysterical,
high spirits.

The "Verses On The Death of Dr. Swift" was one of the wittiest
and pleasantest of these elaborate practical jokes. They were first
circulated anonymously; Swift then wrote letters to the newspapers
indignantly attacking the scurrilous unknown who had written
them; and a whole involved series of mystifications and counter-
accusations was developed before they were finally published as his
in 1739.

They read, in part:

> "O! may we all for death prepare!
> What has he left? and who's his heir?"
> "I know no more than what the news is;
> 'Tis all bequeathed to public uses."—
> "To public uses! there's a whim!
> What had the public done for him?"
> Now Grub-Street wits are all employ'd;
> With elegies the town is cloy'd;
> Some paragraph in every paper
> To curse the Dean, or bless the Drapier.
> From Dublin soon to London spread,
> 'Tis told at court, "The Dean is dead."
> And Lady Suffolk, in the spleen,
> Runs laughing up to tell the queen.
> The queen, so gracious, mild and good,
> Cries, "Is he gone? 'Tis time he should!"
> Here shift the scene to represent
> How those I love my death lament.
> Poor Pope would grieve a month, and Gay
> A week, and Arbuthnot a day.
> The rest will give a shrug, and cry,
> "I'm sorry—but we all must die!"
> My female friends, whose tender hearts
> Have better learn'd to act their parts,
> Receive the news in doleful dumps:
> "The Dean is dead: (Pray, what is trumps?)"
> "His time was come; he ran his race;
> We hope he's in a better place."
>
>   .   .   .   .   .   .
>
> He never thought an honour done him
> Because a duke was proud to own him,
> Would rather step aside and choose
> To talk with wits in dirty shoes;
> And would you make him truly sour,
> Provoke him with a slave in power.
> The Irish Senate if you named,
> With what impatience he declaim'd!
> Fair Liberty was all his cry,
> For her he stood prepared to die;
> For her he boldly stood alone;
> For her he oft exposed his own.
> Two kingdoms, just as factions led,
> Had set a price upon his head;
> But not a traitor could be found,
> To sell him for six hundred pound.

. . . . . .
He gave the little wealth he had
To build a house for fools and mad
And show'd by one satiric touch
No nation wanted it as much.
. That kingdom he had left his debtor,
I wish it soon may have a better.

Madness ran much in his mind; in his *Proposal for the Universal Use of Irish Manufacture*, as early as 1720 he had written: "The Scripture tells us oppression maketh a wise man mad," and in his verses on his own death he referred to the project he later carried out of leaving his estate to found a hospital for the incurably insane—the first of its kind. And when in 1736 the House of Commons passed a bill to facilitate evictions, Swift's wild burlesque attack "The Legion Club" has a particular personal horror mixed with the hatred which describes in detail the inmates of parliament as literal madmen.

In his letters we read of frequent attacks of "age, giddiness, deafness, loss of memory, rage and rancour against persons and proceedings," although we find brief flashes of self-possessed wit reported as late as 1740. One characteristic anecdote tells of his returning from a ride during which he had seen a new armory being built and writing:

Behold a proof of Irish sense;
Here Irish wit is seen!
When nothing's left that's worth defence
They build a magazine.

It was clear his mind was breaking. As Hazlitt was to say when lecturing about Swift three quarters of a century later:

There is nothing more likely to drive a man mad, than the being unable to get rid of the idea of the distinction between right and wrong, and an obstinate, constitutional preference of the true to the agreeable.

In 1742 Dean Swift, then already seventy-four years old, was declared insane. He died in 1745 and was buried, as he had directed, with the utmost privacy and simplicity. The Latin epitaph which he himself had composed when making his will in 1735, was, as he had arranged, chiseled in letters "deeply cut and strongly gilded" on his monument of black stone. Translated, it reads:

Here Lies the Body
of
Jonathan Swift
Once Dean of This Cathedral
Where Savage Indignation
[Ubi Saeva Indignatio]
Can No Longer Tear His Heart
Go, Passerby,
And do, if you can, as he did
A Man's Part in Defense of Human Freedom.

Yeats, a later Irish poet and patriot, not fortunate enough to share Swift's instinctive lifelong loyalty to the people and their interests, has transposed the sonorous Latin into a perhaps somewhat too lightly musical English verse:

Swift has sailed into his rest;
Savage indignation there
Cannot lacerate his breast.
Imitate him if you dare,
World besotted traveller; he
Served human liberty.

Great fighter and superb satirist as Swift was, he cannot be said adequately to represent the progressive force of the early eighteenth century. His hatred of tyranny was deep and strong, and his sympathy with the oppressed a burning painful thing, but although these helped him break through the smug complacency of his class, he could carry on the struggle against its callous corruption only in a desperate and hopeless fashion.

The positive achievements which were made possible by the development of scientific agriculture, skilled manufacture and widespread commerce Swift could not appreciate. Both his essentially aristocratic education and the more or less accidental circumstances of a colonial life made it impossible for him to grasp the limited but real significance of material progress in his age, while his human sympathy for suffering and indignation at injustice kept him keenly aware of the misery, ugliness and destruction involved in the ruthless greed with which it was achieved.

But if he never won, he never surrendered and little as he finally anticipated victory, still less did he ever accept defeat. He did not see how the common man could ever regain his birthright, but he never doubted that he should. Nor did he ever blame the victim for the assault as so many liberal intellectuals have absolved their consciences by doing.

Together with his expressions of furious hatred for those who had stripped and bound man, perhaps the most violent in the great tradition of English literature, we find rare touches of gentleness in his regard for "Esau come fainting from the field . . . [to sell] his birthright for a mess of pottage." And so Swift remains one of the very few who have made satire an effective weapon with which to attack the enemy, rather than merely a shield with which to protect their own sensibilities from him.

DANIEL DEFOE

For a true picture of the real accomplishment of this vigorous postrevolutionary commercial age we must turn to a different figure, a son of lower middle-class nonconformists, a grandson of those who had formed the backbone for Cromwell's New Model Army, and the father of perhaps the greatest art form originated by the bourgeoisie—the novel.

Daniel Foe (he added the "de" forty years later) was born in London, oldest son of an energetic and intelligent London chandler, James Foe, in 1659 or 1660. His family survived both the Great Plague of 1665 and the Great Fire of London in 1666 without mishap, and sometime about the boy's tenth birthday his father, who had evidently been thriving, joined the prosperous London Butchers' Company, securing a membership which carried with it the right to a vote as well as to other substantial benefits.

Defoe, as he was later to call himself, fortunate in his education as well as in his family, was sent to one of the best of the dissenting academies, kept by a Mr. Morton who, like many other nonconformists barred from a clerical career by the Restoration, had turned to teaching.

His school omitted the customary instruction in Greek and spent little time on Latin but stressed English composition, mathematics and even the rudiments of science, then and for long after altogether ignored at both Oxford and Cambridge. Defoe later says that Mr. Morton's "chief excellence lay in Mathematicks, and especially the mechanick part of them," and that he also stressed history, geography, which the boy was to find of absorbing interest all the rest of his life, and political science. This very progressive educator emigrated to New England in 1688 and became the first vice-president of Harvard.

Defoe has also left us a characteristic comment—written as part of a memorial tribute in 1696—on the minister to whose congregation his family belonged, stressing the virtues which seemed to him most important:

> If e'er his Duty focred him to contend,
> Calmness was all his temper, Peace his end.
> His native candor and familiar stile,
> Which did so oft his hearers' hours beguile,

His own religion seems to have been, as indeed it always remained, sincere but by no means immoderate, and he tells us in a characteristically frank and reasonable autobiographical comment that when, on the alarm of a possible Catholic restoration which would confiscate all English Bibles, many of the dissenters copied theirs out in a kind of short-hand:

> . . . I myself, then but a boy, worked like a horse, till I wrote out the whole Pentateuch, and then was so tired I was willing to run the risk of the rest.

Years later in a book of advice called *The Complete English Tradesman*, Defoe ingenuously says that a man must not be "so intent upon religious duties, as to neglect the proper times and seasons of business. . . . Works of superrogation are not required at any man's hands." In discussing James II's Declaration of Indulgence, which we have already noted in relation to Bunyan, he makes clear the relative importance of religious and political liberty as far as he is concerned:

> Was anything ever more absurd than this conduct of King James and his party in wheedling the Dissenters, giving them liberty of conscience by his own arbitrary dispensing authority, and expecting they should be content with their religious liberty at the price of the constitution?

His father had expected his oldest son to enter the ministry, but as Defoe later said of his desire to write about economics rather

than politics: "trade was the whore I really doated upon and designed to have taken up with." When he left school, trade was
growing by leaps and bounds. London's imports, for example,
increased from £7,000,000 in 1672 to £11,500,000 in 1688 and the
establishment of the Penny Post in 1680 was both an indication of,
and an enormous assistance to, the increasing tempo of domestic
trade. Defoe, who never in the course of an incredibly tempestuous
life was to tire of excitement, plunged enthusiastically into the
midst of this busy world of affairs.

About 1680 he became a hose factor or commission merchant,
dealing between manufacturer and retailer, and also acting as a
jobber for wine, tobacco, woolens, and any other merchandise that
seemed interesting.

We have few details of these years but know that he did some
commercial traveling in Spain, France, Holland and Italy during
the eighties and took many business trips, on horseback, throughout large sections of England. He may have begun his study of
French and Italian at school but he evidently became fluent in
both languages during this time, and has written some interesting
notes on the comparative manners, customs and ways of life in
the various European countries he visited. Among the observations
he made during his English travels is a rather noncommittal comment on what may have been something like the first industrial
strike in England:

> As to Spittle-fields, in about 1679 and 80, if I remember
> right, when the Weavers in Spittle-fields mutineed upon some
> occasion of setting up Engine-looms, as they called them, in
> which one Man might do as much Work as 6 or 8, or
> more. . . .

By 1684 he was well established with a large enough business
to enable him to marry an attractive young woman of twenty,
daughter of a rather more important commercial family than his
own, who brought him a dowry of over £3,000. By 1688 he had
been admitted as a member of the powerful group of "Liverymen
of the City of London," had claimed his inherited right to membership in the "Butchers' Company," owned a large warehouse, a
London home and a country residence, had several children and
seemed likely to be able to retire as a wealthy alderman twenty
years later.

Yet, as one of the best of his biographers, James Sutherland, has

said, Defoe was always "a citizen first and a man of business afterwards." Twice during these prosperous four years Defoe had im-
periled not only his business success but life itself, first by joining
in the abortive attempt to place the Protestant Duke of Monmouth
on the throne in 1686, and later in the successful rebellion which
forced James II's abdication and made William of Orange king in
England.

The records of six lawsuits in the next few years show that
when Defoe's business began to bore him by a too routine success
he looked for more adventurous speculations elsewhere. It may also
be true, as he himself claimed, that the war with France caused
Defoe, as it did many other merchants, disastrous losses in ship-
ping. At any rate, in 1692, Defoe was forced into bankruptcy,
failing for the imposing sum of £17,000—the equivalent of at least
$150,000 today.

Years later in one of the many chapters of advice to tradesmen
which he wrote in both periodical and book form, he used what
was no doubt a summary description of this part of his career. He
says:

> . . . nothing is more common than the tradesman when
> once he finds himself grown rich, to have his head full of great
> designs, and new undertakings. He finds his cash flow in upon
> him, and perhaps he is fuller of money than his trade calls
> for; and as he scarce knows how to employ more stock in
> it than he does, his ears are the sooner open to any project
> or proposal that offers itself; and I must add, that this is the
> most critical time with him in all his life; if ever he is in
> danger of ruin, 'tis just then. . . . I think, I may safely ad-
> vance without danger of reprehension, there are more people
> ruined in England by over-trading than for want of trade;
> and I would, from my own unhappy experience, advise all
> men in trade to set a due compass to their ambition.

His creditors seem to have retained faith both in his ability and
in his essential honesty, and agreed to an arrangement which enabled him to keep out of the debtors prison, accepting his unsecured
and legally unenforcable promise to pay in full as soon as he
again made money. (He had paid off over £11,000 by 1705 when
circumstances which we shall note as of more than passing interest
seriously delayed the remainder.)

Two years later he was offered a good position in Cadiz which he refused, being unwilling permanently to leave England, and in 1695 he was appointed accountant for a newly formed glass-tax commission, trustee for a state lottery, and unofficial unpaid advisor on ways and means to several prominent Whig members of the government.

By 1697 he had organized a pantile factory to make bricks—then imported from Holland—and had received a contract to supply them to the large new Greenwich hospital.

It is interesting to note that excavations for a railroad 160 years later on the site of his factory turned up bricks in sufficient quantity to prove that they were exceptionally well made, of a rather novel design, and extremely durable.

But as always, once a business was successful Defoe lost interest in it and, running it with one hand, turned the other to more exciting and generally more dangerous, matters.

In 1698 he published his first real book, *An Essay Upon Projects*. This included suggestions for improved roads; an enlarged banking system; special simplified legal procedures for commercial disputes; bankruptcy laws which would distinguish between honest and fraudulent failures, allowing the former to work out their debts rather than idle in jail; an asylum or hospital for "idiots"—that is, the feeble-minded; higher education for women; fire and shipwreck insurance; and even an Income Tax! Most of these proposals were adopted within the next two or two and a half centuries.

Perhaps the most interesting to us is the one for "An Academy for Women." This begins:

> I have often thought of it as one of the most barbarous customs in the world considering us as a civilized and a Christian country, that we deny the advantages of learning to women. We reproach the sex every day with folly and impertinence, while I am confident, had they the advantages of education equal to us, they would be guilty of less than ourselves.
>
> One would wonder, indeed, how it should happen that women are conversible at all, since they are only beholding to natural parts for all their knowledge. Their youth is spent to teach them to stitch and sew, or make baubles. They are taught to read indeed, and perhaps to write their names, or so; and this is the height of a woman's education. And I would but ask any who slight the sex for their understanding, what is a man (a gentleman, I mean) good for that is taught no more?

Benjamin Franklin says in his autobiography: "I found besides, a work of Defoe's, entitled an 'Essay on Projects' from which, perhaps, I derived impressions that have since influenced some of the principal events of my life."

Advanced as it was, this was nevertheless a fairly safe publication since those who did not like it found no difficulty in ignoring it. But an article Defoe had published some months before made more enemies.

King William, whom he greatly admired, was making serious efforts to stamp out the remnants of Restoration manners, and at his urging several salutary laws had been passed toward the correction of the public brutality, drunkenness, and gross abuse of women which were still prevalent in London.

These were often enforced against poor and unimportant offenders—and there only. On March 31, 1697 Defoe published an open letter entitled *The Poor Man's Plea* which read, in part:

> These are all cobweb laws, in which the small flies are catched, and the great ones break through. My Lord-Mayor has whipt about the poor beggars, and a few scandalous whores have been sent to the House of Correction; some alehousekeepers and vintners have been fined for drawing drink on the Sabbath-day; but all this falls upon us of the mob, the poor plebian, as if all the vice lay among us; for we do not find the rich drunkard carried before my Lord-Mayor, nor a swearing lewd merchant fined, or set in the stocks. The man with a gold ring may swear before the Justice or at the Justice; may reel home through the open streets, and no man take any notice of it; but if a poor man get drunk, or swear an oath, he must to the stocks without remedy.

Dickens, who knew his Defoe well, may have thought of this when, a hundred and fifty years later, he still found it timely to write the brief dialogue:

> "There's something in his appearance quite—dear, dear, what's that word again?"
>
> "What word?" enquired Mr. Lillyvick.
>
> "Why—dear me, how stupid I am," replied Miss Petowker, hesitating. "What do you call it, when Lords break off doorknockers and beat policemen, and play at coaches with other people's money, and all that sort of thing?"
>
> "Aristocratic?" suggested the collector.
>
> "Ah! aristocratic," replied Miss Petowker; "something very aristocratic about him, isn't there?"

There was certainly something aristocratic about this conduct in the eighteenth century, and there were many of the Tories who bore Defoe serious ill will from that time on.

In 1698 and 1700 he further antagonized them by two pamphlets defending the King's Whig pro-trade policies, and in 1701 when the landed interest's dislike of William had led to openly racist attacks on his Dutch followers, and covert sneers at the King himself as racially inferior, Defoe wrote an extremely successful burlesque called *The True Born Englishman.*

It traces with broad humor and accuracy the successive invasions of Danes, Romans, Normans and later-day French, as well as the many other strains which make the truest born Englishman a mongrel:

> Thus from a mixture of all kinds began
> That heterogenous thing, an Englishman.

Then it points out, in defense of the forced abdication of James II and, therefore, of the legitimacy of William's title:

> And punishing of Kings is no such crime,
> But Englishmen have done it many a time.

The following stanza gives us a good idea of the generally unsubtle but effective humor which no doubt helped make the verses so extraordinarily popular that there were nine authorized, and at least twelve pirated, editions.

> A Turkish horse can show more ancestry
> To prove his well-descended family. . . .
> These are the heroes that despise the Dutch,
> And rail at new-come foreigners so much,
> Great families of yesterday we show,
> And lords whose parents were the Lord knows who.

A more important effect of the poem was that it won for Defoe an unusual degree of intimacy with the King and made him, for the short remainder of William's life, almost an unofficial private cabinet member advising on all matters pertaining to trade, and on many others.

That spring Defoe, inspired by this relation with the man whom, all his life, he most respected and perhaps most truly loved, carried out an extraordinary exploit.

The party situation in England was a complicated and, basically, an unimportant one. Both Lords and Commons were now divided into Whigs and Tories and while the latter were generally considered the landed interest, and the former the commercial interest, there was often no line of demarcation between moderate Whigs and moderate Tories insofar as policies were concerned. The party battles were really just irrelevant jockeying for personal position and power. During the last years of William's reign, for example, the House of Lords had a Whig majority and the Commons a Tory one! As Defoe was to write, after many years of political journalism, in 1712:

> I have seen the bottom of all parties, the bottom of all their pretences, and the bottom of their sincerity, and as the Preacher said, that all was vanity and vexation of spirit, so I say of these: all is a mere show, outside, and abominable hypocrisy, of every party, in every age, under every government; when they are OUT to get IN, when IN, to prevent being OUT; every sect, every party, and almost every person that we have an account of, have, for ought I see, been guilty, more or less, of the general charge, viz. that their interests governs their principle.

But a more fundamental question was raised when, in May 1701, five Gentlemen of Kent came up to London to present a petition to the Tory House of Commons for more energetic defense measures in Kent. They argued that if the French armies were planning to effect a landing in England, as was rumored, Kent would be their natural destination.

The Tory majority was probably justified in thinking this a publicity stunt whereby the Whigs meant to force them to vote more generous war supplies, but they were certainly altogether unjustified in summarily arresting and imprisoning all five delegates for daring to petition their parliament!

On May 14, in an altogether unprecedented action, Defoe "guarded" as he says, "by about sixteen gentlemen of quality," simply marched into the House, presented the Speaker with a petition he had written entitled, *Legion's Memorial to the House of Commons*, and prudently marched out again before the Speaker had a chance to read it. The memorial was as simple and direct as all Defoe's writing and said, after bluntly describing the outrageous conduct of which the Commons had been guilty:

And though there is no stated proceeding to bring you to your duty, yet the great law of reason says, and all nations allow that, whatever power is above law, it is burdensome and tyrannical; and may be reduced by extra-judicial methods. You are not above the People's resentments! . . .

It then went on to demand:

That the thanks of the House may be given to those Gentlemen who so gallantly appeared in the behalf of their country with the Kentish Petition and have been so scandalously used for it.

and concluded:

We do hereby claim and declare that if the House of Commons, in breach of the Laws and Liberties of the people, do betray the trust reposed in them; and act negligently or arbitrarily and illegally; it is the undoubted Right of the People of England to call them to account for the same; and by Convention, Assembly, or Force, may proceed against them, as traitors and betrayers of their country.

Gentlemen, you have your Duty laid before you! which it is hoped you will think of! But if you continue to neglect it, you may expect to be treated according to the resentments of an injured Nation! For Englishmen are no more to be Slaves to Parliament than to a king!

Our name is Legion, and we are Many.

Parliament was so intimidated that the five delegates were freed before the House adjourned! Defoe was guest of honor at a dinner given for the Gentlemen of Kent, and an anonymous pamphlet on *The History of the Kentish Petition*, written by Defoe himself, sold in the thousands.

His pantile factory was running smoothly with a minimum of attention; his debts were largely paid; his wife and seven children comfortable; and he himself was busy, effective and happy. But his political enemies were by now very many.

We have already seen how he had earned the anger of the London judges and, now, of most Tories. But he had also had a light-hearted fling at antagonizing a substantial part of the Whigs, particularly those who were, like himself, nonconformists or dissenters.

According to laws, many of which remained in force for more

than another century, it was impossible for anyone to attend the universities, hold government office, or enjoy various other privileges, unless he conformed to the requirements of the Established Church.

As the dissenters became respectable and prosperous, however, the Whig party to which they belonged, had approved of the Whig king's various Acts of Toleration. The most notable one of these provided for "Occasional Conformity" whereby a dissenter need only partake of the communion of the Established Church once or twice a year, while regularly attending his own chapel, to be eligible.

In 1698 Defoe had won the enmity of most of the more important dissenters by publishing a pamphlet, *An Enquiry into the Occasional Conformity of Dissenters in Cases of Preferment,* in which he strongly condemned the illogical and irreligious practise of occasional conformity.

We do not know whether he was moved, as a pious biographer suggests, by a memory of the one sermon Bunyan is reputed to have given at his school; by his lifelong hatred of muddled thinking; by the personal pride which would never allow him to belie his own background and class, however careless, as we shall see, about the literal truth in many matters; or by a shrewd idea that if this evasion was ended there would be far more effective pressure brought to have the disabilities removed altogether.

There is some evidence that the last idea played a considerable part in his thinking. John F. Ross, in an interesting comparative study called *Swift and Defoe,* summarizes Defoe's explicit advice to his fellow dissenters, embodied in a burlesque political allegory, *The Consolidator,* in 1705:

> His long and satiric account of English strife was directed toward action in 1705. First it was a long demonstration that no Anglican-Tory leadership could be trusted—that it would lead the nation to disaster for the trading class and for Dissenters. But it was more than attack; it concluded with long "constructive proposals" for the Whigs to act upon. Basically his advice was, "Don't mourn; organize"—and the word he tried to drive home was "Unite." He pointed out in some detail how an organized labor boycott and an economic freeze-out would bring the Anglican-Tories to their knees. He suggested that the Dissenters remove their deposits from the Bank of England and set up their own credit system. But his master

stroke for financial pressure was to show how the Dissenters could even get control of the privileged and chartered companies, like the East India; on concerted agreement, great stock holders among the Dissenters would sell out and start rumors that the stock was worthless; the market would fall; having sold some stock high, the sellers would secretly buy up all the stock at a low figure; and finally, they would run up the price of Funds again as high as ever. . . . Eventually the Dissenters would have economic control of England, and no Tory government could fail to come to terms. Defoe often speaks as if he were concerned with gaining religious toleration; but the measures he urged so vigorously are economic and political, and, if carried out, would have resulted in the destruction of the Anglican-Tory squirearchy. Defoe's class would have gained religious toleration, but also political and economic supremacy. Defoe was not moving in the world of religion, or of the moon; but in the practical world of modern business politics.

However, none of this was indicated in the pamphlet which had been greeted with amazed indignation by Defoe's co-religionists on its publication in 1698.

When in 1702 King William, whose health had for some time been failing, died of shock after an accidental fall from horseback that broke his collarbone, the loss to Defoe was enormous. He lost not only a political leader and personal friend but also his only powerful well-wisher.

The Whigs distrusted and perhaps disliked him; the Tories resented and feared him. Still, if he could have confined himself to building his second fortune—he was to make and lose several more in the course of a long life—he might have done well enough without the help of either. But, although he did not exactly share Milton's passion for political liberty, or Bunyan's utter devotion to religious freedom, he was in his own less heroic fashion equally unable to ignore what seemed to him his civic responsibilities, or to remain silent when it seemed a word of advice might set so many weaker minds right.

Thus when, on the accession of the deeply religious Queen Anne, many Tory High Churchmen began to introduce proposals for increased discrimination against dissenters, Defoe felt he had to take a hand.

In December, 1702, he published an anonymous pamphlet, *The Shortest Way with Dissenters,* which purported to be written by a member of the right wing of the Tory High Church party, and which advocated the most extreme measures to destroy the prosperity, security, and perhaps even the lives of all dissenters.

Defoe's object was a simple one. He intended this extreme statement as a reductio ad absurdem which would show all moderate Tories to what end the doctrines of intolerance tended, and would deter even the most violent diehards, who had not intimated, and probably did not feel, any desire for real physical violence.

But the pamphlet totally failed of its object. It passed for genuine, but it aroused a warm response from extreme Tories and created real terror in the Whigs. For example, a High Church clergyman wrote a friend about it:

> I join with the author in all that he says, and have such a value for the book that, next to the Holy Bible and Sacred Comments, I take it for the most valuable piece I have. I pray God put it into Her Majesty's heart to put what is there proposed in execution.

A few excerpts from the pamphlet would show how all too convincing Defoe had made it, as far as anyone who did not share his absolutely unquestioning assumption of the irrelevance of religious disputes to the serious business of life, was concerned.

The waste of religious struggles was for him so axiomatic that it evidently never occurred to him anyone could desire their resumption. For example, in 1694 he had written in a fragment of English history:

> the Papist, the Church of England, and the Dissenter have all had their turns in administration. . . . Whenever any of them endeavoured their own settlement by the ruin of the parties dissenting, the consequence was supplanting themselves.

And in 1719 he wrote in Robinson Crusoe:

> It was remarkable, too, we had but three subjects, and they were of three different religions. My man Friday was a Protestant, his father was a Pagan and a Cannibal, and the Spaniard was a Papist; however, I allow'd Liberty of Conscience throughout my Dominions.

But it is easy to see why dissenters should have been outraged when they learned who had written the pamphlet, and why their enemies should first have been taken in, and then have been furious because of their own gullibility.

The immediate result of his exploit was that in January, 1703, the Tories procured a warrant for his arrest on general grounds of seditious writing and disturbing the peace, and although the pamphlet had probably been instrumental in turning the twelve moderate Tory votes which defeated the antitoleration bill, the Whigs eyed Defoe with undiminished suspicion and refrained from coming to his defense.

He was more afraid of a lengthy and indefinite jail sentence— "during her majesty's pleasure"—than of death, and went into hiding, attempting by letter to make a bargain with her majesty whereby he would secure a pardon in return for raising "a troop of horse" (a cavalry regiment) at his own expense, and leading them to fight in the French wars!

This was refused and while still a fugitive Defoe frankly wrote a friend:

> Gaols, pillories, and suchlike, with which I have been so much threatened, have convinced me I want passive courage, and I shall never for the future think myself injured if I am called a coward.

Finally captured, he was given an unprecedently severe sentence whose object was obviously to destroy him rather than merely to punish him.

It included a very heavy fine of 200 marks, an indefinite jail sentence clearly intended to be of great duration, and the crowning and really dangerous indignity of three days in the pillory in three separate parts of London. Not infrequently an unpopular prisoner, stoned by the mob while helpless, was fortunate if he emerged with no greater permanent injury than the loss of an eye. Even death from wounds so inflicted was not altogether unlikely or unprecedented.

Defoe was, of course, really being punished for *Legion's Memorial* and perhaps as he himself always claimed, for his refusal even in jail to betray the secrets of policy and ministerial discussions with which the late king had entrusted him.

But although Defoe had confessed himself frightened in advance, as always he rose to the occasion.

Through his wife, of whom we wish we had more personal knowledge than is afforded by tantalizing glimpses at this and succeeding crises, he sent confidential messages to friends and succeeded in getting a *Hymn to the Pillory* printed for street distribution on his first appearance there, and the nucleus of a friendly "mob" organized for the same occasion.

His courage and the humor of his verses won the immediate sympathy of many, and on that and his two subsequent appearances, he was pelted with nothing worse than flowers.

Perhaps the best stanza of the hymn reads:

> Tell them it was because he was too bold,
> And told those truths which should not ha' been told,
>   Extol the justice of the land,
> Who punish what they will not understand.
>   Tell them he stands exalted there
>   For speaking what they would not hear. . . .
> Tell them the Men that placed him here
> Are scandals to the times,
>   Are at a loss to find his guilt,
>   And can't commit his crimes.

Returned to jail, Defoe saw his business going to pieces while he was unable to do anything to save it or help his large family. In desperation he appealed to the very moderate Tory, Harley, who was minister of state, for assistance. Harley who, as we have seen, had shown himself well aware of the value of a skillful pen in his successful efforts to enlist Swift's assistance, was quite willing to secure Defoe's. However he carelessly or deliberately delayed the fulfillment of his half promise until the end of the year and finally, in November 1703, secured for Defoe a pardon from the queen.

One of the many urgent letters with which the prisoner bombarded his dilatory patron is particularly interesting in containing a rare—and characteristic—reference to his children.

> Seven children whose education calls on me to furnish their heads if I cannot their purses, and which debt if not paid now can never be compounded hereafter, is to me a moving article and helps very often to make me sad.

When Defoe emerged from jail he was again bankrupt, a man of forty-three, with a wife and seven children to feed and clothe as well as educate. But the inexhaustible vitality that made it impossible for him to be depressed whenever there was any possibility of action, was no less in evidence now than it had been twelve years before.

He immediately set to work and, with capital secretly furnished by Harley, issued on February 19, 1704, the first number of *A Weekly Review of the Affairs of France, Purged from the Errors and Partiality of News-Writers and Petty Statesmen of all Sides.*

A year later it began to appear three times a week, and in that state continued for nine years.

The Review, as it was soon familiarly called, is in itself an extraordinary achievement. Defoe wrote it himself from cover to cover, personally handled all correspondence—one of his innovations was a weekly supplement which combined the functions of an "Advice to the Lovelorn" column, with an "Information Please" quiz program—was publisher, business manager, and editor as well as reporter, and never missed an issue! This is the more amazing in that, during those nine years, he was often employed as a secret government agent in circumstances of considerable difficulty, had to travel to Scotland and other parts of Great Britain, and was engaged in all sorts of odd and profitable business ventures as opportunity on his travels offered.

A letter to Harley from Edinburgh, where he had spent some time helping to achieve a successful conclusion of the difficult negotiations for "An Act of Union Between England and Scotland," tells of his having been stoned by the anti-English crowd and ends:

> I baulked no cases, I appeared in print when others dared not open their mouths, and without boasting I ran as much risk of my life as a grenadier storming a counter-scarp.

In the vast number of essays which he wrote during the nine years of *The Review*—the equivalent in volume of some twenty or twenty-five average novels—he touched upon the most diverse and personal topics, recurring frequently to questions of woman's position, relations between parents and children, matters of art, journalism, science and religion, as well as to the more obvious questions of economics and politics.

For the paper to be effective it was necessary that it hold its readers' interest, build its circulation, and create respect for the editor's knowledge, intelligence and good will. Although the closely guarded secret of Defoe's government position prevented complete independence he was, as a matter of fact, in sympathy with most of Harley's policies and kept silent about, without defending or attacking, those of which he disapproved.

That he lied about his independence in the pages of the review and, no doubt, outside them, there is no question. But there seems to be as little reason to disbelieve his assertions that he was nevertheless expressing his own opinion in all the matters he chose to discuss, most of which were, of course, unaffected by party policies.

Even when writing more or less "to order" on a specific political controversy, Defoe frequently developed the broader implications of his position in a way altogether different from, and often startlingly more advanced than, any involved in the concrete proposals at issue.

For example, when in the spring of 1709 the government moved to secure general support for its proposal of an immediate peace—largely opposed by the Whigs—Defoe suggested a sort of early League of Nations, or United Nations, to guard against any recurrence of the war. He wrote, on April 19, 1709:

> Nothing then can be a sufficient guarantee for the present peace, but the whole Confederacy, the body of powers that have now acted, being formed into a politic frame or constitution, upon which they can again act in case of an invasion upon any of the branches. Call this what you please, and let the difficulties be as great as you can propose; . . . but if a constitution be formed by which the whole Confederacy may resume and act as a body, then the peace will be always under the protection of the same power that has procured it.
>
> . . . it is now in the power of the present Confederacy forever to prevent any more war in Europe. It is in their power to make themselves arbiters of all the differences and disputes that ever can happen in Europe, whether between kingdom and kingdom, or between sovereign and subjects. A congress of this alliance may be made a court of appeals for all the injured and oppressed, whether they are princes or people that are or ever shall be in Europe to the end of the world. Here the petty states and princes shall be protected against the terror of their powerful neighbours; the great shall no more oppress the small, or the mighty devour the weak; this very

Confederacy have at this time, and if they please may preserve to themselves, the power of banishing war out of Europe. They are able from henceforward to crush the strongest, and support the weakest. . . . Perhaps this may pass for a wild thought of mine, and I confess it is new and undigested; but I refer it to the consideration of those in whose hands the power of better modelling this thought lies, whether they have not now the only opportunity that ever Providence entrusted with mankind to make sure the peace of all this part of Europe, as long as the world shall last; and if it be neglected, let them answer for it that ought to have improved it.

Two years earlier, in October, 1707, combating the general clamor for territorial acquisition as a part of England's conditions for making peace, Defoe had with amazing prescience declared:

We want not the dominion of more countries than we have; we sufficiently possess a nation when we have an open and free trade to it. We know how to draw wealth from all nations if we can but trade to them; the value and bulk of our own manufactures have found the way to make themselves necessary to all the world, and they force the wealth from the best and richest countries, be they never so remote; our trading to Old Spain has been a full trade to New Spain, and a trade by which England has always drawn as much money from America as Old Spain itself.

He concluded that essay:

And this is the reason why there are fewer English in foreign parts than of any other nation, and fewer soldiers, and harder to be raised than in any other nation. What should they go abroad for, that live so well at home; what should make the soldier fight at 3s. 6d. a week that can work at home and get near that in a day? 'Tis poverty makes nations scatter, and want of bread drives men into the army. But England, happy in herself, seeks no living abroad, nor dominion abroad; give her peace and trade, she is the happiest, and will be the richest, and in time the most populous, nation in the world.

Since English literature is concerned with Defoe chiefly as a novelist, and since he did not write his first novel until he was sixty, it is of special interest to note how many of the ideas, as well as how much of the technique, which fifteen years later made their appearance in *Robinson Crusoe, Moll Flanders,* and *Roxana,* and in his less well-known fiction, were first formulated in the pages of *The Review.*

For example, in response to a reader's question on "What is the worst sort of husband a sober woman can marry?" Defoe described a number of bad husbands, concluding:

> Well, good people, here are four sorts of ill husbands, and take one of them where you will, the best of them is bad enough, and hard is that woman's case, especially if she be a woman of any merit, whose lot it is; but yet I think my first rate is behind still; there is yet a bad husband that is worse than all these, and a woman of sense had better take up with any of these than with him, and that's a *fool husband.* The drunkard, the debauched, the fighting, and the extravagant; these may all have something attendant which in the intervals of their excesses may serve to alleviate and make a little amends to the poor woman, and help her to carry through the afflicting part; but a fool has something always about him that makes him intolerable; he is ever contemptible and uninterruptedly ridiculous—it is like a handsome woman with some deformity about her that makes all the rest be rejected. If he is kind, it is so apish, so below the rate of manhood, so surfeiting, and so disagreeable, that like an ill smell, it makes the face wrinkle at it; if he be forward, he is so unsufferably insolent that there is no bearing it; his passions are all flashes, struck out of him like fire from a flint. If it be anger, 'tis sullen and senseless; if love, 'tis coarse and brutish. He is in good, wavering; in mischief, obstinate; in society, empty; in management, unthinking; in manners, sordid; in error, incorrigible; and in everything ridiculous.
>
> Wherefore upon the whole, my answer is in short, that the worst thing a sober woman can be married to is a FOOL. Of whom whoever has the lot, Lord have mercy, and a cross should be set on the door as of a house infected with the plague.

And in *Roxana, the Fortunate Mistress,* we find the heroine advising us:

> Never marry a fool. . . . No fool, ladies at all, no kind of fool, whether a mad fool or a sober fool, a wise fool or a silly fool; take anything but a fool; nay, *be* anything, be even an old maid, the worst of fortune's curses, rather than take up with a fool.

Similarly, we find in *The Review* that Defoe draws a sharp distinction between the wickedness of cheating to increase wealth, and the naturalness of stealing to satisfy need:

> The world has a very unhappy notion of honesty, which they take up to the prejudice of the unhappy. Such a man is a fair merchant, a punctual dealer, an honest man, and a rich man. Ay, says one, that makes him a rich man; God blesses him because he is an honest man. *It's a mistake*: God's blessing is the effect of no man's merit. God's blessing may have made him a rich man—*but why is he an honest man, a fair dealer, a punctual merchant?* The answer is plain: Because he is a rich man. The man's circumstances are easy, his trade answers, his cash flows, and his stock increases; this man cannot be otherwise than honest, he has no occasion to be a knave. Cheating in such a man ought to be felony, and that without the benefit of clergy. He has no temptation, no wretched necessity of shifting and tricking, which another man flies to, to do deliver himself from ruin. The man is not rich because he is honest, but he is honest because he is rich. . . .
>
> And pray, gentlemen, do not vouch too fast for your own honesty; you that have not been tried with distress and disasters, ye know not what you are yourselves. Many a man that thinks himself as honest as (his) neighbours, will find himself as great a r(ogu)e as many of them all, when he comes to the push. How many honest gentlemen have we in England of good estates and noble circumstances that would be highwaymen and come to the gallows if they were poor? How many rich, current, punctual, fair merchants now walk the Exchange that would be errant knaves if they come to be bankrupt? Poverty makes thieves, as bare walls makes giddy housewives; distress makes k(nave)s of honest men, and the exigencies of tradesmen when in declining circumstances, of which none can judge, and which none can express but those that have felt them, will make honest men do that which at another time their very souls abhor. I own to speak this with sad experience, and am not ashamed to confess myself a penitent. *And let him that thinketh he standeth take heed lest he fall.*
>
> . . . "Give me not poverty, lest I steal," says the wise man; that is, if I am poor I shall be a thief. I tell you all, gentlemen, in your poverty the best of you all will rob your neighbour, ay, and say grace to your meat too. Distress removes from the soul all relation, affection, sense of justice, and all the obligations, either moral or religious, that secure one man against another. Not that I say or suggest the distress makes the violence lawful; but I say it is a trial beyond the ordinary power of human nature to withstand; and therefore that excellent petition of the Lord's Prayer, which I believe

is most wanted and the least thought of, ought to be every
moment in our thoughts, "Lead us not into temptation."

And Roxana says, "Honesty is out of the question when Starvation is the case." To which Moll Flanders adds, in her own defense,
"Vice came in always at the Door of Necessity, not at the Door
of Inclination," and, "As Covetousness is the Root of all Evil, so
Poverty is the worst of all Snares." Her God is evidently well aware
of the facts of life, for she very reasonably addresses him in prayer,
"Give me not poverty, lest I steal."

Defoe himself, in his *Tour through the whole Island of Great
Britain* (1724), adds of a vice which he probably disliked more
than either dishonesty or unchastity: "People tell us that Slothfulness begets Poverty, and it is true; but I must add too, that Poverty
makes slothfulness."

This attitude toward poverty is, of course, diametrically opposite to any we would expect from the proponent of *The Compleat
English Tradesman* and we find in other respects also that Defoe's
breadth of intelligence as well as his practical humanity lead him
to transcend the fast hardening commercial ethics of the rising class
he represents.

The ugly bourgeois ideal of ascetism for profit was not yet,
perhaps, fully developed in its application to the master, but it was
certainly generally applied to the conditions of his workman, and
Defoe was almost alone in the unaffected joy with which he hailed
the possibilities of an economy of plenty for all.

He says enthusiastically in *The Compleat English Tradesman*:

> The same trade that keeps our people at home, is the cause
> of the well living of the people here; for as frugality is not the
> national virtue of England, so the people that get much spend
> much; and as they work hard, so they live well, eat and drink
> well, cloath warm, and lodge soft; in a word, the working
> manufacturing people of England eat the fat, drink the sweet,
> live better, and fare better, than the working poor of any other
> nation in Europe; they make better wages of their work, and
> spend more of the money upon their Backs and Bellies, than
> in any other country; . . .

This leads him naturally into one of his favorite discussions,
with an explicit emphasis on high wages as the basis of all prosperity for the landed as well as the commercial interests:

This expense of the Poor, as it causes a prodigious consumption both of the provisions and of the manufactures of our country at home, so two things are undeniably the consequence of that part.

1. The consumption of provisions encreases the rent and value of the lands, and this raises the Gentleman's estates, and that again encreases the employment of people, and consequently the numbers of them, as well those who are employ'd in the husbandry of land, breeding and feeding of cattle etc. . . .

2. As the people get better wages, so they, I mean the same poorer part of the people, clothe better, and furnish better, and this encreases the consumption of the very manufactures they make; then that consumption encreases the quantity made, and this creates what we call *Inland Trade*, by which innumerable families are employ'd and the increase of the people maintain'd; and by which encrease of trade and people the present growing prosperity of this nation is produced.

This emphasis on the desirability of high real wages is often repeated in *The Review* in such comments as: ". . . nothing can do them any Service, but what raises the Price of their Labour, or sinks the Price of Provisions; . . ."

Defoe issues repeated warnings on the evils of a subsistence economy:

Again, if you lower the Wages of the Poor, you must of Course sink the Rate of Provisions, and that of Course will sink the Value of Lands, and so you wound the Capital at once; for the Poor cannot earn little and spend much, the End of that is, starving and misery . . . there is no possibility of its being otherwise; it has ever been so, and ever will be so, the Nature of the Thing requires it.

While in general one of the earliest proponents of free trade, he even suggested government subsidies and import duties to protect infant industries without lowering wage standards by the use of workhouse labor in their development, as had then been proposed. He says, for example:

All Manufacturers must have a Beginning and in the Infancy of things, the Government must assist; National Benefits should have National Support, and there are several Ways to do that in this Case, . . . by publick Bounties and Allowances to every Pound of Cotton spun and wrought into Calicoe or Muslin, and by laying yet a higher Duty on the Importation of the same Goods from abroad.

He also argued strenuously (against the prevailing opinion) for the free admission of immigrants, feeling that the number of working people added to a nation's real riches, since:

Every labouring man is an increase to the public wealth, by how much what he gains by his labour amounts to more than he or his family eats or consumes—for every increase is an article in the credit of the general stock—and for this reason, I say, it is an addition to the public wealth to have the price of labour dear; of which hereafter.

Every labouring man, then, however poor, increases the public wealth.

This argument he pursued at length in many issues of *The Review*.

At a time when the mercantile theory, with its single emphasis on the balance of gold, stressed only foreign markets and seemed to consider goods consumed at home wasted, Defoe declared:

But if more foreigners came among us, if it were two millions, it could do us no harm, because they would consume our provisions, and we have land enough to produce much more than we do, and they would consume our manufactures, and we have wool enough for any quantity.

He concluded:

. . . 't is upon the Gain they make either by their Labour, or their Industry in Trade, and upon their inconceivable Numbers that the Home Consumption of our own Produce, and of the Produce of foreign Nations imported here; is so exceeding great, and that our Trade is raised up to such a Prodigy of Magnitude. . . .

And, almost three quarters of a century before Adam Smith, he carelessly struck out the phrase that has made the latter famous when, in 1704, his *Review* declared:

The Power of Nations is not now measur'd, as it has been, by Powers, Gallantry and Conduct. 'Tis the *Wealth of Nations* that makes them great.

Defoe was also, as we can see from his fiction, especially interested in the question of colonies whose importance he very early foresaw. In the first year of *The Review* he declared that the growth of the colonies should be England's chief concern for:

> . . . were all, or the greatest part of our Foreign Trade to die, and be no more, our own Colonies in Africk and America are capable of so much Improvement, as is sufficient of themselves to Support our Manufactures, Employ our Shipping, enrich our People, and form all the necessary Articles of Trade within ourselves.

And four years later, in 1707, he rebuked the short-sighted policy which did, indeed, lead to catastrophe in 1776:

> I hinted in a former Review, where I entered on this Subject, that the pernicious Jealousie of making the Colonies independent had always stood in the Way of their Prosperity, and in general in the Way of our own. . . .
> . . . To fear to make our Colonies too great, is, as if a Father, in the educating his Child, should fear to make him too wise, or to give him too much Learning, or in feeding him; should be afraid of making him too strong, or too tall, or too beautiful; for the Plantations being our own Children, the Off-spring of the Commonwealth, they cannot, politically speaking, have too much care taken of them, or be too much tender'd by us.

Other comments of a more personal nature scattered through the issues of *The Review* remind us of the forcible direct style of *Robinson Crusoe* and the realistic insight of *Moll Flanders*.

For example, in one of the first issues, rebutting some attacks upon him in an opposing periodical, he begins:

> But if I must act the Pharisee a little, I must begin thus: God, I thank thee, I am not a drunkard, or a swearer, or a whore-master, or a busie-body, or idle, or revengeful, etc., and I challenge all the world to prove the contrary.

Two years later in response to another attack which evidently dwelt on his writing for profit he replied:

> Oh! but 'tis a scandalous employment, to write for bread!
> . . . What are all employments in the world pursued for, but for bread? What do you sell, run, fetch, carry, stoop, cringe,

> build, pull down, turn and return, what is it all but for bread?
> And what do you sail, travel, fight, nay, without offense, what
> preach for? Is it not bread? I hope there are other ends joined
> in the sacred office, or else I should break in upon my charity,
> but that office would be thinly supplied if bread were not
> annext to it.

This was of course only half true about Defoe, as about any
other unspoiled human being who genuinely enjoys constructive
work. For example, while busy enough with his newspaper, employment as a secret government agent to help bring about the
final union of England and Scotland, and with several minor business projects he was investigating in Edinburgh, Defoe wrote
Harley a long letter on August 7, 1707, which began: "I am never,
you know, for searching an evil to be amazed at it, but to apply
the remedies." The letter continued to present an amazingly well
thought out "project" for "A Pension Office" that was really an
embryo plan of social security insurance by which:

> all mankind, be he never so mean, so poor, so unable, shall
> gain for himself a just claim to a comfortable subsistence
> whensoever age or casualty shall reduce him to a necessity of
> making use of it.

This plan included provision for free medical aid, sick and
disability benefits, the care of widows and orphans, and support
for the families of those confined to debtors' prisons! Defoe concluded: "It is a Shame we should suffer real objects of charity to
beg; and for those who are not so, it is a shame but they should
work."

Years later, in 1728, he wrote in a similar tone a second book
of "projects" which he called *Augusta Triumphan* and which included suggestions for a University of London, and a Hospital, or
home, for foundlings. About the latter proposal he very reasonably
remarked in defense against accusations that his plan would further
immorality:

> I am as much against bastards being begot, as I am against
> their being murdered; but when a child is once begot, it can-
> not be unbegotten . . . and we ought to show our charity
> toward it as a fellow creature and Christian, without any
> regard to its legitimacy or otherwise.

Before leaving this important part of Defoe's work we should remark on how frequently his *Review* discussed woman's position and on how advanced his opinions there were, not only in reference to his own century but even the succeeding one.

We shall have briefly to revert to this in glancing at his second novel, *Moll Flanders,* but should note it here as well.

Defoe not only proposed the education of women (see p. 255), but also repeatedly urged the importance of women's participating in the conduct of their husbands' business or, as widows, of their being able to carry the business on independently; he objected vehemently to the fashion of viewing women simply as sexual objects; and he deplored the injustices of the laws automatically transferring a married woman's property to her husband. We will appreciate Defoe's attitude more adequately if we remember that these laws were still substantially unreformed when Dickens wrote *Nicholas Nickleby,* in which Mr. Mantalini's extravagance bankrupts his wife and forces her to safeguard her reorganized business by conducting it in the name of a spinster forewoman.

Defoe went still further in discussing woman's need for, and right to, full emotional satisfaction in marriage. In several letters of advice to readers he says such things as:

> 'Tis true, Affection is not always Grounded upon Merit; but still they [the imaginary editorial board] reckon Love so Essential to the Happiness of a Conjugal State, that however absurdly that Unaccountable Passion may be Grounded, they think a Woman ought to choose a Man She Loves best. . . .
>
> If She has not Discretion to govern her Affections, by the real Merit of the Person, that's her Misfortune; but 'tis most certain, She will be but Indifferently Happy with the Man, to whose Person she is indifferent before.

Later, in one of his last books startlingly entitled *On Conjugal Lewdness or Matrimonial Whoredom,* and republished under the comparatively discreet title of *Use and Abuse of the Marriage Bed,* Defoe is even more explicit. He says:

> Some are of the opinion, prudential matches, as they call them, are best. They tell us, it is the parents' business to choose wives for their sons, and husbands for their daughters: . . . that property begets affection, and that if all other things

hit, they may run the risk of the love with less in inconvenience. . . .

But I must enter my protest here: . . . they seem to
know little of the misery of those matches who think they are
to be toyed into love after consummation. How often are they
cloyed with one another's company before the affection comes
in? . . .

The man that marries without love must be a knave; the
woman that marries without it must be a fool.

In this book he also advocates a reasonably-sized family—his
own would have been so considered when twelve, fourteen and
even sixteen births and perhaps many miscarriages in addition were
no uncommon lot for a woman—and a divorce law which would
accept incompatibility as adequate grounds.

This argument he pursued in later journalistic work, writing in
Applebee's Journal, April 24, 1725:

If my Wife and I,—by mere agreeing upon Terms,—came
together and married,—why may not my wife and I,—by the
like mere agreeing upon Terms,—separate again? For if mutual Consent be the Essence of the Contract of Matrimony,
why should not the dissolving that mutual Consent dissolve
likewise the Marriage, and disengage the Parties from one another again?

On July 11, 1713 *The Review* came to and end, partly because
of the purposely exorbitant stamp tax, designed rather for prohibition than revenue, which Defoe had consistently opposed, and
partly because of a change in the political situation, which brought
the Whigs into power.

Queen Anne's ill health in that year had raised serious questions of the succession since the choice lay between her Catholic
Stuart brother living in exile in France, and the unfamiliar and
unpopular German House of Hanover, her nearest Protestant relatives, to whom the succession was legally secured.

Defoe had evidently not learned not to joke with strangers, and
burlesqued the Jacobite or Stuart view in two satirical pamphlets,
Reasons Against The Protestant Succession, which he felt would
attract the attention of waverers or opponents and might, if read,
convert them to uphold it.

The pamphlets did have an excellent sale and may have been
the instrument of converting some, but in 1713, when the Whigs

returned to power, Defoe again found himself in jail, on complaint of the Whigs this time, for seditious writing. He succeeded in getting a pardon from the queen in November but immediately after her death, in August 1714, was rearrested for a newspaper squib in which he had attacked a Tory lord who favored the Stuart claims.

Evidently the chief Whig minister thought him useful enough to enlist, and extricated him from his difficulties on condition of certain complicated services which he undertook to perform. Three years later, in 1718, he summarized these in a letter to a new Secretary of State, Lord Stanhope.

He speaks there of the editorship of the *Tory News Letter* which he has been carrying on for the past three years, and traces his negotiations with the Whig ministry preliminary to undertaking it:

> Upon this I engaged in it; and that so far, that though the property was not wholly my own, yet the conduct and government of the style and news was so entirely in me that I ventured to assure his Lordship the sting of that mischievous paper should be entirely taken out, though it was granted that the style should continue Tory, as it was, that the Party might be amused, and not set up another, which would have destroyed the design. And this part I therefore take entirely on myself still. . . .

> Upon the whole, however this is the consequence, that by this management the *Weekly Journal,* and *Dormer's Letter,* as also the *Mercurius Politicus,* which is in the same nature of management as the Journal, will be always kept (mistakes excepted) to pass as Tory papers, and yet be so disabled and enervated; so as to do no mischief, or give any offence to the government.

> I beg leave to observe, Sir, one thing more to his Lordship in my own behalf, and without which, indeed, I may one time or other run the risk of fatal misconstructions. I am, Sir, for this service posted among Papists, Jacobites, and enraged High Tories—a generation who, I profess, my very soul abhors; I am obliged to hear traitorous expressions and outrageous words against His Majesty's person and government and his most faithful servants, and smile at it all as if I approved it; I am obliged to take all scandalous and, indeed, villainess papers that come, and keep them by me as if I would gather materials from them to put them into the news; nay, I often venture to let things pass which are a little shocking, that I may not render myself suspected.

His enthusiasm for verisimilitude seems again to have overcome him, however, and when Mist, the Tory owner of *Mist's Miscellany* was shortly thereafter fined for an extremely antigovernment article it was asserted with apparent truth that Defoe had been personally responsible for its insertion.

This probably ended his employment by the government and in 1719, at sixty, which was then considered a ripe old age, he retired to the comfortable country house he shared with his wife and two unmarried daughters, and wrote *The Life and Strange Surprizing Adventures of Robinson Crusoe, of York, Mariner: Who lived Eight and Twenty years, all alone in an un-inhabited Island on the Coast of America, near the Mouth of the Great River of Oroonoque; Having been cast on Shore by Shipwreck, wherein all the Men perished but himself. With an Account how he was at last strangely deliver'd by Pyrates. Written by Himself.*

The subject of the book was suggested by the then topical recent adventures of the celebrated Alexander Selkirk, marooned for some years on an island very much like Crusoe's. Superficially the story followed the immensely popular tradition of personal travel books, relating real or pretended adventures of their heroes. This form had been well-established in England ever since Othello won a wife by telling her of:

> . . . antres vast and deserts idle,
> Rough quarries, rocks and hills whose heads touch heaven,
>
> . . . .
> And of the Cannibals that each other eat,
> The Anthropophagi and men whose heads
> Do grow beneath their shoulders. . . .

To all appearances, Defoe simply went a step further by inventing the explorer himself as well as the sights he reported.

Robinson Crusoe purported to be a true history of the life and adventures of an adventurous young businessman. Cast away, not on a desert island, but on an island boasting considerable natural resources, a large number of wild but domesticable animals and even a potentially useful native population, Robinson Crusoe uses the tools civilization has given him, both in his education, ingenuity, and skill, and in the more literal form of iron, seed, and so forth, to build a fruitful, prosperous life. This is not, in the old sense, an adventure story. We do not ask at each step, "What happened to him next?" but "What did he do next?" The emphasis is not on wonderful and terrible events but on resourceful and effective activity. The initiative comes from man throughout. Nature is raw material for his shaping, not a god for his worship. Sometimes stubborn and difficult, it is never purposeful or malicious and can therefore be mastered and used by any educated, intelligent, self-reliant, hard working and prudent man who has a reasonable share of good luck—just such a share as the laws of probability (or the goodness of God) is likely to afford him. One can hardly imagine a more perfect representation of primitive capitalist accumulation building the nucleus of its first small fortunes on industry and thrift, as well as appropriation, and the practical Protestant religion it developed as its rationale, than the passages in chapters IX, XI and XII, in which Defoe describes Crusoe's achievement of a store of grain sufficient to safeguard him from all foreseeable vicissitudes of weather and accident. The kernel of almost every other episode, important or unimportant, is in the same way, profoundly correct as well as realistic.

The surface realism enforced by Defoe's pretense of reportage is valuable and interesting, but was already well-developed in such other earlier and contemporary books of an allegorical nature as *Pilgrim's Progress* and *Gulliver's Travels*. *Robinson Crusoe* derives its honorable position as the first English novel from its subject rather than its technique. Defoe was the first fully to accomplish what Lukasch refers to as the novelist's distinctive task—"to deal with the totality of objects," that is, to deal with a person or group of people in their relations not only to each other, but also to the material and social world around them. In other words, even this early and casually written novel uses the concrete historical world not as an unchanged background but as an essential and changing element in the development of character. It uses nature as a necessary factor in the interaction of man's will with the world, an interaction which shapes the personal as well as social course of history. "The world" Defoe uses here is, of course, socially and economically a simple one, restricted to the dimensions of the island; but we always feel that, like an iceberg, it shows only a small fraction of its bulk above the surface. And we soon realize that our pilot is well aware of the whole great mass beneath. In Crusoe himself we find even more clearly represented all the essentials of the energetic, and individualistic, middle-class man when he still had a future before him and could afford to face the reality he had to know in order to master it.

Here in his masterpiece Defoe has unhesitatingly selected as his theme the essential core of all that was still progressive in the role of the bourgeoisie—their leadership in man's great struggle to conquer and use nature.

And while Crusoe, as well as Defoe, perfectly represents this historic achievement of his class, neither of them are simply average members of that class. We have already seen this in Defoe's life. And we must not forget that it is *against* the urging of his middle-class parents that Crusoe sets out on the adventurous voyage which forces him *physically* to come to grips with nature and create his own fruitful estate in the wilderness. Nor must we forget that Crusoe held it one of his greatest hardships when the store of ink with which he recorded his experience was exhausted!

The inexhaustible vitality, the elasticity of spirit, the intelligent curiosity about life, the self-disciplined ability to work for a far off objective, and the capacity to work experimentally and selectively, learning from each experience, were neither exclusively nor universally bourgeois virtues, but they were typically such at the beginning of the eighteenth century. It is that reality which gives its greatness to this truthful myth of the first postrevolutionary capitalist era.

The book became so enormously and immediately popular that a contemporary critic sneered:

> There is not an old woman that can go to the price of it, but buys thy *Life and Adventures*, and leaves it, as a legacy, with the *Pilgrim's Progress, the Practice of Piety*, and *God's Revenge against Murther* to her posterity.

Defoe responded immediately to the tremendous and widespread demand with a second part, relating Crusoe's adventures after his rescue, which was published within a few months. Next year he followed up his success with the (fictional) *Memoirs of a Cavalier*, ostensibly written by the Cavalier himself—until recently it was still listed as a real autobiography in most bibliographies—and *The Life, Adventures and Piracies of the Famous Captain Singleton*.

This latter pretended biography amazed readers a century later by its accurate descriptions of the then newly explored interior of Africa, and led to wildly improbable surmises of Defoe's access to hidden or forgotten records of unknown explorations. Today scholars are agreed that he used no information which could not have been pieced together by a keen geographer who had studied all the maps and other sources available in England, and was able to make shrewd estimates of topographical probabilities. In any case, the achievement is a most impressive one.

In 1722 he followed his previous successes with his second really important novel, *The Fortunes and Misfortunes of the Famous Moll Flanders etc. Who was Born in Newgate, and during a life of contin'ued Variety for Threescore Years, besides her childhood, was Twelve Year a Whore, five times a Wife (whereof once to her own Brother) Twelve year a Thief, Eight Year a Transported Felon in Virginia, at last grew Rich liv'd Honest, and died a Penitent, Written from her own Memorandums. . . .*

Here again Defoe was following a tradition well-established since pre-Elizabethan times. There were frequently cheap broadsides sold in the streets after the execution of notorious criminals, giving the story of their lives. These generally pretended to be based on last minute confessions and were often written in the first person, supposedly in the very words of the late prisoner. They almost invariably concluded with expressions of penitence and exhortations to virtue, offering the speaker's own life as a horrible example of crime and punishment.

Defoe himself wrote a whole series of these in the miscellaneous journalism of his last ten years. And in *Moll Flanders* he again ostensibly went just a step further in creating the heroine as well as the bulk of her adventures. But we have already seen how deeply concerned Defoe was with the position of woman in his society, so it is no surprise to find that his second important novel deals largely with this question.

In the "true history" of *Moll Flanders* we have what is really a companion piece to *Robinson Crusoe*—the story of his feminine counterpart. She is cast away, not on an uninhabited island, but in the midst of London, and struggles with comparable difficulties in order to carve out her portion of security, comfort and wealth from this wilderness. With deep insight Defoe shows us that whereas middle-class man could, at this time, still deal directly with material things, middle-class woman could secure possession of them only indirectly through her dealings with their owner—man— and had to exercise her ingenuity and wits to make as good a bargain with him as she could. That marriage in which she was subjugated nevertheless gave her some legal rights and put certain

limits to her exploitation, and all her shrewdness and resourcefulness is bent upon achieving it on the best possible terms. We have
already noted Moll Flanders' blunt summary of what a woman
owes herself and how she can best secure it. She says succinctly:

> I hold no woman should allow herself to be taken for a
> Mistress that hath the means to make herself a Wife.

But since there can be nothing constructive in her efforts to
sell herself, legally or illegally, to the best advantage, the book
lacks the deeper epic significance we find in *Robinson Crusoe*. Moll
Flanders has no creative moment to which we can thrill as we do
to Crusoe's exultation when he has finally succeeded in baking a
misshapen pot and cries out: "No joy at a thing of so mean a
nature was ever equal to mine, when I found that I had made an
earthen pot that would bear the fire."

Our interest in her exploits is on the lower level of the
picaresque story where we sympathize with society's outlaws and
enjoy seeing them get back something of their own. But the more
comprehensive ethical understanding which would link these isolated raids on society with a struggle to change it was not a part
of Defoe's universe. In his contrast between Swift and Defoe referred to above, Ross correctly says:

> . . . in Defoe's time his culture was at a youthful, vigor-
> ous stage, with a promising future predicated on material
> progress and that useful contradiction in terms, business ethics.
> Thus, though his own life was full of difficulties, and though
> he had failed in whatever ambitious dreams he had dreamed
> in 1702, his work throughout expresses the freshness, the
> vigor, and the unthinking pioneer optimism which properly
> reflected the status of his class.

And thus, although he was still human enough to see woman
as a person and an equal, it was impossible for him to question
the basis of her social degradation—the property relationships which
were also the basis of the material progress of his class.

Yet with her robust common sense, warmth, and vitality, Moll
has stood as comforter and justification, if not champion, to some
of her disinherited sisters in many generations during the past two
centuries. We find a striking illustration of this in George Borrow's
delightful and too little known *Lavengro*, written in 1851.

There an old apple woman on London Bridge offers the young author help if he is, as she mistakenly thinks, running from the police, and he asks in surprise:

"So you think there is no harm in stealing?"

"No harm in the world, dear! Do you think my own child would have been transported for it, if there had been any harm in it? and what's more, would the blessed woman in the book here have written her life as she has done, and given it to the world, if there had been any harm in faking? She, too, was what they call a thief and a cut-purse; ay, and was transported for it, like my dear son; and do you think she would have told the world so, if there had been any harm in the thing? Oh, it is a comfort to me that the blessed woman was transported, and came back—for come back she did, and rich too—for it is an assurance to me that my dear son, who was transported too, will come back like her."

"What was her name?"

"Her name, blessed Mary Flanders."

"Will you let me look at the book?"

"Yes, dear, that I will, if you promise me not to run away with it."

I took the book from her hand; a short, thick volume, at least a century old, bound with greasy black leather. I turned the yellow and dog's-eared pages, reading here and there a sentence. Yes, and no mistake! *His* pen, his style his spirit might be observed in every line of the uncouth— looking old volume—the air, the style, the spirit of the writer of the book which had first taught me to read. I covered my face with my hand and thought of my childhood. . . .

"This is a singular book," said I at last; "but it does not appear to have been written to prove that thieving is no harm, but rather to show the terrible consequences of crime: it contains a deep moral."

"A deep what, dear?"

"A . . . but no matter, I will give you a crown for this volume."

"No, dear, I will not sell the volume for a crown."

"I am poor," said I; "but I will give you two silver crowns for your volume."

"No, dear, I will not sell my volume for two silver crowns; no, nor for the golden one in the king's tower down there; without my book I should mope and pine, and perhaps fling myself into the river; but I am glad you like it, which shows that I was right about you, after all; you are one of our party, and you have a flash about that eye of yours which puts me just in mind of my dear son. No, dear, I won't sell you my book; but if you like, you may have a peep into it whenever

you come this way. I shall be glad to see you; you are one of
the right sort, for if you had been a common one, you would
have run away with the thing; but you scorn such behaviour,
and, as you are so flash of your money, though you say you
are poor, you may give me a tanner to buy a little baccy with:
I love baccy, dear, more by token that it comes from the plantations to which the blessed woman was sent."

In 1722 Defoe also published the amazing "eye witness account"
of *A Journal of the Plague Year,* the less well-known but interesting relation of *Due Preparations for the Plague,* another novel—*The
Adventures of Colonel Jack*—and a four-hundred page book on
Religious Courtship!

In 1724, in addition to undertaking a number of large-scale
business ventures in cheese, oysters and honey and a complicated
real estate-pottery factory deal, Defoe found time to write the only
other one of his books which is today fairly well known, *Roxana,
The Fortunate Mistress,* to complete the first volume of his very
interesting *Tour Thro the Whole Island of ·Great Britain,* and to
dash off *A New Voyage round the World.*

The next year saw the second volume of the *Tour* and a new
very much enlarged edition of the first volume of *The Compleat
English Tradesman, in Familiar Letters, Directing him in all the
several Parts and Progressions of Trade.*

Despite his several bankruptcies Defoe writes with undiminished
enthusiasm about the wonders of trade, not only in this book but
in the novels as well. Roxana, for example, is never so romantic
as when she discusses its possibilities. In weighing the merits of
alternative suitors, she concludes rapturously:

> That an estate is a pond, but that trade is a spring; that
> if the first is once mortgaged it seldom gets clear, but embar-
> rasses the person forever; but the merchant has his estate
> continually flowing; and upon this he named me merchants
> who lived in more real splendour and spent more money than
> most of the noblemen in England could singly expend, and
> that they still grew immensely rich.

Defoe's irrepressible seasoned optimism reminds one of the
famous Greek epitaph:

> A shipwrecked sailor, buried on this coast,
>   Bids you set sail;

> Full many a gallant bark, when ours was lost,
> Weathered the gale.

Some of the chapter heads of the business handbook are startling and almost disarming in their directness. For example, a section entitled: "Of Honesty in Dealing" has a subhead, "Of Telling Unavoidable Trading Lies," and explains: ". . . there are some latitudes which a tradesman is and must be allowed . . . which cannot be allowed in other cases."

With the same simplicity the pirate Captain Singleton's Quaker first mate, who assists him in the most unscrupulous exploits, finally says to him:

> Now that you're rich, have you not had enough of this wicked life, which will certainly lead you to damnation?

And when, after due consideration, the captain agrees that he has, they both retire to prepare for salvation by living peacefully and virtuously on their piratical spoils.

During all this time Defoe was also engaged in such journalistic writing as a whole series of the "lives, trials, last words and executions" of notorious contemporary criminals, as well as some other less sensational pieces.

That year a journalist describing the manners and morals of the lower classes, could write, with a certainty that the general public would understand his reference:

> Down in the kitchen honest Dick and Doll
> Are studying Colonel Jack and Flanders Moll.

And, although men of letters were all properly contemptuous in public, as fashionable an arbiter of polite taste as Pope felt constrained to admit privately:

> The first part of *Robinson Crusoe* is very good. . . . Defoe wrote a vast many things; and none bad, though none excellent, except this. There is something good in all he had written.

A few years later, Dr. Johnson more enthusiastically exclaimed after reading *Robinson Crusoe*:

> Was there ever anything else written by mere man that was wished longer by its readers except *Don Quixote* and *Pilgrim's Progress*?

And it is with those two immortal classics that succeeding generations have ranked Defoe's almost accidental masterpiece ever since.

Almost accidental because, while he might well never have written a novel at all, only a man who both represented and transcended his special class in the particular way Defoe did, could ever have written anything like this first English novel. Its special place in literature is not won by the simple verisimilitude which convinced its contemporary readers that it must be a true story. A story can be true and damnably dull, or even true and interesting enough as it goes along but, finally, insignificant. As Dr. Arnold Kettle, in his *Introduction to the English Novel,* says on this point:

> It is precisely the fact that the human interest story in our newspapers is nearly always presented from a morally neutral standpoint, without significance, that makes it so often rather disgusting. A concern with the texture of life which is not accompanied by an attempt to evaluate the experiences recorded is bound to be in the end irresponsible.

But *Robinson Crusoe* holds our interest in its first nursery presentation and challenges our maturer understanding at each new rereading. It is concerned not merely with the texture of life, but with its innermost core. It represents the essence of any responsible experience because it summarizes man's successful attempt to impose a state of art on the state of nature, and thus create the material prerequisites for all civilization.

1726 saw the *History of the Devil,* 1727 an *Essay on the History and Reality of Apparitions,* including the well-known account of "The Appearance of Mrs. Veal," and the second volume of *The Compleat English Tradesman.*

The next year Defoe published the *Augusta Triumphans* already mentioned as a second book of *Essays on Projects* and a very sound *Plan of the English Commerce.*

His last publication was another fictional autobiography, *The Military Memoirs of Captain George Carleton,* which some bibliographies still list with anonymous factual material of the preceding century.

The last year of the *Life and Adventures of the Incredible Daniel Defoe,* as one of his biographers has aptly put it, was until very recently a mystery.

In the fall of 1729 he wrote a note to his publisher explaining that he had delayed returning some proof sheets because of illness, and then he disappeared.

There remains one long, emotional and somewhat confused letter the following spring in which Defoe speaks of his loneliness, his intense desire to see his newly born grandson if that could be managed with secrecy. He also urges his son-in-law, to whom the letter is addressed, to give Defoe's wife and unmarried daughter any counsel or assistance they may need in claiming their inheritance after his death. The letter makes it clear that Defoe was in hiding from some unnamed enemy, and that although ill and lonely he was determined to keep his whereabouts a closely guarded secret.

Recent research has finally established the fact that there was a large claim against his estate, which had probably been satisfied in one of his bankruptcy proceedings, as he himself said:

> No man has tasted differing fortune more,
> And thirteen times I have been rich and poor—

but which was now fraudulently or mistakenly revived.

According to the law at the time, this particular claim could be pressed only against Defoe in person and not against his heirs after his death. With a characteristic mixture of adventure and prudence, and with his habitual practical unsentimental devotion to his family, Defoe had acted promptly to preserve their inheritance for his wife and children, and succeeded by dying alone and undiscovered in a London lodging in April, 1730.

The cause of death was noted in the burial certificate as "a lethargy"—surely the only one that had ever visited him in all his varied career.

HENRY FIELDING

Although Defoe wrote the first and most widely read English novel, the novel as a form can hardly be said to have come into being for another quarter of a century.

Robinson Crusoe and even *Moll Flanders* are somewhat special in having only one real character; there are serious limitations to the possible development of the first person hero-narrator form; and, perhaps most important of all, both Defoe and his critics took the question of factual accuracy as a fundamental one.

A contemporary article on *The Life and Strange Adventures of Mr. D. De F. — — of London, Hosier, Who had lived above fifty years by himself in the Kingdoms of North and South Britain* represented Defoe as saying to Crusoe, "I have made you out of nothing," and attacked the book as a lie. Defoe first tried to prove it was true and then fell back, in a third part, on interpreting the entire story as a detailed allegory of his own life and business misadventures.

The interpretation is ingenious though unconvincing, but its importance for us is the evidence it gives that not even its creator yet realized a new literary form had come into being.

It is not until a generation later that we find any further experiments with its possibilities. The first conscious novelist, Henry Fielding, born in 1707, was a skilled writer, a dramatist with a good classical education, who saw the real importance of this new development and half-apologetically, half-proudly, and altogether self-consciously, named it a "comic epic in prose."

Fielding began his literary career as a writer for that theatre which Defoe had called "Satan's work-house where all the manufactures of Hell are propagated." He had both a broad knowledge of, and a deep respect for, the classics which Defoe contemned. He was a highly conscious literary pioneer who spent much thought not only on the experiments which resulted in the first complete modern novel, but also on formulating critical aesthetic theories to evaluate them, while Defoe was, as we have seen, simply concerned to convince his readers that his imaginative creations were just long statements of fact. In addition, Fielding was the great-grandson of a Cavalier, the grandson of a church dignitary who served as royal chaplain, and the son of an army officer. His specific taste differed from Defoe's as much as their varying backgrounds would lead one to expect. Yet what they had in common was a far more essential part of that genius which shaped the great eighteenth century English novel than any or all of their specific differences in training, taste and talent.

Fielding was an impecunious member of the younger branch of an aristocratic family, and his education was much more like that of Swift, whom he greatly admired, than like that of Defoe. But he shared Defoe's central intuition that the world's great age lay ahead, Defoe's fundamental faith in the power of men to change their environment, and Defoe's democratic belief in the goodness and vitality of the common man—and woman—whom he, as well as Defoe, respected without idealizing.

To these attitudes Fielding adds a greater breadth of ethical and aesthetic interest than Defoe's, a keener realization of the joys this world can afford man's senses, a more conscious concern with men's and women's personal relations to each other, and perhaps a wider observation of the rich varieties of character and experience on all levels of society.

Dr. Arnold Kettle summarizes Fielding's refinement of Defoe's attitude when he says:

> Even more basic to the impression of assuredness is the nature of Fielding's philosophy, sceptical but optimistic. He takes the world in his stride, always curious, frequently indignant, but never incurably hurt. . . . He is not complacent but he is fundamentally confident—confident that the problems of human society, that is to say *his* society, can and will be solved by humane feeling and right reason.

Fielding's father was an officer with little but his colonel's pay to live on—fair provision for a fashionable bachelor but altogether inadequate for the comfortable support of a wife and family. He improvidently fell in love with the daughter of a substantial country squire and judge, who defied her parents to elope with him. Her father finally forgave her and settled a small estate of £3,000— an income of about £150 a year—on her and her (future) children on condition that her husband "should have nothing to do nor intermeddle therein."

Five years after Fielding's birth his father temporarily retired on half-pay and set up as a gentleman farmer. The venture was not very successful and Mrs. Fielding was indebted to her mother's help in caring for the family which soon included four little girls and a baby boy. When she died, in 1718, Colonel Fielding rejoined his regiment in London, leaving the family to the care of his mother-in-law. A year later he returned with a second wife—a young Italian woman who is said to have been the widow of an innkeeper.

Fielding, already eleven, seems to have led his sisters in open rebellion against their stepmother—the violent anti-Catholicism which was, in later life, almost his only strong prejudice, no doubt dates from this period. The children's maternal grandmother, now a widow of considerable income and great forcefulness, encouraged them; and their easygoing father sent the young boy to Eton, and the girls to a good boarding school in Salisbury. Their grandmother undertook the care of the baby, and rented a home in Salisbury near the girls' school.

Since Colonel Fielding soon had six children by his second wife, he played little part thereafter in Fielding's life, although the two always remained friendly. On his son's graduation he good-naturedly granted him an allowance of £200 a year which, as Fielding later said, "any body might pay that would," since his father was totally unable to do so.

After two years private study at his grandmother's the young man spent a few months in London, getting a play performed for a few nights at the Drury Lane Theatre. He then enrolled at the University of Leyden.

At the end of a year there his remittances from home stopped altogether, and in 1729 he returned to London with, as he said, "no choice but to be a hackney writer or a hackney coachman."

While his first play, *Love in Several Masques*, had made no money, its reception had been encouraging enough to make him look to the theatre for a living. Read today it seems a slight but promising beginning, with a creditable caricature of a greedy squire, Sir Positive Trap, who thought a man should be able to "carry his daughter to market with the same lawful authority as any other of his cattle." There was also much mockery of the fashionable "beau" or "fine gentleman"—that "empty, gaudy nameless thing" possessing "everything of a woman but the sex and nothing of a man besides it." A few lines of dialogue indicate what was, for a twenty-one year old, an unusually easy tone:

> "That's a pretty suit of yours, Sir Apish, perfectly gay, new, and alamode."
> "He, he, he! the ladies tell me I refine upon them. I think I have studied dress long enough to know a little, and I have the good fortune to have every suit liked better than the former."

Fielding was always a very rapid workman and during the next seven years he must have written four or five plays a year, since he had at least twenty-five produced.

These compare favorably with others of the period, and are, for the most part, in the same genre—a sort of free spoken topical comedy of manners leaning heavily on amorous intrigue, and caricaturing such types as the pedantic scholar, the money-grubbing squire, and the hypocritical prude.

Fielding himself also developed a vein of more serious realistic satire, attacking particularly the corrupt magistrates and law enforcement officers who were in league with the most dangerous elements of the teeming London underworld and who assisted its leaders in exploiting the miserable prostitutes, pickpockets and other weaker brethren. For example, in *Rape upon Rape or The Justice Caught in his own Trap,* which was produced as early as June, 1730, we find such a dialogue as the following between Magistrate Squeezum and his clerk who has just returned from an errand to "Mother Bilkum's" bagnio:

> "She says she does not value your worship's protection at a farthing, for that she can bribe two juries a year to acquit her in Hicks' Hall for half the money which she hath paid you within these three months."
>
> "Very fine! I will show her that I understand something of juries as well as herself. Quill, make a memorandum against Mother Bilkum's trial that we may remember to have the panel No. 3; they are a set of good men and true, and hearken to no evidence but mine."

In the same play the magistrate commends his subordinates' discretion in having called off a raid when they learned that two lords patronized the gambling house they were supposed to surprise. He says: "Quite right. The laws are turnpikes, only made to stop people who walk on foot, and not to interrupt those who drive through them in their coaches."

These satires clearly owe their inspiration rather to Moliere, several of whose plays Fielding translated and adapted, than to Congreve, who was the model for most of the postrestoration playwrights.

In the later comedies Fielding's attacks became even sharper, and are frequently directed at specific public officials, easily recognized by the delighted audience and their less well-pleased government protectors.

In April, 1731 he went much further with a play called *The Welsh Opera or The Grey Mare is the Better Horse* whose very title impudently commented on the well-known political relationship between George II and his wife Queen Caroline. The body of the play still more dangerously represented the powerful prime minister, Robert Walpole, in the person of a thieving butler Robin. It glanced at his support by other dishonest government officials and parliamentary leaders in such lines as these of the cook's, who is rebuking the coachman for threatening to expose an especially shameless piece of pilfering:

> Fie upon't, William, what have we to do with master's losses? He is rich, and can afford it. Don't let us quarrel among ourselves; let us stand by one another; for, let me tell you, if matters were to be too nicely examined into, I am afraid it would go hard with us all. . . .

The church is represented by Parson Puzzletext, who ponders:

> I think it is a difficult matter to determine which deserves to be hanged most; and if Robin the butler hath cheated more than other people, I see no other reason for it, but because he hath had more opportunity to cheat.

We have already seen in our consideration of the earlier part of the century that while there was an enormous amount of political intrigue and maneuvering, there were really no fundamental political questions involved and that the conflicts were essentially between individuals and groups struggling for the personal rewards of office. In his *People's History of England,* Morton says:

> In England the whole quality of Whiggery was summed up in the commanding person of Robert Walpole. Enterprising Norfolk landowner, financial genius with an understanding of the needs of commerce as keen as any City merchant's, colleague and leader of the great Whig peers, shrewd, predatory and wholly unidealistic, he symbolised the interests and character of the unique alliance which governed England.
> The policy of the Whigs was simple enough. First to avoid foreign wars as being harmful to trade. Then to remove taxes, so far as was possible, from the merchants and manufacturers and place them upon goods consumed by the masses and upon the land. But, as the leading Whigs were themselves landowners and it was considered dangerous to rouse the active hostility of the [Tory] squirearchy, the land tax was kept fairly low and agriculture stimulated by protection and bounties. By avoiding war Walpole was, indeed, able to reduce the land tax considerably. All the politically active classes were thus satisfied and the masses, in this period between the age of spontaneous armed rising and that of organized political

agitation, had no effective means of expressing any discontents that may have existed.

On such a basis party politics became less and less a matter of policies and more and more of simple personal acquisitiveness. It came to be normal and respectable for a gentleman "to get his bread by voting in the House of Commons," and the main concern of such ministers as the Duke of Newcastle was "to find pasture enough for the beasts that they must feed."

Naturally, then, Fielding's dramatic satire was directed against the bribery in parliamentary elections, the dishonesty of government officials, the corruption of such other representatives of vested interests as lawyers, fashionable physicians, and church dignitaries, and dealt with personalities and types rather than issues. It was, however, stinging enough to attract the special attention of the government, and his plays might be better remembered even today if he had not later adapted their best material for use in his novels.

Meanwhile, with the same prodigious vitality we have already marveled at in Defoe, Fielding was not only writing play after play, and living the fast-paced London theatrical life he describes in many of them, but was also maintaining and improving his affectionate intimacy with the Greek and Latin writers to whom he so often refers, and studying such moderns as Shakespeare, Moliere and Cervantes. In addition he found time, during a visit to his sisters' home in Salisbury, to fall romantically and passionately in love with the beautiful young woman whom he immortalized, as a girl, in Tom Jones' Sophia and as a wife and mother in Amelia.

In 1734 she eloped with him to London, and writing for the theatre became a much grimmer affair when every failure meant deprivation for an adored wife and, soon, her dearly loved "little things."

Fielding was writing out of bitter knowledge when he said, in *Tom Jones*:

> To see a woman you love in distress and to be unable to relieve her, and at the same time to reflect that you have brought her into this situation is perhaps a curse of which no imagination can present the horrors to those who have not felt it.

Two years later he took a bold step and invested the greater part of his wife's small inheritance, a total of about £1,500, in a theatre of his own called The Little Theatre.

From the beginning this venture was prodigiously successful. His first play, which was received with enormous enthusiasm and had what was then a very long run, was called *Pasquin or A Dramatic Satire on The Times.*

The first half of the play dealt with bribery in parliamentary elections and the second with similar corruption in the learned professions. The prologue to the second part begins:

> Religion, law and physic were designed
> By heaven the greatest blessings on mankind;
> But priests and lawyers and physicians made
> These general goods to each a private trade;
> With each they rob, with each they fill their purses,
> And turn our benefits into our curses.

His next play, a classical burlesque, was almost as much of a success, and in March, 1737, he topped both of them with his production of *The Historical Register for 1736.* This was a direct satire of Walpole, openly enough presented to provoke the government's *Daily Gazette* into a stern leading article on "An Adventurer in Politics."

Fielding replied to this by printing his two satirical plays in a mock-apologetic pamphlet with a defiant preface that concluded, after discussing plans for enlarging his theatre:

> If nature hath given me any talents at ridiculing vice and imposture, I shall not be indolent, nor afraid of exerting them, while the liberty of the press and stage subsists, that is to say, while we have any liberty left among us.

The pamphlet sold very well, but the government had the last word. In May, 1737, it rushed through a Licensing Act which forced Fielding's theatre to close and made it most unlikely that any other theatrical management would risk the presentation of his plays.

With a wife and two children to provide for, forced out of the profession in which he had made a considerable, if precarious, success, Fielding at 31 enrolled himself as a law student in the Honourable Society of the Middle Temple. Here he somehow managed to complete the normal seven-year course of study in three years, while doing an enormous amount of literary hack work to support a hand-to-mouth existence.

During the last part of this period, from November, 1739, to June, 1741, he served as editor of *The Champion,* a periodical modeled on *The Spectator* and published by a syndicate of booksellers.

Again, we would be more likely to remember these articles if Fielding had not later included and surpassed them in the incidental essays we find scattered through the novels.

The most distinctive emphasis in *The Champion* was Fielding's characteristic development of the contradiction between property values and human values. For example, in discussing the disproportion of the law, he says:

> A boy should, in my opinion, be more severely punished
> for exercising cruelty on a dog or a cat or any other animal,
> than for stealing a few pence or shillings or any of those
> lesser crimes which our courts of justice take note of.

The paper also enabled him to continue his attacks on Walpole who is, for instance, personified as Mammon in one issue and made to say:

> For doubting, sure, thou canst have no pretence;
> To shun a bribe must argue want of sense.
> A wise man's conscience always hath a price;
> Those that are dear are called by blockheads nice.
> Nature 'twixt men no other bounds has set
> Than that of sums—the little and the great.

That month Fielding read an extraordinary book, *Pamela*. This had been published in November, 1740 by Samuel Richardson who, in most literary histories, disputes or shares with Defoe and Fielding the honor of originating the English novel.

It is important to note that Richardson did not, any more than Defoe, think of the novel as a development of the well-established long story form of prose fiction, but as an instrument for the education of the young. As a printer-bookseller he had already published several collections of letters addressed to imaginary correspondents, which were intended to teach young people how to write letters to employers, parents, and so forth. These not only set forth the manner of writing but attempted to inculcate proper attitudes and moral principles.

One of these compendiums was entitled:

> Letters Written to and For Particular Friends on the Most
> Important Occasions; directing not only the requisite style and
> form to be observed in writing familiar letters, but how to

think and act justly and prudently in the common concerns of human life.

Some of the letters included were described:

"From a Maid-servant in Town, acquainting her Father and Mother in the Country with a Proposal of Marriage, and asking their Consent."
"From a Son reduced by his own Extravagance, requesting his Father's advice on his Intention to turn Player."
"To a young Lady, advising her not to change her Guardians, nor to encourage any Clandestine address."

In this collection there was a certain continuity of personnel and anecdote in one series of five letters, which proved extremely effective. Richardson had thus been inspired to write, in the form of an extremely long series of letters, the story of a maid servant, Pamela, whose master, failing in his three volume attempt to seduce or rape her, finally has recourse to the desperate expedient of marriage.

The only virtue of this extremely cumbersome self-conscious machinery is that it focuses attention, as did Defoe's simpler autobiographical method, on the apparent truth of the narration and the reality of its subject.

The subject is, of course, again, (as always in the great realistic novels), man's attempt to master his environment, to act on it so that he can shape the kind of life he wants. In conscious terms Pamela plays a somewhat passive part, since the initial attraction that moves Squire B—— is rather her good fortune than her planning, but even there "accomplishments," education, dress and manner—all of which have been acquired through hard work as well as natural ability and good luck—are as important as the accident of beauty; and the stubborn resistance of her thoroughly commercial, though not consciously hypocritical, virtue is the means whereby she makes a deservedly profitable marriage.

The inhuman commercial relations to which capitalism reduced men and women were revolting enough, when displayed by so naive and sentimental a petty bourgeois as Richardson, to shock a more generous and discriminating man like Fielding. He dashed off an amusing though rather superficial burlesque, *An Apology for the Life of Mrs. Shamela Andrews,* which appeared that April with some success, and which Richardson never forgave. In this skit he announced his discovery that Squire B——'s real name was Booby and, less plausibly, that Shamela [Pamela] was a conscious hypocrite, already delivered of an illegitimate child, who wrote her mother: "I thought once of making a little fortune by my person. I now intend to make a great one by my virtue."

When Fielding was called to the Bar that year he had to give up his editorship and so had time to begin a far more powerful and amusing satire, which soon turned into a full length novel, *The Adventures of Joseph Andrews, and of his Friend Mr. Abraham Adams.*

This begins with a parody which is, in itself, a powerful denunciation of the double sexual standard in bourgeois society, and the whole degradation of women implied by it. Pamela's brother, Joseph, was the first hero of the book. It was intended to center about his adventures, as a footman, in defending his chastity against determined attacks by his titled mistress and her housekeeper. But the book soon overflowed the narrow channel planned for it and became a positive assertion of Fielding's own human values of warmth, gratitude, love between men and women, and delight in the pleasures of beef, ale, beauty and scholarship.

Joseph's friend and counselor, Parson Adams, is a figure comparable only to the immortal Don Quixote, by whom he was avowedly inspired; and the journey the two undertake across England, accompanied by the sweetheart who is soon introduced to give Joseph a better reason for his virtue, is a homely modern Odyssey.

Hazlitt speaking of the English Comic writers almost a century afterwards says:

> I should be at a loss where to find in any authentic documents of the same period so satisfactory an account of the general state of society, and of the moral, political and religious feeling in the reign of George II, as we meet with in *The Adventure of Joseph Andrews and his Friend Mr. Abraham Adams.*

Kettle, in a detailed analysis of Fielding's first novel, which must be quoted at some length shows that: "In the conflicts of the novel—which are always those of humanity versus hypocrisy and bogus morality—Adams, for all his idealistic impracticability, is always on the right side."

He refers to a conversation between this absent-minded scholar and the typically down-to-earth man of business, the steward Peter Pounce, as an example not only of the vigor of Fielding's dialogue but also of the subtlety of his dialectic saying: "Pounce begins with a typical, apparently common-sense, materialist definition of charity. But by the end of the dialogue his materialism is revealed as an empty idealism ('the distresses of mankind are mostly imaginary'), while the impractical idealist Adams is left asserting the reality of hunger and thirst, cold and nakedness."

His final description of Fielding's accomplishment is perhaps the best summary of the book we have:

> It is this kind of insight which goes beyond a mere hearty sympathy for what is decent and dislike of what is hypocritical that gives *Joseph Andrews* its quality. But neither should we undervalue the sheer common-sense decency and strong (albeit unsubtle) moral concern which is at the basis of Fielding's vision. In the continual conflicts in *Joseph Andrews* around the theme of charity, conflicts in which Adams and Joseph are always in trouble, generally because they have no money, it is interesting that the unkind are invariably the great and fashionable and lustful, the mercenary and servile and hypocritical—while the kind are the humble people—the postilion who gives Joseph his cloak, the common soldier who pays the bill at the inn, the farmer who has seen through the ways of the world. If we stop to analyse the pervading sense, in Fielding's novels, of generous humanity (and it is, when all is said, the dominant quality of his books), we shall find that it springs not from a vague, undifferentiated bonhomie but from a very explicit social awareness and understanding of the people.

A brief excerpt from the scene where Joseph, stripped and beaten by thieves, is discovered bleeding in a ditch by a stage coach full of passengers, will give us some idea of the book's quality.

> The poor wretch, who lay motionless a long time, just began to recover his senses as a stage-coach came by. The postilion hearing a man's groans, stopt his horses, and told the coachman he was certain there was a dead man lying in the ditch, for he heard him groan. "Go on, sirrah," says the coachman, "we are confounded late, and have no time to look after dead men." A lady, who heard what the postilion said, and likewise heard the groan, called eagerly to the coachman to stop and see what was the matter. Upon which he bid the postilion alight, and look into the ditch. He did so, and returned, "That there was a man sitting upright, as naked as ever he was born."—"O, J-sus!" cried the lady; "A naked

man! Dear coachman, drive on and leave him." Upon this the gentlemen got out of the coach; and Joseph begged them to have mercy upon him: for that he had been robbed and almost beaten to death. "Robbed," cries an old gentleman: "Let us make all the haste imaginable, or we shall be robbed too." A young man, who belonged to the law, answered, "He wished they had passed by without taking any notice: but that now they might be proved to have been last in his company; if he should die they might be called to some account for his murder. He therefore thought it advisable to save the poor creature's life for their own sakes, if possible; at least, if he died, to prevent the jury's finding that they fled for it. He was therefore of opinion, to take the man into the coach, and carry him to the next inn." The lady insisted, "That he should not come into the coach. That if they lifted him in, she would herself alight; for she had rather stay in that place to all eternity, than ride with a naked man." The coachman objected, "That he could not suffer him to be taken in, unless somebody would pay a shilling for his carriage the four miles." Which the two gentlemen refused to do. But the lawyer, who was afraid of some mischief happening to himself, if the wretch was left behind in that condition, saying no man could be too cautious in these matters, and that he remembered very extraordinary cases in the books, threatened the coachman, and bid him deny taking him up at his peril; for that, if he died, he should be indicted for his murder; and if he lived, and brought an action against him, he would willingly take a brief in it. These words had a sensible effect on the coachman, who was well acquainted with the person who spoke them; and the old gentleman above mentioned, thinking the naked man would afford him frequent opportunities of showing his wit to the lady, offered to join the company in giving a mug of beer for his fare; till, partly alarmed by the threats of the one, and partly by the promises of the other, and being perhaps a little moved with compassion at the poor creature's condition, who stood bleeding and shivering with the cold, he at length agreed; and Joseph was now advancing to the coach, where seeing the lady who held the sticks of her fan before her eyes, he absolutely refused, miserable as he was, to enter unless he was furnished with sufficient covering to prevent giving the least offence to decency. . . .

Though there were several greatcoats about the coach, it was not easy to get over this difficulty which Joseph had started. The two gentlemen complained they were cold, and could not spare a rag; the man of wit saying, with a laugh, that charity begins at home; and the coachman, who had two greatcoats spread under him, refused to lend either, lest they should be made bloody; the lady's footman desired to be excused for the same reason, which the lady herself, not withstanding her abhorence of a naked man, approved: and it is more than probable poor Joseph, who obstinately adhered to his modest resolution, must have perished unless the postilion (a lad who hath since been transported for robbing a hen-roost) had voluntarily stript off a greatcoat, his only outer garment, at the same time swearing a great oath (for which he was rebuked by the passengers), "that he would rather ride in his shirt all his life than suffer a fellow-creature to lie in so miserable a condition."

The book was ignored by the critics but achieved an immediate popular success, selling about 6,500 copies within the year. This enabled Fielding to pay off his debts and provide some much needed comforts for his wife, who had been prostrated by an illness which proved fatal to their beloved first child that winter, and who was still seriously ill.

Fielding himself now became subject to the frequent and excruciatingly severe attacks of gout which were to afflict him for the rest of his life, and found it increasingly difficult to build the substantial law practise for which he had hoped.

He again had recourse to his pen and on April 12, 1743, published a book of *Miscellanies* for which he received almost £800 by subscription. The most important piece included in that volume was the bitter satire, usually referred to as one of his novels, *The Life of Jonathan Wild The Great.*

Jonathan Wild was a notorious criminal—the head of a gang of cutthroats, bullies and pimps, exceeding them all in his utter callousness—who had been one of the first in eighteenth century London to organize crime on a business basis. He had been executed in the late twenties and was included in the series of *Lives of Criminals* written by Defoe at the time.

Fielding, in his introduction, refers to Defoe's "True and Genuine Account of the Life and Actions of the late Jonathan Wild; not made up out of Fiction and Fable, but taken from his own Mouth, and collected from Papers of his own Writing." He handsomely acknowledges his great indebtedness to "that excellent historian, who, from authentic papers and records, etc. hath already given so satisfactory an account of the life and actions of this great man." But, in truth, the facts furnished by Defoe serve merely as raw material for a powerful satire in which Fielding makes it very clear that this "great man," a reference which to his contemporaries invariably meant Walpole, is only the prototype of all corrupt

political leaders and military bullies, and that it is they rather
than the avowed criminals who merit every decent man's hatred
and contempt.

Byron makes an interesting reference to this book in his discussion of Fielding's work in 1821:

> I have lately been reading Fielding over again. They talk
> of Radicalism, Jacobinism, etc. in England (I am told), but
> they should turn over the pages of Jonathan Wild the Great.
> The inequality of conditions and the littleness of the great,
> were never set forth in stronger terms; and his contempt for
> Conquerors and the like is such, that, had he lived *now*, he
> would have been denounced in "the Courier" as the grand
> Mouth-piece and Factionary of the revolutionists. And yet I
> never recollect to have heard this turn of Fielding's mind no-
> ticed, though it is obvious in every page.

The next winter—November, 1744—his passionately loved wife
died, leaving him with two small children. A devoted young housekeeper who had cared for her for many years continued to care
for the children, and Fielding's favorite sister, Sarah, joined the
little household.

A year later Fielding undertook another periodical, *The True
Patriot and The History of Our Own Time,* intended to arouse
Londoners to the dangers of a new Jacobite attempt at crowning
"The Young Pretender," who actually landed in Scotland and at-
tempted a short-lived invasion of England. Among other interest-
ing nonpolitical notes in the paper was Fielding's brief epitaph for
Dean Swift:

> A genius who deserves to be ranked among the first whom
> the world ever saw. He possessed the talents of a Lucian, a
> Rabelais and a Cervantes, and in his works exceeded them all.
> He employed his wit to the noblest purposes . . . in the de-
> fence of his country against several pernicious schemes of
> wicked politicians.

In November 1746 he married his housekeeper and although he
still and always spoke of his first wife as his only real love, the
marriage was a happy one for both himself and his only surviving
little daughter as well as for his second wife. In his *Journal of A
Voyage to Lisbon,* written during the last year of his life, Fielding
said of her:

My wife, besides discharging excellently well her own, and all the tender offices becoming the female character—besides being a faithful friend, an amiable companion, and tender nurse—could likewise supply the wants of a decrepit husband and occasionally perform his part.

But the attacks upon his taste for "low company," assiduously promoted by Richardson, were, in the thinking of the time, given far more support by this marriage than they would have been by the grossest immorality, and those attacks were partly responsible for his decision to give up his unsuccessful efforts for a legal career.

In 1748 Richardson published his only really fine novel—*Clarissa Harlowe*—which, with all its sentimentality, melodrama and religiosity, nevertheless makes Clarissa an extraordinary spokesman of her sex. Although really in love with her betrayer, she refuses his offer to "make her an honest woman" with the cry "The man who has been the villain to me you have been shall never be my husband," and chooses rather to die in disgrace than to become his wife. In this climax, as well as in her earlier resistance to marrying a wealthy boor of her father's choice, Clarissa stands as an amazingly advanced champion of her sex.

As Kettle says:

> The conflict of Clarissa—the individual hearts vs. the conventional standards of the property-owning class—is one of the essential, recurring conflicts of the modern novel, as of all literature of class society. It is the conflict of love (i.e. human dignity, sympathy, independence) vs. money (i.e. property, position, "respectability," prejudice) which lies at the heart of almost all the novels of Fielding, Jane Austen, the Brontes, . . . unlike as they are in almost every respect.

Fielding, with characteristic candor and generosity, lavished enthusiastic praise upon the book in the pages of a new satirical newspaper, *The Jacobite's Journal,* which had succeeded *The True Patriot.* Richardson was, however, far from mollified and continued the venomous and partially successful attempt to destroy his rival's personal as well as his literary reputation.

It was largely owing to these efforts that two of Fielding's patrons, who had replaced Walpole in the forties, refused his application for the judgeship which had been half promised him in recognition of his voluntary assistance against the Jacobite invasion. The malicious gossip retailed as current stories of dissipation that, insofar as they were at all true, dated from Fielding's bachelor days in the theatre. His indisputably low marriage, his unconventional liking for unfashionable company, and his championship of the unrespectable in *Joseph Andrews,* all gave color to these slanders. They were, in fact, still believed and repeated by most Victorian biographers a century later.

However, in October 1748, Fielding was named as magistrate or justice of the peace for Westminster and a few months later this appointment was extended to include all of Middlesex.

Such a position was then considered lucrative but contemptible. In Fielding's hands it became a most ill-paid but honorable one.

There was no salary attached to the office and the magistrate was still, as all Judges had been in Bacon's time, paid by fees collected from the litigants themselves. Fielding gives an excellent brief description of the duties and rewards of this office in the introduction to his *Voyage to Lisbon* written six years later:

> . . . I will therefore confess . . . that my private affairs at the beginning of the winter had but a gloomy aspect; for I had not plundered the public or the poor of those sums which men, who are always ready to plunder both as much as they can, have been pleased to suspect me of taking; on the contrary, by composing instead of inflaming the quarrels of porters and beggars (which I blush to say hath not been universally practised), and by refusing to take a shilling from a man who most undoubtedly would not have had another left, I had reduced an income of about five hundred pounds a year of the dirtiest money on earth to little more than three hundred pounds; a considerable proportion of which remained with my clerk; and, indeed, if the whole had done so, as it ought, he would be but ill paid for sitting almost sixteen hours in the twenty-four in the most unwholesome, as well as nauseous, air in the universe, and which hath in his case corrupted a good constitution without contaminating his morals.

But before we consider further his work as a magistrate, which Fielding himself thought his major claim to public gratitude, we must turn to the publication of *The History of Tom Jones, A Foundling* on February 20, 1749.

The publisher's advertisement early in March announces the six volumes at eighteen shillings a set and happily adds: "it being impossible to get sets bound fast enough to answer the demand for them, such gentlemen and ladies as please, may have them sewed in blue paper and boards, at the price of 16s. a set." There were five more editions within the year and while critical opinion was divided, there were a fair number of appreciative reviews.

The book is some three times the length of *Joseph Andrews* and is even more richly filled with incidents, scenes, and characters, of the English countryside and its capital. In addition Fielding deliberately develops in this book his theory of this new form which he called a "comic epic in prose," but which we recognize as the first fully conscious novel—the form which has most completely expressed the values, and most adequately explored the possibilities, of modern life.

In discussing this great bourgeois art form Kettle says:

> For literature to the bourgeois writers of this period was, above all, a means of taking stock of the new society. A medium which could express a realistic and objective curiosity about man and his world, this was what they were after. It was the search for such a medium that that led Fielding to describe Joseph Andrews as a "comic epic poem in prose." Their task was not so much to adapt themselves to a revolutionary situation as to cull and examine what the revolution had produced. They were themselves revolutionaries only in the sense that they participated in the consequences of a revolution, they were more free and therefore more realistic than their predecessors to just the extent and in just those ways that the English bourgeois revolution involved in fact an increase in human freedom.

Although Fielding used in this new way the time honored apparatus of story-telling—a narrative method heightened and quickened by his long dramatic apprenticeship—his skill and apparent ease should not make us forget the significance of Defoe's and Richardson's seemingly unnecessary technical difficulties. For the very existence of their experiments emphasize what Fielding's mastery conceals—the essentially didactic or ethical nature of the novel.

Fielding himself repeatedly stressed the novelty of the form he was creating. Later critics have, however, too often taken an essentially formal approach, and treated the novel simply as a development of the long romances and the picaresque stories of an earlier day, made more important by the material conditions of the eighteenth century.

Doubtless the comparatively cheap development of printing and the increasing literacy of the population made the novel possible; but a necessary cause is not a sufficient cause, and either of these technical conditions might more easily have accounted for the increased writing and reading of short or long stories, such as we find in magazines today. An understanding of the rich and immediate development of the eighteenth century novel must, I think, be sought in a complex of causes all essentially related as conditions of the developing bourgeois life. Increased literacy has already been mentioned but it must be combined with the increased leisure of at least a part of the middle class, that is, the women; a certain economic margin for leisure-time recreation without a tradition of formal social activity; and a Protestant tradition that disapproved both of the luxurious display of, and of the content involved in, most earlier theatrical performances. All these, however, except for the increasing importance of feminine readers and, soon, writers, are still only a part of the necessary conditions for some popular reading matter suited to a not too educated public, and we must look further into the problems and needs of this public to see why their literature took the form it did.

When we do so we are first struck by their enormous lack of any clearly formulated philosophy of life or ethical system, and the fact that there was really no authority which could formulate or promulgate such a philosophy for them. The church was perhaps at its lowest point in terms of living influence or general authority and respect. Ways of life both in city and country, and especially in the movement from one to the other, were changing almost under men's eyes. Aristocratic mores, as adapted by most upper-class writers and exemplars, were clearly not applicable to most people. Even family authority could not be exercised in the old way. How, for example, could a shopkeeper tell his son to behave as his father had done when clearly his whole object in life was to raise his son to a sphere of activity in which the grandfather would have been completely lost, and in which he himself could barely hope to set an exploratory foot.

Even Addison indicated how sharply traditional family ties must be broken when the younger son could rise "by an honest industry to greater estates than those of their elder brothers," and the brief excerpt from Morton's history, already cited, amply indicates how impossible it must have been for any of the minority who did change from small freeholders to successful manufacturers authoritatively to tell their children or themselves what model to imitate for a successful life.

It is precisely this all important question to which the earliest novels directly address themselves. How shall a man act, in such and such concrete circumstances, to achieve success? What kind of life will make him happy and how can he secure it? Fielding and the other great early novelists were not preachers delivering a memorized answer. They were scientists reproducing in their pages enough of the actual relevant conditions of the world to make possible a laboratory experiment whose results they, as well as their readers, were anxious to learn. Certainly they had a prior hypothesis. But they watched with genuine curiosity and anxiety for its confirmation or correction as the experiment developed in the course of the novel. It is this that gives these early novels— and those later Victorian ones which, with less scope, still used the same serious approach—such genuine and breathless interest. Even in the limited world of a lady like Jane Austen we will find, restricted though the range of her subjects is, the realism and truth of an honest scientific approach to an important experiment. And in such later giants as Balzac and Tolstoi we find that though the size of our crucibles is greater, our mixtures more complex, and the explosive force of our ingredients more dangerous, the attitude of combined exploration and didacticism remains the sign of the great realistic novelist. This is not the place to enter upon a further examination of those distinguishing characteristics of the novel— the persistent consciousness of an irreversible time, the reality of novelty and change, the emphasis on personal relationships, the development of psychological analysis, the concrete contemporary nontransferable nature—which make it the predominant art form of modern bourgeois culture, and made it inevitable that it should have developed only when that culture itself was expanding most fruitfully in its first period of unquestioned dominance.

Tom Jones is an excellent example of all these qualities. There is a vast wealth of amazingly varied formulations in it, ranging from the perfectly eighteenth century equation, "The Cause of King George is the cause of liberty and true religion. In other words, it is the cause of common sense," to the more surprising twentieth or twenty-first century challenge:

> "The delicacy of your 'sex,'" said Tom, "cannot conceive the grossness of ours, nor how little one sort of amour has to do with the heart." "I will never marry a man," replied Sophia, very gravely, "who shall not learn refinement enough to be as incapable as I am myself of making such a distinction."

The central conflict in the novel between property rights and personal rights—between respectability and humanity—comes to a climax in Squire Western's attempt to force his daughter to marry the man who is heir of an estate that happens to adjoin the squire's. He attempts to persuade her by promising an exceptionally large dowry for, as Fielding gravely observes: "so extravagant was the affection of that fond parent, that, provided his child would but consent to be miserable with the husband he chose, he cared not at what price he purchased him."

She refuses, and, locked up in her room for days, is unable to eat or sleep:

> Western beheld the deplorable condition of his daughter with no more contrition or remorse than the turnkey of Newgate feels at viewing the agonies of a tender wife when taking her last farewell of her condemned husband; or rather he looked down on her with the same emotions which arise in an honest fair tradesman who sees his debtor dragged to prison for £10, which, though a just debt, the wretch is wickedly unable to pay. Or, to hit the case more nearly, he felt the same compunction with a bawd when some poor innocent, whom she hath ensnared into her hands, falls into fits at the first proposal of what is called seeing company. Indeed this resemblance would be exact, was it not that the bawd hath an interest in what she doth, and the father, though perhaps he may blindly think otherwise, can, in reality, have none in urging his daughter to almost an equal prostitution.

Although the final happy ending is a somewhat contrived one, this does not really matter. As Kettle says:

> What does matter, because the whole movement and texture of the book depend on it, is that Tom and Sophia fight conventional society, embodied in the character of Blifil. They fight with every strategem including, when necessary, fists and swords and pistols. Unlike Clarissa, they are not passive in their struggle, and that is why *Tom Jones* is not a tragedy but a comedy. It is not the conventionally contrived happy ending but the confidence we feel throughout the book that Tom and Sophia can and will grapple with their situation and change it that gains our acceptance of Fielding's comic view of life.

This is perhaps the best, and certainly the best-known, of Fielding's novels. Coleridge, who seldom accorded unreserved praise to any work of fiction, said:

> What a master of composition Fielding was! Upon my word, I think the Oedipus Tyrannus, the Alchemist, and Tom Jones,

the three most perfect plots ever planned. And how charming,
how wholesome, Fielding always is! To take him up after
Richardson is like emerging from a sick-room, heated by
stoves, into an open lawn, on a breezy day in May.

And Bernard Shaw concluded a discussion by proclaiming that:

> Between the Middle Ages and the nineteenth century,
> when Fielding was by the Licensing Act driven out of the
> trade of Moliere and Aristophanes into that of Cervantes, the
> English novel has been one of the glories of literature, whilst
> the English drama has been its disgrace.

But while there was still one great novel to come, the next
few years found Fielding busy with other though, as it proved,
not wholly unrelated matters.

He marked his assumption of office with a grave and searching
Charge To The Grand Jury which was later printed at the particular request of the jurymen. In the beginning of 1751 he published
the result of much thought and careful observation, his *Enquiry
into the Causes of the late Increases of Robbers, etc. with some
Proposals for Remedying this Growing Evil.*

This first relates a plain unvarnished tale:

> What indeed may not the public apprehend, when they
> are informed as an unquestionable fact, that there are at this
> time a great gang of rogues, whose number falls little short
> of a hundred, who are incorporated in one body, have offices
> and a treasury, and have reduced theft and robbery into a
> regular system? There are of this society of men who appear in
> all disguises, and mix in most companies. Nor are they better
> versed in every art of cheating, thieving, and robbing than
> they are armed with every method of evading the law, if they
> should ever be discovered, and an attempt made to bring them
> to justice. Here, if they fail in rescuing the prisoner, or (which
> seldom happens) in bribing or deterring the prosecutor, they
> have for their last resource some rotten members of the law
> to forge a defence for them, and a great number of false wit-
> nesses ready to support it.

Then it goes on to speak of the truly indescribable and bestial
conditions of life in the swollen London slums, saying with considerable restraint:

> Among other mischiefs attending this wretched nuisance
> the great increase of thieves must necessarily be one. The
> wonder in fact is that we have not a thousand more robbers
> than we have; indeed, that all these wretches are not thieves

must give us either a very high idea of their honesty, or a very mean one of their capacity and courage.

It concludes with concrete proposals for a new sort of police force, practical suggestions to make impossible, or at least much more difficult, the kind of collusion then existing between the underworld and law enforcement officers, and recommendations for the drastic reform of prison procedures, particularly in regard to the segregation and treatment of first offenders.

At the end of that year Fielding used his experience as a magistrate, as well as his observations of the world of fashion, and his memories of his rapturous first marriage, in a different form in his last novel, *Amelia*.

The first edition of 5,000 copies was exhausted in twelve hours, partly because of the reputation of *Tom Jones* and partly because of a clever "puffing" or advertising stunt by the publisher. But a second uncorrected impression of 3,000 was not yet completely sold at Fielding's death, and the carefully revised edition he had prepared was not published for some years thereafter.

The realistic exposure of slum and prison conditions, the sharp attacks on the whole machinery of the law, and on such accepted institutions as the imprisonment of debtors, and the general exposure of profligacy and corruption in high places, while it forms a comparatively small part of the book, is unforgettable long after one has closed it. In addition, there is little of the rollicking humour of *Tom Jones* and readers led to expect that overlooked other qualities they might otherwise have found almost equally appealing.

At any rate a large part of respectable public opinion, anxious to ignore the unpleasant truth of the book's social criticism, concurred with Richardson's spiteful judgment:

> I could not help telling his sister that I was equally surprised and concerned for his continued lowness. Had your brother, said I, been born in a stable, or been a runner at a sponging-house, we should have thought him a genius, and wished he had had the advantage of a liberal education, and of being admitted into good company; but it is beyond my conception, that a man of family, and who had some learning, and who really is a writer, should descend so excessively low, in all his pieces. Who can care for any of his people?

This criticism was echoed until, a century later, Dickens angrily countered it with:

I am not aware of any writer in our language having a respect for himself, or held in any respect by his posterity, who has ever descended to the taste of the fastidious classes. . . . On the other hand, if I look for examples and precedents, I find them in the noblest range of English literature. Fielding, Defoe, . . . for wise purposes . . . brought upon the scene the very scum and refuse of the land . . . and yet, if I turn back . . . I find the same reproach levelled against them . . . each in his turn, by the insects of the hour; who raised their little hum, and died, and were forgotten . . . when Fielding described Newgate, the prison immediately ceased to exist.

Disgust at the cold reception of *Amelia*, whom he spoke of as his favorite child, together with increasing ill health and the pressure of his almost unpaid duties, made Fielding publicly declare his determination to write no more. This resolution he evidently meant to apply to fiction rather than journalism, for in January, 1752, he instituted his last periodical venture—*The Covent Garden Journal.*

The paper had a curious history. In 1749 he and his youngest half-brother John, an intelligent and energetic young man who had had the misfortune to be blinded at nineteen, had organized a "Universal Register Office"—perhaps the first general employment office in England!

This had expanded under John's direction to include real estate and insurance, a sort of travel agency, and in fact a general exchange of all sorts of goods and services. It furnished a good part of Fielding's income, and all of John's until in 1751, Fielding secured him an appointment as assistant magistrate.

By 1751 several rival agencies had sprung up and most of the available London newspapers for political or business reasons, accepted their advertisements but not those of the Fieldings. The brothers therefore decided to publish their own journal. Fielding, despite much dissuasion, personally assumed the editorship in order to use the paper as an organ through which to press for judicial reforms.

Despite its commercial inspiration this periodical affords us more insight into his personal views than any of Fielding's earlier journalistic ventures have done. In one of the first issues he defined his attitude to the political scene declaring:

I disclaim any dealing in politics. By politics, here, I cannot be understood to mean any disquisitions into those matters which respect the true interest of this kingdom abroad, or

which relate to its domestic economy and government. . . .
By politics I mean that great political cause between *Woodall
Out* and *Takeall In* Esqs, which hath been so learnedly handled in papers, pamphlets, and magazines, for above thirty
years last past.

A number at the beginning of the second month contains an
especially interesting discussion of religion as a means of plunder-
ing the poor, although we know from other sources that Fielding
himself was a convinced if unexcited Christian. However, here he
ironically appeals to gentlemen in power for a revival of religion
on politic if on no other grounds:

> . . . if we look into the doctrines and tenets of that insti-
> tution [Christianity] which was accounted divine by our an-
> cestors . . . we shall find it admirably calculated for the
> preservation of property; . . .
>
> Now what can more effectually establish this . . . than
> the positive assertion of one St. Luke, 20th verse, "Blessed
> are the poor, for theirs is the kingdom of heaven." If the poor
> or the people (for in this country the _____ and the
> _____ are synonymous) could be once firmly per-
> suaded that they had a right to the other world, they might
> surely be well contented to resign their pretensions to this.
> Nay, the rich might in that case very fairly withhold every-
> thing in this world from them: for it would be manifestly un-
> just that the poor should enjoy both. . . .
>
> Could anything, therefore, be so weak in our late gover-
> nors, as to have suffered a set of poor fellows, who were just
> able to read and write, to inform their brethren, that the place
> which the rich had allotted to them was a mere Utopia, and
> an estate, according to the usual sense of the phrase, in
> [limbo] only? Could the poor become once unanimously per-
> suaded of this, what should hinder them from an attempt in
> which the superiority of their numbers might give them some
> hopes of success; and when they have nothing real to risk
> in either world in the trial?
>
> . . . I know so many good people who are pleased with
> . . . the scheme of the late Dean Swift, to force our poor to
> eat their own children, as what would not only afford provi-
> sion for our present poor but prevent their increase.
>
> But with submission, however proper and humane this
> proposal might be in Ireland, I must observe it would be ex-
> tremely cruel and severe here. For there the children of the
> poor being sustained for the most part with milk and potatoes,
> must be very delicious food; but here, as the children of the
> poor are little better than a composition of gin, to force their

parents to eat them would in reality be to force them to poison themselves. . . .

In truth, religion here, as in many other instances, will best do the business of the politician.

As to the restoration of the Christian religion, though I must own the expediency of it, could it be accomplished, I think it is a matter of too much difficulty. . . .

Without further preface then I shall propose the restoration of the ancient heathen religion . . . that consisted in the immolation of human sacrifices.

. . . The objection I would obviate is this; that my scheme is rather too barbarous and inhuman.

To this it might be sufficient to answer that it is for the good of the nation in general; that is to say, for the richer part.

But in truth it is for the advantage of the poor themselves; . . . Do we not daily see instances of men in distressed circumstances, that is to say, who cannot keep a coach and six, who fly to death as to a refuge? What must we think then of wretches in a state of hunger and nakedness; without bread to eat, without clothes to cover them, without a hut or hovel to receive them?

. . . In this light, therefore, I shall be understood by my sensible reader, and instead of that censure of cruelty which hath been bestowed upon Dr. Swift by some very ingenious and learned critics for his above-mentioned proposal, it will be attributed to my humane disposition that I have proposed to lessen the severity of that death, which is suffered by so many persons, who in the most lingering manner do daily perish for want in this metropolis.

Other briefer comments indicate the social views we find developed more fully but sometimes less explicitly in his novels. A good example is his temperate and realistic conclusion:

I do not pretend to say, that the mob have no faults; perhaps they have many. I assert no more than this, that they are in all laudable qualities very greatly superior to those who have hitherto, with much injustice, pretended to look down upon them.

In another article a letter from a purported madman suggests the abolition of money as a cure for many social evils, concluding:

I shall add but one particular more; which is, that my scheme would most certainly provide for the poor, and that by an infallible (perhaps the only infallible) method, by removing the rich. Where there are no rich, there will of consequence be found no poor; for Providence hath in a wonderful manner provided for every country a plentiful subsistence for all its inhabitants; and where none abound, none can want.

After Fielding's ill health had, at the end of 1752, forced him to end the journal, he published one more pamphlet, *A Proposal for Making An Effective Provision for the Poor, for Amending their Morals and for Rendering them Useful Members of the Society.* The specific suggestions are of little interest today, but his description of existing conditions with its indignation at the delicacy that cannot bear to know of horrors but can easily endure their hidden existence is as timely now as then:

> If we were to make a progress through the outskirts of this town, and look into the habitations of the poor, we should there behold such pictures of human misery as must move the compassion of every heart that deserves the name of human. What, indeed, must be his composition who could see whole families in want of every necessary of life, oppressed with hunger, cold, nakedness, and filth, and with diseases, the certain consequences of all these—what, I say, must be his composition, who could look into such a scene as this, and be affected only in his nostrils?

The excellent French literary historian, Louis Cazamian, gives a good description of the strength as well as the limitations of Fielding's thinking in this field when he says:

> As a magistrate Fielding knows well the conflicts of the penal codes and the instincts; he recounts them with the exactitude of a well-informed witness and the zeal of a reformer. For he has a generous conception of justice; no doubt, his ideas on the right to punish, on the responsibility of the criminal, on the social regime, do not go beyond the range of vision of his time; but he quickens them through the susceptibility of a noble conscience, he has felt and shown the crudity of certain legal punishments, the scandals of judicial administration. His calm objective world is at times animated by a humane ardour, just as the independence of his thought does not stop at the inequalities his age deemed necessary.

This pamphlet and the growing fame of Fielding's accomplishments in his district caused the Duke of Newcastle to request in August, 1753, that he submit a plan "for putting an immediate end to those murders and robberies which were everyday committed in the streets."

Although seriously ill, Fielding submitted a plan which he personally undertook to put into effect if supplied with £600 for necessary expenses. This would, he guaranteed, serve to "demolish the then reigning gangs, and to put the civil policy in such order, that no such gangs should ever be able for the future to form themselves into bodies, or at least to remain any time formidable to the public."

The successful upshot of the matter is given very succinctly in an autobiographical fragment, included in the introduction to his *Journal of A Voyage to Lisbon,* which was written two years later and published after his death. Here he says, in part:

> But, not to trouble the reader with anecdotes. . . . I assure him I thought my family was very slenderly provided for; and that my health began to decline so fast that I had very little more of life left to accomplish what I had thought of too late. I rejoiced therefore greatly in seeing an opportunity, as I apprehended, of gaining such merit in the eye of the public, that if my life were the sacrifice to it, my friends [in the government] might think they did a popular act in putting my family at least beyond the reach of necessity, which I myself began to despair of doing. And though I disclaim all pretence to that Spartan or Roman patriotism, which loved the public so well that it was always ready to become a voluntary sacrifice to the public good, I do solemnly declare I have that love for my family.
>
> After this confession therefore, that the public was not the principal deity to which my life was offered a sacrifice, and when it is further considered what a poor sacrifice this was, being indeed no other than the giving up what I saw little likelihood of being able to hold much longer, and which, upon the terms I held it, nothing but the weakness of human nature could represent to me as worth holding at all; the world may, I believe, without envy, allow me all the praise to which I have any title.
>
> My aim, in fact, was not praise, which is the last gift they care to bestow; at least, this was not my aim as an end, but rather as a means, of purchasing some moderate provision for my family, which, though it should exceed my merit, must fall infinitely short of my service, if I succeeded in my attempt.

His health was, actually, so completely destroyed in the work of carrying out his reforms that in April 1754, he retired, happily securing John's appointment to his magistracy. On the urgent advice of his physician, he set sail for Lisbon to attempt recovery in a warm climate.

He was accompanied by his wife and oldest daughter. Unable to walk, suffering from a complication of painful disorders including dropsy, and separated from his children, the "little things," he unfeignedly and unashamedly loved, and with whom he normally spent an extraordinary amount of time, he nevertheless still displayed the liveliest interest in all the incidents of the trip, the eccentricities of the ship's captain, and the novelties to be seen en route.

Two months after reaching his destination he died, and the *Journal* which he had written to defray the expenses of his journey was published posthumously in February, 1755, for the benefit of his wife and children.

His brother John, who published it, also succeeded in getting two of Fielding's old plays produced for their benefit, and in securing them a small pension.

He shared his own income with them for the rest of his life and Fielding's two sons, the only ones of the children to survive their uncle, seem to have been well educated. Charles Lamb half a century later describes the older as a fairly well-known judge whom he went to see for his father's sake.

Hazlitt has, perhaps, written Fielding's best epitaph saying:

> It is a very idle piece of morality, to lament over Fielding for his low indulgence of his appetite for character. If he had been found quietly at his tea, he would never have left behind him the name he had done. There is nothing of a tea inspiration in any of his novels. They are assuredly the finest things of the kind in the language; and we are Englishmen enough to consider them the best in any language. They are indubitably the most English of all the works of Englishmen.

FROM THE AUGUSTANS TO THE ROMANTICS

As late as 1814 a man of letters like Sir Walter Scott could explain the anonymity of his first novel by writing apologetically:

> I shall not own Waverly; . . . In truth I am not sure it would be considered quite decorous of me, as a Clerk of Session, to write novels. . . . I do not see how my silence can be considered as imposing on the public. . . . In point of

emolument everybody knows that I sacrifice much money by withholding my name; and what should I gain by it that any human being has a right to consider as an unfair advantage? In fact, only the freedom of writing trifles with less personal responsibility, and perhaps more frequently than I otherwise might do.

But it must not be supposed that during the preceding fifty years the "official literature" had remained unaffected by this rich and powerful new literary form.

Even a leading intellectual figure like the famous critic and literary dictator Samuel Johnson (1709-1784) read and discussed the novels of Richardson, Fielding and others and, more important, showed in his own writing and way of thinking their influence and that of the social forces which had molded them.

The latter part of the eighteenth century is often referred to as the Age of Johnson, as the earlier one is called that of Addison and Pope, and a comparison of Johnson with the two former writers shows clearly how much even the approved upper-class literature of the period had, insensibly, been changed by the pressure of interests and attitudes from below. Johnson himself was the son of a lower middle-class family. Although he had earned a sort of working scholarship to Oxford, he found it intolerable to remain at the University under the stigma of a sizar's (student waiter's) gown. He was one of the first finally successful representatives of the new class of writers, who made a living entirely by selling their wares to the public through the medium of the new capitalist publisher-booksellers rather than by gaining the patronage of a great nobleman.

His quarrel with Lord Chesterfield is one of the best known anecdotes of literary history, and since it not only marked, but also perfectly summarized, the end of the patronage system—and the establishment of the commodity system—in art, it must again be repeated here.

When Johnson determined to undertake his famous Dictionary, his reason was characteristically eighteenth century, in that he felt the language had reached perfection and must be set in that mold before deterioration, the germs of which were already apparent, overcame it. He naturally thought of securing financial assistance from a leading patron of the arts, and on the hint of some friend or follower of Lord Chesterfield, waited upon him for that purpose. His visits were not encouraged and Johnson, well-known for his independence and touchy pride, made no further efforts in that direction but devoted himself, in great poverty, to doing the work alone. With the assistance of several meager advances from the bookseller who was to bring it out he succeeded. During these years of hardship his wife died.

When the work was about ready for the press its fame had already preceded it. Johnson's literary and critical reputation was also well established by that time, and Chesterfield wrote several very graceful "anonymous" articles in anticipation of its publication, letting it be known that he was not averse to receiving—and rewarding—its dedication to him. Johnson, furious at this belated and unnecessary patronage, wrote his famous letter to Lord Chesterfield on February 7, 1755. In effect this announced the emergence of the modern "independent" intellectual and middle-class professional, free to sell his wares in the market place or starve. The polished style and classical allusions, as well as the gracefully implied insult in the ironically courteous conclusion, all make this an excellent example of the aristocratic eighteenth century style, although the content heralds the end of that epoch.

To the Right Honorable the Earl of Chesterfield

My Lord: I have been lately informed by the proprietor of the World, that two papers, in which my Dictionary is recommended to the public, were written by your Lordship. To be so distinguished is an honor which, being very little accustomed to favors from the great, I know not well how to receive, or in what terms to acknowledge.

When, upon some slight encouragement, I first visited your Lordship, I was overpowered, like the rest of mankind, by the enchantment of your address, and could not forbear to wish that I might boast myself Le vainquer du vainqueur de la terre;—that I might obtain that regard for which I saw the world contending; but I found my attendance so little encouraged that neither pride nor modesty would suffer me to continue it. When I had once addressed your Lordship in public, I had exhausted all the art of pleasing which a retired and uncourtly scholar can possess. I had done all that I could; and no man is well pleased to have his all neglected, be it ever so little.

Seven years, my Lord, have now passed since I waited in your outward rooms, or was repulsed from your door; during which time I have been pushing on my work through difficulties, of which it is useless to complain, and have brought it, at last, to the verge of publication without one act of assistance, one word of encouragement, or one smile of favor. Such treatment I did not expect, for I never had a Patron before.

The shepherd in Vergil grew at last acquainted with Love, and found him a native of the rocks.

Is not a Patron, my Lord, one who looks with unconcern on a man struggling for life in the water, and when he has reached ground, encumbers him with help? The notice which you have been pleased to take of my labors, had it been early, had been kind; but it has been delayed till I am indifferent, and cannot enjoy it; till I am solitary, and cannot impart it; till I am known, and do not want it. I hope it is no very cynical asperity not to confess obligations where no benefit has been received, or to be unwilling that the Public should consider me as owing that to a Patron, which Providence has enabled me to do for myself.

Having carried on my work thus far with so little obligation to any favorer of learning, I shall not be disappointed though I should conclude it, if less be possible, with less; for I have been long wakened from that dream of hope, in which I once boasted myself with so much exultation,

My Lord,
Your Lordship's most humble,
Most obedient servant,
Sam Johnson

Before turning to the emergence of "sentiment" and the last two eighteenth century figures we must here mention, we should say that Johnson as well as Swift—the only eighteenth century writers, besides the novelists, who powerfully expressed hatred of oppression and understanding sympathy for poverty—were Tories. This may seem as contradictory as Balzac's official devotion to royalism in Republican France, or Tolstoy's theory of ascetism, non-resistance, resignation and religion in revolutionary Russia. Actually an understanding of these contradictions is of the utmost importance to the student of literature for it requires him to make, and aids him in making, the effort of historical imagination necessary for any real appreciation of the art and creative thinking of other ages.

It is always easier to feel what is wrong than to find a remedy, and those writers sensitive enough to react at that early date to the evils of capitalism were often forced, by their opposition to its inhumanity, to take sides with any who seemed to oppose it. In eighteenth century England, this meant with the Tories. In specific terms, for example, the Whigs were for the War of the Protestant

Succession. The rising merchants and early manufacturers who grew rich through early exploitation of India and other colonies abroad, and through the rooting up of the independent peasantry at home, were all Whigs. The deliberate destruction of Irish industry, which so infuriated Swift, and the defense and extension of the slave trade which aroused Johnson, were largely organized by the Whig interests. Of course, the Tories were fundamentally no better, and in the few cases where there was a genuine difference between them and the Whigs, their stand was hopeless as well as reactionary. But barring an impossible and unhistorical mental leap, there was no stand but the Tory stand for those who could not stomach the commercial bourgeoisie, unless they withdrew from political participation entirely, and became preoccupied with sentimental personal problems as the few later eighteenth century poets like Cowper, Collins and Gray tended to do.

The argument on the slave trade between the "Reactionary Tory" Johnson and his "Progressive Whig" biographer, Boswell shows how very misleading party labels can be if we do not take the trouble to examine their concrete historical content and background. Thus, although we would agree with Boswell and not Johnson in their attitude to the American Revolution, we would certainly sympathize with Johnson's toast: "Here's to the next insurrection of the Negroes in the West Indies"; his statement about "the natural right of the Negroes to liberty and independence"; his argument that "An individual may, indeed forfeit his liberty by a crime, but he cannot by that crime forfeit the liberty of his children"; and his wry comment, with which Swift would have entirely agreed, "I do not much wish well to discoveries for I am always afraid they will end in conquest and robbery." In fact, much of his unfriendly attitude toward the colonies is explained by the sarcastic question, "How is it we hear the loudest yelps for liberty among the drivers of the Negroes?"

Boswell expressed a typically sanctimonious Whig rationalization when he begged leave:

> to enter my most solemn protest against his [Johnson's] general doctrine with respect to the slave trade. . . . To abolish a status which in all ages GOD has sanctioned and man has continued would not only be robbery to an innumerable class of our fellow subjects; but it would be an extreme cruelty to the African savages, a large portion of whom it saves from massacre, or intolerable bondage in their own country, and

> introduces into a much happier state of life . . . to abolish
> that trade would be to shut the gates of mercy on mankind.

This alone makes us realize why some of the most humane men of
the age were driven to support any opposition to "Whiggism."

Before leaving Johnson we should, perhaps, look at a few more
of the many comments in which he shows how it was his rather
amazing insight into the reality of bourgeois ethics (as they were
more unmistakably to develop after his time) that motivated his
opposition to the party which was their leading representative. The
growing bourgeois ideal of a "wealthy but usurious miser and a
hard working but ascetic slave," which lies at the root of all the
nineteenth century cant about "the deserving poor," was characterized by Johnson as "Whiggism." At one time, in response to a
protest that it was no use giving alms to beggars since they would
spend it on gin or tobacco, Johnson demanded:

> And why should they be denied such sweeteners of their
> existence? It is surely very savage to refuse them every pos-
> sible avenue to pleasure, reckoned too coarse for our own ac-
> ceptance. Life is a pill which none of us can bear to swallow
> without gilding; yet for the poor we delight in stripping it still
> barer, and are not ashamed to shew even visible displeasure if
> ever the bitter taste is taken from their mouths.

He also related to "Whiggism" the growing middle-class cult of
sentimentality at which we must glance before leaving the eighteenth century, and went out of his way to shock his bourgeois
"liberal" friends with such remarks as:

> These are the distresses of sentiment which a man who is
> really to be pitied has no leisure to feel. The sight of people
> who want food and raiment is so common in great cities, that
> a surly fellow like me has no compassion to spare for wounds
> given only to vanity or softness . . . you will find these very
> feeling people are not very ready to do you good. They *pay*
> you by *feeling*.

Like Swift, he felt a deep though muffled indignation at the
infuriating complacency of articulate eighteenth century opinion,
and at the fashionable unfelt world-weariness its successful ex-
ponents sometimes affected. A remark he made in his *Life of Pope*
summarizes and explains much of this attitude:

Swift's resentment was unreasonable, but it was sincere; Pope's was the mere mimickry of his friend, a fictitious part which he began to play before it became him. When he was only twenty-five years old, he related that "a glut of study and retirement had thrown him on the world" and that there was danger lest "a glut of the world should throw him back upon study and retirement." To this Swift answered with great propriety, that Pope had not yet either acted or suffered enough in the world to have become weary of it.

Johnson's own pessimistic stoicism is well-known—his famous comment on the purpose of writing can bear another repetition: "The only end of writing is to enable the readers better to enjoy life or better to endure it." So can his response to a lady's remark on drunkenness: "I wonder what pleasure men can take in making beasts of themselves?" "I wonder, Madam, that you have not penetration enough to see the strong inducement to this excess; for he who makes a *beast* of himself gets rid of the pain of being a man."

Another time when he was approached by a morbidly conscientious young man who, having stolen some packthread and paper from his employer, wanted Johnson's advice on how best to express repentance, he exploded:

> . . . five hours of the four-and-twenty unemployed are enough for a man to go mad in; so I would advise you Sir, to study algebra . . . your head would get less *muddy* and you will leave off tormenting your neighbors about paper and packthread, while we all live together in a world that is bursting with sin and sorrow.

Even the economic analysis of the origin of the family is foreshadowed in such an amazing statement as Johnson's:

> Consider of what importance the chastity of women is. Upon that, all the property in the world depends. We hang a thief for stealing a sheep. But the unchastity of a woman transfers sheep and farm and all from the right owner.

Finally, before closing this brief survey of some of the landmarks of the eighteenth century, we must turn to the timid reemergence of real poetry in the work of Gray and Goldsmith. This refers, of course, to feeling and content; in terms of technical form poetry—metrical rhymed verse—had never gone out of fashion during the eighteenth century, and while less widely read in comparison with the increasing volume of essays, biographies, memoirs and novels, it remained unquestionably the correct thing to write. Even Johnson found it worth his while to achieve a succes d'estime with several long neoclassical poems, and Swift's early and justly forgotten bids for literary fame all took the shape of elaborate rhetorical odes.

Nor would it be true to imply that Swift's astringent wit and Fielding's healthy, sensuous vigor, and Johnson's solid common sense represent all the important facets of the age. Despite its self-chosen title of "The Age of Reason," the eighteenth century had witnessed the rise of a new and most unpleasant phenomenon in the sentimentality consciously expressed as early as 1768 in Sterne's *Sentimental Journey*, less consciously and more unpleasantly in Richardson's *Pamela, Clarissa Harlowe*, and *Richard Grandison* and as we shall see, still more extravagantly developed in the host of minor novelists who imitated these. Cowper's religious melancholia, Collins' more sedate nature poetry, Thomson's "Seasons" and other lesser work, all show traces of this new devotion to sentiment. It is a difficult attitude to define but if we recollect the somewhat cynical description of faith as "a belief in what we know is not true" we may perhaps describe sentimentality as "emotion about what we know does not matter." It is the indulgence of melancholy for its own sake, the luxurious enjoyment of "a good cry" which has persisted from its eighteenth century birth down to the latest "linked sweetness long drawn out" of the agonized soap opera heroine, or woman's magazine serial or (less frequently in this day of film brutality) the vicissitudes of a sad, sweet, motion picture idyll.

As we shall soon note, Jane Austen unmercifully satirizes this tendency of the host of inferior eighteenth century novelists in her juvenilia as well as in her serious novels, and we find its influence strong in the very inferior sentimental drama which monopolized the American as well as the English theatre of the next century.

It is difficult to discuss this attitude briefly or analyze its causes in a reasonable amount of space. Perhaps Leslie Stephens' explanation in his excellent book on *English Literature and Society in the Eighteenth Century* will suffice for our purpose here. He says:

> No distinct democratic sentiment had yet appeared; the aristocratic order was accepted as inevitable or natural; but there was a vague though growing sentiment that the rulers are selfish and corrupt. There is no strong sceptical or anti-religious sentiment; but a spreading conviction that the official pastors are scandalously careless in supplying the wants

of their flocks. . . . The popular books (among this class) of the preceding generation had been the directly religious books (like Pilgrim's Progress) which had been made obsolete by the growth of rationalism. Still the new public wanted something more savoury than its elegant teachers had given; and, if sermons had ceased to be so stimulating as of old, it could find it in secular moralisers. . . .

Richardson was . . . the first writer who definitely turned sentimentalism to account for a new literary genus . . . sentimentalism at the earlier period naturally took the form of religious meditation upon death and judgement. . . .

Sentimentalism, I suppose, means, roughly speaking, indulgence in emotion for its own sake. The sentimentalist does not weep because painful thoughts are forced upon him but because he finds weeping pleasant in itself. He appreciates the luxury of grief. . . . But the general sense that something is not in order in the general state of things, without as yet any definite aim for the vague discontent was shared by the true sentimentalist.

Although it is apparent that no important art could arise from so unreal and essentially dishonest an emotion, it does tinge at least two poems of more than passing importance, which serve as some transition to the extraordinary outburst of poetic genius we find in the romantic poets of the next quarter century. Gray's *Elegy in a Country Churchyard* and Goldsmith's *The Deserted Village* are both directly referred to as sources of inspiration by Burns, and each has some lines of more than historical value, although their chief interest to us is, perhaps, essentially historical.

Thomas Gray (1716-1771), a classmate and friend of the prime minister's son, Horace Walpole, accompanied him on a continental grand tour of several years' duration after they had, together, been graduated from Cambridge. Then, declining all invitations and possible opportunities to a political or literary career, he settled down on a small income to live the life of a semirecluse in rural retirement near the college. He maintained an increasingly desultory correspondence with Walpole and several other worldly patrons of the arts, and did a great deal of work collecting and editing some of the older folk songs and ballads in which he was the first to take a systematic interest. One of the few autobiographical comments we have purports to explain his retirement, and at any rate gives a good thumbnail sketch of the mores of his age:

Too poor for a bribe and too proud t' importune
He had not the method of making a fortune;

Could love and could hate, so was thought somewhat odd,
No very great wit,—he believed in a God.

His single important poem, *Elegy in a Country Churchyard*
maintains a fashionable painless melancholy and uses classical allusions and generalized images from nature in the approved manner,
but is memorable for a few lines which strike out to the immediacy
of death, give us a powerful symbol for the waste of human potentialities and the role of accident in human life, and make a clear
if limited assertion of the claims to consideration, respect, and a
certain kind of equality that should be granted all human beings.

Beginning with the eighth stanza, which Burns quotes as an
introduction to his own "Cotter's Saturday Night," Gray says, in
part:

> Let not Ambition mock their useful toil,
>   Their homely joys, and destiny obscure;
> Nor Grandeur hear with a disdainful smile,
>   The short and simple annals of the poor.
> The boast of heraldry, the pomp of pow'r,
>   And all that beauty, all that wealth e'er gave,
> Awaits alike th' inevitable hour,
>   The paths of glory lead but to the grave.
> Nor you, ye Proud, impute to These the fault,
>   If Mem'ry o'er their Tomb no Trophies raise,
> Where thro' the long-drawn aisle and fretted vault
>   The pealing anthem swells the note of praise.
> Can storied urn or animated bust
>   Back to its mansion call the fleeting breath?
> Can Honour's voice provoke the silent dust,
>   Or Flatt'ry sooth the dull cold ear of Death?
> Perhaps in this neglected spot is laid
>   Some heart once pregnant with celestial fire;
> Hands, that the rod of empire might have sway'd,
>   Or wak'd to extasy the living lyre.
> But Knowledge to their eyes her ample page
>   Rich with the spoils of time did ne'er unroll;
> Chill Penury repress'd their noble rage,
>   And froze the genial current of the soul.
> Full many a gem of purest ray serene,
>   The dark unfathom'd caves of ocean bear:
> Full many a flower is born to blush unseen,
>   And waste its sweetness on the desert air.
> Some village-Hampden, that with dauntless breast
>   The little Tyrant of his fields withstood;
> Some mute inglorious Milton here may rest,
>   Some Cromwell guiltless of his country's blood.

Th' applause of list'ning senates to command,
The threats of pain and ruin to despise,
To scatter plenty o'er a smiling land,
And read their hist'ry in a nation's eyes,
Their lot forbad: nor circumscrib'd alone
Their growing virtues, but their crimes confin'd;
Forbad to wade through slaughter to a throne,
And shut the gates of mercy on mankind.
The struggling pangs of conscious truth to hide,
To quench the blushes of ingenuous shame,
Or heap the shrine of Luxury and Pride
With incense kindled at the Muse's flame.
Far from the madding crowd's ignoble strife,
Their sober wishes never learn'd to stray;
Along the cool sequester'd vale of life
They kept the noiseless tenor of their way.
Yet ev'n these bones from insult to protect
Some frail memorial still erected nigh,
With uncouth rhymes and shapeless sculpture deck'd,
Implores the passing tribute of a sigh.
Their name, their years, spelt by the unletter'd muse,
The place of fame and elegy supply:
And many a holy text around she strews,
That teach the rustic moralist to die.
For who to dumb Forgetfulness a prey
This pleasing anxious being e'er resign'd,
Left the warm precincts of the chearful day,
Nor cast one longing ling'ring look behind?
On some fond breast the parting soul relies,
Some pious drops the closing eye requires;
Ev'n from the tomb the voice of Nature cries,
Ev'n in our Ashes live their wonted Fires.

In Goldsmith's *The Deserted Village*, to which Burns also refers in his conclusion of "the Cotter's Saturday Night," we find a more sustained attempt to question the certainty that all was for the best, which the eighteenth century so complacently assumed. Oliver Goldsmith (1728-1774) had had a more varied and eventful life than most of his contemporaries. The son of an Irish gentleman, he was sent to Trinity College in hopes of securing a position in the Church, but after graduation he failed to do so; an uncle gave him some funds to enable him to study law but he immediately lost or spent these; he made shift with various odd jobs for a year or two and finally studied medicine, first in Edinburgh and then in Leyden.

For some years he played the flute and acted with a traveling theatrical company on the continent, visiting many cities and debating and speaking before a number of university audiences. On his return to London, where he became a member of Dr. Johnson's circle, he settled down as a professional writer, doing much hack work, editing, and so forth, but also writing a number of distinguished pieces of different kinds, including a collection of charming essays in *The Citizen of the World,* a delightful seminovel or novelette, *The Vicar of Wakefield,* one of the best known of sentimental comedies, *She Stoops to Conquer,* and the long poem, *The Deserted Village.*

In this poem, centering about the fate of the village of Lissoy, in which he had spent considerable time as a child, Goldsmith raises his most serious questions as to the changes which he saw taking place in England. It is not surprising that he should idealize the pleasantness of country life, whose real hardship he had never known. The description of peasant farming as "light labour" and the general gaiety and charm of village life as he pictures it, are sufficient evidence of the inaccuracy of his nostalgic memory. But it is much more surprising and important to note the clearness with which he understands what was happening to the whole rural population of England. The conversion from "corn" to sheep, by the end of the small freeholdings, the new inclosure acts, and, in Ireland and Scotland, the use of the land as a playground for men whose fortunes were made in trade, forced the peasant off the land. He was left to emigrate or to become a part of the uprooted vagabond population whose remnants settled in city slums and formed the first reservoir of cheap factory labor in the new industrial (late eighteenth, early nineteenth century) period. This all finds a place in *The Deserted Village.*

It is also surprising to find so clear a statement—and criticism—of the whole mercantile theory as Goldsmith packs into the couplet:

> Proud swells the tide with loads of freighted ore
> And shouting Folly hails them from her shore.

Evidently even a minor poet was not abashed at arguing the wealth of nations with a political economist in an earlier time than ours! However, to quote a few of the lines which most clearly show Goldsmith's perspicacity:

> Sweet smiling village, loveliest of the lawn,
> Thy sports are fled, and all thy charms withdrawn;
> Amidst thy bowers the tyrant's hand is seen,
> And desolation saddens all thy green:
> One only master grasps thy whole domain,
> And half a tillage stints thy smiling plain.

. . . . . .

Sunk are thy bowers in shapeless ruin all,
And the long grass o'ertops the mouldering wall;
And, trembling, shrinking from the spoiler's hand,
Far, far away, thy children leave the land.
Ill fares the land, to hastening ills a prey,
Where wealth accumulates, and men decay;
Princes and lords may flourish, or may fade;
A breath can make them, as a breath has made;
But a bold peasantry, their country's pride,
When once destroyed, can never be supplied.
A time there was, ere England's griefs began,
When every rood of ground maintained its man;
For him light labor spread her wholesome store,
Just gave what life required, but gave no more;
His best companions, innocence and health;
And his best riches, ignorance of wealth.
But times are altered; trade's unfeeling train
Usurp the land and dispossess the swain;
Along the lawn, where scattered hamlets rose,
Unwieldy wealth and cumbrous pomp repose,
And every want to opulence allied,
And every pang that folly pays to pride.

. . . . . .

Ye friends to truth, ye statesmen who survey
The rich man's joys increase, the poor's decay,
'Tis yours to judge how wide the limits stand
Between a splendid and a happy land.
Proud swells the tide with loads of freighted ore,
And shouting Folly hails them from her shore;
Hoards even beyond the miser's wish abound,
And rich men flock from all the world around.
Yet count our gains. This wealth is but a name
That leaves our useful products still the same.
Not so the loss. The man of wealth and pride
Takes up a place that many poor supplied;
Space for his lake, his park's extended bounds,
Space for his horses, equipage, and hounds;
The robe that wraps his limbs in silken sloth
Has robbed the neighboring fields of half their growth;
His seat, where solitary sports are seen,
Indignant spurns the cottage from the green;
Around the world each needful product flies,
For all the luxuries the world supplies;
While thus the land, adorned for pleasures, all
In barren splendor, feebly waits the fall.

. . . . . .

Thus fares the land by luxury betrayed,
In nature's simplest charms at first arrayed,
But verging to decline, its splendors rise,

Its vistas strike, its palaces surprise;
While, scourged by famine, from the smiling land
The mournful peasant leads his humble band;
And while he sinks, without one arm to save,
The country blooms—a garden and a grave.

.   .   .   .

Kingdoms, by luxury to sickly greatness grown,
Boast of a florid vigor not their own.
At every draft more large and large they grow,
A bloated mass of rank unwieldy woe;
Till, sapped their strength, and every part unsound,
Down, down they sink, and spread a ruin round.

Neither Gray nor Goldsmith were truly great poets, and one of the reasons is apparent in the constant quarrel one senses between traditional form and new content. The heroic couplet, excellently contrived to sharpen the swift sting of Pope's satire, and to provide a more specious plausibility for his sententious epigrams, is not at all suited to the mounting tide of indignation or the flow of sympathy which Goldsmith and Gray wish to express. Gray, in fact, loosened the couplet, placing his rhymes at the end of every other line, and thus securing a little more continuity in the four line stanza; he also gave specific directions—since almost universally ignored—forbidding the printer to break his continuity by spaces between the stanzas. Goldsmith, too, in various ways, struggled against the form which, unsuited to his purpose, had become a strait-jacket instead of a support. But neither of them had the real power of poetic imagination which enabled a Walt Whitman to break through a form that had become irrelevant, and establish his own. This was achieved by two greater poets, Burns and Blake, who, although almost contemporary in time, were in spirit no longer transitional figures, but full-fledged pioneer romantics. They must, therefore, be dealt with in the next section. But first comes one more late eighteenth century figure—the last of the great early novelists, and the first of the great women novelists, Jane Austen, born in 1775.

JANE AUSTEN

After Fielding and Richardson had blazed the path two younger contemporaries, a rough Scottish surgeon, Tobias Smollett, and a most irreverent Yorkshire clergyman, Laurence Sterne, experimented further with what is often referred to as the novel of character and incident on the one hand, and the novel of sensibility on the other. These four who are often grouped as "the first English novelists" or "the great eighteenth century novelists" were all men of affairs and their work shows a breadth of worldly knowledge, a concrete practical observation of people of all classes, and an active energetic interest in the business of contemporary life, which are not again fully expressed by any bourgeois English writer but Dickens.

During the second half of the century, although an extraordinary number of novels were written—and an even more extraordinary number of copies were purchased or rented and read—neither the actual literary value of the form nor its place in critical estimation made any significant advance. The two major lines of development were those of the "Gothick Novel"— blood-chilling melange of ruined castles, haunted rooms, insane prisoners, secret murders, hidden wills and spectral figures, and the "novel of sensibility" with heroines who fainted on the slightest provocation, became frenzied or fell into a decline on very little more, and were dissolved in tears or suffused with blushes on no provocation whatsoever. By far the most important proponent of the former group was Mrs. Radcliffe, while Fanny Burney, Dr. Johnson's young protégée, was certainly the most readable of the latter.

Not only these two novelists but the greater part of their lesser colleagues and by far the major portion of their readers were women, an altogether new phenomenon in literary history.

We have already glanced at one of the most important causes for this huge new audience—the increased leisure and widespread but limited literacy of middle-class women.

Furthermore, the ambiguous position of the novel still prevented self-respecting men of letters from seriously turning to it, and left the field open to the competition of the most adventurous and talented of their sisters. These had few other outlets for their ability and, except through marriage, almost no other way of making or supplementing an income.

Actually the novel was not really accepted as literature until some time after the anonymous publication of *Waverly* in 1814. Its enormous success induced Sir Walter Scott, already well-known as a popular poet, to waive his anonymity and stamp subsequent novels with the hallmark of his undoubted gentility.

Writing as late as 1798 or 1799 Jane Austen found reason to exclaim, in *Northanger Abbey*:

> Yes, novels; for I will not adopt that ungenerous and impolitic custom, so common with novel writers, of degrading, by their contemptuous censure, the very performances to the number of which they are themselves adding: joining with their greatest enemies in bestowing the harshest epithets on such works, and scarcely ever permitting them to be read by their own heroine, who, if she accidentally take up a novel, is sure to turn over its insipid pages with disgust. Alas! If the heroine of one novel be not patronised by the heroine of another, from whom can she expect protection and regard? I cannot approve of it. Let us leave it to the Reviewers to abuse such effusions of fancy at their leisure, and over every new novel to talk in threadbare strains of the trash with which the press now groans. Let us not desert one another; we are an injured body. Although our productions have afforded more extensive and unaffected pleasure than those of any other literary corporation in the world, no species of composition has been so decried. From pride, ignorance, or fashion, our foes are almost as many as our readers; and while the abilities of the nine-hundredth abridger of the History of England, or of the man who collects and publishes in a volume some dozen lines of Milton, Pope and Prior, with a paper from the Spectator, and a chapter from Sterne, are eulogised by a thousand pens, there seems almost a general wish of decrying the capacity and undervaluing the labour of the novelist, and of slighting the performances which have only genius, wit and taste to recommend them. "I am no novel reader; I seldom look into novels; do not imagine that I often read novels; it is really very well for a novel." Such is the common cant. "And what are you reading, Miss ....?" "Oh! it is only a novel!" replies the young lady; while she lays down her book with affected indifference or momentary shame. "It is only Cecilia, or Camilla, or Belinda"; or, in short, only some work in which the greatest powers of the mind are displayed, in which the most thorough knowledge of human nature, the happiest delineation of its varieties, the liveliest effusions of wit and humour, are conveyed to the world in the best chosen language.

Jane Austen's remarks indicate that it remained the fashion to scorn novels as suitable only for women and lesser tradesmen long after it had become the custom to read them in far better society. Nor, in truth, were there many novels after Fielding's worth critical attention until Jane Austen herself at the turn of the century picked up and adapted his realistic form to her creation of what are, today, almost universally considered the first modern English novels.

The departure of the other later eighteenth century novels from their realistic predecessors and the development of the ridiculous Gothic and even more intolerable lachrymose novel of fashion, have, I think, been correctly accounted for in Marvin Mudrick's stimulating recent study of Jane Austen, entitled *Irony as Defense and Discovery*. His analysis of these phenomena concludes:

> The middle-class woman of the late eighteenth century had good reason to accept and magnify these values [of sensibility and passionate love]. Living in a society dedicated to possession and dominance, with no opportunity for political or economic expression, with no influence, indeed, but such as she might gain by her maneuverability in courtship and marriage and by reading or writing novels in which this maneuverability was exploited, she could hardly fail to examine, claim, and apotheosize—even at the expense of all others—the only values which centered in courtship and marriage, and which could therefore make her feel possessive and dominant. It is significant that an impressive proportion of both lachrymose and Gothic novels—books which disregarded the man's world of property and its cardinal virtue, discretion, or treated them as no more than detestable clogs on sex and sensibility—were written by women; that, in fact, the English novel of the last quarter of the eighteenth century was almost monopolized by women, Fanny Burney and Mrs. Radcliffe being only the pre-eminent examples; and that Jane Austen was the only woman writer to oppose the tide of feminine sensibility in the novels of her time.

This does not, of course, mean that Jane Austen ignored the specifically feminine problems of her period or the values implicit in varying attempts at their solution. These were, in fact, her essential preoccupation and a great part of her extraordinary power comes from the intensely realistic scrutiny to which she subjected them. But her solutions were serious ones, no matter how ironically presented, and she had nothing but laughter for the escapist fantasies with which sentimental contemporaries solaced their more sentimental readers. In his *Introduction to the English Novel*, Dr. Kettle begins a detailed analysis of perhaps her most mature completed work, *Emma*, by saying:

> . . . a good deal of the moral passion of the book, as of her other novels, does undoubtedly arise from Jane Austen's understanding of and feeling about the problems of women in her society. It is this realistic, unromantic and indeed, by ortho-

dox standards, subversive concern with the position of women
that give tang and force to her consideration of marriage.

Before we consider more fully the peculiarly happy satire and
the small but perfectly truthful world to which she voluntarily confined her novels, let us look briefly at the very similar world in
which she was, perhaps less voluntarily, herself confined all her
life. Her world always consisted so largely of the family and its
connections that we must enumerate its most important members
with some particularity.

Jane Austen was born in 1775 in Hampshire, the sixth of eight
children in a pleasant country parsonage. Her family was, like the
class to which it belonged, still on the way up. Although her father's
father had been a surgeon and so barely a gentleman, and his
mother—widowed early—had actually had to take carefully selected
lodgers in order to manage an education for her five sons, she
had managed, and George Austen had won sufficient distinction as
a scholar to obtain favorable notice and two fairly good church
livings.

His wife, daughter of a clergyman, came of a rather better family with some very wealthy relatives. One of these, a Mr. Knight,
was childless and adopted the third son, Edward,—the oldest,
James, was of course destined to succeed Jane's father and the
second, George, "had fits" and was perhaps feeble-minded from
infancy. At any rate he never lived at home and is never mentioned
by any of the brothers or sisters.

Edward Knight, as the third son was renamed, inherited a very
considerable landed estate and a great deal of Jane's time and that
of her older sister, Cassandra, was spent in pleasant visits to him
and his family.

Since both the sisters rarely left home together, and since they
were always extraordinarily close to each other, the innumerable
letters they exchanged furnish a running commentary on Jane's
daily life and often enable us to compare the raw material with
the highly finished product of the novels. There are, however,
exasperating gaps in this correspondence since Cassandra, who
long outlived Jane, finally destroyed not only all her own letters,
but also all those of Jane's which seemed to her indiscreet, unduly
revealing or too emphatically emotional.

Jane's two youngest brothers, Francis and Charles, both entered the navy as midshipmen and rose rapidly through the danger-

ous opportunities offered by the period of the Napoleonic wars, both finally dying admirals long after Jane's own death.

Her favorite brother, Henry, just a few years older than Jane, had first secured a Colonel's commission in the militia, but resigned this on marrying his cousin Eliza, the Comtesse de Feuillade, widowed by her husband's execution as a royalist emigré in postrevolutionary France. Upon his marriage, Henry entered a London banking house. This venture proved successful and highly remunerative for some time but finally failed in the postwar depression of 1816. With seemingly unclouded spirits Henry, then recently widowed, prepared for ordination, secured a church living, and finished a long life as a highly popular clergyman. He is of particular interest to us because he arranged for the publication of all his sister's six completed novels, and wrote the first brief biographical notice of her after her death.

The family was obviously an extremely energetic, intelligent and good-humored one, and Jane's and Cassandra's enviable position in a household of five brothers was further enhanced by Rev. Austen's custom of tutoring two or three carefully selected young men, sons of friends, who often lived with the family as resident pupils.

The impression of lively good spirits at home which we get from all Jane's early letters is supplemented by her detailed accounts of country balls in which she "danced twenty out of twenty sets" although not fewer than seven less fortunate young ladies were obliged, by the scarcity of gentlemen, to remain partnerless!

Her sophisticated cousin, Eliza Feuillade, wrote on one of her visits to England in 1791: "The two sisters are perfect beauties. They are two of the prettiest girls in England." And after another visit the following year: "Cassandra and Jane are both very much grown and greatly improved in manners as in person. They are, I think, equally sensible and both so to a degree seldom met with, but my heart still gives the preference to Jane."

The Austen brothers were keen hunters, and the whole family enjoyed charades, reading aloud, and the sort of informal youthful hospitality for which such a home easily becomes the center. A number of their rhymed charades have been preserved and enough of Jane's juvenilia—she began writing at twelve or fourteen—exist, formally copied out and ceremoniously dedicated to Henry, Eliza, her father, Cassandra, and other members of the circle, to verify our impression of an unusually happy, spirited and congenial group.

They were evidently much pleased with each other, proud of the abilities of sisters as well as brothers, fond of reading, and confident in their anticipation of future successes of various sorts for all members of the group. There was no luxury, but no feeling of anxiety clouded their easy enjoyment of good health, moderate comfort, and active preparation for the church, the navy, estate managership and marriage.

A cousin of Mrs. Austen's, visiting her for the first time after her marriage wrote of her stay with "the wife of the truly respectable Mr. Austen," saying: "With his sons (all promising to make figures in life) Mr. Austen educates a few youths of chosen friends and acquaintances. When among this Liberal Society, the simplicity, hospitality, and taste which commonly prevail in different families among the delightful valleys of Switzerland ever occurs to my memory."

Cassandra, who had just become engaged to a young clergyman, a former student of her father's, was away on a visit during much of 1796 and Jane wrote her:

> You scold me so much in the nice long letter which I have this moment received from you, that I am almost ashamed to tell you how my Irish friend and I behaved. Imagine to yourself everything most profligate and shocking in the way of dancing and sitting down together. I *can* expose myself, however, *only once* more, because he leaves the country soon after next Friday, on which day *we are* to have a dance at Ashe, after all.

The next year Mrs. Austen welcomed James' second wife—his first wife had died some time before in childbirth, and Jane and Cassandra had been caring for his baby daughter. She wrote her new daughter-in-law: "I look forward to you as a real comfort to me in my old age when Cassandra is gone into Shropshire and Jane the Lord knows where."

However, Jane's Irish friend left to be admitted to the Irish bar, and eight years later married an Irish lady. Many years afterwards, when he had become a Chief Justice and Jane was long dead—and famous—he confided to a nephew that as a boy he had been in love with the younger Miss Austen but there is no strong indication that he was, at most, ever more than one of several possible suitors.

A more serious loss was Cassandra's. Her fiancé died of yellow fever in the West Indies, where he had served as military chaplain while waiting for an appointment to a church living at home.

Yet during this trying period and later, despite all personal vicissitudes, both Jane's letters and her novels breathe undiminished the spirit of stability and security that "characterized the post-revolutionary period of the great English eighteenth century novelists."

For although Jane Austen comes at the very end of that period her general circumstances, family situation, and the somewhat circumscribed practical experiences of a lifelong residence in one of the most prosperous and stable country districts of England, enable her to absorb and recreate its atmosphere with no premonition of an imminent end. Dr. Kettle emphasizes the peculiar advantages this gave her art, while explaining why it was impossible for later English novelists to achieve the same seemingly effortless balance.

> This atmosphere of stability and security Jane Austen emphatically shares. The impulse of realism which permeates her novels is an extension, a refinement of that impulse of controlled and objective curiosity which we have noticed as a by-product of the bourgeois revolution and the underlying characteristic of the eighteenth century novel.
>
> But by the time of Jane Austen the eighteenth century world . . . is almost gone. The industrial revolution is under way and a new and immensely powerful class—that of the industrial capitalists—is in the ascendancy. And the world of the nineteenth century is a world infinitely less amicable to art of any kind than the eighteenth century world.
>
> . . . the [nineteenth century] industrial bourgeoisie as a class . . . hated and feared the implications of any artistic effort of realism and integrity. And throughout the century from the days of Shelley's Castlereagh through those of Dickens' Gradgrind . . . honest writers were bound to feel a deep revulsion against the underlying principles and the warped relationships of the society they lived in.
>
> It is for this reason that, after Jane Austen, the great novels of the nineteenth century are all, in their differing ways, novels of revolt. The task of the novelist was the same as it had always been—to achieve realism, . . . to express the truth about life as it faced them. But to do this, to cut through the whole complex structure of inhumanity and false feeling that ate into the consciousness of the capitalist world, it was necessary to become a rebel. . . .

Jane Austen, needless to say, never became a rebel. And in her satire we find a curious combination of the sharpest and most searching social criticism with a fundamental assurance of social well-being and the likelihood of a reasonable personal happiness. The only analogous satire which comes to mind is found in the early postrevolutionary work of such Russian writers as Ilya Ilf, Eugene Petrov, Valentin Kataeyv, and other minor contemporaries.

This is generally broader and more farcical than anything of Jane Austen's, although the Thorpes and General Tilney in *Northanger Abbey* and Mr. Collins and Lady de Bourgh in *Pride and Prejudice* are almost as explicit. But the fundamental resemblance is that of underlying tone, not that of style. The unsparing exposure of serious social shortcomings, saved from bitterness by a fundamental conviction of the health of the social system, and of its consequent ability to reform itself, are both characteristic of Jane Austen, as they are of those Russian satirists who wrote immediately after the stabilization of the Soviet Union.

When Jane Austen at twenty-one completed her first serious novel—*First Impressions* (later rewritten as *Pride and Prejudice*)—her father evidently esteemed it enough to write a London publisher about the possibilities of its appearance. But he received no answer, and there were no further attempts at negotiation for some time.

That same year, however, she began *Sense and Sensibility* (then named *Elinor and Marianne*) and when that was completed wrote *Northanger Abbey* which she finished in 1799.

We still find some very gay letters to Cassandra, although in many of them it is evident that the gaiety is more a matter of attitude than circumstance. For example, after an entertaining account of a small ball in 1799 she adds: "I do not think it worth while to wait for enjoyment until there is some real opportunity for it." And after a dinner, she writes: "I believe Mary found it dull, but I thought it very pleasant. To sit in idleness over a good fire in a well proportioned room is a luxurious sensation. I said two or three amusing things and Mr. Holder made a few infamous puns."

There is a deliberate—almost a determined—amusement about fashions, as when she reports the result of a buying commission to Cassandra from Bath: "besides, I cannot help thinking that it is more natural to have flowers grow out of the head than fruit. What do you think on that subject?"

There are also pointed observations which might, unchanged, have found their place in the novels. At the conclusion of a dramatic account of a storm, which destroyed some fine elm trees but did no further damage we read: "We grieve therefore in some comfort."

A few years later she more sharply hits at the conventional "mourning in comfort" of her neighbors when she reports the news of a naval engagement in 1811: "How horrible it is to have so many people killed!—And what a blessing that one cares for none of them!"

And a thumbnail sketch is given of "a very young man, just entered of Oxford, wears spectacles and has heard that [Fanny Burney's] Evelina was written by Dr. Johnson."

The unliklihood of publication does not seem to have at all affected Jane's interest in writing, or the high spirits and rapidity with which she wrote. But in 1800 her father's decision to retire (he was already over seventy) and move to Bath with his wife and two daughters, leaving the vicarage and church duties to his oldest son, James, was evidently a great and unwelcome shock to Jane. She was then already twenty-five, and for her this removal evidently put a definite period to youth and its promise of some more significant future. As long as circumstances were relatively unchanged in the home in which she had been born it was still possible to feel that the peaceful, busy, domestic routine was just a pleasant preparation for life. Now, suddenly, a much more circumscribed, less happy domesticity was all too likely to be life itself. When the decision was announced to her, on her return from a visit, she fainted for the first and only time of her life and Cassandra later destroyed all the letters she wrote her during the next month.

Jane had mastered herself enough to announce gaily before their departure: "We plan having a steady cook and a young giddy housemaid, with a sedate middle-aged man, who is to undertake the double office of husband to the former and sweetheart to the latter. No children, of course, to be allowed on either side."

But she was never happy at Bath or, later, Southampton, and despite the sale of Northanger Abbey to a publisher in 1803, wrote nothing but the first few chapters of an unfinished novel—The Watsons—during the next nine years.

Before we look at that period and at this significantly uncompleted novel, as well as at Lady Susan, a rather shocking novelette which had probably been written much earlier, but of which Jane

Austen made a final fair copy in 1805, let us turn to consider the work she had completed before the removal which marked the end of her youth.

The juvenilia to which we have earlier referred was all completed by the time Jane Austen was seventeen, and included a long story told in letters—*Love and Freindship*—which tumultuously parodies the extremes of sensibility fashionable in novels at the time.

The heroine, at fifty, writing the story of her life for the benefit of a friend's daughter, begins in simple burlesque: ". . . I was once beautiful. But lovely as I was the Graces of my Person were the least of my Perfections. Of every accomplishment accustomary to my sex, I was Mistress. When in the Convent, my progress had always exceeded my instructions, my acquirements had been wonderfull for my age, and I had shortly surpassed my Masters."

But even that first letter concludes with more penetrating insight into the relations of sentimentality and egotism: "A sensibility too tremblingly alive to every affliction of my Friends, my Acquaintance and particularly to every affliction of my own, was my only fault, if a fault it could be called. Alas! how altered now! Tho' indeed my own Misfortunes do not make less impression on me than they ever did, yet now I never feel for these of another."

After a doubled and foreshortened but hardly exaggerated version of the then conventional story of love at first sight, elopement and disinheritance, the two young husbands are arrested for debt and the wives: "Ah! what could we do but what we did! We sighed and fainted on the sofa." They refuse to visit the prison for, as one of them explains: "I shall not be able to support the sight of my Augustus in so cruel a confinement—my feelings are sufficiently shocked by the *recital* of his Distress, but to behold it will overpower my Sensibility."

The tenderheartedness that protects itself from any knowledge of suffering was evidently Jane Austen's particular abomination and she returns to the attack later with: "Ah! my beloved Laura (cried Sophia) for pity's sake forbear recalling to my remembrance the unhappy situation of my imprisoned Husband. Alas, what would I not give to learn the fate of my Augustus! to know if he is still in Newgate, or if he is yet hung. But never shall I be able so far to Conquer my tender sensibility as to enquire after him."

Finally they are reunited with their husbands only to see them both perish in a carriage accident. "Sophia immediately sunk again

into a swoon—My grief was more audible. . . . For two Hours did
I rave thus madly. . . . The morning after . . . Sophia complained
of a violent pain in her delicate limbs . . . how could I . . . have
escaped the same indisposition but by supposing that the bodily
Exertions I had undergone in my repeated fits of frenzy had so
effectually circulated and warmed my Blood as to make me proof
against the chilling Damps of Night, whereas, Sophia lying totally
inactive on the ground must have been exposed to all their
severity."

Then, marking the need of common sense even in this fantastic
world of sensibility Sophia expires with a solemn moral: "Beware
of fainting fits. . . . Though at the time they may be refreshing
and agreeable yet believe me they will in the end, if too often
repeated, and at improper seasons, prove destructive to your Constitution. . . . Run mad as often as you chuse; but do not faint."

There are other stories parodying such "language of the heart"
like *Evelyn* whose heroine: ". . . was the darling of her relations—
From the clearness of her skin and the Brilliancy of her Eyes, she
was fully entitled to all their partial affection. Another circumstance contributed to the general Love they bore her, and that was
one of the finest heads of hair in the world."

But there are also some still more interesting fragments which
directly satirize the crudely materialistic values of social snobbery
rather than its seeming contradiction in sentimental fantasy. For
example, in a collection of fictional letters, *From a Young Lady in
distressed Circumstances to her friend* the heroine reports her conversation with a patroness en route to a ball:

"Have you got a new Gown on?"

"Yes Ma'am" replied I with as much indifference as I could
assume.

"Why could not you have worn your old striped one? It
is not my way to find fault with people because they are poor,
for I always think that they are more to be despised and pitied
than blamed for it, especially if they cannot help it, but at the
same time I must say that in my opinion your old striped
Gown would have been quite fine enough for its Wearer—for to
tell you the truth (I always speak my mind) I am very much
afraid that one half the people in the room will not know
whether you have a Gown on or not—But I suppose you intend
to make your fortune tonight—Well, the sooner the better;
and I wish you success."

"Indeed Ma'am I have no such intention—"

"Who ever heard a young Lady own that she was a For-
tune-hunter?"

". . . I dare not be impertinent, as my Mother is always
admonishing me to be humble and patient if I wish to make
my way in the world. She insists on my accepting every invitation of Lady Greville, or you may be certain that I would
never enter either her House or her Coach with the disagree-
able certainty I always have of being abused for my poverty
while I am in them."

It is not surprising that Jane Austen's most recent English
biographer, the pleasant but somewhat sentimental popular novelist, Margaret Kennedy, should feel constrained to admit, apologetically, that:

At some period in her life, probably very early, she seems
to have formed a strong prejudice against rich people and great
land owners. Some startling encounter with boorish complacency or stupid arrogance created a bias from which she never
quite freed herself. Time qualified it. In the course of her life
she met with people in this class whom she could love, admire
and respect, who were her equals in refinement and who possessed, perhaps, a little more of the world's polish. But the
early bias remained and is responsible for the pride of Pem-
berly, the arrogance of Rosings, the cupidity of Norland, the
rustic conviviality of Barton, the instability of Mansfield, the
tasteless splendour of Sotherton, the snobbery of Kellynch. It
is reflected in the avarice of General Tilney; the selfishness of
Lord Osborne, and the insipidity of "our cousins Lady Dal-
rymple and Miss Carteret.

Miss Kennedy would evidently like to think that Jane Austen's
satire was imparatially aimed at all classes but her honesty and
detailed knowledge of the novels forces her to conclude that:

. . . vulgarity of the smaller fry is generally used to set off
the false standards, the lack of discrimination shown by their
betters. Lucy Steele completely imposes upon Barton and on
the Ferrar family. General Tilney knows no better than to
gossip with John Thorpe. The designing Mrs. Clay very nearly
marries Sir Walter Elliot. Snobbery is shown to impair the
judgement; and arrogance has no defence against a toady.

In her last novel, Sandition, left unfinished at her death, Jane
Austen herself, or, rather, her heroine, said:

> But she is very, very mean.—I can see no Good in her. . . .
> And she makes everybody mean about her.—This poor Sir Ed-
> ward and his Sister,—how far Nature meant them to be respect-
> able I cannot tell,—but they are obliged to be Mean in their
> Servility to her.—And I am Mean too, in giving her my atten-
> tion, with the appearance of coinciding with her.—Thus it is,
> when Rich People are Sordid.

Perhaps the most surprising note struck in these very early
experiments is that represented by the indignant comment in
Catharine when the heroine says of a young friend who has been
sent to India to make a "good match" there:

> . . . do you call it lucky, for a Girl of Genius and Feeling,
> to be sent in quest of a Husband to Bengal, to be married
> there to a Man of whose Disposition she has no opportunity of
> judging till her Judgement is of no use to her, who may be a
> Tyrant, or a Fool or both for what she knows to the Con-
> trary. . . .

Although the only copy extant of *Lady Susan,* a more ambitious
novelette in the form of a series of letters, was made in 1805, that
too was probably completed at the end of this early period of inspired preliminary exercises. It is a surprisingly sophisticated
and uncompromising self-portrait by a young widow, *Lady
Susan.* Her complete lack of maternal feeling, her ambitious world-
liness, carefully disciplined self-indulgence, frank physical enjoyment of illicit love, and pride in her power to manipulate both men
and women, would all make one think that Vanity Fair's immortal
Becky Sharp was deeply indebted to her, were it not for the fact
that *Lady Susan* saw the light of print only after Thackeray's death.

The first of Jane Austen's finished novels to be completed in its
present form was *Northanger Abbey* which, written in 1798, was,
with some slight revisions, sold to a publisher in 1803 for £10. More
careful consideration made him hesitate to print so devastating a
mockery of the "Gothick novels" which furnished most of the best-
sellers on his own book list, as well as on those of his rivals. Since
he had no knowledge of the author's identity, her brother Henry
was able in 1816 to purchase the manuscript back for the same
£10, although in the meantime both *Sense and Sensibility* and
Pride and Prejudice had made their successful appearance. *Northanger Abbey* was, therefore, not published until after Jane Austen's

early death in 1817, but its place in the development of her work
is here at the beginning.

In addition to its much more subtle and consistent parody of
other popular literary forms, the beginning of which we have already noted in her juvenilia, *Northanger Abbey* touches, lightly it
is true, on the essential theme of all Jane Austen's novels.

An interesting article by the liberal English economist, Leonard
Woolf, "The Economic Determination of Jane Austen," says:

> . . . It is remarkable to what extent the plots and char-
> acters are determined by questions of money. The whole open-
> ing of Sense and Sensibility turns upon the finance of the
> Dashwood will and the avarice of Mrs. John Dashwood whose
> income is £10,000. The finances of the Bennett family and the
> entail in Pride and Prejudice have an equal importance. The
> axis of the plot in every novel except Emma is money and
> marriage or rank and marriage.

But for the most part *Northanger Abbey* deals with the qualities
and attitudes required of a marriageable miss rather than with the
direct problem of marriage. Its heroine, Jane Austen's youngest,
falling easily in love at seventeen with the first personable and intelligent young man she meets, and happily married within the
year, has no real problems.

It is very rarely that Jane Austen speaks out in her own person,
but in this early book she permits herself the liberty several times.
We have already noted her comment on novels and novelists, and
there are others which generalize about the qualities of a heroine
and the relations of the sexes. For example:

> She was heartily ashamed of her ignorance—a misplaced
> shame. Where people wish to attach, they should always be
> ignorant. To come with a well-informed mind is to come with
> an inability of ministering to the vanity of others, which a
> sensible person would always wish to avoid. A woman, espe-
> cially, if she have the misfortune of knowing anything, should
> conceal it as well as she can.
> The advantages of natural folly in a beautiful girl have
> already been set forth by the capital pen of a sister author;
> and to her treatment of the subject I will only add, in justice
> to men, that though, to the larger and more trifling part of
> the sex, imbecility in females is a great enhancement of their
> personal charms, there is a portion of them too reasonable, and
> too well-informed themselves, to desire anything more in

woman than ignorance. But Catherine did not know her own advantages—did not know that a good-looking girl with an affectionate heart and a very ignorant mind cannot help attracting a clever young man, unless circumstances are particularly untoward.

A more characteristic comment, with its arch side glance at Richardson's solemn moral pronouncements, describes the unromantic opening of the acquaintance:

> They danced again; and when the assembly closed, parted, on the lady's side at least, with a strong inclination for continuing the acquaintance. Whether she thought of him so much, while she drank her warm wine and water, and prepared herself for bed, as to dream of him when there, cannot be ascertained; for if it be true, as a celebrated writer has maintained, that no young lady can be justified in falling in love before the gentleman's love is declared; it must be very improper that a young lady should dream of a gentleman before the gentleman is first known to have dreamt of her.

The unconventionally realistic though happy conclusion is even less compatible with romantic standards.

After Henry had declared his affection:

> . . . that heart in return was solicited, which, perhaps, they pretty equally knew was already entirely his own; for, though Henry was now sincerely attached to her,—though he felt and delighted in all the excellencies of her character, and truly loved her society,—I must confess that his affection originated in nothing better than gratitude; or, in other words, that a persuasion of her partiality for him had been the only cause of giving her a serious thought. It is a new circumstance in romance, I acknowledge, and dreadfully derogatory of a heroine's dignity; but if it be as new in common life, the credit of a wild imagination will at least be all my own.

Before writing *Northanger Abbey* Jane had completed the first version of *Sense and Sensibility*, but this was very considerably rewritten when it became her earliest published work in 1811.

Here there is no element of burlesque, but only a realistic satire; and while the heroine's attitude is obviously influenced by the current novels of sensibility, the criticism is directed at a way of living rather than at a way of writing.

There is much outspoken contempt for the mercenary values of

good society, and the entire work is colored by an informed indignation at the easy assumption of masculine superiority.

Good-natured Sir John, for example, expresses his delight in
telling his attractive but relatively impoverished young cousins of
a valuable new acquaintance by saying: "Yes, yes, he is very well
worth catching, I can tell you, Miss Dashwood; he has a pretty
little estate of his own in Somersetshire."

His widowed cousin, Mrs. Dashwood, Jane Austen's most en-
gaging mother, says with gentle dignity: "I do not believe that Mr.
Willoughby will be incommoded by the attempts of either of *my*
daughters towards what you call *catching him*. It is not an employment to which they have been brought up."

Sir John persists, however: "Aye, aye, I see how it will be, I see
how it will be. You will be setting your cap at him now, and never
think of poor Brandon."

And when Marianne sharply retorts: "I abhor every commonplace phrase by which wit is intended; and 'setting one's cap at
a man,' or 'making a conquest,' are the most odious of all. Their
tendency is gross and illiberal; and if their construction could ever
be deemed clever, time has long destroyed all its ingenuity." Sir
John "did not much understand this reproof; but he laughed as
heartily as if he did, . . ."

Of course, some of the most unpleasant of the characters in the
book are women, and their acquiescence in the mores of male
supremacy is not among the least unpleasant of their characteristics.
For example, after addressing her husband several times with no
response, Charlotte Palmer turns to Mrs. Dashwood:

> "Mr. Palmer does not hear me," said she, laughing, "he
> never does sometimes. It is so ridiculous!"
> This was quite a new idea to Mrs. Dashwood, she had
> never been used to find wit in the inattention of any one, and
> could not help looking with surprise at them both.

Neither Mrs. Palmer nor her mother are among the really unpleasant people, but the same point is illustrated in a number of
their scenes. For example, when Mr. Palmer publicly replies to a
comment of his wife's:

> "I did not know I contradicted any body in calling your
> mother ill-bred."
> "Aye, you may abuse me as you please," said the good-

natured old lady, "You have taken Charlotte off my hands, and
cannot give her back again. So there I have the whip hand
of you."

Charlotte laughed heartily to think that her husband could
not get rid of her, and exultingly said, she did not care how
cross he was to her, as they must live together. It was impossible for anyone to be more thoroughly good-natured or more
determined to be happy than Mrs. Palmer. The studied indifference, insolence, and discontent of her husband gave her no
pain; and when he scolded or abused her, she was highly
diverted.

But the masterpiece of these three early novels, and, for many
people, their favorite Jane Austen novel is *Pride and Prejudice.*
This was the earliest of the three to be completed, under the title
of *First Impressions,* in 1797, but it was the most completely rewritten from its early letter form into its present one just before
publication in 1813.

It was, for some time at least, Jane Austen's own favorite and
she wrote her sister when it appeared: "I must confess that I think
her [the heroine, Elizabeth] as delightful a creature as ever appeared in print; and how I shall be able to tolerate those who do
not like *her* at least I do not know."

Whether Jane Austen realized Elizabeth's resemblance to her
creator we do not know, but it is certainly a striking and satisfactory self-portrait.

Dr. Mudrick develops an excellent analysis of Elizabeth's character saying: "Her point of reference is always the complex individual, the individual aware and capable of choice. Her own pride
is in her freedom to observe, to analyze, to choose; her continual
mistake is to forget that, even for her, there is only one area of
choice—marriage—and that this choice is subject to all the powerful
and numbing pressures of an acquisitive society." He adds: "Irony
here rejects chiefly to discover and illuminate; and though its setting is the same stratified, materialistic, and severely regulated society, its new text and discovery . . . is the free individual."

One of Elizabeth's most delightful scenes is her rejection of Mr.
Collins' proposal despite his reminder that, in view of her small
fortune: "it is by no means certain that another offer of marriage
will ever be made." This scene comes to a climax with a statement
of one of Jane Austen's own favorite themes: "Do not consider me
now as an elegant female . . . but as a rational creature." It reads,
in revealing part:

"You are too hasty, sir," she cried. "You forget that I have made no answer. Let me do it without further loss of time. Accept my thanks for the compliment you are paying me. I am very sensible of the honour of your proposals, but it is impossible for me to do otherwise than decline them."

"I am not now to learn," replied Mr. Collins, with a formal wave of the hand, "that it is usual with young ladies to reject the addresses of the man whom they secretly mean to accept, when he first applies for their favour; and that sometimes the refusal is repeated a second or even a third time. I am therefore by no means discouraged by what you have just said, and shall hope to lead you to the altar ere long."

"Upon my word, sir," cried Elizabeth, "your hope is rather an extraordinary one after my declaration. I do assure you that I am not one of those young ladies (if such young ladies there are) who are so daring as to risk their happiness on the chance of being asked a second time. I am perfectly serious in my refusal. You could not make *me* happy, and I am convinced that I am the last woman in the world who would make you so. Nay, were your friend Lady Catherine to know me, I am persuaded she would find me in every respect ill qualified for the situation."

"Were it certain that Lady Catherine would think so," said Mr. Collins very gravely—"but I cannot imagine that her ladyship would at all disapprove of you. And you may be certain that when I have the honour of seeing her again, I shall speak in the highest terms of your modesty, economy, and other amiable qualifications."

"Indeed, Mr. Collins, all praise of me will be unnecessary. You must give me leave to judge for myself, and pay me the compliment of believing what I say. I wish you very happy and very rich, and by refusing your hand, do all in my power to prevent your being otherwise. In making me the offer, you must have satisfied the delicacy of your feelings with regard to my family, and may take possession of Longbourn estate whenever it falls, without any self-reproach. This matter may be considered, therefore, as finally settled." And rising as she thus spoke, she would have quitted the room, had not Mr. Collins thus addressed her:

"When I do myself the honour of speaking to you next on the subject, I shall hope to receive a more favourable answer than you have now given me; though I am far from accusing you of cruelty at present, because I know it to be the established custom of your sex to reject a man on the first application, and perhaps you have even now said as much to encourage my suit as would be consistent with the true delicacy of the female character."

"Really, Mr. Collins," cried Elizabeth with some warmth, "you puzzle me exceedingly. If what I have hitherto said can

appear to you in the form of encouragement, I know not how
to express my refusal in such a way as may convince you of its
being one."

"You must give me leave to flatter myself, my dear cousin,
that your refusal of my addresses is merely words of course.
My reasons for believing it are briefly these: It does not appear
to me that my hand is unworthy your acceptance, or that the
establishment I can offer would be any other than highly desirable. My situation in life, my connections with the family
of de Bourgh, and my relationship to your own, are circumstances highly in my favour; and you should take it into further
consideration, that in spite of your manifold attractions, it is
by no means certain that another offer of marriage may ever
be made you. Your portion is unhappily so small that it will
in all likelihood undo the effects of your loveliness and amiable
qualifications. As I must therefore conclude that you are not
serious in your rejection of me, I shall choose to attribute it to
your wish of increasing my love by suspense, according to the
usual practice of elegant females."

"I do assure you, sir, that I have no pretensions whatever
to that kind of elegance which consists in tormenting a respectable man. I would rather be paid the compliment of being
believed sincere. I thank you again and again for the honour
you have done me in your proposals, but to accept them is
absolutely impossible. My feelings in every respect forbid it.
Can I speak plainer? Do not consider me now as an elegant
female, intending to plague you, but as a rational creature,
speaking the truth from her heart."

"You are uniformly charming!" cried he, with an air of
awkward gallantry; "and I am persuaded that when sanctioned
by the express authority of both your excellent parents, my
proposals will not fail of being acceptable."

To such perseverance in wilful self-deception Elizabeth
would make no reply, and immediately and in silence withdrew; determined, that if he persisted in considering her repeated refusals as flattering encouragement, to apply to her
father, whose negative might be uttered in such a manner as
must be decisive, and whose behaviour at least could not be
mistaken for the affectation and coquetry of an elegant female."

But Elizabeth, who never hesitates in her determination to prefer even single blessedness to Mr. Collins, is inexpressibly shocked
when her best friend, Charlotte, accepts his hand as soon as it is
offered to her.

Dr. Mudrick explains: "It is not that Elizabeth misjudges Charlotte's capabilities, but that she underestimates the strength of the
pressures acting upon her. . . . She recognizes Mr. Collins' total

foolishness and Charlotte's intelligence, and would never have dreamed that any pressure could overcome so natural an opposition. Complex and simple, aware and unaware, do not belong together—except that in marriages made by economics they often unite, however obvious the mismatching."

But although the twenty-year old Elizabeth Bennet cannot understand this, Jane Austen does. She sadly tells us that after accepting the proposal, Charlotte's:

> . . . reflections were in general satisfactory. Mr. Collins, to be sure, was neither sensible nor agreeable; his society was irksome, and his attachment to her must be imaginary. But still he would be her husband. Without thinking highly either of men or of matrimony, marriage had always been her object; it was the only honourable provision for well-educated young women of small fortune, and however uncertain of giving happiness, must be their pleasantest preservative from want. This preservative she had now obtained; and at the age of twenty-seven, without having ever been handsome, she felt all the good luck of it.

This understanding does not mean that Jane Austen herself was prepared to accept safety on such terms. As we shall see from subsequent biographical events, from her letters, and from her later novels, she explicitly refused to settle for anything less than real respect and affection—that is, a real personal relationship, in marriage. But she did not do so under any illusions as to the unpleasant alternative possibilities.

An interesting English article by D. W. Harding, "Regulated Hatred: An Aspect of the Work of Jane Austen," may perhaps overstate the case, but it provides a valuable insight into the importance of Mr. Collins in *Pride and Prejudice*:

> Consequently the proposal scene is not only comic fantasy, but it is also, for Elizabeth, a taste of the fantastic nightmare in which economic and social institutions have such power over the values of personal relationships that the comic monster is nearly able to get her. . . . Elizabeth can never quite become reconciled to the idea that her friend is the wife of her comic monster. And that, of course, is precisely the sort of idea that Jane Austen herself could never grow reconciled to. The people she hated were tolerated, accepted, comfortably ensconced in the only human society she knew; . . .
> It is important to notice that Elizabeth makes no break

with her friend on account of her marriage. This was the sort of friend—"a friend disgracing herself and sunk in her esteem"—that went to make up the available social world which one could neither escape materially nor be independent of psychologically.

Mr. Harding indicates, though without analysis, the one-sided and therefore somewhat misleading nature of his own comments, on Jane Austen's attitude to her society, and provocatively concludes: "I have tried to underline one or two features of her work that claim the sort of readers who sometimes miss her—those who would turn to her not for relief and escape but as a formidable ally against things and people which were to her, and still are, hateful."

There is a probable but unsubstantiated family story of Jane's meeting with an exceptionally intelligent and attractive young man during a summer trip with Cassandra in 1801. According to Cassandra's account as repeated by a niece, he asked her father's permission to call the following winter but the family were soon shocked to hear of his sudden death.

This may or may not be a true story. Much more important to our understanding of Jane Austen's character and sense of values is an authenticated account of an incident in December, 1802.

Jane and Cassandra had been visiting two friends, sisters, at a large estate near their old home when their friends' younger brother, the heir of Manydown, proposed to Jane and was accepted. After a sleepless night Jane faced him in the morning to declare that she had changed her mind—a broken engagement then had at least as much opprobrium attached to it as a divorce does in most circles today—and she and Cassandra, almost hysterical for the only time in their brother James' knowledge of them, arrived before breakfast Friday morning at his rectory, insisting that he immediately arrange for their transportation home to Bath. Since he felt bound to escort them himself he urged that they wait until he had preached that Sunday, but they felt it impossible to remain an unnecessary hour in the vicinity and he was obliged to arrange for a substitute and leave immediately.

Jane's attempt at twenty-seven to emulate Charlotte's practical prudence—not, indeed with as contemptible a figure as Mr. Collins but with a somewhat younger man in whom she evidently found nothing particular to enjoy or admire—is apparent in this incident, as is her essential inability to accept life on such terms.

This experience, or, rather, the long consideration of bleak alternatives which had shaped it, is apparent in the novel she attempted to write during 1803-4, and left barely begun. There is a note of bitterness and almost of desperation in *The Watsons* which no doubt betrayed far more of her social consciousness than she wished known, and forced her to discontinue it after what seems to be a most promising and absorbing beginning.

A dialogue between two sisters, one, an almost resigned spinster of twenty-nine and the other a very beautiful young girl of nineteen, opens the book. The latter, like Fanny Price in Jane Austen's next novel, *Mansfield Park,* has been brought up by wealthy relatives by whom she was to have been adopted, but has been forced to return to her father's poor and barely genteel home.

Miss Watson begins:

> . . . You know, we must marry. I could do very well single for my own part; a little company, and a pleasant ball now and then, would be enough for me, if one could be young forever; but my father cannot provide for us, and it is very bad to grow old and be poor and laughed at. I have lost Purvis, it is true; but very few people marry their first loves. I should not refuse a man because he was not Purvis. . . .

Emma replies, and in reading her reference to a "school" we must remember the realistic boarding schools of Charlotte Bronte's *Jane Eyre,* with their teachers' salaries ranging *up* to £20 a year. She rather cavalierly says:

> "Poverty is a great evil; but to a woman of education and feeling it ought not, it cannot be the greatest. I would rather be a teacher at a school (and I can think of nothing worse), than marry a man I did not like."
>
> "I would rather do anything than be teacher at a school," said her sister. "I have been at school, Emma, and know what a life they lead; *you* never have. I should not like marrying a disagreeable man any more than yourself; but I do not think there *are* many very disagreeable men; I think I could like any good humoured man with a comfortable income. I suppose my aunt brought you up to be rather refined."

When in January 1805 Reverend Austen died, the major part of his income passed to James, and Mrs. Austen had only £150 a year on which to support herself and her two daughters.

Her five sons agreed among themselves to contribute another £300 a year during her lifetime and were, no doubt, prepared to offer their sisters a home after her death. But the parallel, in circumstances of dependence at least, to the Miss Watsons, was clearly a painful one.

An unmarried friend of Cassandra's, Martha Lloyd, who had been caring for an invalid mother, was at this time left alone by her mother's death, and Mrs. Austen and her daughters invited her to join them. The pooled incomes made living arrangements easier, and her presence made it possible for Jane and Cassandra to pay occasional visits together, but the widowed and essentially rootless household must have been a sad contrast with the busy active life of former years. Anne Elliot's suppressed distaste for Bath, her regret for the duties and dignities of a substantial country residence, and her unspoken comments on the busy littlenesses of a resort town, which later run through Jane Austen's last completed novel, *Persuasion,* all seem to echo the experience of these years.

Jane wrote Cassandra about a visit from James in 1807, when their mother's household had temporarily joined forces with brother Frank's wife, and moved to Southampton for his convenience on brief shore leaves: "I am sorry and angry that his [James'] visits should not give one more pleasure, the company of so good and so clever a man ought to be gratifying in itself; but his chat seems all forced, his opinions on many points, too much copied from his wife's, and his time here I think is spent in walking about the house, banging the doors, and ringing the bell for a glass of water."

The next fall, October 1808, Edward's wife died in childbirth leaving him with eleven children—all under fifteen—and he evidently felt a need for closer relations with his sisters, of whom he had always been very fond.

He offered his mother a choice of two comfortable cottages, one on the estate at which he resided and the other on an estate he owned nearer their former home. They chose the latter and Jane's spirits seemed to rise immediately as they prepared for the move to a new country home of their own in the old neighborhood.

She wrote Cassandra about a last ball at Southampton, to which she had taken a guest: "It was the same room in which we danced fifteen years ago!—I thought it all over,—and in spite of the shame of being so much older, felt with thankfulness that I was quite as happy now as then."

Again, more happily than she had written for years, she jested: "I assure you I am as tired of writing long letters as you can be. What a pity that one should still be so fond of receiving them."

And even when Mrs. Knight, widow of the relative who had made Edward his heir, suggested as one of the advantages of the move that the Rector of Chawton was a middle-aged bachelor, Jane answered imperturbably: "I am very much obliged to Mrs. Knight for such a proof of the interest she takes in me, and she may depend upon it that I *will* marry Mr. Papillon, whatever may be his reluctance or my own."

In her recovered spirits she wrote under an assumed name to the publisher who had six years before purchased *Northanger Abbey*, asking whether he meant to fulfill his contract. He replied that the purchase had carried no obligation to publish but that he was willing to return the manuscript for the £10 he had paid. That was then too large a sum for Jane to spare, and there seemed no advantage in pursuing the matter. She was evidently not seriously discouraged by it, however, for as soon as they had settled in Chawton she turned to a revision of *Sense and Sensibility*, which Henry succeeded in placing with a publisher before the end of the year.

A visit to Henry's home in London enabled her to correct the proofs and although she had undertaken to share any loss the publisher might sustain, she had the great satisfaction of receiving £140 as her share of the profits, the first money she had ever earned.

Her authorship was kept a profound secret, even in the family. Only Cassandra and Henry knew of her negotiations in November, 1812 for the publication of her next book, *Pride and Prejudice*.

During her visit to Henry's to correct those proofs the next May she wrote Cassandra: ". . . I have now therefore written myself in to £250—which only makes me long for more."

The following April Henry's wife, Eliza, died after a long illness and Jane spent over three months with him in London, reporting: "Upon the whole, his spirits are very much recovered.—If I may so express myself, his mind is not a mind for affliction. He is too busy, too active, too sanguine."

She seems genuinely distressed that his pride in her work led him to give away the secret of its authorship on a number of occasions, and she steadfastly resisted his invitations to meet such literary figures as Madame de Stael and others who had expressed a desire to know her. About one lady who wished to meet the author of *Sense and Sensibility*, she wrote: "I am rather frightened by hearing that she wishes to be introduced to me. If I *am* a wild beast I cannot help it. It is not my own fault." And she remarked, on Henry's telling an admirer of *Pride and Prejudice* that she had written that book: "I am trying to harden myself. After all what a trifle it is in all its bearings to the really important part of one's existence, even in this world. . . ."

That August, 1814, she completed the first novel of her second series—*Mansfield Park*—which was published during the fall.

In her letter January 29, 1813, announcing the arrival of her copy of *Pride and Prejudice* Jane had written Cassandra: "I want to tell you that I have got my own darling child from London . . ." and announced the work in progress—*Mansfield Park*: "Now I will try and write of something else, and it shall be a complete change of subject—ordination." The book is not exactly about ordination but it is the only one in which a clergyman's vocation is even hinted at in any terms that would not perfectly well apply to the few other gentlemanly professions.

Whether Jane Austen was practically aware of the increased current demand for books with a religious theme—and she very frankly assured Cassandra she was more interested in gaining money, and independence, by her writing than fame—or whether she was influenced by Cassandra's increasing concern with religious matters, the impulse evidently came from no real interest of her own, and makes *Mansfield Park* with all its added maturity and richness, the only one of her books where we feel a certain distortion of characters and values.

G. K. Chesterton delightfully summarized one aspect of her life and work when he said: "Jane Austen may have been protected from the truth, but precious little of the truth was ever protected from Jane Austen." He discussed her essentially irreligious attitude in his centenary analysis of *Emma* (1917), beginning:

> It is true that Jane Austen did not attempt to teach any history or politics, but it is not true that we cannot learn any history or politics from Jane Austen. . . .
> She is perhaps most typical of her time in being supremely irreligious. Her very virtues glitter with the cold sunlight of the great secular epoch between medieval and modern mysticism. . . .

And a less catholic romantic critic, H. W. Garrod, says indignantly in his frankly named "Jane Austen: A Depreciation": "Human beings act from a variety of motives; but the only motive from which no one ever acts in Miss Austen is the motive of religion."

Another centenary article in the *Quarterly Review* of 1917, by Reginald Farrar, deals generally with the "radiant and remorseless Jane," and discusses her realistic feminism:

> It is not for nothing that "rational" is almost her highest word of praise. . . .
> For her whole sex she revolts against "elegant females," and sums up her ideal woman, not as a "good-natured un-affected girl" (a phrase which, with her, connotes a certain quite kindly contempt), but as a "rational creature." The pre-tences of "Vanity Fair," for instance, to be an historical novel, fade into the thinnest of hot air when one realizes, with a gasp of amazement, that Amelia Sedley is actually meant to be a contemporary of Anne Elliot. And thus one understands what a deep gulf Victorianism dug between us and the past; how infinitely nearer to Jane Austen are the sane sensible young women of our own day than the flopping vaporous fools who were the fashion among the Turkish-minded male novelists of Queen Victoria's fashions.

This centenary statement here anticipates that of a postwar feminist, Mona Wilson, who wrote in 1938 in *Jane Austen and Some of Her Contemporaries*:

> . . . I wanted to express my conviction that her name should be linked with that of the great Vindicator of the Rights of Women, Mary Wollstonecraft, and that the *vis comica* of the one has been as powerful an agency as the *saeva indignatio* of the other.
> Jane Austen and Mary Wollstonecraft were bent on the destruction of the fair sex, of the ". . . milk-white lamb, that bleats for a man's protection," and the evolution of the rational woman.

Reginald Farrar concluded his article by turning to the one novel where the radiant Jane allowed remorse—or some other equally irrelevant sentiment—to blunt her perception.

> . . . Yet alone of all her books Mansfield Park is vitiated throughout by a radical dishonesty. . . . For example, Jane Austen has vividly and sedulously shown how impossible a

home is Mansfield for the young, with the father an august old
Olympian bore, the mother one of literature's most finished
fools, and the aunt its very Queen of Shrews; then suddenly
for edification, she turns to saying that Tom Bertram's illness
converted him to a tardy appreciation of domestic bliss. Having
said which, she is soon over mastered by truth once more, and
lets slip that he couldn't bear his father near him, that his
mother bored him, and that consequently those domestic blisses
resolved themselves into better service than you'd get in lodgings, and the ministration of the uninspiring Edmund. . . .

All through "Mansfield Park" in fact Jane Austen is torn
between the theory of what she ought to see, and the fact of
what she does see. . . . And while in talking of what she
does see she is here at her finest, in forcing herself to what she
ought to see she is here at her worst; to say nothing of the
harm done to her assumptions by her insight and to her insight
by her assumptions.

But if, in this first new work undertaken by Jane Austen as an
acknowledged author, she allowed herself to be intimidated by the
responsibilities of publication, she did not compromise on her
statement of woman's wrongs—it never quite reached the status of
an explicit demand for woman's rights.

Even Fanny, Jane Austen's most "creep-mouse" heroine stands
up to her awe-inspiring uncle with a refusal of a most advantageous
proposal, and the daring heresy: "I think it ought not to be set
down as certain that a man must be acceptable to every woman
he may happen to like himself."

And in her next novel, *Emma*, perhaps her most perfect mature
accomplishment, Jane Austen has completely turned her back on
any standards but her own.

This novel was, unpredictably, dedicated to the Prince Regent
at his own request.

There is almost no other pleasant thing recorded of this monarch—whom we shall have occasion to meet more seriously in the
next section—and Jane Austen had herself written to Cassandra
when, in February, 1813, he scandalously attempted to divorce his
wife: "Poor woman, I shall support her as long as I can, because
she *is* a Woman, and because I hate her Husband."

But he evidently had the good taste to enjoy *Sense and Sensibility, Pride and Prejudice,* and *Mansfield Park.* When in 1814 his
librarian, Mr. Clarke, learned that Henry Austen's sister had written them, he wrote her telling her that His Royal Highness had a

complete set of her books in each of his palaces, and that he would be pleased with the dedication of her next work.

Jane Austen sent a suitable acknowledgment and accepted an invitation to visit the famous library at Carleton House.

Mr. Clarke, a clergyman who might well be compared with Jane Austen's Mr. Elton if not with Mr. Collins himself, was evidently much struck with her on this visit and suggested that in her next novel she should choose as a subject his prototype. He urged:

> Do let us have an English clergyman after your fancy— much novelty may be introduced—show, dear Madam, what good would be done if tithes were taken away entirely, and describe him burying his own mother—as I did—because the High Priest of the parish in which she died did not pay her remains the respect he ought to do. . . . Carry your clergyman to sea as the friend of some distinguished character about a court.

Jane Austen hurriedly replied, with as much trepidation as amusement:

> I am quite honoured by your thinking me capable of drawing such a clergyman as you gave me the sketch of in your note of Nov. 16th. But I assure you I am *not*. The comic part of the character I might be equal to, but not the good, the enthusiastic, the literary. Such a man's conversation must at times be on subjects of science and philosophy, of which I know nothing; or at least be occasionally abundant in quotation and allusions which a woman who, like me, knows only her own mother tongue and has read little in that would be totally without the power of giving. A classical education, or, at any rate, a very extensive acquaintance with English literature, ancient and modern, appears to me quite indispensable for the person who would do any justice to your clergyman; and I think I may boast myself to be, with all possible vanity, the most unlearned and uninformed female who ever dared to be an authoress.

He persisted with offers of virtual collaboration and told her he was sending her two "Sermons I wrote and preached on the ocean" which she was free to use. He also had a new project to suggest. He had just been appointed English Secretary to the Prince Regent's son-in-law, Prince Leopold of Saxe Coburg, and felt that Miss Austen might well write a historical romance dealing with the history of Saxe Coburg.

She ended the correspondence by replying:

> You have my best wishes. Your recent appointments are I
> hope a step to something still better. In my opinion, the ser-
> vice of a court can hardly be too well paid, for immense must
> be the sacrifice of time and feeling required by it. . . .
>
> I am fully sensible that an historical romance, founded on
> the House of Saxe Coburg, might be much more to the pur-
> pose of profit or popularity than such pictures of domestic life
> in country villages as I deal in. But I could no more write a
> romance than an epic poem. I could not sit seriously down to
> write a serious romance under any other motive than to save
> my life; and if it were indispensable for me to keep it up and
> never relax into laughing at myself or other people, I am sure
> I should be hung before I had finished the first chapter. No, I
> must keep to my own style and go on in my own way; and
> though I may never succeed again in that, I am convinced that
> I should totally fail in any other.

During this same period we get another rare glimpse of her
conscious artistry in the course of a correspondence with her oldest
niece. Anna had begun to write a novel and was sending it to Aunt
Jane, chapter by chapter, for criticism.

There are many notes which indicate how scrupulous Jane was
about facts—the distance of one town from another, for example,
the probability of a small resort being talked of sixty miles away,
and such social minutia as: "I have also scratched out the introduction between Lord Portnam and his brother and Mr. Griffin. A
country surgeon (don't tell Mr. C. Lylord) would not be introduced to men of their rank."

But there are also more self-revealing comments: "You are now
collecting your People delightfully, getting them exactly into such
a spot as is the delight of my life;—3 or 4 Families in a Country
Village is the very thing to work on." And: "You had better not
leave England. Let the Portmans go to Ireland, but as you know
nothing of the Manners there, you had better not go with them.
You will be in danger of giving false representations. Stick to Bath
and the Foresters. There you will be quite at home."

Another note reminds us that Jane Austen's superbly unaccented
and effective use of words was not as unconscious as it seems. She
writes Anna about one installment: "Devereux Forester's being
ruined by his Vanity is extremely good; but I wish you would not
let him plunge into a 'Vortex of Dissipation'. I do not object to the
Thing, but I cannot bear the expression. . . ."

She would, I think, have been rather pleased by the indignant complaint of Mr. Garrod, in his "Depreciation of Jane Austen," that: "When I call her writing truthful and apt, I have said all that should be said in praise of it. . . . Its qualities, indeed, are, I should be inclined to say, rather those of science than of literature. It does just what it is meant to do, no more, no less. It appears of course a more telling language than the language of science; but that is merely because it has been transferred from the analysis of matter to the analysis of manners."

Another chapter, with one of the interpolated stories so common in the novels of the time, elicited a playful comment which reminds us how carefully prearranged all the most detailed effects in Jane Austen's novels are, even though their freshness and spontaneity often give the effect of improvisation. She writes: "St. Julian's history was quite a surprise to me. You had not very long known it yourself I suspect," and continues with more personal amusement about the antecedent plot complication St. Julian's history had evidently revealed: "His having been in love with the Aunt gives Cecilia an additional interest in him. I like the idea, a very proper compliment to an aunt! I rather imagine indeed that nieces are seldom chosen but out of compliment to some aunt or other." She concludes with a comment on Ben Lefroy—her niece's fiancé, and a nephew of the young Irish gentleman with whom she had flirted so outrageously twenty years before: " I daresay Ben was in love with me once, and would never have thought of you if he had not supposed me dead of scarlet fever."

Two further family correspondences of these years give us valuable glimpses of her personal attitude to several of the major ideas presented, with seeming detachment, in her novels.

Her other motherless niece, Fanny, was involved in a series of courtships, and not sure as to her own feelings, encouraged first one suitor, then another, then decided "never" to marry, then feared lest she would be criticized as fickle for drawing back so late, and wrote her Aunt Jane a day-by-day series of requests for comfort and advice.

Many of the replies might well have been written by Elinor Dashwood or Elizabeth Bennet or Anne Elliot after they had stopped being heroines and become Aunts.

For example, the playful warning in response to her niece's fervent vows of celibacy: "single women have a dreadful propensity for being poor,—which is one very strong argument in favour of matrimony."

And the more serious warning when it seemed the pressure of public opinion might force Fanny into maintaining her consistency even at the cost of an unhappy marriage: "The unpleasantness of appearing fickle is certainly great—but if you think you want Punishment for Past Illusions, there it is—and nothing can be compared to the misery of being bound without Love. . . . That you do not deserve."

These letters came to an end in March, 1817, only a few months before Jane Austen's death. They close happily: "You can hardly think what a pleasure it is to me to have such a thorough picture of your heart.—Oh, what a loss it will be when you are married. You are too agreeable in your single state, too agreeable as a niece —I shall hate you when your delicious play of mind is all settled down into conjugal and maternal affections."

The last letter reads, prophetically as it turned out: "Well, I shall say, as I have often said before, Do not be in a hurry; depend upon it, the right Man will come at last; . . . And then, by not beginning Mothering quite so early in life, you will be young in Constitution and spirits, figure and countenance."

This last bit of advice which would seem, even to many twentieth century readers, remarkably freespoken from a maiden lady to a girl barely out of her teens, reminds us of a whole series of such comments in Jane's letters to Cassandra.

Birth control was evidently altogether unknown in eighteenth century England and three of Jane's own sisters-in-law died in childbirth despite their unusual command of medical attention and care.

Writing of one sister-in-law's pregnancy the twenty-three year old Jane had told Cassandra, evidently with no fear of shocking her, that she had visited Mary: "who is still plagued with the rheumatism, which she would be very glad to get rid of, and still more glad to get rid of [give birth to] her child, of whom she is heartily tired. . . . I believe I never told you that Mrs. Caulthard and Ann, late of Manydown, are both dead, and both died in child-bed. We have not regaled Mary with this news."

Again, some years later, commenting on a neighbour's difficult delivery: "Good Mrs. Deedes!—I hope she will get the better of this Marianne, and then I would recommend to her and Mr. D. the simple regimen of separate rooms."

And in the last years of her life, just a few months after her niece Anna's marriage had put a stop to her novel writing, Jane wrote Cassandra: "Anna has not a chance of escape; her husband called here the other day, and said she was *pretty well* but not *equal* to so long a walk; she *must come in her Donkey Carriage.* Poor animal, she will be worn out before she is thirty. I am very sorry for her. Mrs. Clement too is in that way again. I am quite tired of so many children. —Mrs. Benn has a 15th."

Unlike her other concerns this one was not directly reflected in the novels—unless we can take the very limited sizes of her heroines' families (all but the first one)—presumably attained by the Spartan regime of separate rooms—as evidence on the matter. But it is important for us to see how fearlessly Jane Austen had considered such aspects of "the woman question" in the light of whatever information was then available.

One other family note, not from her pen, may be instructive before we consider *Emma* and *Persuasion,* the work of her last three years.

A niece, long after Jane Austen's death, when she was already famous and her novels had gone into many editions, described the way in which she had to write even after the successful publication of her first two books. (Jane had never again had a private or semi-private sitting room after the first move from Steventon, where she had shared a dressing room with Cassandra.)

The unconscious contrast her niece's vocabulary assumes between woman's real work and any such personal occupation as authorship, which may be indulged only if not taken too seriously, tells us volumes about the special practical and emotional problems of the woman writer.

According to this undoubtedly accurate account Jane: "would sit quietly working [sewing] beside the fire in the library, saying nothing for a good while, and then would suddenly burst out laughing, jump up and run across the room to a table where pens and paper were lying, write something down, and then come back to the fire and go on quietly working as before."

In this way much of *Emma,* like her other masterpieces, was written.

Dr. Kettle chooses this novel as the greatest and most representative of the works she lived to write (she was only forty-two when she died a year after its publication) and says:

> How does Jane Austen succeed in thus combining intensity with precision, emotional involvement with objective judgment? Part of the answer lies, I think, in her almost complete lack of idealism, the delicate and unpretentious materialism of

her outlook. . . . The clarity of her social observations (the
Highbury world is scrupulously seen and analysed down to
the exact incomes of its inmates) is matched by the precision
of her social judgments, and all her judgments are, in the
broadest sense, social. Human happiness not abstract principle
is her concern. Such precision—it is both her incomparable
strength and her ultimate limitation—is unimaginable except in
an extraordinarily stable corner of society. . . .

Sufficient has perhaps been said to suggest that what gives
Emma its power to move us is the realism and depth of feeling
behind Jane Austen's attitudes. She examines with a scrupulous
yet passionate and critical precision the actual problems of her
world. That this world is narrow cannot be denied. How far
its narrowness matters is an important question.

The reason that its narrowness finally does not matter is that
none of the implications which could be drawn from the examination of this little corner of society are evaded. Just as the smallest
possible section of a circular arc will, when properly examined,
allow us to locate the center of the circle from which it was taken,
determine the radius, and so reconstruct the circle in its original
size and position, so this small section of middle-class relations
enables Jane Austen to reach many profound conclusions about her
whole society none of which are shirked. She pulls no punches.
Her heroine is deliberately presented as a spoiled child and a
snobbish, conceited, egotistical young woman, whose false upper-
class values are only partially excused as the logical and almost
inevitable result of her upbringing. She is, however, both intelligent and warmhearted and the theme of the book is the reeduca-
tion of Emma who is, finally, able to learn from her own painful
experience.

The cardinal sin in Jane Austen's hierarchy—that one should
treat other human beings like inanimate objects, simply as means
to one's own ends—is committed by Emma before the end of the
third chapter, and the falsity of her relation to her new protégée
is lightly and indelibly indicated when she muses about the convenience for companionship of "*a* Harriet Smith," now that Miss
Taylor, her former governess-companion, has married.

Emma's genuine affection for Miss Taylor has led her to promote this very happy marriage, but her wealthy father, far more
stupid and hopelessly self-engrossed, cannot be brought to believe
that anything even mildly inconvenient to him can be at all desir-

able to anyone, and spends a large part of the first chapter pitying "poor Miss Taylor":

> . . . from his habits of gentle selfishness, and of being never able to suppose that other people could feel differently from himself, he was very much disposed to think Miss Taylor had done as sad a thing for herself as for them, and would have been a great deal happier if she had spent all the rest of her life at Hartfield.

This "gentle selfishness," shown in relation to all who come in contact with him, finally gives us as profound and exasperated an understanding of the completely impenetrable righteous self-regard of a ruling class as we could get from the most indignant economic expose of a paternalistic employer. Incidentally it makes us the more ready to welcome even long delayed efforts at self-criticism by his daughter.

Nor is Emma, from the very beginning, with all her deliberate self-delusions, lacking in a certain honesty and understanding of objective facts. For example, although Emma at the beginning sees marriage, as Dr. Kettle says, in "terms of class snobbery and property qualifications . . . typical of the ruling class," she has a saving humorous realism about her position. She tells Harriet she has now (at twenty-one) determined never to marry:

> I have none of the usual inducements of women to marry. Were I to fall in love, indeed, it would be a different thing; but I never have been in love; it is not my way or my nature; and I do not think I ever shall. And without love, I am sure I should be a fool to change such a situation as mine. Fortune I do not lack; employment I do not lack; consequence I do not lack; I believe few married women are half as much mistress of their husband's house as I am of Hartfield; . . .

In response to Harriet's horrified exclamation: "But still, you will be an old maid—and that's dreadful!" she replies:

> Never mind, Harriet, I shall not be a poor old maid; and it is poverty only which makes celibacy contemptible to a generous public! A single woman with a very narrow income must be a ridiculous, disagreeable old maid! the proper sport of boys and girls; but a single woman of good fortune is always respectable, and may be as sensible and pleasant as anybody else!

However, the real meaning of poverty for a lady is stated not by Emma, but by Jane Fairfax. She is a well-educated, beautiful and exceptionally accomplished young woman whose father's early death has left her, with only a few hundred pounds, to support herself. She must, necessarily, seek a position as governess but has decided to postpone the evil day a few months until her twenty-first birthday.

In reply to the officious vulgarity with which a self-appointed patroness offers to help her find a post she says:

> When I am quite determined as to the time, I am not at all afraid of being long unemployed. There are places in town, offices, where inquiry would soon produce something—offices for the sale, not quite of human flesh, but of human intellect."
> "Oh! my dear, human flesh! You quite shock me; if you mean a fling at the slave trade, I assure you Mr. Suckling was always rather a friend to abolition."
> "I did not mean—I was not thinking of the slave trade," replied Jane; "governess—trade, I assure you, was all that I had in view; widely different, certainly, as to the guilt of those who carry it on; but as to the greater misery of the victims, I do not know where it lies. . . ."

And later Emma herself, despite her snobbish jealousy of Jane's accomplishments, replies to some one who, excusing a serious breach of decorum on Jane's part, has urged:

> "And how much may be said, in her situation, for even that error."
> "Much, indeed!" cried Emma feelingly. "If a woman can ever be excused for thinking only of herself, it is in a situation like Jane Fairfax's." Of such, one might almost say, that "the world is not theirs, nor the world's law!"

Again we see how far an honest, intelligent examination of even the smallest most stable corner of a class society will carry us toward a reexamination of its professions and the values it really lives by. As Kettle concludes:

> Against the element of complacency other forces, too, are at work. . . . Among these positive forces are, as we have seen, her highly critical concern over the fate of women in her society, a concern which involves a reconsideration of its basic values. . . .

It is Jane Austen's sensitive vitality, her genuine concern (based on so large an honesty) that captures imagination. . . . And the concern does not stop at what, among the ruling class at Highbury, is pleasant and easily solved.

It gives us glimpses of something Mr. Woodhouse never dreamed of—the world outside the Hartfield world and yet inseparably bound up with it; the world Jane Fairfax saw in her vision of offices and into which Harriet in spite of (no, *because* of) Emma's patronage was so nearly plunged: the world for which Jane Austen had no answer. It is this vital and unsentimental concern which defeats, to such a very large extent, the limitations.

There were, of course, many contemporary criticisms like those of a church dignitary who "thought the Authoress wrong in such times as these, to draw such Clergymen as Mr. Collins and Mr. Elton."

The Prince Regent's secretary sent formal thanks for the presentation of the "dedicated" Emma. Jane evidently found them somewhat inadequate for she wrote to her publisher: "You will be pleased to hear that I have received the Prince's thanks for the *handsome* copy I sent him of *Emma*. Whatever he may think of *my* share of the work, yours seems to have been quite right."

Not only clergymen and princes, but evidently ladies as well, were rendered somewhat uneasy by the unsparing realism and utter lack of sentimentality in *Emma*. Lady Shelley, for example, wrote in 1819, when Jane's first novel, *Northanger Abbey*, and her last, *Persuasion*, were posthumously published together: "the same objection may be made to all Jane Austen's novels. . . . Surely works of imagination should raise us above our everyday feelings, and excite in us those élans passagères of virtue and sensibility which are exquisite and ennobling."

But perhaps one of the most interesting contemporary criticisms was a long article which Sir Walter Scott wrote anonymously for *The Quarterly* in October 1816.

Although well-known for his poetry, Scott was just entering upon his career as a novelist when Jane Austen was concluding hers, and his position as a lawyer and man of business, influential in literary and political circles in both Edinburgh and London, subjected him to influences quite different from any Jane Austen knew. It is no exaggeration to say that he wrote in an England at least a generation further along the road to industrialism than hers, and that the forces which shaped his world had barely impinged on hers.

His work as a novelist should, therefore, be considered in the context of the great romantic writers of the early nineteenth century rather than in this transitional eighteenth century period (see pp. 617-620).

The review of Jane Austen's work which he wrote in 1816, while friendly, and appreciative enough of some of her minor talents, utterly fails to grasp the essential meaning of her novels. It gives us a glimpse of the good-natured Tory who, unable to face the implications of his own position in an increasingly ruthless capitalist world, turned to a glorification of the medieval past and of luxury emotions which neither he nor any of his readers would have dreamed of obeying in their real lives.

He begins with a good if somewhat patronizing summary of Jane Austen's most obvious subjects and abilities:

> But the author of Emma confines herself chiefly to the middling classes of society; her most distinguished characters do not rise greatly above well-bred country gentlemen and ladies; and those which are sketched with most originality and precision, belong to a class rather below that standard. The narrative of all her novels is composed of such common occurrences as may have fallen under the observation of most folks; and her dramatis personae conduct themselves upon the motives and principles which the reader may recognize as ruling their own and that of most of their acquaintances. . . .
>
> The author's knowledge of the world, and the peculiar tact with which she presents characters that the reader cannot fail to recognize, reminds us something of the merits of the Flemish school of painting. The subjects are not often elegant, and certainly never grand; but they are finished up to nature; and with a precision which delights the reader. . . .

He is, however, troubled by the unromantic tone in which she discusses marriage. Not that he would recommend *acting* imprudently, but he holds a decent reticence about the real considerations involved more becoming, and would rather the hand were quicker than the eye. It is interesting to note how completely and unquestioningly he assumes that the subject who significantly feels love must be a young man—woman is essentially just its object. And it is also instructive to see how imperceptibly his idealistic argument in favor of romantic self-disregarding early love merges into its utilitarian justification by the practical benefits it may confer.

> One word, however, we must say in behalf of that once powerful divinity, Cupid, king of gods and men, who in these times of revolution has been assailed, even in his own kingdom of romance, by the authors who formerly were his devoted priests. We are quite aware that there are few instances of first attachment being brought to a happy conclusion, and that it seldom can be so in a state of society so highly advanced as to render early marriages among the better class, acts, generally speaking, of imprudence. But the youth of this realm need not at present be taught the doctrine of selfishness. It is by no means their error to give the world or the good things of the world all for love; and before the authors of moral fiction couple cupid indivisibly with calculating prudence, we would have them reflect, that they may sometimes lend their aid to substitute more mean, more sordid, and more selfish motives of conduct, for the romantic feelings which their predecessors perhaps fanned into too powerful a flame. Who is it, that in his youth has felt a virtuous attachment, however romantic or however unfortunate, but can trace back to its influence much that his character may possess of what is honourable, dignified and disinterested? If he recollects hours wasted in unavailing hope or saddened by doubt and disappointment; he may also dwell on many which have been snatched from folly or libertinism, and dedicated to studies which might render him worthy of the object of his affections, or pave the way perhaps to that distinction necessary to raise him to an equality with her.

It is most instructive to see here how Sir Walter's panegyric on disinterested love assumes that its romantic object is inevitably chosen from a higher—and richer—social circle and that its occasional result, and natural if unconscious purpose, is to enable the romantic lover to enter that charmed sphere.

"In Belmont is a lady richly left *and* she is fair, and fairer than that word, of wondrous virtue." But Shakespeare knew what he was doing, whereas Sir Walter sees the aristocratic Bassanio as a noble and disinterested hero.

> Even the habitual indulgence of feelings totally unconnected with ourself and our own immediate interest, softens, graces, and amends the human mind; and after the pain of disappointment is past, those who survive (and by good for-

tune those are the greater number) are neither less wise nor
less worthy members of society for having felt, for a time, the
influence of a passion which has been well qualified as the
"tenderest, noblest and best."

Jane Austen said noncommittally that the authoress of *Emma*
could not complain of her treatment by the anonymous *Quarterly
Reviewer* who was evidently a very clever man.

The depression which followed the peace of 1815-16 forced
Henry's banking house into bankruptcy, along with many others,
but Jane had only £13 on deposit there, the rest of her earnings—
less than £1,000—being with patriotic or more likely sisterly pride,
invested in Navy Funds.

However for the first time in her life she now became seriously
unwell. Her illness, which proved fatal in little more than a year,
was never really diagnosed but the detailed description of her
"decline" available from family letters seems clearly to indicate a
cancerous affection of some internal organ.

She had begun a new novel shortly after *Emma* was completed
and later wrote to Fanny: "I have a something ready for publication which may perhaps come out in a twelve months time." The
plan for such a delay was deliberate. Henry in his biographical
memoir wrote: "Though in composition she was equally rapid and
correct, yet an invincible distrust of her own judgment induced her
to withhold her works from the public till time and many perusals
had satisfied her that the charm of recent composition was dissolved."

And although *Persuasion* was completed by August 1816, it is
likely that had she lived, some scenes—notably that of Mrs. Smith's
story—would have been largely rewritten and enriched. The end,
too, as far as such important minor characters as Mrs. Clay and
Mr. Elliot are concerned, was rather "huddled together" and the
novel is, of course, much shorter than any of the others except the
first, *Northanger Abbey*. On the whole it seems that while her
failing energy made no significant change in the development of
characters or theme it did prevent completion of the multitude of
felicitous touches which overflow the main channel of all her other
books.

But there are also important positive changes that add to our
regret for the unwritten novels which should have followed this
transitional one.

For the first time we have a mature heroine—Anne Elliot is twenty-seven—and a really sympathetic account of a long-standing love affair.

There is far more sensitivity to the beauty of nature and, on the whole, more emotional awareness of many varied physical sensations.

Relative poverty is touched upon in a daringly uncritical manner. Here again, as in her discussion of childbirth, Jane Austen's private correspondence reveals her awareness of things not directly mentionable in a lady's public writing. Her two favorite contemporary authors were Dr. Johnson, whose discussions of poverty we have already had occasion to note, and a now largely forgotten poet, George Crabbe, who wrote, attacking the sentimental pictures of rural plenty in *The Deserted Village* and elsewhere:

> Will you praise the healthy homely fare
> Plenteous and plain, that happy peasants share?
> O trifle not with wants you cannot feel,
> Nor mock the misery of a stinted meal,
> Homely, not wholesome, plain, not plenteous, such
> As you who praise would never deign to touch;
> By such examples taught, I paint the cot
> As Truth will paint it and as Bards will not.

But while *Persuasion* does not, of course, go so far down the social scale, it does touch almost the very lowest income group in the lower middle class.

Only Miss Bates in *Emma* was previously shown as hospitable in poverty, and she is a sympathetic and amusing, rather than an attractive, character. But here a half-pay navy captain—surely no better off than Captain Price of whose uncomfortable household we have so painfully convincing a view in *Mansfield Park*—is the head of an exceptionally harmonious and generous family.

> Mrs. Harville, a degree less polished than her husband, seemed, however, to have the same good feelings; and nothing could be more pleasant than their desire of considering the whole party as friends of their own, because the friends of Captain Wentworth, or more kindly hospitable than their entreaties for their all promising to dine with them; . . . they seemed almost hurt that Captain Wentworth should have brought any such party [five total strangers] to Lyme without considering it as a thing of course that they should dine with them.

There was so much attachment to Captain Wentworth in all this, and such a bewitching charm in a degree of hospitality so uncommon, so unlike the usual style of give-and-take invitations and dinners of formality and display, that Anne felt her spirits not likely to be benefited by an increasing acquaintance among his brother-officers. "These would have been all my friends" was her thought; and she had to struggle against a great tendency to lowness.

On quitting the Cobb, they all went indoors with their new friends, and found rooms so small as none but those who invite from the heart could think capable of accommodating so many. Anne had a moment's astonishment on the subject herself; but it was soon lost in the pleasanter feelings which sprang from the sight of all the ingenious contrivances and nice arrangements of Captain Harville to turn the actual space to the best possible account, to supply the deficiencies of lodging-house furniture, and defend the windows and doors against the winter storms to be expected. . . .

. . . He drew, he varnished, he carpentered, he glued, he made toys for the children, he fashioned new netting-needles and pins with improvements; and if everything else was done, sat down to his large fishing net at one corner of the room.

Another new departure is a warm study of a deeply united elderly couple—Admiral and Mrs. Crofts. She especially is an unconventional character who has insisted upon living with her husband aboard ship, and rebukes her brother: "But I hate to hear you talking so, like a fine gentleman, and as if women were all fine ladies instead of rational creatures. We none of us expect to be in smooth water all our days."

Our last glimpse of Mrs. Croft is in Bath where the Admiral:

was ordered to walk to keep off the gout, and Mrs. Croft seemed to go shares with him in everything, and to walk for her life to do him good. . . . Anne . . . delighted to see the Admiral's hearty shake of the hand when he encountered an old friend, and observe their eagerness of conversation when occasionally forming into a little knot of the navy, Mrs. Croft looking as intelligent and keen as any of the officers around her.

The plot of *Persuasion* is much the same as that of Jane Austen's other novels. Dr. Marvin Mudrick says, in discussing the question of Jane Austen's "comedy":

Anne and Wentworth neither overlook nor rebel against the material base of their society: if they overlooked it, they would be deluded, which they are not; if they rebelled, they would be outcasts, which they do not wish to be. Their problem—and they are both wholly aware of it—is to determine just how far the claim of feeling can yield, without effacing itself altogether, to the claim of economics; and this central problem of *Persuasion* is not comic.

And Mark Schorer, in an interesting analysis of the language of the novel, makes a very striking point, although he ignores the presence of those characters who share the author's viewpoint, notably those active or wounded naval officers we have seen who, in a sense, work for their living:

> *Persuasion* is a novel of courtship and marriage with a patina of sentimental scruple and moral punctilio and a stylistic base derived from commerce and property, the counting house and the inherited estate. The first is the expression of the characters, the second is the perception of the author . . . the essence of her comedy resides . . . in the discrepancy between social sentiment and social fact, and the social fact is to be discovered not so much in the professions of her characters as in the texture of her style.

This is true, and his article's subsequent detailed analysis of the language is extremely valuable, but as we have seen, the "essence of the comedy" is not altogether the essence of the book, for "the central problem of *Persuasion* is not comic."

The last novel Jane Austen began, which she found herself unable to continue beyond the first few uncorrected chapters, is an even more apparent departure.

Here for the first time she introduces—and apparently as a center to the book—a commercial scheme for making money.

Sandition is the name of a new health resort or watering place created by speculative landlords to increase the value of their land.

In previous novels all commercial activities have been pursued off stage, usually before the first chapter began—and money was to be inherited or married but not made. The sole exception lay in the odd system of war office rewards for taking prize-ships referred to by the naval passages of *Persuasion*. Mr. Knightley in *Emma* was a working landlord supervising his farms, and his brother was an energetic barrister, but all the clergymen draw their salaries in dignified repose and no one else comes even that close to earning a living.

Yet Mr. Parker, the first and most important character we meet in *Sandition,* is on a business errand intended to increase the number of guests at his resort, and we are immediately informed:

> . . . the success of Sandition as a small fashionable Bathing Place was object, for which he seemed to live. A very few years ago, and it had been a quiet Village of no pretensions; but some natural advantages in its position and some accidental circumstances having suggested to himself, and the other principal Land Holder, the probability of its becoming a profitable Speculation, they had engaged in it, and planned and built and praised and puffed and raised it to something of young Renown—and Mr. Parker could now think of very little besides. . . . Sandition was a second Wife and 4 children to him—hardly less Dear—and certainly more engrossing.—He could talk of it forever.—It had indeed the highest claims; not only those of Birthplace, Property, and Home,—it was his Mine, his Lottery, his Speculation and his Hobby Horse; his Occupation his Hope and his Futurity. . . .

The wealthy Lady Denham, his greedy but niggardly coinvestor, complains that an increase of visitors will mean higher prices for her household necessities and Jane Austen actually ventures into an economic discussion when Mr. Parker replies:

> My dear Madam, They can only raise the price of consumeable Articles, by such an extraordinary Demand for them and such a diffusion of Money among us, as must do us more Good than harm. Our Butchers and Bakers and Traders in general cannot get rich without bringing Prosperity to *us.*—If they do not gain, our rents will be insecure—and in proportion to their profit must be ours eventually in the increased value of our Houses.

There is a return to the high-spirited burlesque of *Northanger Abbey* but this time it is, significantly, aimed not at an overemotional young heroine but at a determinedly profligate young "villain" with whom the heroine is obviously perfectly competent to deal.

> The truth was that Sir Edw: whom circumstances had confined very much to one spot had read more sentimental novels

than had agreed with him. His fancy had been early caught
by all the impassioned, and most exceptionable parts of Richardson's; and such Authors as have since appeared to tread in
Richardson's steps, so far as Man's determined pursuit of
Woman in defiance of every opposition of feeling and convenience is concerned, had since occupied the greater part of
his literary hours, and formed his character. . . .

Clara saw through him; and had not the least intention of
being seduced—but she bore with him patiently enough to
confirm the sort of attachment which her personal charms had
raised.—A greater degree of discouragement indeed would not
have affected Sir Edw:—, He was armed against the highest
pitch of Disdain or Aversion—If she could not be won by affection he must carry her off. He knew his Business.—

This tantalizing fragment strikes out into such completely new
territory that it is impossible even to guess its future development.
One can only regret its abrupt termination when, on March 18,
1817, Jane Austen found herself too ill to continue.

On March 28 her wealthy and childless uncle died but the
£1,000 legacies of which his sisters' children had been assured were,
by the terms of his will, not to be paid until his wife's death—an
event which actually did not take place until many years after
Jane's.

She had evidently been counting heavily upon the independence which might be assured to Cassandra and herself, and wrote
one of her brothers a week later:

I am ashamed to say that the shock of my uncle's will
brought on a relapse and I was so ill on Friday and thought
myself so likely to be worse, that I could but press for Cassandra's returning with Frank after the funeral last night, which
of course she did, and either her return, or my having seen
Mr. Curtis or my disorder choosing to go away, have made me
better this morning. I live upstairs however for the present and
am coddled. I am the only one of the legatees who has been
so silly, but a weak body must excuse weak nerves.

The rally was a very temporary one and on May 24 she and
Cassandra took lodgings in the nearby cathedral town of Win-
chester where there was a surgeon of some reputation who had
offered to undertake her treatment.

She wrote gaily enough to a nephew: "Mr. Lyford says he will
cure me, and if he fails, I shall draw up a memorial and lay it

before the Dean and Chapter, and have no doubt of redress from that pious, learned, and disinterested body." But she also made her will, leaving everything to Cassandra except for one £50 legacy to Henry and another to an old housekeeper who had lost that amount in the failure of his bank.

The disease made rapid progress and on July 18, 1817 she died at the age of forty-two.

Northanger Abbey, of which Henry had repurchased the manuscript, and *Persuasion,* were published in one volume in 1818, and her fame grew slowly but steadily from then on.

Half a century later George Eliot and George Henry Lewes agreed that she was the most perfect artist who had yet used the novel form, unequalled by any male writer—and her popularity with a special but very large public has persisted even though most of the more astringent elements of her art have often been ignored. The best of this traditional appreciation is illustrated by Virginia Woolf who calls her: "the most perfect artist among women," and says:

> Think away the surface animation, the likeness to life, and there remains to provide a deeper pleasure, an exquisite discrimination of human values. . . . Her fool is a fool, her snob is a snob, because he departs from the model of sanity and sense which she has in mind, and conveys to us unmistakably even while she makes us laugh. Never did any novelist make more use of an impeccable sense of human values. It is against the disc of an unerring heart, an unfailing good taste, an almost stern morality, that she shows up those deviations from kindness, truth, and sincerity which are among the most delightful things in English literature.

And Cazamian emphasizes her position as the first *modern* novelist, saying:

> all that a Rochefoucauld had shown up in the strong and bitter note of a straight forward denunciation, and which at a later date the pessimistic novel will dissect with such profuseness and intensity of method, is here indicated or suggested so calmly and with so sober a touch that the author's personal reaction is reduced to a minimum. There is nothing more objective than those stories . . . if a subtle suggestion of irony did not hover over every page, revealing a sharpness of vision that could be unmercifully severe.

This insight into her continuing contemporary relevance is completed by Dr. Kettle with his statement that:

> The intensity of Jane Austen's novels is inseparable from their concreteness and this intensity must be stressed because it is so different from the charming and cosy qualities with which the novels are often associated. Reading . . . [Jane Austen] is a delightful experience but it is not a soothing one. On the contrary, our faculties are aroused, we are called upon to participate in life with an awareness, a fineness of feeling and a moral concern more intense than most of us normally bring to our everyday experience. Everything matters. . . . And in none of the issues of conduct arising in the novel[s] is Jane Austen morally neutral. The intensity with which everything matters to us . . . is the product of this lack of complacency, this passionate concern of Jane Austen for human values.

These widely varied evaluations do not supplant, but rather supplement each other. The fact that as perceptive and sympathetic a critic as Virginia Woolf left so much of Jane Austen's depth unplumbed shows how deceptive the sparkling surface of her work is. For Jane Austen was compelled to accomplish an almost unprecedented feat—to become an artist while remaining a lady.

Only by reading between the lines can one follow the unsparing analysis beneath the imperturbable surface. And then one finds an especial piquancy in the rapid and skillful social dissection carried on while the lady's air of courteous attention to the story disclaims all knowledge of her right hand as well as her left. And of course the need for such a pose is in itself Miss Austen's sharpest comment on woman's position in the best of polite society.